DATE DUE			

SEX, DRUGS, DEATH,
AND THE
LAW

PHILOSOPHY AND SOCIETY
General Editor: MARSHALL COHEN

Also in this series:

SEX, DRUGS, DEATH,
AND THE
LAW

*An Essay on Human Rights
and Overcriminalization*

David A. J. Richards

ROWMAN AND LITTLEFIELD
Totowa, New Jersey

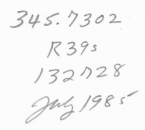

First published in the United States 1982 by Rowman and Littlefield,
81 Adams Drive, Totowa, New Jersey 07512.

Copyright © 1982 by Rowman and Littlefield

Library of Congress Cataloging in Publication Data

Richards, David A. J.
  Sex, drugs, death and the law.

  (Philosophy and society)
  Includes index.
    1. Crimes without victims—United States.   2. Decrimi-
nalization—United States.   3. Crimes without victims.
4. Decriminalization.   I. Title.   II. Series.

KF9434.R5   345.73'02   81-23392
ISBN 0-8476-7063-5   347.3052   AACR2

Distributed in the U.K. and Commonwealth by
George Prior Associated Publishers Limited
High Holborn House
53154 High Holborn
London WC1 V 6RL
England

Printed in the United States of America

To Donald Levy

"The more I reflect, the more I find that the question may be reduced to this fundamental proposition: to seek happiness and avoid misery in that which does not affect another is a natural right . . . If there is a self-evident and absolute maxim in the world, I think it is this one, and if anyone succeeded in subverting it, there is no human action which might not be made a crime."

Jean-Jacques Rousseau, *La Nouvelle Héloïse,*
(J. H. McDowell trans. 1968), page 264

Contents

Acknowledgments

In this book, I integrate various articles published in diverse law journals over the last five years into a coherent general theory. In chronological order, these articles are "Unnatural Acts and the Constitutional Right to Privacy: A Moral Theory," 45 *Fordham L. Rev.* 1281 (1977); "Sexual Autonomy and the Constitutional Right to Privacy: A Case Study in Human Rights and the Unwritten Constitution," 30 *Hastings L.J.* 957 (1979); "Commercial Sex and the Rights of the Person: A Moral Argument for the Decriminalization of Prostitution," 127 *U. Pa. L. Rev.* 1195 (1979); "Constitutional Privacy, the Right to Die and the Meaning of Life: A Moral Analysis," 22 *William & Mary L. Rev.* 327 (1981); and "Drug Use and the Rights of the Person: A Moral Argument for Decriminalization of Certain Forms of Drug Use," 33 *Rutgers L. Rev.* 607 (1981).

These articles profited from the able research assistance of various law students; Diana R. Lewis at Fordham Law School and, at New York University, Becky Palmer and Robert Freedman (on prostitution), Jon Dubin, Linda Ecksmith, and Lynn Paltrow (on drugs), and Linda Ecksmith, J. Fortier Imbert, William Kaplan, and Lynn Paltrow (on death). Work on most of these articles was made possible by generous research grants from the Law Center Foundation of New York University School of Law.

Conversations with many colleagues at New York University School of Law assisted work on various of these articles: I am grateful, especially, to Paul Chevigny, Ronald Dworkin, Lewis Kornhauser, Sylvia Law, Lawrence Sager, and Laurence Tancredi.

All my work on these articles and this book has profited from the stimulus, patience, intelligence, criticism, and kindness of Professor Donald Levy of Brooklyn College (Department of Philosophy).

Introduction

This book is written from the perspective of a teacher of law in the areas of constitutional and criminal law and of a moral and legal philosopher concerned with the investigation of concepts of law, justice, and human rights. Accordingly, the approach here taken is interdisciplinary: the adequate analysis of these, as of many other, legal problems requires that one be a philosopher in doing law, or, alternatively, that one do law philosophically. Indeed, the approach here is even more ambitiously interdisciplinary than a training in law and philosophy would warrant. For, in the investigation and criticism of the gross and unjust overcriminalization typical of American criminal justice, I have found it necessary not only to draw on forms of legal and philosophical argument, but to trace the links of the subjects under investigation to history, psychology, social science, and even literature. The deeper criticism of overcriminalization requires a form of empirical inquiry into the background assumptions that often uncritically underlie the common American sense of proper criminalization. Accordingly, as the argument evolves, we will explore such assumptions and other often detailed empirical arguments establishing factual premises fundamental to the rational discussion of these issues.

My intent here is to develop a new form of moral, legal, and political argument that connects the moral criticism of overcriminalization not to utilitarianism but to antiutilitarian conceptions of human rights (Chapter 1). This argument of general political theory is used to delineate deep commitments of American constitutionalism and thus to explain and justify specific forms of judicially enforceable constitutional argument, grounded on the constitutional right to privacy, and more general forms of liberal argument, which urge legislatures to replace the improper use of the criminal sanction with reasonable forms of regulation more consistent with basic respect for the rights of the person. The implications of this general argument are explored in detail in three general areas of proposed decriminalization: consensual adult sexual relations (in particular, homosexuality in Chapter 2 and commercial sex in Chapter 3), drug use in Chapter 4, and decisions on the right to die in Chapter 5. The resulting argument connects the limits of the criminal sanction to a general conception of personal responsibility for the meaning of individual human life (Chapters 5 and 6).

1

Human Rights and Public Morality under Constitutional Democracy

As an initial matter, it is important to put the moral criticism of over-criminalization in some historical context. Any coherent account of the ethical foundations of the substantive criminal law and its connections to constitutional principles must take seriously the radical vision of the rights of the person that underlies the United States Constitution and its precepts of criminal law. The idea of human rights was a major departure in civilized moral thought. When Locke, Rousseau, and Kant progressively gave that idea its most articulate and profound theoretical statement,[1] they defined a way of thinking about the moral implications of human personality that was radically new. One central critical focus of this new perspective was the criminal law. The Constitution and Bill of Rights of the United States, in implementing these ideas, not only required just forms of criminal procedure,[2] but also placed limits on the substantive scope of the criminal law. These limits included not only mens rea, actus reus, legality, and proportionality requirements,[3] but also the limitations imposed by the religion and free speech clauses of the first amendment on federal and (after incorporation) state power to criminalize certain kinds of conduct.[4]

Several provisions of the French Declaration of the Rights of Man and of Citizens, adopted by the French National Assembly in 1789, went beyond the United States Constitution in placing express constraints on the scope of the substantive criminal law.[5] Specifically, persons were to have "the power of doing whatever does not injure another," free of the threat of criminal penalties.[6] The Napoleonic Code, whose conception of the proper scope of the substantive criminal law appears to have been inspired by the provisions, accordingly imposed no criminal sanctions on consensual adult sexual acts, such as homosexuality and prostitution.[7]

No comparable general principle then existed in the Anglo-American political and legal tradition. In the United States, the largely unexamined governing assumption, which continues to have vitality, was that the public morality, which the criminal law enforces, is simply the set of moral values at the core of the Calvinist religious conception and its derivatives. America is, after all, a nation founded by religious extremists who conceived their task as building a New Jerusalem in express contrast to European decadence.[8] The American invention of prisons and the extravagant hopes for moral reform that they embodied for groups like the Quakers[9] were of the same spirit as the later American commitment to the "noble" experiment, Prohibition. The criminalization of alcohol was one manifestation of the power of the Calvinistic purity reformers of the nineteenth and early twentieth centuries. It was their tradition that decisively shaped America's common sense of morality and created the expectation that criminal justice could and should radically reform corrupt human nature.[10] Many Americans today, responding to felt injustices in our criminal justice system at every stage of its operation, question the assumptions underlying this conception of criminal justice. A natural means of examining the conception is to conduct a philosophical analysis of its assumptions. One available theory for such an analysis is utilitarianism, which radically questions the whole perspective on human rights implicit in American constitutionalism; another is an antiutilitarian natural rights theory, which takes seriously ideas of human rights implicit in American constitutional practice but affords a critical organon for reinterpreting their implications for criminal justice.

I. THE UTILITARIAN CRITIQUE OF OVERCRIMINALIZATION

The utilitarian argument against the Anglo-American conception of criminal justice began with the publication in 1859 of John Stuart Mill's *On Liberty*.[11] Mill proposed a general doctrine that may be termed the "harm principle." This principle limits the scope of the criminal law in the following ways:

1. Acts may properly be made criminal only if they inflict concrete harms on assignable persons.[12]

2. Except to protect children, incompetents, and "backward" peoples,[13] it is never proper to criminalize an act *solely* on the ground of preventing harm to the agent.[14]

3. It is never proper to criminalize conduct solely because the mere thought of it gives offense to others.[15]

Although Mill's harm principle places a constraint on the criminal law comparable to the one embodied in the French Declaration of Rights, Mill did not justify the constraint on the basis of the human rights paradigm, as did the French Declaration. Rather, Mill appealed to a general utilitarian argument, derived from Jeremy Bentham,[16] that failing to follow the harm principle reduces the aggregate surplus of pleasure over pain. Mill was less doctrinaire in his opposition to the language and thought of rights than Bentham,[17] and some find in *On Liberty* rights-based arguments of personal autonomy.[18] But although Mill did give great weight to preserving the capacity of persons to frame their own life plans independently, he appears—in accordance with his argument in *Utilitarianism*[19]—to have incorporated this factor into the utilitarian framework of preferring "higher" to "lower" pleasures. Thus, the argument of *On Liberty* is utilitarian: the greatest aggregate sum by which pleasure exceeds pain, taking into account the greater weight accorded by utilitarianism to higher pleasures, is secured by granting free speech and observing the harm principle.

The Anglo-American tradition of opposition to overcriminalization, initiated by Mill, has—following Mill—conceived of the issue in utilitarian terms. This tradition relies, when seeking the decriminalization of "victimless crimes,"[20] on efficiency-based arguments deploring the pointless or counterproductive use of valuable and scarce police resources in the enforcement of these laws. The pattern of argument and litany of evils are familiar. H. L. A. Hart, for example, in his defense of the recommendation of Great Britain's Wolfenden Committee to decriminalize consensual adult homosexuality and prostitution,[21] conceded that some "victimless crimes" are immoral, and then discussed in detail the countervailing and excessive costs of preventing them.[22] In the United States, commentators have emphasized pragmatic arguments that are implicitly utilitarian, identifying tangible evils that enforcement of intangible moralism appears quixotically to cause.[23] Victimless crimes typically are consensual and private, and as a result, there is rarely either a complaining victim or a witness. In such cases, police must resort to enforcement techniques, such as entrapment, that are often unconstitutional or unethical and that tend to corrupt police morals.[24] Enforcement costs also include the cost of forgoing opportunities to enforce more"serious" crimes.[25] When the special difficulty of securing sufficient evidence for conviction and the ineffectiveness of punishment in deterring these acts are considered, the utilitarian balance sheet condemns criminalization as simply too costly.

The utilitarian cast of these arguments is understandable in a nation like Great Britain, where they must be made to a parliament that enjoys constitutional supremacy. In the United States, however, arguments of this kind are made not only to legislatures but also to countermajoritarian courts empowered with judicial supremacy in the elaboration of a charter of human rights. Since 1965, the United States Supreme Court has invoked a constitutional right of privacy to invalidate the use of criminal sanctions against the purchase or use of contraceptives by adults, married[26] and unmarried,[27] and, more recently, minors;[28] the use of pornography in the home;[29] and the use of abortion services by adults[30] and, more recently, minors.[31] In addition, state courts have elaborated a similar right under state constitutions to permit the withdrawal of life support systems from irreversibly comatose, terminally ill patients.[32] One state court has interpreted the privacy right in its state constitution to permit the use of marijuana in the home,[33] and another court has held that the use of peyote by Native Americans in religious ceremonies is a constitutionally protected form of free exercise of religion.[34]

It is difficult, if not impossible, to reconcile the notion of privacy rights that these cases embody with the utilitarian policy arguments that decriminalization proponents generally use. Indeed, the status and rationale of the constitutional right of privacy are at the center of contemporary controversy over constitutional theory and practice. It is argued that the right of privacy is policy-based, legislative in character, and unneutral, and therefore may not properly be adopted by courts, whose decisions must be governed by neutral principles of justification.[35] If the deployment in these cases of the constitutional privacy right or other rights must be construed in utilitarian terms, such objections may be conclusive, and decriminalization arguments would be properly directed only to legislatures, not to courts.

It is quite natural to interpret the harm principle as derivative from some more general utilitarian argument. Harm appears to be a quasi-utilitarian concept at least insofar as utilitarianism seeks to avoid pain. There are several powerful objections to this interpretation, however.

First, utilitarian arguments for decriminalization proselytize the already converted and do not seriously challenge the justifications that defenders of criminalization traditionally offer. For these defenders, the consensual and private character of prohibited acts, even when coupled with the consequent higher enforcement costs, is not sufficient to justify decriminalization. They point out that many consensual acts, such as dueling, are properly made criminal and that many nonconsensual acts are also properly criminal despite comparably high enforcement costs. The prosecution of intrafamilial homicide, for example, requires intrusion into intimate family relations, and yet intrafamilial homicide is not therefore legalized.[36] Certainly, if there is a good moral reason for criminalizing certain conduct, quite extraordinary enforcement costs will justly be borne. Accordingly, efficiency-based arguments for decriminalization appear to beg the question. They have weight only if the conduct in question is not independently shown to be immoral. But the decriminalization literature concedes the immorality of such conduct, and then elaborates arguments, based on efficiency and costs, that can have no decisive weight.[37]

The absence of critical discussion of the focal issues that divide proponents and opponents of criminalization has made decriminalization arguments much less powerful than they can and should be. In practice, efficiency-based arguments have not been very successful in reducing the scope of "victimless crimes," whether by legislative penal code revision or by judicial invocation of the constitutional right to privacy. The wholesale or gradual decriminalization of contraception, abortion, consensual noncommercial sexual relations between or among adults, and decisions by the terminally ill to decline further treatment[38] has resulted from a shift in moral judgments: these acts are no longer believed to be morally wrong.[39] In contrast, where existing moral judgments have remained unchallenged—as, for example, with commercial sex[40] and many forms of drug use[41]—movement toward decriminalization has been either negligible[42] or haphazard.[43] Yet the decriminalization literature has failed to address these moral questions, perhaps because utilitarianism is presumed to be the only enlightened critical morality.[44] In order to give decriminalization arguments the full force they should have, it is necessary to supply the missing moral analysis. The absence of such analysis has prevented us from seeing the moral needs and interests that decriminalization in fact serves. To this extent, legal theory has not responsibly brought to critical self-consciousness the nature of an important and humane legal development.

A second objection may be made to the utilitarian interpretation of the harm principle. The harm principle is not a necessary corollary of

utilitarian tenets. The basic desideratum of utilitarianism is to maximize the surplus of pleasure over pain. If certain plausible assumptions about human nature are made, however, utilitarianism would
require the criminalization of certain conduct in violation of the harm
principle. Assume, for example, that an overwhelming majority of
people in a community take personal satisfaction in their way of life
and that their pleasure is appreciably increased by the knowledge
that conflicting ways of life are forbidden by the criminal law. Suppose, indeed, that hatred of the nonconforming minority, legitimated
by the application of criminal penalties, reinforces the pleasurable
feelings of social solidarity, peace of mind, self-worth, and achievement in a way that tolerance, with its invitation to self-doubt, ambivalence, and insecurity, could not. In such circumstances, the greater
pleasure thus secured to the majority may not only outweigh the pain
to the minority but, as compared to the toleration required by the
harm principle, may result in a greater aggregate of pleasure; accordingly, utilitarianism would call for criminalization in violation of the
harm principle.

Utilitarians defend the harm principle against such a plausible interpretation of utilitarianism by excluding the offense taken at the
mere thought of certain conduct as a ground for criminalization.[45]
Yet, how, on utilitarian grounds, can *any* form of pleasure or pain be
thus disavowed as morally irrelevant? Mill appears to have argued
that this exclusion follows from the greater weight accorded to autonomy by utilitarianism, both in and of itself (as a higher pleasure) and
instrumentally as a means of encouraging innovations and experiments that may enable people to realize more pleasure in their lives.
Mill did not, however, explain why autonomy should be given such
decisive weight, either as a pleasure in and of itself or as an instru-
ment whose value is so great that other pleasures should be wholly
excluded from the utilitarian calculus in order to preserve it. Certainly, the exercise of the competences that accompany rational autonomy often gives pleasure, but it also yields the pain of self-doubt,
ambivalence, and insecurity. In any event, why should these pleasures and pains be considered more important within the utilitarian
scheme than the pleasures of security, peace of mind, and solidarity,
which Mill appears to have disavowed? Although the claims for autonomy on instrumental grounds introduce consequentialist arguments to which utilitarians must give weight, it is difficult to see how
these arguments can be regarded as decisive. As an empirical matter,
autonomy may lead to creative innovation and experiment, but it also
may lead to empty distractions, idle fantasies, and wasted lives. The

potential effects weigh on both sides of the utilitarian scales, with perhaps some tilt toward protecting autonomy, but not to the degree that Mill's argument requires.

In order to place the principle of not criminalizing conduct that does not harm others on sound foundations, its moral basis must be interpreted in a non-utilitarian way.[46] Such an interpretation would be more consistent with the historical origins of the principle in the rights-based conception of the French Declaration of the Rights of Man and of Citizens, with the American constitutional tradition, which has based decriminalization arguments on the constitutional right to privacy, and with the texture and resonance of Mill's own intuitive spirit in *On Liberty*.

This alternative approach entirely abandons Mill's strategy of interpreting the role of autonomy in the defense of the harm principle as an aspect of the ultimate utilitarian good of maximizing the surplus of pleasure over pain. Instead, this chapter will show the harm principle to be a natural consequence of an ethical conception of human rights, in which autonomy is an ultimate good.

II. HUMAN RIGHTS AND THE MORAL FOUNDATIONS OF THE CRIMINAL LAW

In order to present an alternative conception of proper criminalization of acts in a constitutional democracy fundamentally committed to human rights, this chapter will first introduce an explanation of the concept of human rights. It will then show that recent deontological moral theory expresses this concept in a sharply antiutilitarian fashion, and will analyze the implications of this theory for the proper limits of the criminal law. Finally, it will show how this conception elucidates the harm principle in a way that utilitarianism cannot.

A. *The Concept of Human Rights*

As suggested above, when Locke, Rousseau, and Kant progressively gave the idea of human rights its most articulate and profound theoretical statement, they defined a way of thinking about the moral implications of human personality that was radically new.[47] Recent deontological moral theory, particularly as articulated by John Rawls[48] and Alan Gewirth,[49] enables us to understand and explicate these conceptions in a forceful way, as a plausible alternative to utilitarianism. It also provides us with an effective tool for rebutting familiar Benthamite criticisms of the idea of human rights.[50]

Specifically, these neo-Kantian moral theorists have explicated the concept of human rights in terms of an autonomy-based interpretation of treating persons as equals.

1. AUTONOMY. Autonomy, in the sense fundamental to the idea of human rights, begins with the conception that persons have a range of capacities that enables them to develop, to want to act on, and in fact to act on higher-order plans of action that take as their object their lives and the way they are lived, and to evaluate and order their lives according to principles of conduct and canons of ethics to which they have given their rational assent.[51] The philosopher Harry Frankfurt made this point when he argued that an "essential difference between persons and other creatures is to be found in the structure of a person's will."[52] The difference between human beings and animals is not, Frankfurt argued, that the former have desires and motives, or that they make decisions based on prior thought; certain lower animals may have these characteristics as well. Rather, besides wanting, choosing, and being moved to do this or that, persons may want to have or not to have certain desires. As Frankfurt put it, persons

are capable of wanting to be different, in their preferences and purposes, from what they are. Many animals appear to have the capacity for . . . "first-order desires" or "desires of the first order," which are simply desires to do or not to do one thing or another. No animal other than man, however, appears to have the capacity for reflective self-evaluation that is manifested in the formation of second-order desires.[53]

The complex human capacities that constitute autonomy include language, self-consciousness, memory, logical relations, empirical reasoning about beliefs and their validity (human intelligence), and the capacity to use normative principles, including, *inter alia*, principles of rational choice, to decide which among several ends may be most effectively and coherently realized. These capacities permit persons to make independent decisions regarding their lives: which of their first-order desires will be developed and which disowned, which capacities cultivated and which left fallow, with what or with whom in their life histories they will or will not identify, what they will define and pursue as basic goals, and what they will strive toward as an aspiration. For example, persons establish priorities and schedules for the satisfaction of first-order desires. The satisfaction of certain wants, such as hunger, is regularized; the satisfaction of others is sometimes postponed—marriage, for example, may be delayed in order to first secure other objectives. Persons sometimes gradually eliminate certain desires (smoking or gluttonous appetite) or encourage the development over time of others (cultivating their sensibility to love and tender mutual response).[54] The mark of personhood is precisely this capacity to assess and change one's life in such ways: to see certain aspects of one's life as irrational, self-defeating, or morally wrong, while seeing other aspects as rational, competent, or morally desirable, and to take corresponding critical attitudes expressed in uniquely *personal* emotions—regret, shame, or guilt, or, on the other hand, self-respect, pride, or a sense of integrity.[55]

Crucially, the idea of "human rights" respects this capacity of persons for rational autonomy—their capacity to be, in Kant's memorable phrase, free and rational sovereigns in the kingdom of ends.[56] Kant characterized this ultimate normative respect for the revisable choice of ends as the dignity of autonomy,[57] in contrast to the heteronomous, lower-order ends (pleasure, talent) among which the person may choose. Kant thus expressed the fundamental liberal imperative of moral neutrality with regard to the many disparate visions of the good life: the concern embodied in the idea of human rights is not with maximizing the agent's pursuit of any particular lower-order ends, but rather with respecting the higher-order capacity of the agent to exercise rational autonomy in choosing and revising his ends, whatever they are.

2. TREATING PERSONS AS EQUALS. The idea of human rights also views all persons' capacities for autonomy as being of equal value. Recent neo-Kantian moral theory has articulated the idea of equality in three ways: (1) equal concern and respect,[58] (2) universalizability,[59] and (3) that all persons are equal parties to the social contract.[60]

The notion of treating persons as equals is, of course, ambiguous. A fundamental way to distinguish among moral theories is to focus on how they differently resolve this ambiguity. For example, John Stuart Mill, following Bentham, argued that utilitarianism treated people as equals in the sense that everyone's pleasures and pains were impartially registered by the utilitarian calculus; thus, utilitarianism satisfies[61] the fundamental moral imperative of treating persons as equals, where the criterion of equality is pleasure or pain. To humane liberal reformers like Mill the great attraction of utilitarianism was precisely its capacity to interpret sensibly the basic moral imperative of treating people as equals in a way that enabled reformers concretely to assess institutions in the world in terms of human interests.[62] Any alternative to utilitarianism must provide a coherent interpretation of treating people as equals which also enables critical moral intelligence concretely to assess institutions in terms of relevant consequences. The great challenge to antiutilitarian moral theory is to explain why it better explicates the moral imperative of treating persons as equals in a way that also supplies coherent substantive principles of humane moral criticism of existing institutions.

From the perspective of neo-Kantian deontological moral theory, utilitarianism fails to treat persons as equals in the morally fundamental sense. To treat persons in the way utilitarianism requires is to focus obsessionally on pleasure alone as the *only* ethically significant fact and to aggregate it as such. Pleasure is treated as a kind of impersonal fact, and no weight is given to the separateness of the creatures who experience it. But this treatment flatly ignores that the only *ethically* crucial fact can be that *persons* experience pleasure and that pleasure has significance and weight only in the context of the life that a person chooses to lead.[63] Utilitarianism thus fails to treat persons as equals in that it literally dissolves moral personality into utilitarian aggregates. In contrast, neo-Kantian deontological moral theory interprets treating *persons* as equals not in terms of lower-order ends persons may pursue, pleasure or pain, but in terms of personhood, the capacity of each person self-critically to evaluate and give order and personal integrity to one's system of ends in the form of one's life. The fundamental and ethically prior fact is not pleasure and the maximum impersonal aggregations thereof, but so expressing equal concern and respect for the capacities of personhood that people may equally develop the capacities to take ultimate responsibility for how they live their lives and revise them accordingly. It is no accident that from Kant[64] to Rawls[65] and Gewirth[66] this perspective has been supposed to justify human rights that are not merely nonutilitarian, but antiutilitarian. Thus to express equal respect for personal autonomy is to guarantee the minimum conditions requisite for autonomy; ethical principles of obligation and duty rest upon and insure that this is so and correlatively define human rights. Without such rights, human beings would lack, *inter alia*, the basic opportunity to develop a secure sense of an independent self. Instead they simply would be the locus of impersonal pleasures that which could be manipulated and rearranged in *whatever* ways would aggregate maximum utility overall, for all individual projects must, in principle, give way before utilitarian aggregates. Rights insure that this not be so, a point Dworkin has made by defining rights as trumps over countervailing utilitarian calculations.[67]

B. *Recent Neo-Kantian Theory and Human Rights*

The task of interpreting human rights in terms of the autonomy-based interpretation of treating persons as equals has been substantially furthered by the recent revival of contractarian theory in the work of John Rawls and the similar neo-Kantian construction of Alan Gewirth.

1. JOHN RAWLS. Rawls's contractarian theory explicates human rights and their institutionalization in American constitutional law in a way that the existing moral theories of constitutional theorists—utilitarianism[68] and value skepticism[69]—cannot imitate. The great early theories of human rights—those of Locke, Rousseau, and Kant—elements of which underlie American constitutionalism, all invoked, explicitly or implicitly,[70] contractarian metaphors in explaining the concrete implications of autonomy and equal concern and respect. The basic moral vision of these theorists was that human institutions and relationships should be based on equal concern and respect for personal autonomy or, as I have put it above, on an autonomy-based interpretation of treating persons as equals. The requirements of this moral point of view were expressed by the idea that a just society was one governed by an agreement or social contract arrived at by the consent of all persons starting from a position of basic equality. Rawls's contractarian model has the great virtue of showing the continuing intellectual and moral vitality of this kind of metaphor.

The basic analytic model is this:[71] moral principles are those that perfectly rational persons, in a hypothetical "original position" of equal liberty, would agree to as the ultimate standards of conduct applicable at large.[72] Persons in the original position are thought of as ignorant of any knowledge of their specific situations, values, or identities, but as possessing all knowledge of general empirical facts, capable of interpersonal validation, and holding all reasonable beliefs. Because Rawls's concern is to apply this definition of moral principles to develop a theory of justice, he introduces into the original position the existence of conflicting claims to a limited supply of general goods and considers a specific set of principles to regulate these claims.[73]

The original position presents a problem of rational choice under uncertainty. Rational people in the original position have no way of predicting the probability that they will end up in any given situation of life. If a person agrees to principles of justice that permit deprivations of liberty and property rights and later discovers that he occupies a disadvantaged position, he will, by definition, have no just claim against deprivations that may render his life prospects meager and servile. To avoid such consequences, the rational strategy in choosing the basic principles of justice would be the conservative "maximin" strategy:[74] one would seek to maximize the minimum condition, so that if a person were born into the worst possible situation of life allowed by the adopted moral principles, he would still be better off than he would be in the worst situation allowed by other principles.

The choice of which fundamental principles of justice to adopt requires consideration of the weight assigned to general goods by those in the original position. "General goods"[75] are those things or conditions that all people desire as the generalized means to fulfillment of their individual life plans.[76] Liberty, understood as the absence of constraint, is usually considered to be one of these general goods. Similarly classifiable are powers, opportunities, and wealth.[77]

Among these general goods, self-respect or self-esteem, a concept intimately related to the idea of autonomy, occupies a place of special prominence.[78] Autonomy, seen now in the light of contractarian theory, is the capacity of persons to plan, shape, and revise their lives in accordance with changing desires and aspirations assessed in terms of arguments and evidence to which the person gives rational assent. As such, autonomy involves such essentially human capacities as thought and deliberation, speech, and craftsmanship. The competent exercise of such abilities in the pursuit of one's life plan forms the basis of self-respect,[79] without which one is liable to suffer from despair, apathy, and cynicism. Thus persons in the original position, each concerned to create favorable conditions for the successful pursuit of his life plan but ignorant of the particulars of his position in the resulting social order, would agree to regulate access to general goods so as to maximize the possibility that every member of society will be able to achieve self-respect. Accordingly, self-respect may be thought of as the primary human good.[80]

Thus Rawls's contractarian construction provides an interpretation of the moral weight of autonomy—autonomy as a feature of the primary human good—and equality—the original position of equal liberty—and affords a decisionmaking procedure, the maximin strategy, which provides a determinate substantive account for the content of human rights as minimum conditions of human decency. An important feature of the contractarian interpretation of autonomy is the assumption of ignorance of specific identity and the consequent requirement that a decision be reached on the basis of empirical facts capable of interpersonal validation. This assumption assures that the principles decided on in the original position will be neutral as between divergent visions of the good life, for the ignorance of specific identity deprives people of any basis for illegitimately distorting their decisions in favor of their own vision. Such neutrality, a fundamental feature of the idea of political right,[81] insures to people the right to choose their own lives autonomously.[82]

2. ALAN GEWIRTH. Both Rawls and Gewirth give expression to the autonomy-based interpretation of treating persons as equals in terms of variant interpretations of Kantian universalizability. Rawls does so in terms of the veil of ignorance which enables the agent to abstract from her or his particular ends, so that one captures the idea that in thinking ethically one respects higher-order capacities of person-hood, not lower-order ends which happen to be pursued; also in terms of the idealized contractual hypothesis whereby what persons would agree to therein comes to the same thing as what each person, thus idealized, would universalize for all persons alike. Gewirth follows Kant more literally. He argues that ethical reasoning, as such, is marked by a certain phenomenology—namely, in reasoning ethically, an agent abstracts from her or his particular ends—thinking in terms of human action *in general* versus any particular ends of human action, which turns out to be what we previously called rational auton-omy—and considers what general requirements for rational auton-omy the agent would demand for the self, so idealized, on the condition that the requirements be consistently extended to all other agents alike.[83] Clearly Rawls's argument is more abstract but to simi-lar effect: we start not from the particular agent, but from the concept of rational persons who must unanimously agree upon, while under a veil of ignorance as to who they are, the general critical standards in terms of which their personal relations will be governed.

Both the theories of Rawls and Gewirth are deontological: the idea of moral right is not defined teleologically in terms of maximizing the good, however defined, but in terms of certain principles that express the autonomy-based interpretation of treating persons as equals.[84] It is important to see that this kind of deontological moral perspective, while it rejects as an ultimate moral principle the utilitarian maximiza-tion of the aggregate of pleasure over pain, is not incompatible with the relevant assessment of consequences in thinking ethically. Both these theories appeal to consequences in arguing that certain substan-tive principles would be universalized (Gewirth) or agreed to (Rawls). Thus Gewirth has argued that the universalizing agent would assess the necessary substantive or material conditions for rational autonomy and would universalize these conditions; the consequences of universalization thus determine what would be universalized. Correspondingly, Rawls's contractors consider the consequences of agreeing to certain standards of conduct as part of their deliberations.

The main substantive difference between these two theories is in Rawls's argument that the contractors of the original position, in the conditions of uncertainty—not knowing who they are and thus how they will be specifically affected by agreeing to certain principles—would find it rational to maximin, viz., agree to that set of principles which would make the worst off best off. Gewirth has resisted the thoroughgoing application of this strategy on the ground that, through the veil of ignorance, it too radically treats as morally arbitrary differences between people, not all of which can easily be regarded as ethically fortuitous[85] and thus properly regulated by a principle like maximining (which, in making the worst off best off, tends to be equalizing) because, in many cases, the way rationally to make the worst off best off is to abolish the worst off classes altogether by mandating equality. We do not have to pursue this disagreement here, as its substantive upshot is in terms of narrow issues of economic distributive justice, which are not our present concern. For present purposes it is important to keep in mind the broad common ground shared by Rawls and Gewirth. Even in the area of distributive justice, both agree about the justice of maintaining a social and economic minimum. Even as regards their differences over maximining, it seems clear that Gewirth's insistence, over a wide range of cases, that each person, idealized in terms of rational autonomy, should demand for himself or herself whatever can be universalized to other persons converges with maximining, viz., insuring that each person equally has access to certain conditions of well-being and self-respect.[86] With respect to human rights, the consequence of both approaches would be a set of general principles of critical morality, some of which would involve such fundamental interests that coercion would be justified in enforcing them.[87] These principles, which we can denominate the principles of obligation and duty, would define correlative rights.[88] Let us consider the relevance of this general account of human rights to the analysis of the moral foundation of the criminal law and related constitutional principles.

C. *The Moral Foundations of the Substantive Criminal Law*

It is an uncontroversial truth that the criminal law rests on the enforcement of public morality, viz., that criminal penalties, *inter alia*, identify and stigmatize certain moral wrongs that society at large

justifiably condemns as violations of the moral decency whose observance defines the minimum boundary conditions of civilized social
life.[89] Little critical attention yet has been given in Anglo-American
law to the proper explication of the public morality in light of considerations of human rights to which constitutional democracy in
general is committed; rather, legal theory and practice have tended to
acquiesce in a questionable identification of the public morality with
social convention.[90] We are now in a position to articulate an alternative account of the moral foundations of the substantive criminal law,
which can illuminate various criminal law and related constitutional
law doctrines and the proper direction of criminal law reform.

The substantive criminal law and cognate principles of constitutional law rest on the same ethical foundations: the fundamental ethical imperative that each person should extend to others the same
respect and concern that one demands for oneself as a free and rational being with the higher-order capacities to take responsibility for
and revise the form of one's life. Whether one uses Rawls's maximining contractarian hypothesis or Gewirth's universalization of rationally autonomous people, the consequence is the same for purposes of
the criminal law. Certain basic principles are agreed to or universalized as basic principles of critical morality, because they secure, at
little comparable cost to agents acting on them, forms of action or
forbearance from action that rational persons would want guaranteed
as minimal conditions of advancing the responsible pursuit of their
ends. Furthermore, these principles will be so fundamental in securing either a higher lowest (Rawls)[91] or the conditions of rational autonomy (Gewirth)[92] that, in general, coercion will be viewed as
justified, as a last resort, in getting people to conform their conduct to
these principles. Accordingly, these principles are commonly referred
to as the ethical principles of obligation and duty which define correlative rights.[93]

One fundamental distinction between these principles of obligation
and duty is that some apply in a state of nature, whether or not
people are in institutional relations to one another, whereas others
arise because of the special benefits that life in institutions and communities makes possible; I shall refer to the former as natural duties[94]
and to the latter as institutional duties and obligations.[95] With respect
to natural duties, the principles include, at a minimum, a principle of
nonmaleficence[96] (not inflicting harm or gratuitous cruelty), mutual
aid[97] (securing a great good, like saving life, at little cost to the agent),
consideration[98] (not annoying or gratuitously violating the privacy of
others), and paternalism[99] (saving a person with impaired or undeveloped rationality likely to result in severe and irreparable harm).
With respect to institutional duties and obligations, the principles

include basic principles of justice[100] which regulate such institutions—legal and economic systems, conventions of promise-keeping and truth-telling, family and educational structure—and, in appropriate circumstances, require compliance with the requirements of such institutions,[101] for example, respecting certain property rights. All these principles of obligation and duty—natural and institutional—are formulated in complex terms, and priority relations are established among them to determine, in general, how conflicting obligations should be resolved and what the relative moral seriousness of offenses should be; the infliction of death, for example, is a more grave violation of integrity than a minor battery[102] The general nature of such principles and their derivation from the moral imperative of treating persons as equals, however, seems clear. Such principles secure to all persons, on fair terms, basic forms of action and forbearance from action which rational persons would want enforceably guaranteed as conditions and ingredients of living a life of self-critical integrity and self-respect; correlatively, such principles define human or moral rights, the weight of which as grounds for enforceable demands rests on the underlying moral principles of obligation and duty that justify such enforceable demands. Other moral principles are also agreed to or universalized, but they fall in an area, supererogation,[103] which is not our present concern.

In understanding the moral foundations of the criminal law, two classes of these moral principles are relevant at different points: (1) the moral principles that define the forms of action and forbearance from action which the criminal law enforces, for example, nonmaleficence, and (2) the principles of justice that regulate the ways in which these moral principles may be enforced.

With respect to (1), the principles in question require forms of action and forbearance from action that express basic respect for the capacity of persons responsibly to pursue their ends. Such principles impose stringent constraints on the kinds of action and forbearance from action which permissibly may be made subjects of criminal penalty; only those forms of action and forbearance may properly be criminalized which violate rights of the person to forms of respect defined by the underlying principles of obligation and duty.

With respect to (2), the principles of justice, since the moral principles of (1) are the proper objects of enforcement by forms of force or coercion, ethical principles of justice that govern the proper distribution of such force or coercion are agreed to or universalized[104] Such principles include the general requirement that sanctions be applied only to persons who broke a reasonably specific law, who had the full capacity and opportunity to obey the law, and who reasonably could have been expected to know that such a law existed. In this way, each person is guaranteed the greatest liberty, capacity, and opportunity of controlling and predicting the consequences of her or his actions, compatible with a like liberty, capacity, and opportunity for all. Such a principle can be agreed to or universalized because it is a reasonable way to secure general respect for and compliance with the moral principles of (1) at a tolerable cost; for these conditions provide the fullest possible opportunity for people to avoid these sanctions if they so choose or, at least, the fullest possible opportunity within the constraint that some system of coercive enforcement is justified to insure compliance with the moral principles of (1).[105] In addition, the principles of (2) would include principles of proportionality[106] and effectiveness,[107] which would place constraints on degrees and kinds of sanction that may be used as just criminal sanctions.

D. *The Harm Principle Reinterpreted*

Consistent with the autonomy-based interpretation of treating persons as equals, the principles underlying a just criminal law require forms of action and forbearance from action that express, on terms fair to all, basic respect for the capacity of persons responsibly to pursue their ends, whatever they are. Such principles impose this constraint: only those forms of action and forbearance that violate rights of the person to forms of respect defined by the underlying principles of obligation and duty may properly be criminalized. This is a salient feature of the perspective of human rights on criminal justice. Thus, Rousseau observed in *La Nouvelle Héloïse* that "to seek happiness and avoid misery in that which does not affect another is a natural right," without which "self-evident and absolute maxim . . . there is no human action which might not be made a crime,"[108] and the French Declaration of the Rights of Man and of Citizens declares that people are to have liberty from the criminal law "in the power of doing whatever does not injure another."[109] It is striking that Rousseau and the French Declaration formulated the constraint in terms of effect on or injury to others. This is certainly analogous to Mill's harm principle. The harm principle may, however, now be interpreted in a nonutilitarian way as a consequence, not of maximizing pleasure over-all, but of protecting, on fair terms to all, the higher-order rational interests of persons.

Consider, for example, the derivation of one of the natural duties enforceable by the criminal law, the principle of nonmaleficence: the requirement that persons not intentionally, knowingly, or negligently inflict harms on other persons, except in cases of necessary and proportional self-defense, or in certain extreme cases of just necessity or duress.[110] The principle of nonmaleficence would be agreed to or universalized, consistent with the autonomy-based interpretation of treating persons as equals, because it secures the fundamental interest of personal integrity by means of a prohibition that does not typically require the sacrifice of substantial interests.[111] Self-defense and the like are expressly exempt from this principle because to prohibit them would impose substantial sacrifices.[112]

The principle of nonmaleficence is thus no broader than necessary to prevent frustration of the rational interests of persons in their personal integrity as a condition of their other aims. It is important to see the part played by *harm* in properly interpreting the requirements of nonmaleficence. Not all forms of pain infliction, for example, are forbidden by the principle of nonmaleficence, for some are voluntarily undertaken or otherwise reasonable and thus serve the rational interests of persons (for example, in cure). These are not harms. Consider, in this connection, the pain of self-knowledge that good education or therapy sometimes indispensably involves.[113]

Correspondingly, the principle of nonmaleficence does not forbid killing as such, but only those killings that are harms.[114] Clearly, most killings of persons are harms,[115] in that persons typically have a rational interest in living, which killing frustrates. The rational interest in life, however, is an interest not just in life as such, but also in the realization of plans and aspirations that life makes possible.[116] As we shall later see, persons with coherent and rationally affirmed plans of life may, in certain circumstances, find death to be reasonably justified. One whose illness frustrates all his projects, for whom death is, in any event, highly probable, and for whom pointless pain and physical decline violate ideals of personal integrity and control may find a more rational choice in death than in prolonged life.

If death in such cases cannot be regarded as harmful, killing in such cases cannot properly be regarded as within the scope of the principle of nonmaleficence. These cases, however, form a limited exception to the principle. As we shall later see, the infliction of death causes no harm only when the individual voluntarily requests it (or it can reasonably be shown that he or she would request it) and the request is a rational outgrowth of the system of ends that the person would, with full freedom and rationality, affirm. It is central to the autonomy-based interpretation of treating persons as equals that the rational self-determination of the person is ethically fundamental, and cannot be parsed in terms of some more basic moral element like pleasure or pain.

This analysis of the crucial role of harm in the autonomy-based interpretation of nonmaleficence can be extended, with some modifications, to other moral principles. In all such cases the idea of harm and related concepts would be seen, not as components of utilitarian aggregation, but as expressions of the higher-order rational interests of the person that, on fair terms to all, are secured by the relevant moral principles and their enforcement through the criminal law.

There are three corollaries to this interpretation of the harm principle as a constraint on just criminalization, each of which converges with aspects of Mill's account and suggests that the proper basis for his account is some argument of the form here presented. First, Mill clearly ruled out, as a justification for criminalization, the interest of others in punishing acts that are offensive to their thoughts[117] (no matter how conventional, historically common, or sincerely held). It is difficult to understand how, on purely utilitarian grounds, Mill could have *entirely* excluded such interests from some weighting in the utilitarian calculus. The autonomy-based interpretation here proposed, however, clearly gives no weight at all to such interests, because they are not rooted in moral principles that respect the rights of the person. Indeed, criminalization on such a basis must itself be the object of moral criticism and constitutional attack, for to give any weight to such interests would violate the rights of the person in the service of mere majoritarian distaste and, possibly, prejudice. From the perspective of the autonomy-based interpretation of treating persons as equals, the extension of the criminal law beyond the confines of the harm principle, properly understood, creates a tyranny of majoritarian convention which, if left without any moral constraint, erodes the foundations of autonomous personhood. Instead, moral precepts, grounded in the harm principle, should limit personal autonomy only where necessary to protect countervailing rights; other-- wise, persons should have a general right of personal autonomy.[118] The source of this general right is the fundamental value of liberalism, a focal concern with the capacity of each person, compatibly with a like capacity for all, to address with dignity the central problem of personhood—how to live one's life. Only by refraining from coercive interference with this right do we respect the basic higher-order interests of the person in taking responsibility for his or her own life.[119]

Second, although the account here proposed, unlike Mill,[120] would not entirely rule out paternalism as a ground for state interference, it does explain why paternalism is suspect and must, to be acceptable, satisfy rigorous scrutiny. If majority prejudices can support the extension of the criminal law beyond the confines of the harm principle, as here interpreted, it is but a small step to the supposition that conduct alleged to be morally wrong is also sufficiently self-destructive to warrant interference on paternalistic grounds.[121] Mill expressed his criticism of such overreaching by ruling out paternalistic arguments entirely. An autonomy-based interpretation of the harm principle need not go so far. As will shortly be shown,[122] the autonomy-based interpretation implies a natural duty of paternalism. This duty will be defined, however, so as to exclude precisely those forms of criminalization that Mill criticized.

Finally, the account here proposed not only better explains and justifies Mill's argument, it also clarifies the terms of the argument and, in particular, the notion of harm. If the harm principle is interpreted in utilitarian fashion, as Mill's argument appears to suggest, it is difficult to see how it can bear the critical weight that Mill wished to place on it. If we feel the intuitive appeal of harm as a criterion but are puzzled by Mill's ad hoc use of it, we naturally are led to an alternative theory of what harm should mean. The autonomy-based interpretation appears to supply this need. But this can perhaps best be seen in the examination of particular decriminalization controversies.

NOTES

1. See I. Kant, *Foundations of the Metaphysics of Morals* (L. W. Beck trans. 1959) [hereinafter cited as *Foundations*]; I. Kant, "On the Common Saying: 'This May Be True in Theory, But It Does Not Apply in Practice,'" in *Kant's Political Writings* 61–92 (H. Reiss ed. 1970) [hereinafter cited as Kant, "On the Common Saying"]; I. Kant, *The Metaphysical Elements of Justice* (J. Ladd trans. 1965); J. Locke, "Second Treatise," in *Two Treatises of Government* 284–446 (P. Laslett ed. 1960); J.-J. Rousseau, "The Social Contract," in *The Social Contract and Discourses* (G.D.H. Cole trans. 1950).

2. These include requirements for probable cause on arrest, for the issuance of warrants by impartial magistrates for searches and seizures, for jury trials and adversarial procedures, and for the privilege against self-incrimination. See *U. S. Const.* amends. IV, V, VI, VII.

3. For discussions of these principles, see D. Richards, *The Moral Criticism of Law* (192–259 (1977); Richards, "Human Rights and the Moral Foundations of the Substantive Criminal Law," 13 Ga. L. Rev. 1395 (1979) [hereinafter cited as Richards, "Human Rights and Criminal Law"].

4. See generally L. Tribe, *American Constitutional Law* 576–736, 812–85 (1978).

5. See, for general provisions relevant to the criminal law, French Declaration of the Rights of Man and of Citizens, especially arts. IV, V, VI, VII, VIII, IX, X, XI.

6. Id. art IV. For text, see T. Paine, *Rights of Man* 133 (H. Collins ed. 1976).

7. See generally V. Bullough, *Homosexuality: A History* 37 (1979); J. Decker, *Prostitution: Regulation and Control* 49–53 (1979). For various revisions in the French sexual code, see G. Mueller, *The French Penal Code* arts. 330–40, at 113 (n.d.).

8. See E. Morgan, *The Challenge of the American Revolution* 88–138 (1976).

9. See D. Rothman, *The Discovery of the Asylum* 79–108 (1971).

10. See discussion hereof in Chapter 4.

11. J. S. Mill, *On Liberty* (A. Castell ed. 1947).

12. Id. at 9.

13. Id. at 10.

14. Id. at 9–10.

15. Id. at 90–91. One of Mill's examples (stopping a person from crossing an unsafe bridge where there is no time to warn, id. at 97–98) suggests, in fact, that he believed there could be just paternalism even in the case of adults.

16. For Bentham's views, unpublished during his lifetime, on the decriminalization of homosexuality, see Bentham, "Offences Against One's Self: Paederasty" (part 1), 3 *J. Homosexuality* 389 (1978); "Jeremy Bentham's Essay on 'Paederasty'," 4 *J. Homosexuality* 91 (1978).

17. See generally J. Bentham, "Anarchical Fallacies: Being an Examination of the Declaration of Rights Issued During the French Revolution," in 2 *Works of Jeremy Bentham* 448 (J. Bowring ed. 1962) [hereinafter cited as Bentham, "Anarchical Fallacies"].

18. See, e. g., Arneson, "Mill versus Paternalism," 90 *Ethics* 470 (1980).

19. See J. S. Mill, *Utilitarianism* 9–20 (O. Piest ed. 1957).

20. Often the liberal critique is characterized as directed toward "victimless crimes," defined as drug and alcohol abuse, gambling, prostitution, and homosexuality. See N. Morris & G. Hawkins, *The Honest Politician's Guide to Crime Control* 8–10 (1970); H. Packer, *The Limits of the Criminal Sanction* 266 (1968); Kadish, "The Crisis of Over-criminalization," 374 *Annals* 157, 163–165 (1967) [hereinafter cited as Kadish, "Overcriminalization"]. See also *Model Penal Code* §§ 207.1–.6, Comments (Tent. Draft No. 4, 1955); Committee on Homosexual Offenses and Prostitution, *The Wolfenden Report* (1963) [hereinafter cited as *Wolfenden Report*].

21. See *Wolfenden Report*, supra note 20.

22. H. L. A. Hart, *Law, Liberty, and Morality* 45–46, 52, 67–69 (1963).

23. See e. g., N. Morris & G. Hawkins, supra note 20; H. Packer, supra note 20; Kadish, "Overcriminalization," supra note 20.

24. See generally J. Skolnick, *Justice Without Trial* (1966).

25. See works cited at note 23, supra.

26. See *Griswold v. Connecticut*, 381 U. S. 479 (1965).

27. See *Eisenstadt v. Baird* 405 U. S. 438 (1972).

28. See *Carey v. Population Servs. Int'l*, 431 U. S. 678 (1977).

29. See *Stanley v. Georgia*, 394 U. S. 557 (1969).

30. See *Roe v. Wade*, 410 U. S. 113 (1973).

31. See *Bellotti v. Baird*, 443 U. S. 622 (1979); *Planned Parenthood v. Danforth*, 428 U. S. 52 (1976).

32. See *Superintendent of Belchertown State School v. Saikewicz*, 373 Mass. 728, 370 N.E. 2d 417 (1977); *In re Quinlan*, 70 N. J. 10, 335 A 2d 647, cert denied, 429 U. S. 922 (1976); *In re Eichner v. Dillon*, 73 A. D. 2d 431, 426 N. Y. S. 2d 517 (1980), aff'd and modified, *N. Y. L. J.*, April 2, 1981, at 1, col. 2 (N. Y. March 31, 1981).

33. See *Ravin v. State*, 537 P. 2d 494 (Alaska 1975); cf. *People v. Sinclair*, 387 Mich. 91, 194 N. W. 2d 878 (1972) (plurality opinion) (classification of marijuana as a narcotic is violative of equal protection). But cf. *State v. Kantner*, 53 Hawaii 327, 493 P. 2d 306, cert. denied, 409 U. S., 948 (1972) (classification of marijuana as a narcotic is not violative of equal protection).

34. See *People v. Woody*, 61 Cal. 2d 716, 394 P. 2d 813, 40 Cal. Rptr. 69 (1964); Note, "Native Americans and the Free Exercise Clause," 28 *Hastings L. J.* 1509 (1977).

35. See generally Ely, "The Wages of Crying Wolf: A Comment on *Roe v. Wade*," 82 *Yale L. J.* 920 (1973); Comment, "*Roe v. Wade*—The Abortion Decision—An Analysis and Its Implication," 10 *San Diego L. Rev.* 844, 848–51 (1973); Note, "*Roe v. Wade* and *Doe v. Bolton*: The Compelling State Interest Test in Substantive Due Process," 30 *Wash. & Lee L. Rev.* 628, 634–35, 642–43 (1973).

36. For one example of this form of criticism, see Junker, "Criminalization and Criminogenesis," 19 *U.C.L.A. L. Rev.* 697 (1972). Contra, Kadish, "More on Over-criminalization: A Reply to Professor Junker," *U.C.L.A. L. Rev.* 719 (1972) (supporting excessive cost rationale).

37. In his argument for decriminalization, H. L. A. Hart did distinguish between "conventional" and "critical" morality, but did not explicate the latter concept. See

H. L. A. Hart, supra note 22 at 17–24. For the purposes of his argument, Hart assumed the immorality of the acts in question, and then made various points about the costs that would attach to strict enforcement.

38. See notes 26–32 and accompanying text supra. The United States Supreme Court recently upheld a decision that the constitutional right to privacy did not extend to consensual adult homosexuality. See *Doe v. Commonwealth's Attorney for Richmond*, 425 U. S. 901 (1976), aff'g mem. 403 F. Supp. 1199 (E. D. Va. 1975) (three-judge court). There has been, however, a gradual movement toward decriminalization of consensual sodomy by legislative repeal. A recent overview indicates that 21 state legislatures have decriminalized. Rivera, "Our Straight-Laced Judges: The Legal Position of Homosexual Persons in the United States," 30 *Hastings L. J.* 799, 950–51 (1979).

39. For an attempt to explain the nature of these changes in moral judgments, see Chapter 2.

40. See chapter 3.

41. There have been shifts toward decriminalization only in the area of marijuana use and possession. See 1976 *Ann. Survey Am. L.* 343–57. This shift has been limited to the reduction of penalties for the possession and use, but not the sale, of marijuana, and has had no effect on penalties for other forms of drug use. Indeed, some states have increased penalties for other forms of drug use quite drastically. See, e. g., Joint Committee on New York Drug Law Evaluation, *The Nation's Toughest Drug Law: Evaluating the New York Experience* (1978); *Staff Working Papers of the Drug Law Evaluation Project* (1978).

42. See Chapter 3.

43. See Chapter 4.

44. H. L. A. Hart appeared to acknowledge the existence of a critical morality that is not necessarily utilitarian, although he did not explore the content of this morality in his discussion of decriminalization. See H. L. A. Hart, supra note 22 at 17–24. But see H. L. A. Hart, *Punishment and Responsibility* (1968), where he repeatedly insisted that principles of fairness and equal liberty, independent of utilitarian considerations, are needed to account for the principles of punishment, id. at 72–73, and for the form of excuses in the criminal law, id. at 17–24. For a striking attempt by Hart to construct a nonutilitarian theory of natural rights from Kantian premises, see Hart, "Are There Any Natural Rights?" in *Society, Law, and Morality* 173 (F. Olafson ed. 1961).

45. See text accompanying note 15 supra.

46. For a recent excellent analysis of Mill's argument, which concurs in my view that the argument cannot be grounded in utilitarianism, see C. L. Ten, *Mill on Liberty* (1980). The account here offered affords the kind of nonutilitarian foundation for Mill's argument which is clearly needed, and is thus congruent with Ten's account. Ronald Dworkin has attempted to afford such an account in terms of the exclusion of external preferences from the utilitarian calculation. See R. Dworkin, *Taking Rights Seriously* 223–39 (1977). But this account begs many important questions. See H. L. A. Hart, "Between Utility and Rights," in *The Idea of Freedom*, ed. Alan Ryan (1979) at 86–97; V. Haksar, *Equality, Liberty, and Perfectionism* 258–69 (1979). In particular, it assumes some nonutilitarian form of argument for excluding such preferences. The account here given supplies the kind of nonutilitarian argument which is needed.

47. See text accompanying note 1 supra.

48. See J. Rawls, *A Theory of Justice* (1971).

49. See A. Gewirth, *Reason and Morality* (1978).

50. See Bentham, "Anarchical Fallacies," supra note 17.

51. For an elaboration of this idea, see D. Richards, *A Theory of Reasons for Action* 65–68 (1971) [hereinafter cited as D. Richards, *Reasons for Action*].

52. Frankfurt, "Freedom of the Will and the Concept of a Person," 68 *J. Phil.* 5, 6 (1971). For related accounts, see Benn, "Freedom, Autonomy and the Concept of a Person," 1976 *Proc. Aristotelian Soc'y* 109–30; Dworkin, "Autonomy and Behavior Control," 6 *Hastings Center Rep.* 23 (1976); Dworkin, "Acting Freely," 4 *Nous* 367 (1970); Richards, "Rights and Autonomy," *Ethics*, October 1981; Watson, "Free Agency," 72 *J. Phil.* 205 (1975).

53. Frankfurt, supra note 52, at 7.

54. For an account of the relation of the person to rational choice, including choices of these kinds, see D. Richards, *Reasons for Action*, supra note 51, at ch. 3.

55. For an account of the bases for these personal emotions, see id. at 250–67.

56. *Foundations*, supra note 1, at 51–52. See also Rawls, "A Kantian Conception of Equality," *Cambridge Rev.* Feb. 1975, at 94; Rawls, "Kantian Constructivism in Moral Theory," 77 *J. Phil.* 515, 535–54 (1980).

57. *Foundations*, supra note 1, at 53.

58. See R. Dworkin, supra note 46, at 150.

59. See A. Gewirth, supra note 49.

60. See J. Rawls, supra note 42.

61. See J. Mill, *Utilitarianism* 76–79 (1957) (lst ed. London 1863).

62. See id. at 73.

63. See Williams, "A Critique of Utilitarianism," in J. Smart & B. Williams, *Utilitarianism For and Against* 77 (1973).

64. I. Kant, *Foundations*, supra note 1, at 59–64.

65. J. Rawls, supra note 43 at 22–27.

66. A. Gewirth, supra note 49, at 200–01.

67. R. Dworkin, supra note 46, at 90–94, 188–92.

68. The majoritarian appeal in Thayer, "The Origin and Scope of the American Doctrine of Constitutional Law," 7 *Harv. L. Rev.* 129 (1893), is implicitly utilitarian, as are Bickel's later works, A. Bickel, *The Morality of Consent* (1975); A. Bickel, *The Supreme Court and the Idea of Progress* (1970).

69. See generally L. Hand, *The Bill of Rights* (1958). Compare A. Bickel, *The Supreme Court and the Idea of Progress*, supra note 68, in which a value skepticism similar to Hand's leads to a critique of moral reform through constitutional adjudication. Moral reflection and reform in the light of principles are to be replaced by unconscious moral historicism. Id. at 174–75. These ideas represent a significant retreat from Bickel's earlier work. See A. Bickel, *The Least Dangerous Branch* (1962). Value skepticism and utilitarianism are often inextricably intertwined in the work of these theorists. The idea, invoked seminally by Holmes, appears to be that one is skeptical of any nonutilitarian ideas but that utilitarian ideas are to be invoked in any proper analysis of the law. For the latter, see O. W. Holmes, *The Common Law* (2d ed. 1963). For a good statement of Holmes's value skepticism as a theory of the first amendment, see his dissent in *Abrams v. United States*, 250 U.S. 616, 624 (1919) (Holmes, J., dissenting). See also his famous dissenting observation, "The Fourteenth Amendment does not enact Mr. Herbert Spencer's Social Statics," *Lochner v. New York*, 198 U. S. 45, 75 (1905) (Holmes, J., dissenting).

70. Kant did not expressly invoke a contractarian model in the way Locke and Rousseau did, but he clearly suggested it. See Kant, supra note 1. For Locke, see Locke, supra note 1. For Rousseau, see Rousseau, supra note 1.

71. J. Rawls, supra note 48 at 11–22. See also D. Richards, *Reasons for Action*, supra note 61, at 75–91.

72. J. Rawls, supra note 48, at 11–22.

73. If there were goods in abundant superfluity or if people were more willing to sacrifice their interests for the good of others, the need for a moral system might be significantly different or even nonexistent. For David Hume's remarkable discussion of the conditions of moderate scarcity, see D. Hume, *A Treatise of Human Nature* bk III, pt. 2, § 11 (London 1739), reprinted in *Society, Law and Morality* 307–19 (F. Olafson ed. 1961). See also J. Rawls, supra note 48, at 128.

74. See J. Rawls, supra note 48, at 150–61.

75. Rawls describes these general goods as "things which it is supposed a rational man wants whatever else he wants." Id. at 92. The notion of rationality considered here is developed in D. Richards, *Reasons for Action*, supra note 57, at 27–48, and J. Rawls, supra note 48, at 407–16. The general view of the good is discussed in J. Rawls, supra note 49, at 395–452, and in D. Richards, *Reasons for Action*, supra note 51, at 286–91.

76. For the notion of a life plan, see C. Fried, *An Anatomy of Values* 97–101, 155–82

(1970); J. Rawls, supra note 48 at 407–16; D. Richards, *Reasons for Action*, supra note 51, at 27–48, 63–74.

77. J. Rawls, supra note 48 at 92. See also Richards, "Equal Opportunity and School Financing: Towards a Moral Theory of Constitutional Adjudication," *U. Chi. L. Rev.* 32, 41–49 (1973).

78. J. Rawls, supra note 48 at 433, 440–46.

79. See D. Richards, *Reasons for Action*, supra note 51, at 257, 265–68; R. White, *Ego and Reality in Psychoanalytic Theory* (1963).

80. In Rawls' terminology, self-respect is "the most important primary good." J. Rawls, supra note 48 at 440. See also id. at 178–80.

81. Dworkin, "Liberalism," in *Public and Private Morality* 113–43 (S. Hampshire ed. 1978).

82. In later elaborations of his theory, Rawls has laid great stress on the primacy of the argument for religious toleration as the paradigm for his argument. See Rawls, "Fairness to Goodness," 84 *Phil. Rev.* 536, 539–40, 542–43 (1975); Rawls, "Reply to Alexander and Musgrave," 88 *Q. J. Econ.* 633, 636–37 (1974). The self-conscious primacy of religious toleration in Rawls' theory is a striking correlate to the place of the free exercise and anti-establishment clauses of the first amendment. See also Rawls, "Kantian Constructivism in Moral Theory", supra note 56, at 539–40.

83. A. Gewirth, supra note 49, at 48–198.

84. J. Rawls, supra note 48, at 30, 40.

85. A. Gewirth, supra note 49, at 108–09. See also id. at 331.

86. See id. at 199–365; Gewirth, "The Basis and Content of Human Rights," 13 *Ga. L. Rev.* 1143 (1979).

87. For a contractarian derivation of such rights, see D. Richards, *Reasons for Action*, supra note 51, at 92–195.

88. See id. at 96–106.

89. See, e.g., Butler, "Upon Resentment," in *Fifteen Sermons at the Rolls Chapel* 102 (1913); J. Feinberg, "The Expressive Function of Punishment," in *Doing and Deserving* 95–118 (1970); Hart, "The Aims of the Criminal Law," 23 *Law & Contemp. Prob.* 401 (1958); F. Stephen, "Punishment and Public Morality," in 2 *A History of the Criminal Law of England* 30–37, 90–93 (1883).

90. See discussion in Chapter 2, infra.

91. See D. Richards, *Reasons for Action*, supra note 51, at 92–195.

92. See note 86 & accompanying text supra.

93. See note 88 & accompanying text supra.

94. See D. Richard, *Reasons for Action*, supra note 51, at 92–95, 176–95.

95. Id. at 27–175. See also id. at 92–95.

96. Id. at 176.

97. Id. at 185.

98. Id. at 189.

99. Id. at 192.

100. Id. at 107–47. See also J. Rawls, supra note 48, at 195–394.

101. D. Richards, *Reasons for Action*, supra note 51 at 148–75.

102. For attempts to formulate such complex principles which appear broadly convergent in substantive requirements, see id. at 8–10; A. Gewirth, supra note 49, at 199–365.

103. D. Richards, *Reasons for Action*, supra note 51, at 196–211.

104. I discuss these principles at greater length in Richards, "Human Rights," supra note 3, at 1416–20.

105. See id. at 1428–34.

106. See id. at 1418, 1442–45.

107. See id. at 1418–19, 1442–45.

108. J.-J. Rousseau, *La Nouvelle Héloïse* 264 (J. H. McDowell trans. 1968) (lst ed. Paris 1761).

109. *French Declaration of the Rights of Man and of Citizens* art. IV.

110. See generally D. Richards, *Reasons for Action*, supra note 51, at 176–85. For a

similar formulation, see Brandt, "A Moral Principle About Killing," in *Beneficent Euthanasia* 106–14 (M. Kohl ed. 1975).

111. The condition, that actions required by a principle should not call for substantial sacrifices of personal interests (for example, death, ill health, or penury), is a central reason that duties or obligations may be coercively enforced; otherwise, justifiable coercion would never be agreed to. Cf. D. Richards, *Reasons for Action,* supra note 51, at 177.

112. Self-defense is permitted because the agent would be unjustly harmed unless harm were used in defense. See generally id. at 181; Richards, "Human Rights and Criminal Law," supra note 3, at 1435–36. See also C. Fried, *Right and Wrong* 42–53 (1978). In cases of just necessity, harm is inflicted only as a way of fairly avoiding greater harm. See Richards, "Human Rights and Criminal Law," supra note 3, at 1437–39. In cases of duress, the agent is threatened with harm that a reasonable person could not resist. See id. at 1431–32.

113. Cf. D. Richards, *Reasons for Action,* supra note 51 at 180. Even masochistic pleasure may, in some cases, be regarded as a good not forbidden by nonmaleficence. Cf. id. at 178.

114. See generally Brandt, "A Moral Principle About Killing," supra note 110, see also Brandt, "The Morality and Rationality of Suicide," in *Ethical Issues in Death and Dying* 122 (T. Beauchamp & S. Perlin eds. 1978).

115. Joel Feinberg has discussed the question whether the murderer harms his victim. See Feinberg, "Harm and Self-Interest," in *Law, Morality and Society* 285, 299 (P. Hacker & J. Raz eds. 1977).

116. See generally Silverstein, "The Evil of Death," 77 *J. Phil.* 401, 405–10 (1980).

117. J. S. Mill, supra note 11, at 90–91.

118. See chapter 2, infra; see also Richards, "Human Rights and Moral Ideals: An Essay on the Moral Theory of Liberalism," 5 *Soc. Theory and Prac.* 461 (1979) [hereinafter cited as Richards, "Human Rights and Moral Ideals"].

119. See generally Richards, "Human Rights and Moral Ideals," supra note 118 at 472–75.

120. See J. S. Mill, supra note 11 at 9–10.

121. See discussions hereof in Chapters 2 and 3, infra.

122. See Chapters 2–5, infra.

Part One
SEX

2

Consensual Homosexuality and the Constitutional Right to Privacy

From its recognition in *Griswold v. Connecticut*,[1] the constitutional right to privacy commonly has been attacked as expressing subjective judicial ideology, as lacking a constitutionally neutral principle, and as being, in substance, a form of legislative policy not properly pursued by the courts.[2] In particular, critics, both on[3] and off the Supreme Court,[4] have questioned the methodology of the Court in inferring an independent constitutional right to privacy that is not within the contours of the rights expressly guaranteed by the Constitution; in brief, how can the Court legitimately appeal to an unwritten constitution when the *point* of the constitutional design was to limit governmental power by a written text?

The summary affirmance in *Doe v. Commonwealth's Attorney for Richmond*,[5] which could be read as excluding homosexual acts between consenting adults from the scope of the constitutional right to privacy, may give compelling force to these kinds of objections. The Court may have summarily limited the right to privacy in a way that suggests fiat, not articulated principle, for how can the Court in a principled way sustain the constitutional right to privacy of married and unmarried people to use contraceptives,[6] or to have abortions,[7] or to use pornography in the privacy of one's home,[8] and not sustain the rights of consenting adult homosexuals to engage in the form of sex they find natural?

I believe that the constitutional right to privacy is a sound and defensible development in our constitutional jurisprudence that *Doe* betrays. The argument of this chapter will attempt to explicate the jurisprudential foundations of the constitutional right to privacy and to explain, *pari passu,* wherein *Doe* errs. This chapter begins with a discussion of how the philosophical explication of human rights, suggested in Chapter 1, may be used to clarify the idea of an unwritten constitution underlying the terms of the written Constitution. The chapter then examines three interconnecting variables—antimoralism, antipaternalism, and the moral value of autonomy—to explain how the idea of human rights justifies a constitutional right to privacy correctly applied to contraceptives, abortions, and the private use of pornography, as well as to consensual adult homosexual acts.

I. THE CONCEPT OF HUMAN RIGHTS AS AN UNWRITTEN CONSTITUTION

The constitutional power of judicial review is marked by two salient structural features. First, such review is intrinsically countermajoritarian. The Constitution clearly was intended to put legal constraints on majority power, whether exercised by the legislature or by the executive. Second, the basis of this countermajoritarian appeal appears to be ideas of human rights that, by definition, government has no moral title to transgress. Under the constitutional order, certain human rights are elevated into legally enforceable rights, so that if a law infringes on these moral rights, the law is not valid.[9]

Ronald Dworkin has recently described these structural features in terms of his rights thesis,[10] which rests on an analytical claim regarding the force of rights as trump cards that, by definition, outweigh utilitarian or quasi-utilitarian considerations and can legitimately be weighed only against other rights. Moreover, the weighing of *rights* cannot be a sham appeal to vague and speculative consequences. Finally, the force of the rights thesis in American constitutional law is shown by the fact that violation of constitutional rights establishes not merely a permission but an affirmative right and even a duty to disobey the challenged law. This principle derives from the force of the case or controversy requirement for federal litigation,[11] which typically requires that people have standing to make constitutional arguments about violations of human rights only when they have disobeyed the law in question and are about to be prosecuted for violations thereof.[12] Accordingly, the vindication and elaboration of constitutional rights require willingness to disobey the law on a suitable occasion.

Dworkin's description of the institutionalization of the rights thesis in American constitutional law directly challenges current constitutional theories that do not take seriously the rights thesis and the consequent proper scope of the countermajoritarian judicial review that enforces constitutional rights. These theories rest either on utilitarianism,[13] which became the dominant American moral jurisprudence in the late nineteenth century with Holmes's *The Common Law*,[14] or on twentieth-century value skepticism.[15] Neither moral view can be squared with the rights thesis as it underlies American constitutional law. Accordingly, the constitutional theories that assume or presuppose these viewpoints either skeptically question the very legitimacy of judicial review[16] or urge that the scope of judicial review be sharply circumscribed.[17] The American practice of constitutional law, as Dworkin's descriptive thesis shows, does not conform to this theory; American judges, like Holmes and Hand, did not decide constitutional cases in the way their theory of law would require.[18] This dissonance of American theory and practice indicates, I believe, not a defect in the practice of American constitutional law, which rests on sound moral foundations, but a focal inadequacy in American legal theory that has not, in a memorable phrase of Dworkin's, taken rights seriously.

In order to understand and interpret the constitutional design, we must take seriously the radical vision of human rights that the Constitution was intended to express and in terms of which the written text of the Constitution was intended to be interpreted; I call this vision the unwritten constitution.[19]

We have already mentioned in Chapter 1 that the idea of human rights was a major departure in human thought, and that the philosophers who best articulated its radical implications for the significance of respect for moral personality (Locke, Rousseau, and Kant) called for corresponding practical reforms. The political implications of this way of thinking are a matter of history. The idea of human rights was among the central moral concepts in terms of which a number of great political revolutions conceived and justified their demands.[20] Once introduced, the idea of human rights could not be confined. In this country it provided the foundation for the distinctly American innovation of judicial review—the idea that an enforceable charter of human rights requires a special set of governing institutions that, in principle, protect these rights from incursions of the governing majority.[21] Thus, there is little question that the Bill of Rights was part of and gave expression to a developing moral theory regarding the rights of individuals that had been theoretically stated by Milton[22] and Locke[23] and that was given expression by

Rousseau[24] and Kant.[25] The founding fathers believed some such theory[26] and regarded the Bill of Rights, inter alia, as a way of institutionalizing it.[27] Nevertheless, attempts to define the specific content of constitutionally protected moral rights are frustrated by the fact that articulation of such rights typically rests on constitutional provisions strikingly general in form (e.g., "freedom of speech or of the press"; "due process of law"; "equal protection of the law") and often lacking any convincing legal history regarding the intended application of the provision. A consensus, to the extent one existed when these clauses were drafted, was reached on the ambiguous generalities of political compromise.[28] Even when circumstances at the time strongly suggest a certain interpretation, such legal history has not conventionally been regarded as dispositive.[29] In order to understand how constitutional provisions of these kinds are interpreted, we must advert to the underlying concepts of human rights that they express.

Often, in order to articulate a hermeneutics of the meanings that language properly bears, we invoke an underlying theory of the kind of communication that a specific form of discourse exemplifies.[30] When a critic of the arts, for example, interprets the meaning of a complex work of art, he or she invokes, inter alia, conventions of communication of the genre in question, because such conventions are part of the assumed and well-understood background of shared communicative understandings that the artist invoked in creating the work.[31] In the law, the canons of statutory interpretation importantly attempt to specify an underlying theory of the proper communicative purposes that may reasonably be imputed to the choice of legislative language in the context of constitutional values and the institutional separation of powers.[32] Correspondingly, the meaning of constitutional provisions necessarily rests on the background theory of human values that the Constitution assumes as its communicative context.

When referring, then, to the concept of human rights as the unwritten constitution, I do not mean to suggest that these underlying understandings are in some sense a secret and impalpable mist.[33] On the contrary, the idea of human rights is the necessary hermeneutical principle that alone enables us to understand how it is that constitutional provisions have any meaning at all. Indeed, alternative, legal-realist constitutional theories are notoriously inadequate in that they fail to take seriously the kinds of normative meaning that constitutional provisions conventionally and often unambiguously express. That the interpretation of constitutional meaning should invoke background communicative understandings is *in principle* no more mysterious than the fact of human linguistic communication.[34]

Since the central task of a constitutional theory is to explicate the background understandings that constitutional language invokes, we must take as our central analytical focus the unwritten constitution, the idea of human rights. Accordingly, the philosophical explication of the concept of human rights, offered in Chapter 1, necessarily must clarify the proper structure of constitutional argument relevant to many issues. Let us consider how the earlier suggested autonomy-based interpretation of treating persons as equals—in particular, the contractarian interpretation of equal concern and respect for autonomy—clarifies the moral basis of the constitutional right to privacy in general and the application of this right to consensual homosexuality in particular.

II. A MORAL THEORY OF THE CONSTITUTIONAL RIGHT TO PRIVACY

All discussions of the right of privacy must begin with the famous law review article by Warren and Brandeis in which they recommended the recognition of privacy as an independent legal right.[35] Warren and Brandeis were immediately concerned with the failure of existing tort law to provide a clear remedy for the public disclosure of private facts. Nevertheless, basing their argument on the rights "of an inviolate personality,"[36] they spoke more broadly of the human need for "some retreat from the world,"[37] of the effect of unwarranted intrusion on a person's "estimate of himself and upon his feelings,"[38] and of the "general right of the individual to be let alone."[39] The latter suggestion that the right of privacy is broader than the tort remedies under immediate examination was confirmed by the famous dissent in *Olmstead v. United States*[40] in which Brandeis invoked "the right to be let alone," not in support of a private tort remedy but in support of an expanded interpretation of fourth amendment constitutional rights of private parties against the state.[41]

Of course, we now perceive the interests of privacy torts and fourth amendment guarantees as analytically similar—rights of information control protected in the one case against individuals, in the other against the state.[42] But the spirit of Brandeis's argument cuts deeper than this analytical point on which he places no great weight. Brandeis, rather, is appealing to an underlying moral argument about the place of human rights in the American contractarian conception of the relation of individuals among themselves and to the state. In his *Olmstead* dissent, for example, he notes:

The makers of our Constitution undertook to secure conditions favorable to the pursuit of happiness. They recognized the significance of man's spiritual nature, of his feelings and of his intellect. They knew that only a part of the pain, pleasure and satisfactions of life are to be found in material things. They sought to protect Americans in their beliefs, their thoughts, their emotions and their sensations.[43]

When Brandeis summarized this foundational right as "the most comprehensive of rights and the right most valued by civilized men,"[44] he was, I believe, invoking the general conception of human rights, founded on autonomy and equal concern and respect. Certain of the principles of constitutional justice upon which Brandeis relied are concerned with issues having deep connection with personal dignity and the right to control highly personal information about oneself. Such information control is one of the primary ways in which persons autonomously establish their self-conception and their varying relations to other persons through selective information disclosure.[45] Without some legally guaranteed right to control such information, personal autonomy is degraded at its core. From *personal* self-definition and self-mastery it is debased into the impersonal and fungible conventionalism that uncontrolled publicity inevitably facilitates.[46] Accordingly, arguments, premised on the foundational values of equal concern and respect for autonomy, justify the protection of conventional privacy interests under tort law, as well as under various constitutional guarantees.

Actions protected by principles enunciated in *Griswold* and subsequent cases are denominated "private," not because they rest on information control, but because substantive constitutional principles define conclusive reasons why they may not properly be the subject of encroachment by the state or by private individuals. Such rights are sensibly called "rights to privacy" in the sense that constitutional principles debar forms of state and private regulatory or prohibitory intrusion into the relevant areas of people's lives; on the basis of these principles, interference in these areas is unwarranted.

What is at stake here is nothing less than the basic moral vision of persons as having human rights: that is, as autonomous and entitled to equal concern and respect. This vision, correctly invoked by Warren and Brandeis in developing rights to information control, similarly underlies the constitutional right to privacy. In order to explain with care how this is so, we now turn to a deeper examination of the content of the moral principles involved in this latter right, and how they express the underlying values of autonomy and equal concern and respect to which Brandeis appeals. This examination will show why the constitutional right to privacy is a natural and defensible development rooted in the unwritten constitution, which gives sense to the constitutional design.

A. *The Concept of Morality and the Transvaluation of Values*

The constitutional right of privacy cases typically arise in areas where there is a strong conventional wisdom that certain conduct is morally wrong and where the justice of that wisdom is under fundamental attack. It is no accident that the right of privacy is conceived by its proponents not merely as an advisable or charitable or even wise thing to concede, but as a *right*.[47] Proponents conceive matters involving rights, not as human weaknesses or excusable defects that others should benevolently overlook, but as positive moral goods that one may demand and enforce as one's due. Accordingly, the constitutional right to privacy is, in part, to be understood in terms of a transvaluation of values: certain areas of conduct, traditionally conceived as morally wrong and thus the proper object of public regulation and prohibition, are now perceived as affirmative goods the pursuit of which does not raise serious moral questions and which thus is no longer a proper object of public critical concern.[48]

How, philosophically, are we to interpret and understand such changes? First, as used here to explain the constitutional right to privacy, transvaluation of values refers to changes in the lower-order rules and conventions—namely, in the light of contemporary evidence and conditions, certain lower-order conventions are no longer justified by ultimate moral considerations. For example, according to one influential model, sex is proper only for the purpose of procreation. Many would argue, however, that the distinctive force of human, as opposed to animal, sexuality is that it is *not* rigidly procreational. To the extent that the traditional model of sexuality is discarded in favor of a nonprocreational model, rigid moral rules prohibiting forms of nonprocreational sex are no longer perceived as justified by ultimate moral considerations.

In order to provide reasonable criteria to assess the justifiability of such shifts, we must return to our discussion of the foundations of constitutional morality. As we saw, autonomy and equal concern and respect justify the constitutional immunity of human rights from political bargaining. Since one crucial ground for political bargaining is public morality, constitutional values require that the content of the public morality must be squared with the underlying values of constitutional morality. The primacy of the free exercise and establishment of religion clauses shows that at the core of constitutional values is religious toleration, understood as neutrality between those visions of the good life that are fundamental to autonomous capacities. Conceptually, contractarians give expression to this moral value by the ignorance assumption that deprives the contractors of any basis for keying the choice of ultimate principles to their possibly parochial vision of the good life. These values of constitutional morality ineluctably put determinate constraints on the content of the public morality which is the foundation of the criminal law and the enforcement of which pervades the entire legal system.[49]

What is the constitutionally permissible content of the legal enforcement of morals? Regarding this question, recent moral philosophy has been increasingly occupied with the clarification of the conceptual structure of ordinary moral reasoning.[50] The concept of morality or ethics is not an openly flexible one; there are certain determinate constraints on the kind of beliefs that can be counted as ethical in nature.[51] Some examples of these constraints are the principles of mutual respect—treating others as you would like to be treated in comparable circumstances;[52] universalization—judging the morality of principles by the consequences of their universal application;[53] and minimization of fortuitous human differences (like clan, caste, ethnicity, gender, and color) as a basis for differential treatment.[54] It follows from this conception that a view is not a moral one merely because it is passionately and sincerely held, or because it has a certain emotional depth;[55] or because it is the view of one's father or mother or clan, or because it is conventional. On the contrary, the moral point of view affords an impartial way of assessing whether any of these beliefs, which may often press one to action, is in fact worthy of ethical commitment.[56]

In similar ways and for similar reasons, not everything invoked by democratic majorities as justified by "public morality" is, in fact, morally justified. From the moral point of view, we must always assess such claims by whether they can be sustained by the underlying structure of normal reasoning—by principles of mutual respect, universalization, and minimization of fortuity. In this regard, constitutional morality is at one with the moral point of view. The values of equal concern and respect for personal autonomy, which we have unearthed at the foundations of American constitutionalism, are the same values that recent moral theory, following Kant,[57] has identified as the fundamental values of the moral point of view. This kind of moral analysis affords definite constraints on what may permissibly or justifiably be regarded as an ethical belief.[58] In an area where public attitudes about public morality are, in fact, demonstrably not justified by underlying moral constitutional principles, laws resting on such attitudes are constitutionally dubious. There being no defensible moral principle to sustain state interference, the matter is not a proper object of state concern. In this soil, the constitutional right to privacy took root in *Griswold*.

The understanding of *Griswold* and its progeny begins with repudiation of the procreational model of sexual love which was given its classic formulation by St. Augustine.[59] For Augustine, sexuality was a natural object of continuing shame because it involved loss of control.[60] Accordingly, the only proper form of sex was that which was done with the controlled intention to procreate; sexuality without procreation or independent of such intentions was, for Augustine, intrinsically degrading. It follows from this view that certain rigidly defined kinds of intercourse in conventional marriage, always with the intention to procreate, are alone moral; contraception, whether within or outside marriage, extramarital and, of course, homosexual intercourse are forbidden since these do not involve the intent to procreate.[61]

Augustine's argument rests on a rather remarkable fallacy. Augustine starts with two anthropological points about human sexual experience: first, humans universally insist on having sex alone and unobserved by others,[62] and second, humans universally cover their genitals in public.[63] Augustine argues that the only plausible explanation for these two empirical facts about human sexuality is that humans experience sex as intrinsically degrading because it involves the loss of control;[64] this perception of shame, in turn, must rest on the fact that the only proper form of sex is having it with the controlled intention to procreate;[65] sexuality is intrinsically degrading because we tend to experience it without or independent of the one intention that alone can validate it.[66] Assuming, *arguendo,* the truth of Augustine's anthropological assumptions,[67] it does not follow that humans must find sex intrinsically shameful. These facts are equally well explained by the fact that people experience embarrassment in certain forms of publicity of their sexuality, not shame in the experience of sex itself. Shame is conceptually distinguishable from embarrassment in that its natural object is a failure of personally esteemed competent self-control, whether the failure is public or private; embarrassment, in contrast, is experienced when a matter is made public that properly is regarded as private.[68] The twin facts adduced by Augustine are, indeed, better explained by the hypothesis of embarrassment, not shame. Surely many people experience no negative self-evaluations when they engage in sex in private, which is what the hypothesis of embarrassment, not shame, would lead us to expect. For example, people may experience pride in knowing that other people know or believe that they are having sex (the recently married young couple). There is no shame here, but there would be severe embarrassment if the sex act were actually observed. That people would experience such embarrassment reveals something important about human sexual experience, but it is not Augustine's contempt for the loss of control of sexual passion. Sexual experience is, for human beings, a profoundly personal, spontaneous, and absorbing experience in which they express intimate fantasies and vulnerabilities which typically cannot brook the sense of an external, critical observer. That humans require privacy for sex relates to the nature of the experience; there is no suggestion that the experience is, *pace* Augustine, intrinsically degrading.

The consequence of Augustine's fallacy is to misdescribe and misidentify natural features of healthy sexual experience, namely, the privacy required to express intimate sexual vulnerabilities, in terms of putatively degraded properties of sexual experience per se. In fact, this latter conception of sexuality relies on and expresses an overdeveloped willfulness that fears passion itself as a form of loss of control,[69] as though humans cannot with self-esteem indulge emotional spontaneity outside the rule of the iron procreational will. Such a conception both underestimates the distinctly human capacity for self-control and overestimates the force of sexuality as a dark, unreasoning, Bacchic possession whose demands inexorably undermine the rational will. It also fails to fit the empirical facts, indeed contradicts them. Human, as opposed to animal, sexuality is crucially marked by its control by higher cortical functions and thus its involvement with the human symbolic imagination, so that sexual propensities and experience are largely independent of the reproductive cycle. Consequently, humans use sexuality for diverse purposes—to express love, for recreation, or for procreation. No one purpose necessarily dominates; rather, human self-control chooses among the purposes depending on context and person.

The constitutional right to privacy was developed in *Griswold* and its progeny because the procreational model of sexuality could no longer be sustained by sound empirical or conceptual argument. Lacking such support, the procreational model could no longer be legally enforced on the grounds of the "public morality," for it failed to satisfy the postulate of constitutional morality that legally enforceable moral ideas be grounded on equal concern and respect for autonomy and demonstrated by facts capable of empirical validation. Accordingly, since anticontraceptive laws are based on the concept that nonprocreational sex is unnatural, the *Griswold* court properly invoked the right of privacy to invalidate the Connecticut statute. For similar reasons, laws prohibiting the use of pornography in the home were invalidated.[70] Subsequently, abortion laws were also struck down because the traditional objection to them rested, in large part, on the procreational model and the residuum of moral condemnation that was not clearly sustained by sound argument.[71]

If the right to privacy extends to sex among unmarried couples[72] or even to autoeroticism in the home,[73] it is difficult to understand how in a principled way the Court could decline to consider fully the application of this right to private, consensual, deviant sex acts. The Court might distinguish between heterosexual and homosexual forms of sexual activity, but could this distinction be defended rationally? At bottom, such a view must rest on the belief that homosexual or deviant sex is unnatural. Under this view, such practices would have to be excluded altogether from the scope of the constitutional right to privacy, just as obscenity is excluded from first amendment protection. However, an analysis of the application of the notion of the "unnatural" to deviant sexual acts and an examination of the moral force of the constitutional right to privacy seems to compel the clear and decisive rejection of such a view.

The use of so imprecise a notion as "unnatural" to distinguish between those acts not protected by the constitutional right to privacy and those which are so protected is clearly unacceptable. The case where the constitutional right to privacy had its origin was one involving contraception—a practice which the Augustinian view would deem unnatural. Yet the Court has apparently concluded that the "unnaturalness" of contraception or abortion is constitutionally inadmissible and cannot limit the scope of the right to privacy. In considering the constitutional permissibility of allowing majoritarian notions of the unnatural to justify limitations on the right to privacy, the Court must take into account two crucial factors: (1) the absence of empirical evidence or sound philosophical argument that these practices are unnatural; and (2) the lack of any sound moral argument, premised on equal concern and respect, that these practices are in any sense immoral. In particular, as we saw in the contraception and abortion decisions, the Court impliedly rejected the legitimacy of both the classic Augustinian view of human sexuality and the associated judgments about the exclusive morality of marital procreational sex. The enforcement of majoritarian prejudices, without any plausible empirical basis, could be independently unconstitutional as a violation of due process rationality in legislation.[74] To enforce such personal tastes in matters touching basic autonomous life choices violates basic human rights. The moral theory of the Constitution, built as a bulwark against "serious oppressions of the minor party in the community,"[75] requires that such human rights be upheld and protected against majoritarian prejudices.

For the same reasons that notions of the unnatural are constitutionally impermissible in decisions involving contraception, abortion, and the use of pornography in the home, these ideas are also impermissible in the constitutional assessment of laws prohibiting private forms of sexual deviance between consenting adults. No empirical evidence compels a finding that homosexuality is unnatural.[76] Indeed, there have been cultures that possessed normative assumptions of what is natural that nevertheless did not regard homosexuality as unnatural.[77] Some societies (including ancient Greece) have included or include homosexuality among legitimate sexual conduct, and some prescribe it in the form of institutional pederasty.[78] Individuals within our own culture have assailed the view that homosexuality is unnatural by adducing various facts which traditionalists either did not know or did not understand.[79] For example, it is now known that homosexual behavior takes place in the animal world, suggesting that homosexuality is part of our mammalian heritage of sexual responsiveness.[80]

Some have attempted to distinguish between individuals who are exclusively homosexual and the general population based on symptoms of mental illness[81] or measures of self-esteem and self-acceptance.[82] In general, however, apart from their sexual preference, exclusive homosexuals are psychologically indistinguishable from the general population.[83]

The view sometimes expressed that male homosexuality necessarily involves the loss of desirable character traits probably rests on the idea that sexual relations between males involve the degradation of one or both parties to the status of a woman.[84] This view, however, rests on intellectual confusion and unacceptable moral premises since it confuses sexual preference with gender identity, whereas, in fact, no such correlation exists. Male homosexuals or lesbians may be quite insistent about their respective gender identities and have quite typical "masculine" or "feminine" personalities. Their homosexuality is defined only by their erotic preference for members of the same gender.[85] The notion that the status of woman is a degradation is morally repugnant to contemporary jurisprudence[86] and morality.[87] If such crude and unjust sexual stereotypes lie at the bottom of antihomosexuality laws, they should be uprooted, as is being done elsewhere in modern life.

Finally, homosexual preference appears to be an adaptation of natural human propensities to very early social circumstances of certain kinds,[88] so that the preference is settled, largely irreversibly, at a quite early age.[89]

The cumulative impact of such facts is clear. The notion of "unnatural acts," interpreted in terms of a fixed procreational model of sexual functioning, deviations from which result in inexorable damage or degradation, is not properly applied to homosexual acts performed in private between consenting adults. Such activity is clearly a natural expression of human sexual competences and sensitivities, and does not reflect any form of damage, decline, or injury.[90] To deny the acceptability of such acts is itself a human evil, a denial of the distinctive human capacities for loving and sensual experience without ulterior procreative motives—in a plausible sense, itself unnatural.

There is consequently no logically consistent explanation for the Court's refusal to enforce concepts of the "unnatural" in the case of contraception while permitting statutes based on similar concepts to prohibit sexual deviance. Indeed, the moral arguments in the latter case are more compelling. For one thing, at the time *Griswold* was decided, statutes condemning and prohibiting forms of contraception probably no longer reflected a majoritarian understanding of the unnaturalness of this form of birth control.[91] Accordingly, the need for constitutional protection, while proper, was not exigent.[92] In the case of homosexuality, however, there is good reason to believe that, as a group, homosexuals are subject to exactly the kind of unjust social hatred that constitutional guarantees were designed to combat.[93]

A second way by which the Court might justify its restricted application of the right of privacy would be to focus on the morality of the acts in question. Presumably, the naturalness of homosexual experience would not in itself legitimize such experience, if homosexuality were shown to be immoral. There is, however, no sound moral argument any longer to sustain the idea that homosexuality is intrinsically immoral.

The concept of morality, proposed herein, puts certain constraints—mutual respect, universalization, minimization of fortuity—on the kinds of beliefs and arguments that can properly be regarded as ethical in nature. Certainly, such constraints would dictate certain prohibitions and regulations of sexual conduct. For example, respect for the development of capacities of autonomous rational choice would require that various liberties, guaranteed to mature adults, might not extend to persons presumably lacking rational capacities, such as children. Nor is there any objection to the reasonable regulation of obtrusive sexual solicitations or, of course, to forcible forms of intercourse of any kind. Such regulations or prohibitions would secure a more equal expression of autonomy compatible with a like liberty for all, thus advancing underlying values of equal concern and respect. In addition, forms of sexual expression would be limited by other moral principles that would be universalized compatibly with equal concern and respect, for example: principles of not killing, harming, or inflicting gratuitous cruelty; principles of paternalism in narrowly defined circumstances; and principles of fidelity.[94] Thus, as formulated, the relevant limiting moral and constitutional principles permit some reasonable, legitimate restrictions on complete individual freedom.

Statutes that absolutely prohibit deviant sexual acts such as that considered in *Doe*[95] cannot be justified consistently with the principles just discussed. Such statutes are not limited to forcible or public forms of sexual intercourse, or to sexual intercourse by or with children, but extend to private, consensual acts between adults as well. To say that such laws are justified by their indirect effect of stopping homosexual intercourse by or with the underaged would be as absurd as to claim that absolute prohibitions on heterosexual intercourse could be similarly justified. There is no reason to believe that homosexuals as a class are any more involved in offenses with the young than heterosexuals.[96] Nor is there any reliable evidence that such laws inhibit children from being naturally homosexual who would otherwise be naturally heterosexual. Sexual preference is settled, largely irreversibly, in very early childhood, well before laws of this kind could have any effect.[97] If the state has any legitimate interest in determining the sexual preference of its citizens, which is doubtful,[98] that interest cannot constitutionally be secured by overbroad statutes that tread upon the rights of exclusive homosexuals of all ages[99] and that, in any event, irrationally pursue the claimed interest.

Other moral principles also fail to justify absolute prohibitions on consensual sexual deviance. Homosexual relations, for example, are not generally violent. Thus, prohibitory statutes could not be justified by moral principles of nonmalefience.[100] There is no convincing evidence that homosexuality is either harmful to the homosexual or correlated with any form of mental or physical disease or defect.[101] To the contrary, there is evidence that antihomosexuality laws, which either force homosexuals into heterosexual marriage unnatural for them or otherwise distort and disfigure the reasonable pursuit of natural emotional fulfillment, harm homosexuals and others in deep and permanent ways.[102] Accordingly, principles of legitimate state paternalism do not here come into play.

One relevant set of facts that would justify prohibitions of homosexuality would be empirical support for the view that homosexuality is a kind of degenerative social poison that leads directly to disease, social disorder, and disintegration.[103] Principles of constitutional justice must be compatible with the stability of institutions of social cooperation. Thus, if the above allegation were true, prohibition of homosexuality might be justified on the ground that such prohibition would preserve the constitutional order, so that justice on balance would be secured. These beliefs are quite untenable today, however. Many nations, including several in Western Europe,[104] have long allowed homosexual acts between adults, with no consequent social disorder or disease.

One final moral argument has been used to justify a general prohibition upon homosexualty—the argument invoked by the district court in *Doe* as "the promotion of morality and decency."[105] That court believed this to be the ultimate ground for the legitimacy of the Virginia sodomy statute. The argument takes three forms: (1) a general jurisprudential thesis about the relation of law and morals; (2) an interpretation of the moral principles discussed previously; and (3) the point of view of a certain form of theological ethics. None of these views can be sustained.

The classic modern statement of the jurisprudential thesis was made by Devlin[106] against Hart,[107] repeating many of the arguments earlier made by Stephen[108] against Mill.[109] The Devlin-Hart debate centered on the jurisprudential interpretation of the Wolfenden Report,[110] which recommended, *inter alia*, the abolition of the imposition of criminal penalties for homosexual acts between consenting adults. Devlin, in questioning the Report, focused on the proposition that certain private immoral acts are not the law's business. The criminal law, Devlin argued, is completely unintelligible without reference to morality, which it enforces. The fact that two parties agree to kill one another, for example, does not relieve the killer of criminal liability, for the act in question is immoral. The privacy of the act (between consenting adults, perhaps in the privacy of the home) is irrelevant. Similarly, the criminal law in general arises from morality. Morality, Devlin maintains, is the necessary condition of the existence of society. Thus, to change the law in such a way as to violate that morality is to threaten the stability of the social order. Morality, in this connection, is to be understood in terms of the ordinary man's intuitive sense of right and wrong, as determined, Devlin suggests, by taking a man at random. Just as we prove the standards of negligence for purposes of civil or criminal liability by appealing to the judgment of ordinary men acting as jurors, so may we prove applicable standards of morality. Ordinary men morally loathe homosexuality; accordingly, homosexuality is immoral and must be legally forbidden.

Superficially, Devlin's argument appears to be constitutionally acceptable. There should be no constitutional objection to prohibiting clearly immoral acts that threaten the existence of society. Further, it is surely plausible that law and morals have a deep and systematic connection of the kind Devlin suggests.[111] Nevertheless, such abstractly plausible propositions will not support the specific argument that Devlin propounds. Although Devlin is probably correct in asserting that the criminal law arises from the morality that it enforces, he nevertheless falsely identifies morality with conventional social views in a way that renders unthinkable, if not unintelligible, the whole idea of moral criticism and reform of social convention. Adoption of this view would effectively turn the measure of legally enforceable moral ideas into an interim victory of one set of contending ideological forces over another.[112] Moreover, there is no good reason to make this identification of morality and social convention, since it is based on an indefensible and naive moral philosophy as well as an unexamined and unsound sociology.[113]

The attraction of Devlin's theory for judges is its apparent objectivity; it affords a definite criterion for the morality that the law enforces without appeal to subjective considerations.[114] But the empirical objectivity of existing custom has nothing to do with the notions of moral impartiality and objectivity that are, or should be, of judicial concern in determining the public morality on which the law rests. The idea that the pursuit of the latter must collapse into the former is a confusion of inquiries, arising from an untenable and indefensible distinction between subjective moral belief and the public morality of the law. There is no such distinction. Views, to be moral, require a certain kind of justification. Judges, in interpreting legally enforceable moral ideas, must appeal to the kind of reasoning that is moral. They do not as judges abdicate their responsibility for moral reasoning as persons. On the contrary, competence and clarity in such reasoning comprise the virtue that we denominate judicial.

Devlin's theory is, for such reasons, theoretically and practically unacceptable. Even if it could be defended on such grounds, however, it must be rejected as it is incompatible with the moral theory of human rights implicit in the constitutional order. The Constitution rests on the idea that moral rights of individuals cannot be violated, notwithstanding majoritarian sentiments to the contrary. Accordingly, the Supreme Court has rightly upheld constitutional rights against popular racial and sexual prejudices.[115] Prejudices against the vulnerable, largely powerless homosexual minority must be similarly circumscribed.[116]

That this popular argument for preserving moral standards is objectionable in moral and constitutional principle is then apparent. The district court in *Doe*, however, employed another form of argument not similarly objectionable, as it rests on an interpretation of the moral principles that do relevantly regulate sexual conduct. It suggested that the moral issue before it was not that homosexuality is objectionable per se, but rather that in the present state of society homosexuality tends to evade certain moral principles—for example, principles of fidelity intrinsic in heterosexual marriage and family obligations.[117] The court's use of this argument is, however, fundamentally fallacious. In support of its proposition, the court cited a case that involved fellatio among a married couple and a third adult and distribution of pictures of the said acts in school by the couple's daughters (aged 11 and 13). The latter fact was alleged to show that conduct not immoral in itself may be condemned because "the conduct is likely to end in a contribution to moral delinquency."[118] The citation of a case of apparently heterosexual sodomy, involving clear elements of a waiver of privacy rights, as evidence for the propriety of proscribing clearly private homosexual sex is a remarkable nonsequitur, illustrating the kind of shabby reasoning to which courts are driven in order to lend a shred of moral plausibility to these prohibitions.

Aside from this specific argumentative fallacy, there remains the general intuition that homosexuality, if allowed, would violate moral principles implicit in the institution of the heterosexual family. While this line of thought has the general form of an acceptable moral and constitutional argument, its factual assumptions are utterly unsupported by evidence. For example, the argument makes the unsupported assumption that prohibiting homosexuality would encourage heterosexual marriage. But, as Judge Merhige indicated in his dissent in *Doe,* such a claim is so empirically flimsy as to be "unworthy of judicial response."[119] For one thing, historical and contemporary data show that homosexual connections are compatible with heterosexual marriage.[120] The many countries which have legalized homosexual relations show no decline in the incidence of heterosexual marriage.[121] It thus appears that prohibitions of homosexual relations have no effect on heterosexual marriage.[122]

The intuition regarding homosexuality and the decline of the heterosexual family is ancient.[123] According to this view, consensual homosexual acts in private are not of social concern, but the way of life that such sex acts exemplify is. To legitimate these sex acts is to legitimate an undesirable way of life; thus these sex acts, even in private between consenting adults, may justly be prohibited.

The substance of this intuitive allegation should be examined with care, for a form of it bears the imprimatur of the Supreme Court itself.[124] The suggestion is this: public knowledge of the legitimacy of homosexual acts would undermine the capacity of heterosexuals to sustain the way of life required for the monogamous nuclear family and the personal sacrifices that such a way of life requires. But no one in the Western cultural tradition could reasonably claim that the existence of legitimate alternative ways of life outside heterosexual marriage undermines social stability. The legitimacy of remaining unmarried has not undermined the heterosexual family. Indeed, one form of the unmarried state, religious celibacy, has long been regarded by influential Western religions as sanctified; this fact has not, however, made the heterosexual family less stable.

Why, then, should the recognition of homosexuality as a legitimate way of life be treated in a radically different way? The suggestion must be that homosexual preference is so strong and universal and heterosexual preference so weak (and conventional family life so unattractive) that people would on a massive scale tend to shun heterosexual marriage if homosexuality as a way of life were legitimate. But, as we have seen, not even a shred of empirical evidence supports these views. While a small minority of the population naturally experiences erotic pleasure exclusively with people of the same gender, the great majority is exclusively heterosexual.[125]

Aside from the facts of natural eroticism, the attractions of heterosexual marriage are deep-seated and permanent features of the human condition. Human beings, generally raised in the nuclear heterosexual family, naturally regard the cooperation and creative sharing that typifies the heterosexual family as the answer, or part of the answer, to the recurrent human problem of loneliness and isolation. For most people, conventional marriage is and will remain the standard—supplying a natural response to human needs for sexual release, intimacy, and the desire for tangible immortality (childrearing). It is a bizarre failure of imagination and perspective so to underestimate the attractions of family life as to suppose that the legitimacy of homosexuality as a way of life would have any significant effect on it at all. Even in this era of growing sexual freedom and rising divorce rates, there is no sign that heterosexual marriage as an institution is in general less attractive. The rising divorce rates show not a distaste for marriage, but only less willingness to stick with the original partners in marriage. The important and striking feature of this phenomenon is that divorced people typically remarry; they reject their previous partner, not the institution of marriage itself.[126]

Certainly, the crude argument that if everyone were homosexual there would, disastrously, be an end of the human species universalizes absurdly a principle not seriously debated, namely, that everyone should or must be homosexual. Rather, the principle under discussion is whether, given the overwhelming naturally heterosexual majority and the small naturally homosexual minority, the state should, at a minimum, be tolerantly neutral between sexual preferences.

The "way of life" argument cannot be sustained as an empirical proposition, even though it can be understood as the psychological residue of fear and loathing unmistakably left by the long tradition that condemned homosexuality and nonprocreative sex in general as unnatural.[127] The existence and nature of these prejudices, which take the form of homophobia, are interesting and important psychological questions. They are probably significantly connected to a standard masculine fear of passivity and to a feminine rejection of aggressive activity,[128] of which male or female homosexuality, respectively, is mistakenly supposed the ultimate symbol.[129] Homophobia thus appears as a form of intrapsychic defense against any suggestion of "unmasculine" passivity or "unfeminine" aggressiveness.[130] Such underlying stereotypes are under widespread attack today: many men and women, heterosexual and homosexual, justly refuse any longer to dichotomize and disfigure their natures along poles of conventional masculine-feminine stereotypes that are unjust in principle, no longer socially sensible, and inhumanely unfulfilling to individuals.[131] As a matter of law, the prejudices based on such stereotypes clearly should have no force independent of the empirical assumptions on which they rest. Undoubtedly, residues of guilt and fear remain long after we reject on rational grounds the beliefs on which those guilts and fears rest. But this psychological truth does not validate such regressive emotions as a legitimate basis for law. If the life of reason requires us to circumscribe such negative emotions as a basis for ethical conduct, the morality of law can require no less.[132]

In any event, it is difficult to understand how the state has the right, on moral grounds, to protect heterosexual love at the expense of homosexual love. Equal concern and respect for autonomous choice seem precisely to forbid the kind of calculation that this sort of sacrifice contemplates. In principle, these values, as we have seen, forbid the sacrifice of the fundamental interests of one group in order to secure the greater happiness of other groups or of the whole. These values prescribe moral and constitutional benchmarks of human decency, resting on respect for the interest of all persons equally in general goods; thereby the power of majority rule to plough under the interests of minorities is limited.

Finally, there is reason to believe that the argument for protecting marriage and the family is hypocritically proposed. If the argument were meant seriously, state laws against fornication and adultery would be vigorously pressed in addition to the antihomosexuality laws. But in many states, such laws either do not exist or penalize homosexuality much more severely than heterosexual offenses.[133] This suggests what should by now be reasonably clear: antihomosexuality laws rest not on reasonable moral argument consistently pursued, but on ancient prejudice and the last remaining vestige of ideas, elsewhere eschewed, of unnatural sexual witchcraft and demonology.[134]

The last available form of moral argument in support of absolute prohibitions of consensual adult homosexual relations, certainly implicit in Devlin's argument, is that of theological ethics—the moral principles enforceable at law are dictated by the Judaeo-Christian God. Since traditional Judaeo-Christian thought appears to condemn nonprocreative sex in general and homosexuality in particular,[135] these condemnations, being by definition moral, may be enforced at law. There are two conclusive objections to this argument: one moral, the other constitutional.

Morally, invoking theological ethics in support of the moral condemnation of homosexuality runs afoul of a philosophical argument of metaethical principle and a normative argument of casuistry. Metaethically, there are powerful objections to a theological analysis of morality without appeal to the constraints of mutual respect, universalization, and minimization of fortuity previously discussed. The traditional view of Christian theology certainly has been that moral concepts have a natural authority antecedent to divine revelation;[136] accordingly, moral concepts even for theologians must be explicable without a circular appeal to divine revelation. Metaethically, moral reasoning is logically independent of religious reasoning. Accordingly, it is fallacious to invoke purely theological reasoning to rebut the independent force of a valid moral argument. Psychological studies of moral development suggest that ethical reasoning is, in fact, unrelated to religious training or affilation.[137] Normatively, the tradition of theological casuistry, on which Devlin rests his case, is now under critical scrutiny from within theology. There is growing controversy within religious groups as to the proper interpretation of Biblical prohibitions conventionally believed to condemn homosexuality,[138] and indeed invoked to this end by the lower court in *Doe*.[139] This tradition of rational theology, including attacks by Catholic theologians on the procreational model of sexuality,[140] indicates that even the religious foundations on which these laws were constructed are now seen to be jerry-built.

Finally, whatever the constitutional permissibility of the frank invocation of theological ethics in Devlin's England, where Church and State are not constitutionally separate, in the United States the free exercise and establishment of religion clauses of the first amendment stand as an absolute bar to the enforcement of theological ethics of the form implicit in Devlin's argument.[141] Our earlier analysis of the structure of constitutional morality clarifies why this is so. The primary postulate of the American Constitution is the moral principle of religious tolerance, the idea of fundamental constitutionally mandated neutrality between the disparate visions of the good life at the profound level of personal self-definition occupied by religious and philosophical beliefs. Accordingly, constitutional principles require that only those principles may be legally enforced which express the values of equal concern and respect for autonomous self-definition in terms of the many permissible visions of the good life compatible with these values. These principles require, inter alia, that any legally enforceable standards of conduct must rest on generally acceptable empirical standards and must not contravene the underlying values of equal concern and respect.

B. *Sexual Autonomy, the Rational Choice of One's Self, and Human Rights*

It is elementary that moral principles define the boundaries within which a person may rationally pursue her or his ends.[142] For example, human beings clearly possess much larger capacities for aggressiveness than it is morally appropriate for them to develop and cultivate either in themselves or in others. Accordingly, since applicable moral principles forbid the full development and display of these capacities, we do not regard it as appropriate that individuals design their lives to give such capacities full and untrammelled expression, however much in the individual's interests this might be. An uncontroversial truth is the extraordinary adaptability of human psychology, compared to that of the lower animals.[143] Sacrifices of personal interests, regarded as unthinkably onerous and burdensome in a later historical period, are undertaken with natural facility in an earlier period. To the extent that applicable moral principles demand it, human nature can sustain quite onerous demands or, at least, demands eventually perceived to be onerous.

Such shifts in the concept of morally permissible demands are well illustrated by the kind of transvaluation of values that underlies the development of the constitutional right to privacy. Certain ranges of conduct, previously conceived as tightly regulated by moral principles, are now no longer morally determined in the same way. For reasons previously discussed, forms of sexual intimacy once judged immoral per se are no longer so judged.[144] To the extent that moral principles no longer rigidly prohibit certain forms of conduct, the scope of permissible liberty in rationally designing one's life is enlarged. Human capacities, previously narrowly and rigidly confined, are now permissibly cultivated and explored.

The right to privacy was recognized because it is associated with and intended to facilitate the exercise of autonomy in certain basic kinds of choice that bear upon the coherent rationality of a person's life plan. Ordinary people, uncontaminated by philosophical discussions of personal identity,[145] typically identify other people (in response to the query, who is x?) in certain characteristic ways. Certain choices in life are taken to bear fundamentally on the entire design of one's life, for these choices determine the basic decisions of work and love, which in turn order many of the subsidiary choices of human life. Obvious examples of such choices are matters of whether and where to be educated, choice of occupation and avocations, choice of whether and whom to love and befriend and on what terms, and the decision whether and to what extent children will be a life's concern. Classic studies of the human life cycle make clear that the exercise of autonomy in life choices of these kinds occurs throughout the life cycle.[146] Different sorts of choices cluster at different age periods: adolescents struggle with basic questions of identity;[147] persons in their twenties make basic decisions on the form of sexual love;[148] the thirties appear to mark crucial struggles for vocational competence and recognition;[149] the forties appear to call for realistic stock taking, concern for aiding and teaching the young,[150] and so forth. From the earliest life of the infant to quite old age, the development and exercise of autonomous choice underlie the deepening individuation of the person.

Clearly there has been a transvaluation of values whereby many traditional moral judgments regarding the proper exercise of these life choices are no longer justified. In such cases, where reasonable moral argument no longer can sustain absolute prohibitions and the issue in question is one among the fundamental life choices, the constitutional right to privacy, understood as a right of personal autonomy, finds its natural home. It is natural to call this autonomy a right of privacy in the sense that moral principles no longer define these matters as issues of proper public concern but as matters of highly personal self-definition. The constitutional right to privacy as an autonomy right is premised on principles of obligation and duty that secure equal concern and respect for autonomy. The right to privacy does not merely signify that it is no longer not morally wrong to do certain things, but that there is an affirmative moral right to do them which it is, by definition, a transgression of moral duty to violate.

In order to understand this claim, let us recall Chapter 1's contractarian interpretation of the ultimate moral values of equal concern and respect. It was argued that in the deliberations of the original position, self-respect based on one's ability to exercise personal capacities competently would have a special prominence and thus could be called the primary human good. People desire general goods—liberties, opportunities, wealth—in order to attain the self-respect that those conditions facilitate. People in the original position would regulate access to the general goods so as to enhance the possibility that each member of society will be able to attain self-respect.

Another conclusion of contractarian theory is that, in reaching an agreement upon a system of morality and justice, at least in an economically advanced society like the United States, people give priority to the maximization of liberties. After a minimal level of wealth has been secured to all people, the original contractors would not accept limitations on their freedom in exchange for enhanced economic well-being. Maximization of liberty best enables *all* people to attain self-respect by opening up myriad possible areas of experience and endeavor.[151]

The liberties distributed by the principles of justice typically include liberties of thought and expression (freedom of speech, press, religion, and association), civic rights (impartial administration of civil and criminal law in defense of property and person), political rights (the right to vote and participate in political affairs), and freedom of physical, economic, and social movement. The importance of these liberties rests on their relation to the primary good of self-respect, since these liberties nurture personal competences, for example, full expression of the spirit, self-direction, security of the person, and the possibility of unhampered movement.[152] In the United States, this has been accomplished through the constitutional guarantees of the Bill of Rights and the fourteenth amendment.[153]

Contemporary understanding of the strategic importance to self-respect and personhood of sexual autonomy requires that we similarly guarantee full liberty to enjoy and express love. At the core of this understanding lies Freud's central idea, independently confirmed by comparative ethology and anthropology,[154] that human sexuality, rooted in the high degree of cortical control of sexuality, serves complex imaginative and symbolic purposes, and thus is extraordinarily plastic and malleable.[155] Freud thus introduced into scientific psychology what artists have always known and expressed: that for humans to experience sex is never, even in solitary masturbation, a purely physical act, but is embued with complex evaluational interpretations of its real or fantasied object, often rooted in the whole history of the person from early childhood on.[156] Freud's theory of the defenses clarifies some of the imaginative manipulations of sexual feelings that are sometimes destructive,[157] but are also sometimes adaptive.[158] For the latter, consider Freud's own celebration of the eroticism of work that he called sublimation.[159]

Understanding of unconscious imaginative processes was, for Freud, not a concessive plea for irrationalism but a deepening of our understanding of the concept of autonomy and of the person; for knowledge of the unconscious mind and its processes deepens the range and strength of the ego or self in controlling id and superego impulses: "Where id was, there shall ego be."[160] Through our self-conscious retrieval and investigation of the fantasy data of the unconscious (dreams, free associations, slips, and the like), we may achieve a remarkable capacity to extend our control and understanding of mental processes that are otherwise inexplicable, and often stupidly, rigidly, and self-destructively repetitive. Through our knowledge of the unconscious defenses and their form in our own lives, we are able to assess consciously the work of the unconscious, deciding whether desires disowned by the unconscious should be reclaimed (repression) or desires promoted by the unconscious should be cut back (sublimation and projection).[161] We may, in addition, render ourselves self-conscious and independent of our earliest, most intense emotional identifications, achieving an understanding of our life history so that we may see our lives and what we want from them individually as our own and not as the unconscious derivative of the wishes of significant others; with this kind of understanding, we nurture our autonomy to decide with what or with whom in our life history we will or will not identify or continue to identify.[162]

To see human autonomy in this deeper way and to understand the powerful role of sexuality as an independent force in the imaginative life and general development of the person is to acknowledge the central role of sexual autonomy in the idea of a free person. This view of autonomy has necessary implications for the widening application of human rights to sexuality. Sexuality, in this view, is not a spiritually empty experience that the state may compulsorily legitimize only in the form of rigid, marital procreational sex, but one of the fundamental experiences through which, as an end in itself, people define the meaning of their lives. Consider the following specific ways in which this is so.

First, sexual love is profoundly misdescribed by the sorrowing Catholic dismissal of sexuality as an unfortunate and spiritually empty concomitant of propagation, for sexuality has for humans the independent status of a profound ecstasy that makes available to a modern person experiences increasingly inaccessible in public life: self-transcendence, expression of private fantasy, release of inner tensions, and meaningful and acceptable expression of regressive desires to be again the free child—unafraid to lose control, playful, vulnerable, spontaneous, sensually loved.[163] While people may choose to forego this experience, any coercive prohibition of it amounts to the deprivation of an experience central in human significance.

Second, sexual love is sometimes a crucial ingredient in forming lasting personal relationships and thus can facilitate the good that these relationships afford in human life.[164] Such durable relationships founded on sexual intimacy are happily denominated a form of knowledge, in Biblical locution, for they afford to people the capacity for a secure disclosure of self, not only through exposure of sexual vulnerabilities, but also through the sharing of recesses of the self otherwise remote and inaccessible.[165] Accordingly, choices involving these relationships are among the most important strategic decisions in one's life plan.[166] The choice of one's lover, whether in or outside marriage, involves one's entire self-conception. As one major recent study of the human life cycle clarifies, the choice of one's lover is one with one's life "dream";[167] as the "dream" changes, so must the relationship.[168] The disclosure of self that love involves, the mutual shaping of expectations and life styles, the sharing of common aspirations and hopes—all these, and others, suggest the extraordinary significance of decisions about matters of love in the design of a human life.

Third, the force of sexual love in human life expresses itself in the desire to participate with the beloved in the development of and care for common projects created by the relationship.[169] Some of these projects take on a durable character in terms of objects or activities or even persons who survive the relationship. In so doing they embody the lasting value of the relationship and perhaps thus satisfy, in some measure, the longing of human self-consciousness for evidence of the immortal and imperishable self.

In summary, one may appeal to the plausible thought that love is part of what is commonly meant by the meaning of life. Surely, such love may not necessarily take sexual forms; it may, for example, take the form of a diffuse benevolence toward larger or smaller groups of people, or even devotion to an abstract entity. But the absence of love in any form from a human life renders a life plan incoherently empty at its core and the life of the spirit deformed and miserably twisted.

Love plays a role, too, in the contractarian model. As noted earlier, that choice in the original position is choice under uncertainty: rational people in the original position have no way of predicting the probability that they may end up in any given situation of life. By definition, none of the contractors knows his or her own sex, age, native talents, particular capacity for self-control, social or economic class or position, or in general the particular forms of his or her personal desires (e.g., whether one likes asparagus or spinach; or is homosexual or heterosexual). Each contractor will be concerned not to end up in a disadvantaged situation with no appeal to moral principles to denounce deprivations that may render life's prospects bitter and mean. To avoid such consequences, the rational strategy in choosing the basic principles of justice would be the "maximin" strategy.

As we have suggested, the contractors in the original position would regard self-respect as the primary good. Accordingly, their focus would be on principles that would ensure that people have the maximum chance of attaining self-respect. Sexual autonomy, the capacity to choose whether or how or with whom one will have sexual relations, is, for reasons previously discussed, one crucial ingredient of this self-respect; it is one of the forms of personal competence in terms of which people regulate basic issues of what kind of person they will be. Because liberties, opportunities, and capacities relating to love figure so importantly in the quest for self-respect, the rational contractors would not agree to any principle that would permit restrictions upon these liberties, opportunities, and capacities that were not compatible with the greatest equal liberty for all. Use of the "maximin" strategy in choosing principles relating to liberty, opportunity, and capacity to love, then, tends to eliminate the disadvantaged class: the lowest (as well as the highest) condition is equality for all persons.

Because of the profound relation of sexual autonomy to basic self-respect, the following principle of obligation and duty, defining correlative human rights, would be accepted in the original position—*the principle of love as a civil liberty*. Basic institutions are to be arranged so that every person is guaranteed the greatest equal liberty, opportunity, and capacity to love, compatible with a like liberty, opportunity, and capacity for all.

The derivation of this principle, being a specification of the more general principles of justice, depends on the preliminary assumption that the contractors are ignorant of their specific identity and can take into account only facts subject to general empirical validation. The contractors thus cannot appeal to special religious duties to procreate to override the equal liberty to love; nor can there be appeals to any taste or distaste for certain forms of the physical expression of love in order to override the equal liberty to love; nor can they appeal to concepts of love that illegitimately smuggle in covert premises or prejudices of such kinds. The concept of love says nothing about the form of its physical expression other than, for example, that it involves forms of intimate closeness expressing the evident intention of good to another. There is no ideal, exclusive, or proper physical expression of sexual love, because a large and indeterminate class of forms of sexual intercourse is compatible with the aims of love.

This principle explains and justifies the sense in which the constitutional right to privacy is a *right*. The constitutional concept expresses an underlying moral principle resting on the enhancement of sexual autonomy: the self-determination of the role of sexuality in one's life, which protects the values foundational to the concept of human rights, equal concern and repect for autonomy. Accordingly, in the absence of countervailing moral argument, laws that determine how one will have sex and with what consequences are constitutionally invalid. Such considerations explain the unconstitutionality of laws proscribing contraception, abortion, and the use of pornography in the home.[170] They also explain why antihomosexuality laws violate a constitutional right.

Freedom to love means that a mature individual must have autonomy to decide how or whether to love another.[171] Restrictions on the form of love, imposed in the name of the distorting rigidities of convention, that bear no relation to individual emotional capacities and needs would be condemned. Individual autonomy, in matters of love, would ensure the development of people who could call their emotional nature their own, secure in the development of attachments that bear the mark of spontaneous human feeling and that touch one's original impulses. In contrast, restrictions on this individual autonomy would starve one's emotional capacities, withering individual feeling into conventional gesture and strong native pleasures into vicarious fantasies.[172]

Antihomosexuality laws egregiously violate these considerations. First, laws prohibiting homosexual conduct inhibit persons inclined toward this form of sexual activity from obtaining sexual satisfaction in the only way they find natural. Second, these laws probably encourage blackmail by providing a means by which homosexuals can be threatened with exposure and prosecution. Such vulnerability to blackmail may discourage employers from hiring homosexuals, on the ground that they are security risks.[173] Third, laws prohibiting consensual adult homosexual activity provide a ground for discrimination against people of homosexual preference in employment, housing, and public accommodation.[174]

Consider the effects of such laws on exclusive homosexuals who find only homosexual relations naturally satisfying. Traditionally, these individuals do one of three things. First, they may utterly disown sexuality and the sexual aspect of their selves, dedicating themselves, perhaps, to an impersonal benevolence.[175] Second, they may heterosexually marry, using homosexual fantasies when engaging in sex with their spouse.[176] Third, they may be practicing covert homosexuals, either exclusively or in some combination with the second alternative.[177] Each of these options, compelled by the state of the law, outrageously violates human rights.

First, the legal compulsion of celibacy, in the absence of any good reason, unfairly compels homosexuals to personal sacrifices that would be regarded as unthinkable if demanded of heterosexuals. Of course, celibacy may be, for some people, a rational life choice. But to compel people to disown their most basic emotional propensities is to demand that life be gesturally lived behind impersonal masks, that expression be always artfully choreographed and never naturally spontaneous, and that the body be experienced as an empty sepulchre.[178]

Second, the experience of heterosexual marriage without natural eroticism is hollow, frequently leading to marital instability and divorce, both of which may be damaging to the children.[179] In the place of the kinds of relationships found natural, homosexuals fail to experience forms of deep personal release, pointlessly and sometimes dishonestly inflict harms on others, and inflict on themselves unnecessary burdens of self-sacrifice.

Third, the cumulative effect of antihomosexuality laws is to deprive practicing homosexuals of the experience of a secure self-respect in their competence in building personal relationships. The degree of emotional sacrifice thus exacted for no defensible reason seems among the most unjust deprivations that law can compel.[180] Persons are deprived of a realistic basis for confidence and security in their most basic emotional propensities. Criminal penalty, employment risks, and social prejudice converge to render dubious a person's most spontaneous native urges, dividing emotions, physical expression, and self-image in a cruelly gratuitous way.[181] The deepest damage is to the spiritual and imaginative dimension that gives human sexual love its significance. Persons surrounded by false social conceptions that are supported by law find it difficult to esteem their own emotional propensities and natural expression. Without such self-esteem love finds no meaningful or enduring object. Instead of being assured a fair opportunity to develop loving capacities and fair access to love, the homosexual's capacity to express such feelings is driven into a secretive and concealed world of shallow and often anonymous physical encounters.[182] The achievement of emotional relationships of any depth or permanence is made a matter of heroic individual effort when it could, like heterosexual relations, be part of the warp and woof of the ordinary social possibility.[183] In thus forbidding exclusive homosexuals to express sexual love in the only way they find natural, the law deprives them of the good in life that love affords.[184]

C. *Inappropriate Paternalistic Arguments*

Even if no other moral judgment may appropriately be made about the probity of certain conduct, we may still believe that such conduct is sufficiently irrational to permit interference on paternalistic grounds.

Clearly, the contractarian model, as used to articulate a structure of reasons expressing mutual concern and respect, universalization, and minimization of natural fortuity, would justify a principle of paternalism and explain its proper scope and limits. From the point of view of the original position, the contractors would know that human beings would be subject to certain kinds of irrationalities with severe consequences, including death and the permanent impairment of health, and they would, accordingly, agree on an insurance principle against certain of these more serious irrationalities in the event they might occur to them.[185]

There are two critical constraints on the scope of such a principle. First, the relevant idea of irrationality cannot itself violate the constraints of morality. Legally enforceable moral ideas must be formulated with ignorance of specific identity and must be based on facts capable of empirical validation; in particular, idiosyncratic personal values cannot be smuggled into the content of "irrationality" that defines, inter alia, the scope of the principle. Rather, the notion of irrationality must be defined in terms of a neutral theory that can accommodate the many visions of the good life that are compatible with moral constraints. For this purpose, the idea of rationality is defined relative to an agent's system of ends, as determined by the agent's appetites, desires, capacities, aspirations, and the like. The principles of rational choice specify the most coherent and satisfying plan of accommodating the agent's ends over time.[186] Accordingly, only those acts are irrational which frustrate the agent's own system of ends, whatever those ends are. Paternalistic considerations come into play only when irrationalities of these kinds exist (for example, the agent's jumping out the window will cause his death, which the agent does not want but which he falsely believes will not occur). Second, within the class of irrationalities so defined, paternalistic considerations would properly come into play only when the irrationality was severe and systematic (due to undeveloped or impaired capacities, or lack of opportunity to exercise such capacities) *and* a severe and permanent impairment of interests was in prospect. Interference in irrationalities outside the scope of this second constraint is forbidden, in large part because allowing people to make and learn from their own mistakes is a crucial part of the development of mature autonomy.[187]

When we examine the application of paternalistic considerations of these kinds to basic life choices, we face the question of how to assess the rationality of these kinds of choices. Again, the idea of rationality, employed in the context of life choices, importantly takes as the fundamental datum the agent's ends, as determined by his or her appetites, desires, aspirations, capacities, and the like. In such contexts principles of rational choice call for the assessment of basic life choices (for example, choice of occupation) in terms of effects over time, since such choices determine a number of subchoices having effects throughout the agent's life, and indeed may determine the duration of that life.[188] Such choices are assessed in terms of the degree to which they satisfy the system of the agent's ends over time (for example, whether they call upon the exercise of competences which the agent could take pleasure in over a lifetime, the degree to which human contacts satisfy whatever one's desires for sociability are, the level of remuneration in relation to the level of satisfaction of other wants, the degree of leisure to pursue and cultivate avocations or personal interests, and the like). Since the agent's ends over time are often quite complex and difficult to anticipate with exactitude, a number of such choices may be or seem equally rational. Nonetheless, there is a coherent sense to the application of rationality criteria to such choices. Some such choices are clearly irrational if they, compared to other available alternative plans, frustrate the agent's every significant end.[189] Such choices, if they satisfy the stringent constraints of the principle discussed above, may be the proper object of paternalistic interference.

As we have seen, one radically inappropriate form of paternalistic interference is that which is grounded in the substitution of the interferer's own personal ends for the ends of the agent. This form is objectionable because it does not take seriously the fundamental datum of proper paternalism—that the agent's ends are given and that the agent acts irrationally only when his action frustrates those ends. This form of inappropriateness is, I believe, a general problem in the paternalistic assessment of life choices, for in this context people find it all too natural facilely to substitute their own personal solutions for the kind of imaginative understanding of the perspectives of others required properly to examine these matters. The temptations to such paternalistic distortions are irresistibly strong in cases properly covered by the constitutional right to privacy, which is, in part, to be understood as a prophylaxis against such abuses.

No good argument can be made that paternalistic considerations would justify interferences in basic choices such as whether to marry, bear children, or be heterosexual. Indeed, in many cases such choices seem clearly rational. There is widespread consensus that it is rational for many people to limit family size by contraceptives; in such ways, people satisfy their desires for having children and have additional resources better to advance their ends in general. It is no more irrational, I believe, to suppose that for some people not having children would better advance their ends; whatever ends having children advances can be secured in alternative ways (for example, being in a profession that cares for the young, investing one's immortal longings in other forms of enduring projects, etc.), and not having children may free people to advance their own and others' good in ways otherwise improbable. Finally, the idea that it is per se irrational to engage in homosexual relations is no more defensible. Suppose one is an exclusive homosexual, who from early age has experienced natural eroticism, either in fact or in fantasy,[190] only with people of the same gender. Such an individual experiences spontaneous self-expression and fulfillment and meaningful relations only in homosexual relations. Since love is such a fundamental good in human life, it would surely be rational to develop a personal life in which one's natural sexual self can find meaningful expression. The idea of change of sexual preference is unacceptable, not merely because it is painful and probably doomed to failure[191] but because, given the depth of sexuality, it would transmogrify the self in which one has self-esteem. The appeal to social opprobrium rests on a circular appeal to the still extant force of invalid and unjust moral judgments. It is entirely rational to refuse to sacrifice the foundations of one's personal happiness to vicious social prejudices, for such sacrifices degrade the foundations of autonomous self-respect and thus reduce freedom to cowardly, servile, and fear-ridden conventionalism. For many, such a life is simply not worth living. How, then, are we even to *understand* the invocation of paternalistic arguments of irrationality in this context? The answer, I believe, is that in making such judgments people do not take seriously or responsibly what it is to be the agent, in this case, an exclusive homosexual. They suppose that these people are somehow real heterosexuals who must be prodded to realize their latent desires. This fantasy cannot be sustained as an empirical proposition; it is simply a make-weight psychiatric correlate to already accepted moral judgments.[192] This substitution of personal values for the ends of the agent is, of course, improper paternalism. The development of the constitutional right to privacy is, in part, to be understood as a bar to such arguments, allowing the agent the scope of personal autonomy in these matters that is their moral and human right.

It is fair to regard the judgments of conventional family life as "the meaning of life" as a kind of metaphysical familism. It is, however, important to see the limited force that such normative judgments should be accorded. Certainly, such normative judgments are important and deeply significant; indeed, nothing can be more important to individuals than basic life choices. But it is crucial to see that such judgments are not properly regarded as ethical or moral judgments, in the sense of expressing moral requirements applicable at large on the basis of mutual concern and respect, universalization, and minimization of fortuity.[193] In making basic life choices, we undoubtedly assume moral principles of such kinds as background conditions; we assume, typically, that none of the available life choices violates moral requirements. But the substance of such life choices is not dictated by such ethical boundary conditions. Rather, typically, we are morally *at liberty* to adopt any of a number of life plans. In an important sense, then, metaphysical familism is an expression of a nonethical judgment, a view of the more satisfying, and thus more rational, basic life plan. Accordingly, such judgments are entitled to no more legal or constitutional force than any other ideological vision of the good life not dictated by ethical principles. In particular, it is *deeply* mistaken to confuse the moral depth of the constitutional right to privacy, as a right to autonomy, with the ideology of metaphysical familism.[194]

Such confusions are, of course, familiar to many moral traditions. One thinks, for example, of the many religious codes of detailed casuistry that regulate, in the name of "morality," the most detailed features of people's personal lives.[195] Plato's moral theory appears to embody a philosophical form of this confusion, namely, Plato's idea that there are no limits to legitimate state paternalism (a claim I have elsewhere analyzed as a form of deep paternalism inconsistent with basic respect for the person and human rights).[196] Against such views stands the radical vision of autonomy and mutual concern and respect, which accords to persons *as such* the right to create their own lives on terms fair to all. To see people in this way is to affirm basic intrinsic limits on the degree to which, even benevolently, one person may control the life of another. Within ethical constraints, people are free to adopt a number of disparate and irreconcilable visions of the good life. Indeed, the adoption of different kinds of life plans, within these constraints, affords the moral good of different experiments in living by which people can more rationally assess such basic life choices.[197] Since rigid moral prescriptions in many of these areas are no longer appropriate, people *should* make these choices in as imaginative, creative, exploratory, and inventive a way as human wit can devise, consulting one's personal desires, wants, needs, competences and how one most harmoniously wishes them concurrently and complementarily to develop and be satisfied over a lifetime. Perhaps, people fear freedom in this sense,[198] preferring conventional solutions. That is their right. But such choices deserve no special moral approbation; they do not help us more rationally and courageously to choose our lives. In this sense, the constitutional right to privacy protects not only the autonomy rights of individuals, but facilitates the social and moral good that experiments in living afford to society at large—refreshing and deepening the social imagination about the role of children in human life, about the improper force of "masculine" and "feminine" stereotypes in human love and work,[199] and about the varieties of humane sexual arrangements.[200]

III. IN CONCLUSION: THE JUDICIAL METHODOLOGY OF THE CONSTITUTIONAL RIGHT TO PRIVACY

We have proposed a theory of the *form* of considerations which must be assessed in considering issues involving the constitutional right to privacy, namely, (1) whether, in the light of contemporary evidence, there is any good moral reason to believe that certain conduct, traditionally conceived as morally wrong, is wrong at all; (2) whether the conduct relates to basic life plan choices; and (3) consequent on (2), whether paternalistic considerations are radically inappropriate.

This chapter began by taking up the familiar challenge that the constitutional right to privacy is unsound in principle and methodology. We have now discussed at some length the substantive basis of constitutional principles on which the constitutional right to privacy rests, and this analysis may now be used in explaining why the judicial methodology, used in inferring the right, is sound.

Substantively, we have argued that there is an inner moral coherence in the development of the right to privacy. Beginning in the interstices of tort law, used in the interpretation of specific constitutional guarantees, finally invoked as an independent constitutional right—the right to privacy has appealed to a common moral argument, that is, the interpretation of basic rights in terms of the foundational values of autonomy and equal concern and respect. When Warren and Brandeis invoked ideas of the inviolate personality in their seminal article,[201] they appealed to underlying concepts of human rights that, in their view, most deeply explain the moral foundations of tort law and the proper direction in which tort law should judicially evolve. When Brandeis invoked similar arguments in his dissent in *Olmstead*,[202] he made an argument of basic moral principle that he supposed to underlie the fourth amendment and the constitutional design in general. These arguments express the ultimate moral vision of human rights—that there are intrinsic limits on the power of individuals and the state to violate basic interests of the person. Legal doctrines, expressing ideas of human rights, are thus interpreted in terms of the underlying moral concepts which give these doctrines some ultimate coherent sense. Accordingly, when Justice Douglas inferred the constitutional right to privacy in *Griswold*,[203] he correctly appealed, like Brandeis, to an underlying argument of moral principle that he took to explain a number of constitutional provisions and the constitutional design in general. This underlying argument is here called the unwritten constitution, a body of understandings that gives a coherent meaning to the constitutional design. This meaning is the basic constitutional commitment to the ultimate values of human rights, the guarantee to persons of effective institutional respect for their capacities, as free and rational beings, to define the meaning of their own lives. Like the Warren and Brandeis article and the Brandeis dissent and like good judges in general,[204] Douglas thus made sense of existing legal materials in terms of underlying principles and showed how those principles make sense today. Constitutional principles, insuring equal concern and respect for autonomy, require the invalidation of state prohibitions and regulations in matters not properly of public concern (antimoralism and antipaternalism) and implicating basic issues of the definition of the self. In particular, the argument has appealed focally to the matrix of values expressed in the first amendment, principles of basic toleration and respect for the disparate ways in which persons may conscientiously organize their lives. Criminal laws, whose condemnation rests solely on hatred of ways of life which deviate from those of others, fail precisely to accord persons the kind of equal dignity for self-determination which is distinctive of the human rights perspective embodied in the first amendment's charter of basic toleration. Accordingly, the constitutional right to privacy was inferred.[205] Whether derived as an implication of various amendments,[206] as a right reserved to the people by the ninth amendment,[207] or as a substantive right required by due process of law,[208] the constitutional right to privacy makes ultimate moral sense of the constitutional design.

Of course, as we have noted, the constitutional right to privacy is analytically distinguishable from the informational control issues of the tort and fourth amendment concepts.[209] The unity of these disparate rights is not in the definition of the ultimate rights, but in the common moral arguments they invoke: the concern for the exacting protection of matters not properly of public concern, in the interest of protecting the ultimate resources of individuation that lie at the heart of the concept of human rights. Accordingly, the judicial methodology of *Griswold* and its progeny is eminently proper. Analogies are properly drawn to the privacy interests protected by tort law and the fourth amendment, not because the constitutional right to privacy is the same right as these, but because there is an underlying moral principle that the analogy clarifies.[210]

The critics of the constitutional right to privacy are wrong.[211] It is they, not the Court, who have lost touch with the moral vision underlying the constitutional design. The institutional protection of moral personality requires that this right be recognized. A case like *Doe*[212] shows not that the constitutional right to privacy is incoherent, but that the Court has failed consistently to apply or articulately to understand its underlying principle. *Doe* is deeply, morally wrong. Sexual autonomy is a human right in terms of which people define the meaning of their lives. In particular, the persecution of homosexuals, for that is the name we may now properly give it, deserves not constitutional validation, but systematic and unremitting attack. To appeal to popular attitudes, in the way in which *Doe* implicitly does, is precisely to withhold human rights when, as a shield against majoritarian oppression, they are most exigently needed. Homosexuals have the right to reclaim the aspects of the self that society has traditionally compelled them to deny; they, like other persons, have the right to center work and love in a life they can authentically call their own.

NOTES

1. 381 U.S. 479 (1965).
2. See generally Ely, "The Wages of Crying Wolf: A Comment on *Roe v. Wade*," 82 *Yale L.J.* 920 (1973); Comment, "*Roe v. Wade*—The Abortion Decision—An Analysis and Its Implications," 10 *San Diego L. Rev.* 844, 848–51 (1973); Note, "*Roe v. Wade* and *Doe v. Bolton:* The Compelling State Interest Test in Substantive Due Process," 30 *Wash. & Lee L. Rev.* 628, 634–35, 642–43 (1973).
3. Thus, Justice Black complained in his dissent that the majority opinion was "natural justice" in disguise. *Griswold v. Connecticut*, 381 U.S. 479, 511–12 (1965) (Black, J., dissenting).
4. See note 2 supra.
5. 425 U.S. 901 (1976), aff'g without opinion 403 F. Supp. 1199 (E.D. Va. 1975) (three-judge court). In *Doe*, two homosexuals challenged the constitutionality of Virginia's criminal sodomy statute as applied to private acts between consenting adults. The challenge was based on the due process clauses of the fifth and fourteenth amend-

ments, the first amendment guarantee of freedom of expression, the first and ninth amendment guarantee of the right to privacy, and the eighth amendment proscription against cruel and unusual punishment. Nevertheless, the district court found no constitutional bar to the criminalization of homosexual conduct.

6. *Griswold v. Connecticut*, 381 U.S. 479 (1965).

7. *Roe v. Wade*, 410 U.S. 113 (1973).

8. *Stanley v. Georgia*, 394 U.S. 557 (1969).

9. See D. Richards, *The Moral Criticism of Law* 39–56 (1977).

10. R. Dworkin, *Taking Rights Seriously* 81–90 (1977) [hereinafter cited as Dworkin].

11. *U.S. Const.* art. III, § 2.

12. See *United Public Workers v. Mitchell*, 330 U.S. 75 (1930) (federal employees held to have no standing where they desired to engage in political activity in violation of the Hatch Act but did not actually do so); cf. *Cramp v. Board of Pub. Instruction*, 368 U.S. 278 (1961) (loyalty oath).

13. Dworkin, supra note 10, at 212–13, 219–20. Dworkin fails to develop this point. For an elaboration, see M. Kadish & S. Kadish, *Discretion to Disobey* (1973). Compare the majoritarian appeal in Thayer, "The Origin and Scope of the American Doctrine of Constitutional Law," 7 *Harv. L. Rev.* 129 (1893), which is implicitly utilitarian. Also compare the implicit utilitarianism in Bickel's later works, A. Bickel, *The Supreme Court and the Idea of Progress* (1970); A. Bickel, *The Morality of Consent* (1975).

14. See O. W. Holmes, *The Common Law* (M. Howe ed. 1963) (originally published 1881). On its influence on American legal thought, see Richards, "Taking 'Taking Rights Seriously' Seriously: Reflections on Dworkin and the American Revival of Natural Law," 52 *N.Y.U.L. Rev.* 1265, 1334–38 (1977).

15. See L. Hand, *The Bill of Rights* (1958) [hereinafter cited as Hand]. Compare A. Bickel, *The Supreme Court and the Idea of Progress* 174–75 (1970), in which a value skepticism similar to Hand's leads to a critique of moral reform through constitutional adjudication. Moral reform and reflection in the light of principles is to be replaced by unconscious moral historicism. These ideas represent a significant retreat from Bickel's earlier work. See, e.g., A. Bickel, *The Least Dangerous Branch* (1962). Value skepticism and utilitarianism are often inextricably related by these theorists. The idea, invoked by Holmes himself, appears to be one that is skeptical of any nonutilitarian ideas, but that utilitarian ideas are to be invoked in any proper policy analysis of the law. See O. W. Holmes, *The Common Law* (M. Howe ed. 1963). For a good statement of the Holmes value skepticism as a theory of the first amendment, see his dissent in *Abrams v. United States*, 250 U.S. 616, 624–31 (1919).

16. See Hand, supra note 15.

17. See Thayer, "The Origin and Scope of the American Doctrine of Constitutional Law," 7 *Harv. L. Rev.* 129 (1893).

18. For example, consider the famous Holmes-Brandeis dissents urging a more expansive vindication of first amendment rights. See *Pierce v. United States*, 252 U.S. 239 (1920); *Schaefer v. United States*, 251 U.S. 466 (1920); *Abrams v. United States*, 250 U.S. 616 (1919). Holmes bottoms this view on value skepticism expressed in the form that the value of controverted ideas is to be judged by the capacity of such beliefs to win the battle for men's minds on the fair terms insured by the first amendment requirement that the state be a neutral observer. See *Abrams v. United States*, 250 U.S. 616, 630 (1919) (Holmes, J., dissenting). But, the argument that the first amendment is thus necessary to advance truth is not the best argument to support the result Holmes and Brandeis correctly wanted. The search for truth might be secured by much less expansive constitutional guarantees than Holmes and Brandeis urged. For example, the first amendment could have been limited to certain kinds of educated elites or confined to certain limited categories of communication. This shows not that the recommended expansionist interpretation of the first amendment is wrong, but that Holmes' theory of justification is inadequate to his moral aims. For an attempt to formulate a more adequate account, see Richards, "Free Speech and Obscenity Law: Toward a Moral Theory of the First Amendment," 123 *U. Pa. L. Rev.* 45 (1974). For a more extended critique of legal realism along these lines, see Richards, "Book Review," 24 *N.Y.L. Sch. L. Rev.* 310 (1978).

19. See Grey, "Do We Have an Unwritten Constitution?," 27 *Stan. L. Rev.* 703 (1975).
20. The political revolutions of the seventeenth and eighteenth centuries witnessed such landmarks as the English Petition of Rights (1627), the Habeas Corpus Act (1679), the American Declaration of Independence (1776), the United States Constitution (1787), the American Bill of Rights (1791), and the French Declaration of the Rights of Man and Citizen (1789).
21. Although the idea of judicial review is American in origin, it did have European antecedents. See Cappelletti & Adams, "Judicial Review of Legislation: European Antecedents and Adaptations," 79 *Harv. L. Rev.* 1207 (1966). The current American form of judicial review is striking in that it is tied to the function of ordinary litigation regarding private rights, whereas judicial review in other countries, which followed the American example in generally adopting the institution, is not tied to private litigation in this way. See Kauper, "The Supreme Court: Hybrid Organ of State," 21 *Sw. L.J.* 573, 574–76, 590 (1967). For descriptions of non-American models, see M. Cappelletti, *Judicial Review in the Contemporary World* 45–68 (1971). See also Rosenn, "Book Review," 81 *Yale L.J.* 1411, 1417–20 (1972).
22. See J. Milton, "Areopagitica," in *Areopagitica, and Of Education* (G. Sabine ed. 1951).
23. See J. Locke, *The Second Treatise of Government* (T. Peardon ed. 1952); J. Locke, "A Letter Concerning Toleration," in *Treatise of Civil Government and A Letter Concerning Toleration* (D. Sherman ed. 1937).
24. See J. Rousseau, "The Social Contract," in *The Social Contract and Discourses* (G. Cole trans. 1930).
25. See I. Kant, *The Metaphysical Elements of Justice* (J. Ladd trans. 1965); I. Kant, "Concerning the Common Saying: This May Be True in Theory, But Does Not Apply in Practice," *Society, Law, and Morality* 159–72 (F. Olafson ed. 1961).
26. Among the more important works that illustrate the impact of European natural rights and general Enlightenment thought on American thought are B. Bailyn, *The Ideological Origins of the American Revolution* (1967); H. Commager, *The Empire of Reason: How Europe Imagined and America Realized the Enlightenment* (1977); H. May, *The Enlightenment in America* (1976); G. Wood, *The Creation of the American Republic, 1776–1787*, at 282–305 (1969). One important recent book debunks the specific influence of Locke on Jefferson and the Declaration of Independence. See G. Wills, *Inventing America: Jefferson's Declaration of Independence* 167–92 (1978). The case is probably overstated. See Morgan, "The Heart of Jefferson," *N.Y. Review of Books*, August 17, 1978, at 38. Wills does acknowledge general Lockean influence (Wills, supra, at 175) but his main emphasis is on the specific influence of Scottish moral sense theorists, in particular Hutcheson, on Jefferson. Id. at 167–255. The emphasis of these theorists on a fundamental moral equality based on the equal moral sense of all persons, id. at 207–17, clearly prefigures Kantian ideas of the equality of all persons in respect of the Moral Law. Jefferson clearly accepted ideas of fundamental moral equality and clearly believed in forms of natural rights. See Wills, supra, at 229–39. Wills's argument is not against Jefferson's belief in natural rights, but against a certain interpretation of his beliefs in the content of those rights, i.e., the primacy of property.
27. Of course, morally informed constitutional provisions have not always been applied uniformly and consistently with their underlying moral principles. For example, the first amendment clearly rests on the substantive moral idea that all men have certain inalienable rights, including freedom of speech and rights of religious tolerance. The Constitution did not consistently extend these basic rights to all persons, however. For example, the institution of slavery was nowhere condemned, but was rather impliedly endorsed by three clauses in the Constitution that refer to slavery in a way that contemplates the continued existence of that institution. See *U.S. Const.* art. I, § 9, cl. l; art. I, § 2, cl. 3; art. IV, § 2, cl. 3. This flaw in the constitutional charter of basic moral rights was resolved only by the Civil War and the constitutional amendments that followed in its wake. Of these amendments, the due process and equal protection clauses of the fourteenth amendment have been especially fertile sources for the enlargement of constitutional rights. The equal protection clause, for example, has been interpreted to require forms of equal protection well beyond the original intent to

abolish slavery and concomitant state practices. For an excellent account of this development, see "Developments in the Law—Equal Protection," 82 *Harv. L. Rev.* 1065 (1969). The due process clause has been interpreted to require not only application to the states of many of the original amendments comprising the Bill of Rights, but has also been viewed as a means of protecting basic liberties not expressly articulated in the Bill of Rights, including, as we shall see, the constitutional right to privacy. See, e.g., *Griswold v. Connecticut*, 381 U.S. 479 (1965) (right of married couples to use contraceptives); *Pierce v. Society of Sisters*, 268 U.S. 510 (1925) (right to educate a child in a school of the parents' choice); *Meyer v. Nebraska*, 262 U.S. 390 (1923) (right of a child to study a foreign language).

28. For example, the legal history of free speech in England and America prior to the adoption of the first amendment renders doubtful any consensus on the specific application of the amendment. See generally L. Levy, *Legacy of Suppression; Freedom of Speech and Press in Early American History* (1960).

29. Consider the following examples. First, the adopters of the fourteenth amendment quite clearly did not contemplate that the amendment would abolish segregation. See Bickel, "The Original Understanding and the Segregation Decision," 69 *Harv. L. Rev.* 1 (1955). Yet, the Court in *Brown v. Board of Educ.*, 347 U.S. 483, 489 (1954), expressly put such history aside in reaching its decision. Second, the existence, at the time of the adoption of the first amendment, of laws such as those against seditious libel has never been supposed to conclude the question of the constitutionality of such laws. For a discussion of the crime of seditious libel at common law, see L. Levy, *Legacy of Suppression; Freedom of Speech and Press in Early American History* (1960). For the view that seditious libel was abolished by the first amendment, see *Beauharnais v. Illinois*, 343 U.S. 250, 272 (1952) (Black, J., dissenting); *Abrams v. United State*, 250 U.S. 616, 630–31 (1919) (Holmes, J., dissenting). See also *Bridges v. California*, 314 U.S. 252, 264–65 (1941); *Grosjean v. American Press Co.*, 297 U.S. 233, 248–49 (1936) (first amendment prohibits taxes that restrict newspaper circulation, although such taxes were employed in England and America at the time of that amendment's adoption).

30. Even with respect to ordinary word meanings, dictionaries are often only the starting place for inquiries into meaning. Sometimes, historical accounts are useful supplements. See, e.g., C. S. Lewis, *Studies in Words* (1960). In others, we seek deeper philosophical analysis in order to afford an elucidating theory of the underlying concepts invoked by the use of certain language.

31. See, e.g., E. Panofsky, *Meaning in the Visual Arts* (1955).

32. See generally, H. Hart & A. Sacks, "The Legal Process: Basic Problems in the Making and Application of Law" 1144–416 (1958) (mimeographed materials published by Harvard Law School).

33. The famous legal positivist appeal to "wash the law in cynical acid" derives from O. W. Holmes, "The Path of the Law," in *Collected Legal Papers* 167–202 (1952). Compare Holmes's derogatory reference to viewing the common law as "a brooding omnipresence in the sky" rather than as "the articulate voice of some sovereign or quasi sovereign that can be identified." *Southern Pacific Co. v. Jensen*, 244 U.S. 205, 222 (1917) (Holmes, J., dissenting). For the application of these ideas to constitutional law, see Hand, supra note 16, at 1–3, 33–34.

34. The question of the philosophical status of meaning in constitutional interpretation has recently been strikingly raised in Munzer & Nickel, "Does the Constitution Mean What It Always Meant?" 77 *Colum. L. Rev.* 1029(1977). The authors equate constitutional meaning with utterer's meaning, so that constitutional meaning changes as the utterer's meaning (here, Supreme Court interpretation) changes. But even utterer's meaning typically depends on the background conventions that speakers of a language assume, so that analysis of even utterer's meaning often requires analysis of these background conventions. See S. Schiffer, *Meaning* 118–66 (1972). Meaning in constitutional interpretation, which of course expresses a complex legal institution, correspondingly requires analysis of these background conventions that are much more stable than Munzer and Nickel suppose. Dworkin's distinction between concepts and conventions expresses this important truth, namely, that the stability of constitutional

meaning rests on quite general concepts which are valid over time. See Dworkin, supra note 10 at 136.

35. Warren & Brandeis, "The Right to Privacy," 4 *Harv. L. Rev.* 193 (1890).

36. Id. at 205.

37. Id. at 196.

38. Id. at 197.

39. Id. at 205.

40. 277 U.S. 438, 471 (1928).

41. The Brandeis view was finally accepted by a majority of the Supreme Court in *Katz v. United States*, 389 U.S. 374 (1967). For citation and discussion of the intervening cases on mechanical and electronic surveillance, see. J. Vorenberg, *Criminal Law and Procedure: Cases and Materials* 628–45 (1975); Parker, "A Definition of Privacy," 27 *Rutgers L. Rev.* 275, 288–91 (1973).

42. As regards the law of torts, Dean Prosser in 1960 examined three hundred privacy cases in an attempt to discover what interest was being protected. He concluded that no single thing was common to every loss of privacy but noted four characteristics, at least one of which was present in each case: (1) intrusion upon the plaintiff's seclusion or solitude, or into his private affairs; (2) public disclosure of embarrassing private facts about the plaintiff; (3) publicity that places the plaintiff in a false light in the public eye; (4) appropriation, for the defendant's advantage, of the plaintiff's name or likeness. Prosser, "Privacy," 48 *Calif. L. Rev.* 383 (1960). Subsequent commentary has sought to reduce Prosser's list to one unifying theme, privacy as the capacity to control highly personal information about oneself or one's experiences.

The connections between the tort and constitutional concepts of privacy are problematic in the following way. *Griswold* established that married couples have a constitutional privacy right to use contraceptives which the state may not abridge. The Court justified its holding by the ancillary likelihood that anticontraceptive prosecutions would violate conventional privacy interests (bugging the bedroom), which are protected from intrusion against private parties by one of the privacy torts and against the state by fourth amendment guarantees against unreasonable searches and seizures. *Griswold v. Connecticut*, 381 U.S. 479, 485–86 (1965). However, the constitutional right of privacy, as developed since *Griswold*, cannot be characterized as merely a right protecting conventional privacy interests in information control. It rests, rather, on affirmative personal rights to act in certain ways that the state, in principle, cannot abridge. This feature of the constitutional right to privacy cases, which commentators had observed even in *Griswold*, was made quite clear in *Roe v. Wade*, 410 U.S. 113 (1973). In *Roe*, the challenged law subjected the person performing the abortion to criminal sanctions and was held unconstitutional because it made it difficult for women to obtain the desired service. There is not the remotest suggestion in *Roe* that the state could cure the constitutional infirmity by removing any criminal sanction from the woman while continuing effectively to restrict abortion by attacking suppliers of the service. Indeed, since *Roe*, the Court has insisted that the *Roe*-defined right extends to "the doctor's office, the hospital, the hotel room, or as otherwise required to safeguard the right to intimacy involved." *Paris Adult Theatre I v. Slaton*, 413 U.S. 49, 66 n. 13 (1973). In short, there is no evidence that the constitution right to privacy depends on outrageous government surveillance violative of conventional right-to-privacy interests.

43. *Olmstead v. United States*, 277 U. S. 438, 478 (1928).

44. Id.

45. See C. Fried, *An Anatomy of Values* 137–52 (1970).

46. See Bloustein, "Privacy as an Aspect of Human Dignity: An Answer to Dean Prosser," 39 *N.Y.U.L. Rev.* 962, 1003 (1964).

47. See generally Wasserstrom, "Rights, Human Rights, and Racial Discrimination," 61 *J. Philosophy* 628 (1964).

48. When Nietzsche formulated and celebrated the idea of a transvaluation of values, he gave the idea an unwarrantably extreme interpretation by changing the underlying concept of morality from a universalistic concept that embodies equal concern and respect to a perfectionist morality that maximizes the only ultimate moral

good—the excellences of military virtue, artistic and intellectual achievements, and the like. For the main works, see F. Nietzsche, *Beyond Good and Evil: Prelude to a Philosophy of the Future* (H. Zimmern trans. 1909); F. Nietzsche, *Twilight of the Idols* (1889), reprinted in *The Portable Nietzsche* 465 (W. Kaufmann trans. 1954); F. Nietzsche, *Thus Spake Zarathustra*, reprinted in id. at 121; F. Nietzsche, *The Antichrist*, reprinted in id. at 568. Undoubtedly there have been changes of values at this foundational level. One example is the change from Aristotelian perfectionism, which Nietzsche attempts to reintroduce, to Kantian ethics of mutual respect. See Aristotle, *Nicomachean Ethics* bk. 10 (M. Ostwald trans. 1962) (shows the special weight Aristotle gave to the excellence of theoretical wisdom); I. Kant, works cited supra note 25; F. Nietzsche, *Twilight of the Idols*, supra. at 534. However, the transvaluation of values, relevant to the understanding and justifiability of the constitutional right to privacy, does not describe such a foundational shift in the concept of morality itself, but rather it does so with reference to the lower order conventions that the concept of morality justifies. See text accompanying note 115 infra.

49. For support for this kind of position from constitutional history, see Perry, "Abortion, The Public Morals and the Police Power: The Ethical Function of Substantive Due Process," 23 *U.C.L.A. L. Rev.* 689 (1976).

50. See K. Baier, *The Moral Point of View* 187–213 (1958); R. B. Brandt, *A Theory of the Right and the Good* 163–335 (1979); A. Donagan, *Theory of Morality* 210–43 (1978); C. Fried, *Right and Wrong*, 7–29 (1978); D. Gauthier, *Practical Reasoning* (1963); B. Gert, *The Moral Rules* 60–75 (1973); A. Gewirth, *Reason and Morality* 129–98 (1978); G. Grice, *The Grounds of Moral Judgment* 1–35 (1967); R. M. Hare, *The Language of Morals* (1952); R. M. Hare, *Freedom and Reason* 86–185 (1963); J. Mackie, *Ethics* 83–102 (1977); J. Rawls, *A Theory of Justice* (1971); D. Richards, *A Theory of Reasons for Action* (1971).

51. See G. Warnock, *Contemporary Moral Philosophy* 55–61 (1967); G. Warnock, *The Object of Morality* 35–70 (1971); Foot & Harrison, "When Is a Principle a Moral Principle?" 28 *Proc. Aristotelian Soc'y* 95 (1954); Foot, "Moral Arguments," 67 *Mind* 502 (1958); "Moral Beliefs," 59 *Proc. Aristotelian Soc'y* 83 (1958–59).

52. See K. Baier, *The Moral Point of View* 187–216 (1958); D. Gauthier, *Practical Reasoning* 81–94 (1963); G. Grice, *The Grounds of Moral Judgment* 1–35 (1967); J. Mackie, *Ethics* 83–102 (1977); J. Rawls, *A Theory of Justice* 130–32 (1971); D. Richards, *A Theory of Reasons for Action* 75–91 (1971).

53. See R. Hare, *Freedom and Reason* 91–94 (1963); D. Richards, *A Theory of Reasons for Action* 83–85, 216 (1971).

54. This idea is the basis of Kant's theory of autonomy. See I. Kant, *Foundations of the Metaphysics of Morals* 65–71 (L. Beck trans. 1959). Also note J. S. Mill's remark that the true idea of distributive justice consists in "redressing the inequalities and wrongs of nature." J. S. Mill, 2 *Principles of Political Economy* 398 (5th ed. 1864). Mill thus concludes that primogeniture is unjust in that distinctions are grounded on accident. Id. at 505. Note also Sidgwick's claim that justice rewards voluntary effort, not natural ability alone. H. Sidgwick, *The Principles of Political Economy* 505–06, 531 (1887).

55. "What is important is not the quality of the creed but the strength of the belief in it," P. Devlin, *The Enforcement of Morals* 114 (1965).

56. See authorities cited note 50 supra.

57. See A. Gewirth, *Reason and Morality* (1978), J. Rawls, *A Theory of Justice* (1971), D. Richards, *A Theory of Reasons for Action* (1971).

58. For example, equal concern and respect for autonomy clearly rule out as a form of legitimate morality Aristotelian and Nietzschean perfectionism, for such moral systems identify as the only morally relevant factors forms of elitist excellence that most persons lack; such systems show no concern and respect for autonomous persons. See D. Richards, *A Theory of Reasons for Action* 116–17 (1971); G. Warnock, *Contemporary Moral Philosophy* (49–51 (1967). Similarly, we may use moral theories, for example, contractarianism, that express the values of autonomy and equal concern and respect, to assess which beliefs are within the constitutionally permissible content of the public morality.

59. See Augustine, *The City of God* 577–94 (H. Bettenson trans. 1972). St. Thomas is in

accord with Augustine's view. Of the emission of semen apart from procreation in marriage, he wrote: "[A]fter the sin of homicide whereby a human nature already in existence is destroyed, this type of sin appears to take next place, for by it the generation of human nature is precluded." T. Aquinas, *On the Truth of the Catholic Faith: Summa Contra Gentiles*, pt. 2, ch. 122(9), at 146 (V. Bourke trans. 1946).

60., "In fact, this lust we are now examining is something to be the more ashamed of because the soul, when dealing with it, neither has command of itself so as to be entirely free from lust, nor does it rule the body so completely that the organs of shame are moved by the will instead of by lust. Indeed if they were so ruled they would not be *pudenda*—parts of shame." Augustine, *The City of God* 586 (H. Bettenson trans. 1972).

61. One prominent account of the Catholic view notes that Catholic canon law "holds, as a basic and cardinal fact, that complete sexual activity and pleasure is licit and moral only in a naturally completed act in valid marriage. All acts which, of their psychological and physical nature, are designed to be preparatory to the complete act, take their licitness and their morality from the complete act. If, therefore, they are entirely divorced from the complete act, they are distorted, warped, meaningless, and hence immoral." Gardiner, "Moral Principles Towards a Definition of the Obscene," 20 *Law & Contemp. Prob.* 560, 564 (1955); cf. T. Bouscaren, A. Ellis, & F. Korth, *Canon Law* 930 (1963); H. Gardiner, *Catholic Viewpoint on Censorship* 62–67 (1958) (sanctions against immorality by lay persons). For a critique, see R. Haney, *Comstockery in America* 88–96 (1960).

62. Augustine, *The City of God* 579–80 (H. Bettenson trans. 1972).

63. Id. at 578–79.

64. Indeed, Augustine objects to the intensity of the experience in that it overwhelms mental functions: "This lust assumes power not only over the whole body, and not only from the outside, but also internally; it disturbs the whole man, when the mental emotion combines and mingles with the physical craving, resulting in a pleasure surpassing all physical delights. So intense is the pleasure that when it reaches its climax there is an almost total extinction of mental alertness; the intellectual sentries, as it were, are overwhelmed." Id. at 577.

65. Augustine speculates that, prior to the Fall in the Garden of Eden, man could will erections for procreation without any lust just as some extraordinary people now can wiggle their ears at will or even pass air musically "without any stink." Id. at 588.

66. Indeed, Augustine notes that not only is sexual impulse "totally opposed to the mind's control, it is quite often divided against itself." Id. at 577. That is, when we want to experience such feelings, we often cannot; and when we don't want to experience them, we do.

67. The leading anthropological study of cross-cultural sexual practices reports that, universally, sexual intercourse occurs in private. See C. Ford & F. Beach, *Patterns of Sexual Behavior* 68–72 (1951) [hereinafter cited as Ford & Beach]. This is not a characteristic of animal sexual behavior. "A desire for privacy during sexual intercourse seems confined to human beings. Male-female pairs of other animal species appear to be unaffected by the presence of other individuals and to mate quite as readily in a crowd as when they are alone." Id. at 71.

68. See D. Richards, *A Theory of Reasons for Action* 254 (1971).

69. This very conception (that sexuality is a proper object of the will) appears to have disastrous effects on natural sexual function. Masters and Johnson, for example, report that a main feature of certain kinds of inadequate sexual function is the very attempt to will it. See W. Masters & V. Johnson, *Human Sexual Inadequacy* 198–99, 202–03 (1970). This conception, thus, of certain religious traditions (namely, that "proper" sexual experience must be accompanied by certain kinds of wills and intentions) may account for the association of defective sexual function with rigid religious sexual conceptions. See generally id. at 10, 24, 70, 117–20, 133, 135, 139, 144, 175–76, 177–79, 189, 213, 253–56.

70. *Stanley v. Georgia*, 394 U. S. 557 (1969)

71. *Roe v. Wade*, 410 U. S. 113 (1973). For an examination of the Catholic response to the Supreme Court's abortion cases, see Bresnahan, "The Interaction of Religion and

Law—a Post-Vatican II Roman Catholic Perspective," 29 *Hastings L. J.* 1361, 1377–82 (1978). For philosophical arguments against the status of the foetus as a person, see Tooley, "A Defense of Abortion and Infanticide," in *The Problem of Abortion* (51–91) (J. Feinberg ed. 1973); Engelhardt, Jr., "The Ontology of Abortion," in *Moral Problems in Medicine* 318–34 (1976); J. Feinberg, "Abortion," in *Matters of Life and Death* 183–217 (Tom Regan ed. 1980). For various other positions, see note 57, chapter 5, infra.

72. The right to privacy is clearly applicable to nonmarital contexts. See *Roe v. Wade*, 410 U. S. 113 (1973) (abortion); cf. *Eisenstadt v. Baird*, 405 U. S. 438 (1972) (contraceptives and the unmarried); *Stanley v. Georgia* 394 U. S. 557 (1969) (private use of pornography).

73. The constitutional protection for the use of pornography in the home, *Stanley v. Georgia*, 394 U. S. 557 (1969), is arguably protection for the masturbatory practices for which the pornography may be used.

74. See Justice Stewart's remark, in the context of the permissibility of isolating the harmless mentally ill on the ground that they failed to conform to normal behavior: "One might as well ask if the State, to void public unease, could incarcerate all who are physically unattractive or socially eccentric. Mere public intolerance or animosity cannot constitutionally justify the deprivation of a person's physical liberty." *O'Connor v. Donaldson*, 422 U. S. 563, 575 (1975).

75. *The Federalist* No. 78 (A. Hamilton) at 359 (Hallowell ed. 1857).

76. For a fuller account of the concept of the unnatural here employed (namely, a damaging impairment of proper function), see D. Levy, "Perversion and the Unnatural as Moral Categories," 90 *Ethics* 191 (1980); see also Richards, "Unnatural Acts and the Constitutional Right to Privacy: A Moral Theory," 45 *Fordham L. Rev.* 1281, 1287–98 (1977). The history of the application of the concept to consensual homosexuality and the Anglo-American criminalization may be briefly summarized as follows.

The earliest literate explanation of the association of the unnatural and sexual deviance appears in Plato's *Laws*. See Plato, *Laws*, Book VIII 835d–842a, which gives crucial significance to whether homosexuality has been acquired through no fault of the homosexual. See also Aristotle, *Nicomachean Ethics*, at Book VII, 1148b–1149a. Plato's view of the unnaturalness of homosexual acts in the *Laws* is not a departure from the views of the earlier dialogues, which imply or state such a view. See G. Vlastos, "The Individual as an Object of Love in Plato," in *Platonic Studies* 27–28 (1973). Plato argued that male homosexual acts are unnatural on two grounds. First, such acts undermine the development of desirable masculine character traits—for example, courage and self-control. This idea probably rested on the assumption that homosexual acts degrade men to the status of women. See note 84, infra, and text accompanying. Second, Plato argued that male sexuality has one proper form or nature, namely, procreation within marriage, and that homosexuality is unnatural because it is sterile. This latter thought rests on the pervasive Greek conception that everything in the physical world has a precisely defined proper function. Thus, for example, Aristotle argued that usury is unnatural and violative of the proper function of money. Aristotle, *Politics* 1257a–1258b. See J. Noonan, "Tokos and Atokion: An Examination of Natural Law Reasoning Against Usury and Against Contraception," 10 *Nat. L. For.* 215 (1965).

The idea that homosexuality involves the degradation of a man to the status of a woman is at least strongly suggested by the seeming prohibitions on male homosexuality in the Old Testament, see note 84, infra, and by St. Paul's statement of these prohibitions in the context of rigidly defined sex roles. See, e.g., Romans 1:26, 27; 1 Corinthians 6:9, 10; 1 Corinthians 11:14, 15. But see note 138, infra. The early Christian Church absorbed the Platonic-Aristotelian notion that homosexual acts are unnatural. The church's view was further grounded on a probable misinterpretation of the Old Testament prohibitions, note 84, infra, perhaps caused by the influence of the Pauline prohibitions. These homosexuality prohibitions, when enacted into Roman law by the early Christian emperors, were interpreted not merely as prohibiting the unnatural for Plato's reasons, but also as combatting pestilence, plague, and natural disaster. See note 103, infra.

Finally, the Christian interpretation of the unnaturalness of homosexuality was consolidated and given theoretical statement by St. Thomas's reformulation of St. Augustine's view that the only proper "genital commotion" is that aimed toward the reproduction of the species in marriage. See notes 59–69, supra, and text accompanying. Building on these Augustinian foundations, St. Thomas argued that, even granting that homosexual acts between consenting adults harm no one, it is still unnatural and immoral, for it is an offense to God himself who has ordained procreation as the only legitimate use of sexuality. *Summa Theologica,* II–II, Q. cliv, I, II, and XII. St. Thomas thus takes the Platonic view—namely, that human sexuality has a distinct purpose— and gives it a theological interpretation. Homosexuality is unnatural not primarily because it degrades proper human function, but because it violates divine law, which sanctions that function.

On the basis of such views, there arose the conviction that homosexuality was a heresy, a clear and flagrant violation of express divine command. Accordingly, throughout the Middle Ages, homosexuals were prosecuted as heretics, often being burned at the stake. See Bailey, *Homosexuality and the Western Christian Tradition* 135 (1955). See generally S. Runciman, *The Medieval Manichee* (1947). Thus, "buggery," one of the names of homosexual acts, derives from a corruption of the name of one heretical group alleged to engage in homosexual practices. See Bailey, supra, at 141, 148–49. With the association of religious and secular law, one can further understand the association even in contemporary literature of homosexuality and treason. See P. Devlin, *The Enforcement of Morals* 9–13 (1965). Homosexuality was perceived as undermining the foundations of the state because it was a defiance of the divine law, which was conceived to be the basis of the state.

This religious condemnation of sexual deviance strongly influenced the Anglo-American secular prohibitions. Thus, during the Middle Ages in England, homosexuality was, along with heresy, blasphemy, witchcraft, adultery, and the like, within the jurisdiction of the ecclesiastical courts. See W. Barnett, *Sexual Freedom and the Constitution* 80–81 (1973). The first English statute forbidding homosexual acts, 25 Hen. 8, c. 6 (1533) (repealed by 9 Geo. 4, c. 31 [1828]), was not enacted until the English Reformation when Henry VIII transferred powers of the ecclesiastical courts to the king's courts. Barnett, supra, at 80. When Henry's statute was revived under Elizabeth I, the new statute, confirming the religious grounds of its legitimacy, recited that the law was made necessary to combat the prevalence of the "horrible and detestable vice of buggery, aforesaid, to the high displeasure of Almighty God." 5 Eliz. 1, c. 17 (1562). See Barnett, supra, at 81. Blackstone refused, following St. Thomas, even to mention sexual deviance, referring to it as "the infamous crime against nature, committed either with man or beast . . . the very mention of which is a disgrace to human nature," citing Old Testament prohibitions and the Sodom and Gomorrah legend for the appropriateness of capital punishment (preferably, it seems, by burning). 4 W. Blackstone, *Commentaries* 215, 216.

The very Blackstonian language of condemnation was imitated in American colonial statutes and continues to be used in statutes of some American states. See, e.g., *Mass. Ann. Laws* c. 272 § 34 (1968). However, because of constitutional objections to the vagueness of the term "unnatural" in criminal statutes (doubts, now laid to rest, as a matter of federal constitutional law, by the Supreme Court, *Rose v. Locke,* 423 U. S. 48 [1975]), the prohibitions are often described with a specificity which Blackstone would have found shocking. See, e.g., *Ga. Code Ann.* § 26-2002 (1970); *Wis. Stat. Ann.* § 944.17 (1958).

77. See K. Dover, *Greek Popular Morality in the Time of Plato and Aristotle* 213–16 (1974); Ford & Beach, supra note 67, at 130–33; J. Henderson, *The Maculate Muse: Obscene Language in Attic Comedy* 204–22 (1975); H. Licht, *Sexual Life in Ancient Greece* 307–498 (1974); J. Money & A. Ehrhardt, *Man & Woman, Boy & Girl* 125–44 (1972) [hereinafter cited as Money & Ehrhardt]; G. H. Herdt, *Guardians of the Flutes: Idioms of Masculinity* (1981).

78. Id.

79. See W. Churchill, *Homosexual Behavior Among Males* 267–68 (1971); Ford & Beach, supra note 67, at 264–66; A. Kinsey, W. Pomeroy & C. Martin, *Sexual Behavior in the Human Male* 659–60 (1948) [hereinafter cited as Kinsey]; cf. M. Hoffman, *The Gay World* 100–13 (1968) [hereinafter cited as Hoffman].

80. Ford & Beach, supra note 67, at 134–43, 257–59. Contrast the traditional view,

expressed by philosophers as disparate as Plato and Kant, that sexual deviance degraded human beings even below animals, since animals were supposed not to be sexually deviant. Thus, Kant argues that homosexuality is unnatural in that it "degrades mankind below the level of animals, for no animal turns in this way from its own species." I. Kant, *Lectures on Ethics* 170 (L. Infield trans. 1963). See also Plato, *Laws*, Book VIII 835d–842a. On Plato, see Vlastos, *Platonic Studies* 27–28 (1973). For the powerful and influential medieval conception of the animality of homosexuality, see J. Boswell, *Christianity, Social Tolerance, and Homosexuality* 308 ff. (1980).

81. See, e.g., Hooker, "The Adjustment of the Male Overt Homosexual," 21 *J. of Projective Techniques* 18 (1957); *The Wolfenden Report* 31–33 (1963). In late 1973 the Board of Trustees of the American Psychiatric Association (APA) decided to remove homosexuality from the list of mental diseases. *N. Y. Times*, Dec. 16, 1973, § 1, at 1, col. 1. The Board's action was approved by a general vote of the APA membership in April, 1974. *N. Y. Times*, April 9, 1974, § 1, at 12, col. 4. See, in general R. Bayer, *Homosexuality and American Pyschiatry: The Politics of Diagnosis* (1981). The position there rejected receives its classic statement in I. Bieber, *Homosexuality: A Psychoanalytic Study of Male Homosexuals* (1962). See also H. Hendin, *The Age of Sensation*, ch. 4 (1975); C. Socarides, *Beyond Sexual Freedom*, ch. 7 (1975); R. Stoller, *Perversion: The Erotic Form of Hatred* (1975). This position has now been repudiated largely on the ground that it is based only on those homosexuals who have sought psychiatric help, many of whom suffer from neurotic symptoms, as do most patients who seek psychiatric help, heterosexual and homosexual. Thus, from the class of neurotic homosexuals who seek psychiatric help, the view argues fallaciously that all homosexuals are neurotic. See M. Hoffman, supra note 115, ch. 9; J. Marmor, "Homosexuality and Sexual Orientation Disturbances," in 2 *Comprehensive Textbook of Psychiatry* 1510–20 (Freedman, Kaplan & Sadock eds 2d ed. 1975). In fact, when correct scientific method is used to test whether homosexuals as a class exhibit neurotic symptoms, no evidence appears. Hooker, supra. Freud himself well understood these distinctions. Of homosexuality, Freud wrote: "Homosexuality is assuredly no advantage but it is nothing to be ashamed of, no vice, no degradation; it cannot be classified as an illness; we consider it to be a variation of the sexual function." *Letters of Sigmund Freud 1873–1939*, at 419–20 (E. Freud ed. 1961). In the absence of neurotic symptoms, he thus regarded homosexuals as improper subjects for treatment. See A. Freud, "The Psychogenesis of a Case of Homosexuality in a Woman," in 18 *The Complete Psychological Works of Sigmund Freud* (Standard ed. 1920). In the recent Kinsey Institute study of homosexuality, the authors divide homosexuals into five functional categories (Close-Coupleds, Open-Coupleds, Functionals, Dysfunctionals, and Asexuals) and observe that failure to make such distinctions distorts one's realistic picture of the complex and diverse reality of homosexual relations. The Close-Coupleds, essentially monogamous and stable unions, evince considerable psychological health, which may exceed that of comparable heterosexual unions. In contrast, the Asexuals appear to be quite psychologically ill-adjusted. The conflation of these distinct categories presents, the Kinsey study proposes, an unrealistic picture of homosexuality that fails to capture fundamental distinctions among forms of adaptation to homosexual preference in a hostile society. See A. Bell & M. Weinberg, *Homosexualities: A Study of Diversity Among Men and Women* 195–231 (1978) [hereinafter cited as Bell & Weinberg].

82. See M. Weinberg & C. Williams, *Male Homosexuals* 148–49 (1974).

83. See Bell & Weinberg, supra note 81; W. Churchill, *Homosexual Behavior Among Males* 36–59 (1967).

84. That is, it would be self-degradation for men to allow themselves to make love to, or to be made love to by a man, which is the proper role of a woman. This conception is also implicit in the idea, pervasive in the ancient Greek and Roman worlds, that while homosexuality per se was not wrong, to allow oneself to be the passive partner (i.e., the woman) was shameful and degrading. The aggressively bisexual Julius Caesar, thus, was criticized not for his homosexual connections, but for permitting himself at one time to be the passive partner. See *Catullus* 57 where Caesar is insulted by being called "morbosus," i.e., passive (equivalent to the Greek "pathicus"). See T. Vanggaard, *Phallos* 87–99 (1972); J. Boswell, *Christianity, Social Tolerance, and*

Homosexuality 74–75 (1980). This interpretation of the condemnation of homosexuality (degrading a man into a woman) explains why lesbianism was never condemned with the force that was directed against male homosexuality. The Old Testament prohibitions clearly seem to be directed against men. "Thou shalt not lie with mankind, as with womankind: it is abomination." Leviticus 18:22. "If a man also lie with mankind as he lieth with a woman, both of them have committed an abomination; they shall surely be put to death; their blood shall be upon them." Id. 20:13. Note that lesbianism carried far lighter penalties than did male homosexuality under later rabbinical law. See D. Bailey, *Homosexuality and the Western Christian Tradition* 61–63 (1955). For a similar view of the extreme condemnation of male homosexuality, see J. McNeill, *The Church and the Homosexual* 83–87 (1976). The same has been true under Christian religious law. Id. at 160–65.

85. See, e.g., Simon & Gagnon, "Femininity in the Lesbian Community," in *Sexual Deviance and Sexual Deviants* 256–67 (E. Goode & R. Troiden eds. 1974).

86. *Stanton v. Stanton*, 421 U.S. 636 (1975); *Frontiero v. Richardson*, 411 U.S. 677 (1973); *Reed v. Reed*, 404 U.S. 71 (1971); *Sail'er Inn, Inc. v. Kirby*, 5 Cal. 3d 1, 485 P.2d 529, 95 Cal. Rptr. 329 (1971) (en banc). See generally L. Kanowitz, *Women and the Law* (1969). On the need for a constitutional amendment to accelerate judicial and legislative developments, see "Equal Rights for Women: A Symposium on the Proposed Constitutional Amendment," 6 *Harv. C. R.-C. L. L. Rev.* 215 (1971); Brown, Emerson, Falk & Freedman, "The Equal Rights Amendment: A Constitutional Basis for Equal Rights for Women," 80 *Yale L. J.* 871 (1971); Note, "Sex Discrimination and Equal Protection: Do We Need a Constitutional Amendment?" 84 *Harv. L. Rev.* 1499 (1971). For a review of judicial developments and a commentary on the justifiability thereof, see D. Richards, *The Moral Criticism of Law* 162–78 (1977).

87. See S. de Beauvoir, *The Second Sex* (1952); E. Janeway, *Man's World, Woman's Place* (1971); J. S. Mill, *The Subjection of Women* (1869); D. Richards, *The Moral Criticism of Law* 162–78 (1977); V. Woolf, *A Room of One's Own* (1929).

88. The origin of homosexual preference is unclear. Some experimental studies claim to adduce evidence that sexual preference is genetically determined. See D. West, *Homosexuality* 169 (1967). These studies, however, are given little credence. See C. Berg & C. Allen, *The Problem of Homosexuality* 41 (1958); B. Oliver, *Sexual Deviation in American Society* 126 (1967); Sex Information and Education Council of the United States, *Sexuality and Man* 78–80 (1970). The theory that homosexuality is due to hormonal imbalance has been rejected. Berg & Allen, supra, at 41; Ford & Beach, supra note 67, at 236–37; Money & Ehrhardt, supra note 77, at 235–44; Oliver, supra, at 126; West, supra, at 155–60. The prevailing view now seems to be that homosexual preference results, not from inborn physical characteristics, but from experiences during the individual's lifetime. West, supra, at 262. See also Oliver, supra, at 126. One psychoanalytic explanation of male homosexuality suggests that it results from a parent-child relationship that includes a seductive over-attached, domineering mother and a detached, hostile of remote father. I. Bieber, *Homosexuality: A Psychoanalytic Study of Male Homosexuals* 310–13 (1962). Other explanations focus on more general social experience, rejecting the crucial significance of parent-child relationships of these kinds. C. Tripp, *The Homosexual Matrix*, chs. 4–5 (1975). The increasing weight of modern evidence points to the importance of very early social experience. See Hoffman, supra note 79, at 112–27; Money & Ehrhardt, supra note 77, at 153–201. Thus, one study hypothesizes that gender identity and sexual object choice coincide with the development of language, i.e., from 18 to 24 months of age. See Money, Hampson & Hampson, "An Examination of Some Basic Sexual Concepts: The Evidence of Human Hermaphroditism," 97 *Bull. John Hopkins Hosp.* 301 (1955). A recent Kinsey Institute study suggests a deep seated predisposition, possibly biological in origin. See Jane E. Brody, "Kinsey Study Finds Homosexuals Show Deep Predisposition," *N.Y. Times*, Aug. 23, 1981, at 1, 30. In particular, a psychoanalytic aetiology is debunked. See A. P. Bell, M. S. Weinberg, & S. K. Hammersmith, *Sexual Preference* (1981).

89. For the substantial irreversibility of sexual preference, see W. Churchill, *Homosexual Behavior Among Males* 283–91 (1971); C. Tripp, *The Homosexual Matrix* 251 (1975); West, supra note 88, at 266. Claimed cure rates by psychotherapists probably

include instances in which the individual is merely refraining from homosexual conduct while retaining his or her homosexual inclination, and fail to indicate whether those alleged to be changed remained heterosexually oriented. W. Barnett, *Sexual Freedom and the Constitution* 227 (1973). For a discussion of change techniques employed by therapists. see L. Hatterer, *Changing Homosexuality in the Male* (1970).

90. See note 81 supra. Venereal disease is one health problem that might be adduced in this connection on the ground that it is common among homosexuals. In fact, however, there is no necessary connection between homosexuality and the incidence of venereal disease; in any event, there is reason to believe that the incidence of venereal disease among homosexuals has been fostered, not prohibited, by sodomy statutes. As regards the incidence of venereal disease among homosexuals, two significant classes of homosexuals do not involve the venereal disease problem: (1) Lesbians do not in general suffer from venereal disease in that they "practically never become infected except through contact with men," G. Henry, *All the Sexes* 366 (1955); (2) Stable homosexual relations, male and female, do not implicate the disease. In general, the root of the venereal disease problem among homosexuals arises from isolated, promiscuous relations among male homosexuals, not from the form of intercourse itself. This promiscuity among homosexuals is fostered by absolute prohibitions on all forms of homosexual relations and concomitant forms of economic and social discrimination. Indeed, medical attempts to treat the problem are made more difficult by lack of candor by homosexuals about their sexual life and preference, arising from fears of criminal penalties and related forms of discrimination. See generally Note, "The Constitutionality of Laws Forbidding Private Homosexual Conduct," 72 *Mich. L. Rev.* 1613, 1631–33 (1974).

91. In *Poe v. Ullman*, 367 U.S. 497 (1961), the predecessor case to *Griswold*, an important reason for judicial abstention was Justice Frankfurter's view that lack of enforcement of the Connecticut contraception law evinced complete lack of belief in the law by enforcement officials and the citizenry of Connecticut. See A. Bickel, *The Least Dangerous Branch* 143–56 (1962).

92. See A. Bickel, *The Least Dangerous Branch* 143–56 (1962).

93. Like racial and ethnic minorities, exclusive homosexuals constitute a small percentage of the nation's population. Kinsey stated that four percent of white males are exclusively homosexual throughout their lives. Kinsey, supra note 79, at 650–51. Kinsey's figures may even overstate the incidence of male homosexuality. See *Playboy*, Mar. 1974, at 54–55. No major political party has yet espoused the rights of homosexuals. American popular and legal attitudes toward homosexuals derive from traditional Christianity's abhorrence of homosexuality. See "Unnatural Acts," supra note 76 at 1292–98. The cases are replete with expressions of judicial revulsion at homosexuality, something now unthinkable in the racial or gender area. See, e.g., *Schlegel v. United States*, 416 F.2d 1372, 1378 (Ct. Cl. 1969), cert. denied, 397 U.S. 1039 (1970); *In re Labady*, 326 F. Supp. 924, 927 (S. D. N. Y. 1971); *H. v. H.*, 59 N. J. Super. 227, 237, 157 A.2d 721, 727 (1959); *In re Schmidt*, 56 Misc. 2d 456, 460, 289 N. Y. S. 2d 89, 92 (Sup. Ct. 1968). Not surprisingly, empirical surveys confirm the attitudes expressed or commented on in judicial opinions. Fifty percent of respondents in one study, all "from large cities in the United States agree 'very much' that homosexuality is obscene and vulgar." M. Weinberg & C. Williams, *Male Homosexuals* 84 (1974).

94. For a more extended argument for principles of these kinds, see D. Richards, *A Theory of Reasons for Action* 148–95 (1971).

95. *Doe v. Commonwealth's Attorney for Richmond*, 425 U.S. 901 (1976), aff'g without opinion 403 F. Supp. 1199 (E. D. Va. 1975) (three judge court). See note 5 supra.

96. See P. Gebhard, J. Gagnon, W. Pomeroy, & C. Christenson, *Sex Offenders* (1965); Hoffman, supra note 79, at 89–92. Analysis of imprisonment statistics of homosexuals sometimes shows high percentages of arrests for offenses against children. See, e.g., C. Berg, *Fear, Punishment, Anxiety and the Wolfenden Report* 33–34 (1959); cf. R. Mitchell, *The Homosexual and the Law* 11 (1969). However, these higher percentages probably simply reflect the fact that homosexuals who molest children are far more frequently apprehended than homosexual people who engage only in consensual relations with

adults. In general, seduction of the young appears to be more centered on heterosexual rather than homosexual relations. See Bell & Weinberg, supra note 81, at 230. Importantly, the failure to note the distinction between homosexuality and pedophilia is deplored by the majority of homosexual people who "do not share, do not approve, and fear to be associated with pedophiliac interests." D. West, *Homosexuality* 119 (1967); see Rivera, "Our Straight-Laced Judges: The Legal Position of Homosexual Persons in the United States," 30 *Hastings L. J.* 799, 860 n. 367 (1979). On the impropriety of forbidding adults access to obscene books on the ground that access to such books harms children, see *Butler v. Michigan,* 352 U.S. 380 (1957).

97. See note 88 supra.

98. It is not at all self-evident that it has such a constitutionally legitimate interest. See generally *Pierce v. Society of Sisters,* 268 U.S. 510 (1925) and *Meyer v. Nebraska,* 262 U.S. 390 (1923), which question the propriety of certain types of state regulation of the education of children.

99. Consider, for example, the claims that prohibiting all homosexual conduct and homosexual teachers protects the young. In fact, homosexual preference has its origins in very early social experience within the family often prior to any formal education. See note 88, supra. Prohibitions of this kind accordingly have no effect on sexual preference and thus are not rationally related to this end, but do inflict great and unfair harms on homosexuals of all ages. Adult homosexuals are often gifted teachers. See J. McNeill, S. J., *The Church and the Homosexual* 135–38 (1976). These prohibitions either penalize their being teachers or allow them to do so only on hypocritical terms which violate their rights of self-respect based on personal integrity. Society is thus deprived of a social asset or secures it only on immoral terms.

In addition, there is a fundamental unfairness in allowing teachers to be publicly heterosexual, which affords the heterosexual young role models of how to build a life around their sexuality, and not to allow teachers to be publicly homosexual, thus depriving the homosexual young of the education that is any person's right in how to build a life of sexual self-respect. The effect of such public knowledge on the heterosexual young is to discourage in them immoral stereotypes and to develop desirable ethical attitudes of tolerance and respect for the diversities of human fulfillment. Present prohibitions, on the contrary, teach and support immoral and inhumane attitudes that are destructive to the young and to society at large.

Consider, as a useful analogy, the first attacks on racial segregation in the area of elementary education, attacks that have since been enlarged to encompass all forms of state-supported racial discrimination. Such constitutional attacks understandably began in the area of elementary education because undoing racial segregation at this point cuts racist isolation and misunderstanding at its roots. A comparable argument of equivalent force could be made regarding the sexist stereotypes that underlie much antihomosexuality prejudice. These sexist stereotypes retain their force because of compelled ignorance about the nature of homosexuality and homosexuals and the failure of people publicly to acknowledge the irrelevance of sexual preference to any fair measure of moral decency, humanity, or good citizenship. In order to cut at the roots of these unjust and immoral attitudes in ignorance and isolation, public acknowledgement and toleration of sexual diversity in teachers and students in early education appears as necessary and useful here as it was and is in the case of racism. Finally, of course, no teacher or guradian of the young, heterosexual or homosexual, has the right to seduce the underage young.

100. See R. Mitchell, *The Homosexual and the Law* 12 (1969). In fact, there is evidence that homosexuals are less violent than heterosexuals. See Hoffman, supra note 79, at 90–91.

101. See note 81 supra.

102. See discussion, infra, of inappropriate paternalistic arguments.

103. Justinian, for example, prohibited homosexual acts on pain of death or torture or both. See Justinian, *Novellae* 77 and 141, reprinted in Bailey, supra note 84, at 73–75. The issuance of these imperial edicts seems to have been prompted by contemporary earthquakes, floods and plagues, which Justinian, drawing an analogy to the Sodom

and Gomorrah episode, supposed to be caused by homosexual practices. Id. at 76–77. For a description of some tortures inflicted upon homosexuals, see id. at 78–79. Blackstone similarly cites the Sodom and Gomorrah episode, in support of the appropriateness of the death penalty for homosexual acts, indeed suggesting—since God there punished by fire—the special appropriateness of death by burning. 4 W. Blackstone, *Commentaries* 216.

104. See Barnett, *Sexual Freedom and the Constitution* 293, 305–7 (1973). England has also recently legalized sexual conduct between consenting adults. *Sexual Offenses Act*, 1967, c. 60.

105. 403 F. Supp. 1199, 1202 (E. D. Va. 1975), aff'd without opinion, 425 U.S. 901 (1976).

106. See generally P. Devlin, *The Enforcement of Morals* 9–13 (1965).

107. See H. L. A. Hart, *Law, Liberty and Morality* (1963).

108. J. Stephen, *Liberty, Equality, Fraternity* 135–78 (1967).

109. J. S. Mill, "On Liberty," in *The Philosophy of John Stuart Mill* 271–93 (M. Cohen ed. 1961) [hereinafter cited as "On Liberty"].

110. Committee on Homosexual Offenses and Prostitution, *Report*, Cmmd. No. 247 (1957). See the similar view taken in *Model Penal Code* § 207.5(1), comment (Tent. Draft No. 4, 1955).

111. See D. Richards, *A Theory of Reasons for Action*, chs. 7–10 (1971).

112. See Gussfield, "On Legislating Morals: The Symbolic Process of Designating Deviance," 56 *Calif. L. Rev.* 54, 58–59 (1968).

113. See Hart, "Social Solidarity and the Enforcement of Morality," 35 *U. Chi. L. Rev.* 1 (1967).

114. For the classic statement of this view by an American judge, see B. Cardozo, *The Nature of the Judicial Process* 108–11, 112, 131, 136 (1921).

115. Historically, racial and sexual prejudices were interdependent; the inferiority of blacks was used as a ground for arguments for the inferiority of women, and conversely. See G. Myrdal, *An American Dilemma* 1073 (2d ed. 1962); J. Haller & R. Haller, *The Physician and Sexuality in Victorian America* 48–61 (1974); Fitzhugh, "Sociology for the South," in *Slavery Defended* 34 (E. L. McKitrick ed. 1963). For evidence of the psychological interrelationships of racial and sexual prejudice, see T. Adorno, E. Frendel-Brunswick, D. Levinson & R. Sanford, *The Authoritarian Personality*, 399–441, 452–54, 506–17, 866–72 (1950). See, e.g., *Roe v. Wade*, 410 U.S. 113 (1973) (abortion), *Eisenstadt v. Baird*, 405 U.S. 438 (1972) (contraception for unmarried persons); *Loving v. Virginia*, 338 U.S. 1 (1967) (miscegenation); *Griswold v. Connecticut*, 381 U.S. 479 (1965) (contraception); *Brown v. Board of Educ.*, 347 U.S. 483 (1954) (segregated education). See also note 86 supra.

116. See note 93 supra.

117. *Doe v. Commonwealth's Attorney for Richmond*, 403 F. Supp. 1199, 1202 (E. D. Va 1975). The Court, thus, focused on the analysis of *Lovisi v. Slayton*, 363 F. Supp. 620 (E. D. Va 1973), aff'd, 539 F.2d 349 (4th Cir.) (en banc), cert. denied, 429 U.S. 977 (1976). This case involved both a breach of the traditional marital bond (a threesome, two of whom are a married couple, engaging in fellatio) and elements of degradation of the young (the children, aged 11 and 13, who distributed pictures of their parents' activities in school).

118. 403 F. Supp. at 1202.

119. Id. at 1205 (Merhige, J., dissenting).

120. For example, in ancient Greece and in many primitive societies, the preferred model was homosexual relations and heterosexual marriage. See note 77 supra. The United States data illustrates that this pattern still persists; homosexual and heterosexual relations can coexist in the same person either at one time or over time. See Kinsey, supra note 179, at 610–66.

121. See Barnett, *Sexual Freedom and the Constitution* 293 (1973).

122. Some homosexuals do marry and have children. P. Wilson, *The Sexual Dilemma* 52–53 (1971). In general, those whose sexuality is entirely homosexual can function heterosexually for periods of time. D. West, *Homosexuality* 233–34 (1968); Knight,

"Overt Male Homosexuality," in *Sexual Behavior and the Law* 442–43 (R. Slovenko ed. 1965). By employing sexual fantasies of a person for whom they experience erotic feeling, people can thus have intercourse with people in whom they experience nothing erotic. Note Kinsey's description of how people have intercourse with prostitutes they find unattractive: "As far as his psychologic responses are concerned, the male in many instances may not be having coitus with the immediate sexual partner, but with all of the other girls with whom he has ever had coitus, and with the entire genus Female with which he would like to have coitus." A. Kinsey, W. Pomeroy, C. Martin & P. Gebhard, *Sexual Behavior in the Human Female* 684 (1953). In the case of exclusive homosexuals, the effect of thus frustrating natural feeling to conform to conventional models of conduct is probably to starve and waste resouces of spontaneous and individual human feeling.

123. See Plato's suggestion that the prohibition of homosexuality "wins men to affection of their wedded wives." Plato, *Laws*, bk. VIII, at 337 (T. Saunders trans. 1970). For commentary, see G. Grube, *Plato's Thought* 118–19 (1964).

124. See the development of this argument in the obscenity context in *Paris Adult Theatre I v. Slaton*, 413 U.S. 49 (1973); for critical commentary thereon, see Richards, "Free Speech and Obscenity Law: Toward a Moral Theory of the First Amendment," 123 *U. Pa. L. Rev.* 45, 83–90 (1974).

125. See note 93 supra.

126. See generally M. Bane, *Here to Stay* (1976). For a discussion of the gravity of the overpopulation problem, see M. Mesarovic & E. Pestel, *Mankind at the Turning Point, The Second Report to the Club of Rome* 70–82 (1974); for an argument for moral duties to limit population, see D. Richards, *A Theory of Reasons for Action* 134–35 (1971). Given the state of the facts as we have discussed them above and the growing moral concerns for overpopulation, the direction of good moral reasoning appears to support, at a minimum, toleration, and suggests that, so far from mandatory universal heterosexuality being the moral course, if any sexual preference is to be encouraged by the state it is certainly not heterosexuality.

127. See "Unnatural Acts," supra note 76 at 1292–98; also, note 76, supra.

128. See G. Weinberg, *Society and the Healthy Homosexual* 1–20 (1972); cf. note 84 supra.

129. See note 84 & accompanying text supra.

130. See note 128 supra.

131. For the position of men, see H. Goldberg, *The Hazards of Being Male* (1976); H. E. Kaye, *Male Survival: Masculinity Without Myth* (1974); J. Nichols, *Men's Liberation: A New Definition of Masculinity* (1975); *Men and Masculinity* 21–29, 32–35, 35–41, 41–52, 139–49 (J. H. Pleck & J. Sawyer eds. 1974). For the position of women, see C. G. Heilbrun, *Toward a Recognition of Androgyny* (1973); *Men and Masculinity*, supra, at 134–39; and sources cited note 87 supra.

132. Cf. Dworkin, "Lord Devlin and the Enforcement of Morals," 75 *Yale L.J.* 986 (1966), reprinted in Dworkin, *Taking Rights Seriously* 240–58 (1977).

133. See statutes cited in Note, "The Constitutionality of Laws Forbidding Private Homosexual Conduct," 72 *Mich. L. Rev.* 1613, 1622–23 nn. 63–67 (1974).

134. See generally R. Masters, *Eros and Evil: The Sexual Psychopathology of Witchcraft* (1962). For the more general social significance of notions of witchcraft, see *Witchcraft and Sorcery* (M. Marwick ed. 1970).

135. See Barrett, "Legal Homophobia and the Christian Church," 30 *Hastings L.J.* 1019 (1979); "Unnatural Acts," supra note 76 at 1292–98; note 76, supra.

136. St. Thomas, for example, postulates a "special natural habit, which we call synderesis" which contains the first principles of morality. *Summa Theologica*, pt. I, at 116 (Fathers of the Dominican Province trans. 1912). These principles of natural law, prior to any divine revelation, are known as true by "one standard of truth or rightness of everybody," *Summa Theologica*, in *Aquinas: Selected Political Writings* 123–25 (D'Entreves trans. 1959), for "natural law corresponds to the order of our natural inclinations," id. at 123. Francisco Suarez similarly argues that the essence of morality is independent of divine will. See F. Suarez, "On Laws and God the Lawgiver," in

Selections from Three Works 205–06 (Williams, Brown, Waldron, & Davis trans. 1944). The separation of the concepts of ethics and divine will is explicit in Grotius, who observes: "And what we have said would still have great weight, even if we were to grant what we cannot grant without wickedness, that there is no God," Grotius, "Prolegomenon," in *De Jure Belli et Pacis* xlvi (W. Whewell trans. 1853). "Natural law is so immutable that it cannot be changed by God himself." Id. at 12. Indeed, the view that natural law depended on divine law seems to have been theologically revolutionary and heretical. See Oakley, "Medieval Theories of Natural Law: William of Ockham and the Significance of the Voluntarist Tradition," 6 *Nat. L.F.* 65 (1961).

For a useful view of the objections to an ethics based on religious authority alone, see R. Brandt, *Ethical Theory* 56–82 (1959). Cf. P. L. Quinn, *Divine Commands and Moral Requirements* (1978); B. Mitchell, *Morality: Religious and Secular* (1980).

137. L. Kohlberg, "Moral and Religious Education and the Public Schools: A Developmental View," in *Religion and Public Schools* 164, 179–81 (T. Sizer ed. 1967).

138. Thus, the Sodom and Gomorrah episode, Genesis 19, traditionally taken to show that homosexuality is contrary to God's will in that He punished those cities by fire and brimstone, is apparently not about homosexuality at all. See D. Bailey, *Homosexuality and the Western Christian Tradition* 1–28 (1955); J. McNeill, *The Church and the Homosexual* 42–50 (1976); J. Boswell, *Christianity, Social Tolerance, and Homosexuality* 92–99 (1980). Even the seemingly clear Leviticus prohibitions, supra, note 120, have been analyzed by Biblical scholars as not being about homosexuality per se. See, e.g., S. Driver, *Deuteronomy* 264 (1896); McNeill, supra, at 56–60; N. Snaith, *The Century Bible: Leviticus and Numbers* 126 n. 22 (New ed. 1967): J. Boswell, supra, 100–103. Other scholars, however, disagree about this latter prohibition. See Bailey, supra, at 30. Even Catholic theologians have argued that these prohibitions do not attack or condemn exclusive homosexuals: "[The Scriptures'] aim is not to pillory the fact that some people experience this perversion inculpably. They denounce a homosexuality which had become the prevalent fashion and had spread to many who were really quite capable of normal sexual sentiments. . . . Lack of frank discussion has allowed a number of opinions to be formed about [homosexuals] which are unjust when applied generally, because those who have such inclinations in fact are often hard-working and honourable people." *A New Catechism* 384–85 (K. Smith trans. 1967), cited in *In re Labady*, 326 F. Suppl. 924, 930 (S.D. N.Y. 1971). Consistent with and supportive of this viewpoint, Christian scholars argue that relevant New Testament texts of St. Paul, cited at note 76, supra, do not apply to exclusive homosexuals. See Bailey, supra, at x–xii (distinction between invert and pervert); J. McNeill, supra, at 37–66; J. Boswell, supra, 106–17. Boswell emphasizes, in this connection, that any possible condemnation of homosexuality in the Old Testament should, for a Christian, be superseded by the toleration of the New Testament. See J. Boswell, id., 100–103. But cf. "Homosexuality, Intolerance, and Christianity," Gai Saber Monograph No. 1, 1981, the Scholarship Committee, Gay Academic Union, New York City.

139. 403 F. Supp. at 1202 n. 2. Such citation of Old Testament texts in support of the intrinsic evil of homosexuality is common in American judicial opinions. See, e.g., *Dawson v. Vance*, 329 F. Supp. 1329 (S.D. Tex. 1971), which cites the Sodom and Gomorrah episode at Genesis 19:1–29 in support of the proposition that the "practice is inherently inimical to the general integrity of the human person." Id. at 1322.

140. See, e.g., M. Valente, *Sex: The Radical View of a Catholic Theologian* (1970); J. McNeill, S.J., *The Church and the Homosexual* 89–107 (1976). See also J. Boswell, *Christianity, Social Tolerance, and Homosexuality* (1980).

141. See *Epperson v. Arkansas*, 393 U.S. 97 (1968); W. Barnett, *Sexual Freedom and the Constitution* 74–93 (1973); Henkin, "Morals and the Constitution: The Sin of Obscenity," 63 *Colum. L. Rev.* 391 (1963).

142. See D. Richards, *A Theory of Reasons for Action* 75–91, 212–42 (1971).

143. On the contrasts of animal and human intelligence, see J. Bennett, *Rationality* 35–43, 80, 85, 94 (1964). For examples of the instinctive rigidities of animal behavior, see N. Tinbergen, *The Herring Gull's World* 28–32, 140–41, 144–45, 153, 186–210, 232–33 (1953).

144. See generally B. Russell, *Marriage and Morals* (1958); R. Atkinson, *Sexual Morality* (1965); J. Wilson, *Logic and Sexual Morality* (1965).

145. For examples of recent philosophical discussions of issues of personal identity, see B. Williams, *Problems of the Self* 1–81 (1973); *Personal Identity* (J. Perry ed. 1975); *The Identities of Persons* (A. O. Rorty ed., 1976).

146. The major works include the following: E. Erikson, *Childhood and Society* (1963); E. Erikson, *Identity and the Life Cycle* (1959); D. Levinson, *The Seasons of a Man's Life* (1978); G. Vaillant, *Adaptation to Life* (1977); R. White, *Lives in Progress* (1952).

147. See E. Erikson, *Identity and the Life Cycle* 101–64 (1959).

148. See E. Erikson, *Childhood and Society* 263–66 (1963); D. Levinson, *The Seasons of a Man's Life* 71–135 1978).

149. See D. Levinson, *The Seasons of a Man's Life* 139–88 (1978).

150. Id. at 191–313.

151. See Rawls, supra note 57, at 544.

152. For a fuller development of the moral theory of free speech, see Richards, "Free Speech and Obscenity Law: Toward a Moral Theory of the First Amendment," 123 *U. Pa. L. Rev.* 45 (1974).

153. See generally, D. Richards, *The Moral Criticism of Law* (1977).

154. See Ford & Beach, supra note 67, at 199–267 (1951).

155. "The sexual instinct . . . is probably more strongly developed in man than in most of the higher animals; it has almost entirely overcome the periodicity to which it is tied in animals. It places extraordinarily large amounts of force at the disposal of civilized activity, and it does this in virtue of its especially marked characteristic of being able to displace its aim without materially diminishing in intensity. This capacity to exchange its original sexual aim for another one, which is no longer sexual but which is psychically related to the first aim, is called the capacity for sublimation." S. Freud, " 'Civilized' Sexual Morality and Modern Nervous Illness," in 9 *The Complete Psychological Works of Sigmund Freud* 181, 187 (Standard ed. 1908).

156. For an exploration of the importance of fantasy in human sexuality, see A. K. Offit, *The Sexual Self* 206–19 (1977).

157. Freud's conception of the ego was classically formulated in S. Freud, "The Ego and the Id," in 19 *The Complete Psychological Works of Sigmund Freud* 87 (Standard ed. 1923). In this essay, the ego appears as the passive mediator between id and superego impulses. This passive battleground ego conception was expressly disapproved by Freud in his important later work, "Inhibitions, Symptoms and Anxiety" in 20 *The Complete Psychological Works of Sigmund Freud* 87–172 (Standard ed. 1926), wherein he seeks to characterize the independent power of the ego to deal with internal and external dangers (both realistic and intra-psychic id and superego impulses) by triggering the protective system of defenses. Freud's theory of the defenses was elaborated by Anna Freud. See A. Freud, *The Ego and the Mechanisms of Defense* (1936). Later ego psychology has sought to characterize further the reality functions of the ego in addition to its unconscious defensive mechanisms, on which Freud focused. Heinz Hartmann developed accordingly his conception of ego autonomy, focusing on the capacities of the person to engage in adaptive reality testing in a conflict free zone, i.e., a zone free of the warring id and superego impulses. See H. Hartmann, *Ego Psychology and the Problem of Adaptation* (D. Rapaport trans. 1958). In the light of the subsequent work of Piaget, Erikson, and studies of animal and child behavior, these notions of ego functions have been developed into a theory of the competent exercise of the capacities of persons as such with independent desires to exercise these capacities competently. See R. White, *Ego and Reality in Psychoanalytic Theory* (1963).

158. For a recent treatment of the changing and adaptive functions of defenses in the context of the life cycle, see G. Vaillant, *Adaptation to Life* 75–126 (1977).

159. See note 155 supra. See generally, S. Freud, "Civilization and its Discontents," in 21 *The Complete Psychological Works of Sigmund Freud* 64 (Standard ed. 1930).

160. See S. Freud, "New Introductory Lectures on Psycho-Analysis," in 22 *The Complete Psychological Words of Sigmund Freud* 80 (Standard ed. 1933).

161. See A. Freud, *The Ego and the Mechanisms of Defense* ch. 4 (C. Baines trans. 1946).

162. For an example of a possibly self-destructive identification that may profitably be undone, see the discussion of identification with the aggressor, id., ch. 9.

163. See M. Balint, *Primary Love and Psychoanalytic Technique* 109–17 (1952).

164. On the values of these relationships, see S. Benn. "Privacy, Freedom, and Respect for Persons," in *Privacy* 16 (J. Pennock & J. Chapman eds. 1971).

165. See C. Fried, *An Anatomy of Values*, ch. 9 (1970).

166. The gravity of this choice was stressed as early as Aristotle's seminal discussion of friendship. See Aristotle, *Nicomachean Ethics*, bk. 8 (H. Rackham trans. 1926); cf. D. Richards, *A Theory of Reasons for Action* 266–67 (1971).

167. See D. Levinson, *The Seasons of a Man's Life* 91–111 (1978).

168. Id. at 237, 245–51.

169. The thought that falling in love involves thinking of the love object as the parent of a common child, understood physically or metaphorically as a common interest fostered by the relationship, is as old as Plato. Plato, *Symposium* § 206c; for other statements of this view, see M. Scheler, *The Nature of Sympathy* (P. Heath trans. 1954); A. Schopenhauer, 2 *The World as Will and Representation* 531–67 (E. Payne trans. 1966).

170. See notes 70–72 & accompanying text supra.

171. Compare Fourier's striking conception that, just as the utopian state has a duty to supply a minimum of food, it has a duty to supply a minimum of sexual gratification to all citizens. C. Fourier, *The Utopian Vision of Charles Fourier* 336–40 (J. Beecher & R. Bienvenu eds. 1971).

172. See also the similar arguments in "On Liberty," supra note 109, ch. 3.

173. See Rivera, "Our Straight-Laced Judges: The Legal Position of Homosexual Persons in the United States," 30 *Hastings L.J.* 799, 829–37 (1979): Note, "Security Clearances for Homosexuals," 25 *Stan. L. Rev.* 403, 410–11 (1973).

174. See *N.Y. Times*, Dec. 23, 1973 § 4, at 5, col. 1. Engaging in any homosexual activity still conclusively bars an individual from admission to the military. R. Mitchell, *The Homosexual and the Law* 49–50 (1969). Some courts have allowed a general presumption that the commission of homosexual acts makes one unfit for government-service. See *Schlegel v. United States*, 416 F.2d 1372, 1378 (Ct. Cl. 1969), cert. denied, 397 U.S. 1039 (1970). But cf. *Norton v. Macy*, 417 F.2d 1161 (D.C. Cir. 1969); *Acanfora v. Board of Educ.*, 359 F. Supp. 843 (D. Md. 1973), aff'd on other grounds, 491 F.2d 498 (4th Cir.), cert. denied, 419 U.S. 836 (1974); *Morrison v. State Bd. of Educ.*, 1 Cal. 3d 214, 461 P.2d 375, 82 Cal. Rptr. 175 (1969). See generally Rivera, "Our Straight-Laced Judges: The Legal Position of Homosexual Persons in the United States," 30 *Hastings L.J.* 799, 829–37 (1979). For an argument that homosexuality should be a constitutionally suspect classification, see D. Richards, *The Moral Criticism of Law* 162–78 (1977).

175. See e.g., J. McNeill, *The Church and the Homosexual* 164–72 (1976).

176. See note 122 supra.

177. See notes 120 & 122 supra.

178. Of the conventional idea "that all who do not contract a legal marriage shall remain abstinent throughout their lives," Freud observed: "The position, agreeable to all the authorities, that sexual abstinence is not harmful and not difficult to maintain, has also been widely supported by the medical profession. It may be asserted, however, that the task of mastering such a powerful impulse as that of the sexual instinct by any other means than satisfying it is one which can call for the whole of a man's forces. Mastering it by sublimation, by deflecting the sexual instinctual forces away from their sexual aim to higher cultural aims, can be achieved by a minority and then only intermittently, and least easily during the period of ardent and vigorous youth. Most of the rest become neurotic or are harmed in one way or another. Experience shows that the majority of the people who make up our society are constitutionally unfit to face the task of abstinence." S. Freud. " 'Civilized' Sexual Morality and Modern Nervous Illness," in 9 *The Complete Psychological Works of Sigmund Freud* 193 (Standard ed. 1908).

The recent Kinsey Institute study of homosexuals indicates that the Asexuals are a relatively dispirited and depressed lot. See Bell & Weinberg, supra note 81, at 226–28.

179. There is evidence that heterosexual marriages of exclusive homosexuals typically end unhappily for all concerned. One authority, for example, reports that one-

third of the divorce cases he handled arose from the homosexuality of one of the parties. See J. McNeill, *The Church and the Homosexual* 136 (1976). The recent Kinsey Institute study confirms the short-lived character of homosexual marriages. See Bell & Weinberg, supra note 81, a 160–70.

180. See generally H. Hart, *Law, Liberty, and Morality* 22 (1963); G. Weinberg, *Society and the Healthy Homosexual* 78–82, 142–43 (1972).

181. See generally Hoffman, supra note 79. For an account of the damaging effects of prejudice on the self-conception of the group discriminated against, see G. Allport, *The Nature of Prejudice* ch. 9(1954).

182. See Bell & Weinberg, supra note 81, at 81–102; Hoffman, supra note 79; L. Humphreys, *Tearoom Trade* 1–15 (1970).

183. See Note, "The Legality of Homosexual Marriage," 82 *Yale L.J.* 573 (1973). But cf. *Jones v. Hallahan*, 501 S.W.2d 588 (Ky. 1973); *Baker v. Nelson*, 291 Minn. 310, 191 N.W.2d 185(1971).

184. See notes 163–169 & accompanying text supra. The recent Kinsey Institute study of homosexuality indicates that the Close-Coupleds, who maintain relatively monogamous stable relationships, appear to be psychologically better fit, on the whole, than other homosexuals. Bell & Weinberg, supra note 81, at 219–21. Male homosexuals appear to have more difficulty in forming and maintaining such unions than lesbians. Id. at 81–102. Bell & Weinberg suggest that this difference appears to be due to the greater societal condemnation of male homosexuality, which inhibits men from forming such unions either expressly through fear of various legal, economic, or social sanctions or psychologically through internalization of self-hating stereotypes that defensively overvalue the sexist masculine role as sexual predator, not sensitive lover. Id. at 101–2. For a comparable attempt in the legal literature to elaborate an argument supportive of a fundamental constitutional right in this area, see K. I. Karst, "The Freedom of Intimate Association," 89 *Yale L.J.* 624 (1980).

185. For similar arguments to this effect, see D. Richards, *A Theory of Reasons for Action* 192–95 (1971); G. Dworkin, "Paternalism," in *Morality and the Law* 107–26 (R. Wasserstrom ed. 1971); cf. Feinberg, "Legal Paternalism," 1 *Can. J. Phil.* 105–24 (1971).

186. For a more detailed development of this account of rationality, see D. Richards, *A Theory of Reasons for Action* 27–71 (1971).

187. In addition, this requirement is justified by the fact that the agent is typically in the better position to judge his or her own ends, and thus a person's interests are best advanced by limiting any principle of paternalistic interference only to where the probability of third-party error is clearly outweighed by extremes of palpable irrationality and severe harm. See id. at 193.

188. For an exploration of the role of mortality in life plans, see C. Fried, *An Anatomy of Values* 155–82 (1970).

189. One plan dominates the other in terms of rationality criteria. See D. Richards, *A Theory of Reasons for Action* 28, 40–3 (1971).

190. See note 88 supra.

191. See note 89 supra.

192. A striking form of this fallacy appears in one psychiatric formulation of the aetiological theory that homosexuality originates in very early parent-child relationships. In the case of male homosexuality, that theory hypothesizes a seductive, overattached, domineering mother and a detached, hostile or remote father. See I. Bieber, *Homosexuality: A Psychoanalytic Study of Male Homosexuals* 310–13 (1962). From such an aetiological explanation, Bieber fallaciously infers that homosexuality is a disturbance of people's naturally heterosexual underlying impulses which can easily be given expression if certain fears are overcome. Id. at 220–54. Freud, of course, had originated this form of aetiological explanation of homosexual preference. See generally S. Freud, "Leonardo da Vinci and a Memory of his Childhood," in 11 *The Complete Psychological Works of Sigmund Freud* 63–137 (Standard ed. 1910). But he insisted throughout his writings that there was no original or natural direction of sexual prference but rather an undifferentiated original bisexuality. See, e.g. S. Freud, "Three Essays on Sexuality," in

7 *The Complete Psychological Works of Sigmund Freud* 219–20 (Standard ed. 1905); "An Outline of Psychoanalysis," in 23 *The Complete Psychological Works of Sigmund Freud* 188 (Standard ed. 1940). This original bisexuality was shaped, for Freud, by early social experience into the relevant forms of sexual preference in later life. Let us assume, *arguendo*, that this general form of aetiological explanation is true. See F. Fisher & R. P. Greenberg, *The Scientific Credibility of Freud's Theories and Therapy* 231–54 (1977); cf. note 88 supra. It does not follow that because male homosexual preference originates from a domineering mother and remote father that there is a latent heterosexual bent underneath any more than the origin of male heterosexuality in a domineering father and affectionate mother shows a latent homosexual bent beneath. Nothing follows from either aetiological explanation about the natural underlying primacy of either preference, as Freud well understood. For Freud, it is a general truth that sexual development originates in primitive conflicts in the family. The form of these conflicts, whether leading to homosexual or heterosexual preference, was of therapeutic interest only in the presence of neurotic symptoms. See note 81 supra. Bieber's interpretation and the correlative "disease" theory of homosexuality have now been largely repudiated by psychiatrists. Id. They represent, I believe, a striking example of Kinsey's caveat: "Nothing has done more to block the free investigation of sexual behavior than the almost universal acceptance, even among scientists, of certain aspects of that behavior as normal, and of other aspects of that behavior as abnormal. The similarity of distinctions between the terms normal and abnormal, and the terms right and wrong, amply demonstrates the philosophic, religious, and cultural origins of these concepts . . . and the ready acceptance of those distinctions among scientific men may provide the basis for one of the severest criticisms which subsequent generations can make of the scientific quality of nineteenth century and early twentieth century scientists." Kinsey, supra note 79, at 7.

193. See D. Richards, *A Theory of Reasons for Action* 231–32 (1971).

194. This deplorable confusion arguably underlies the Supreme Court's recent statement that the constitutional right to privacy had never been found to protect the private consensual sexual relations of adults. *Carey v. Population Serv.*, 431 U.S. 678, 688 n. 5 (1977). If the constitutional right to privacy is limited to family-linked rights of child rearing, the ideology of metaphysical familism will become the measure of constitutionally enforceable morality in violation of the deepest constitutional values of autonomous self-definition and self-respect. See, in general, Richards, "The Individual, the Family, and the Constitution: A Jurisprudential Perspective," 55 *N.Y.U. L. Rev.* 1, 37–39 (1980).

195. See, e.g., T. L. Bouscaren, A. Ellis & F. Korth, *Canon Law* (1946).

196. See Richards, note 194 supra, at 11–15.

197. See "On Liberty," supra note 109, ch. 3.

198. See E. Fromm, *Escape From Freedom* (1941).

199. See note 131 supra.

200. See e.g., R. Brain, *Friends and Lovers* (1977).

201. See note 35 supra.

202. *Olmstead v. United States*, 277 U.S. 438 (1928) (Brandeis, J., dissenting).

203. *Griswold v. Connecticut*. 381 U.S. 479 (1965).

204. See Richards, "The Theory of Adjudication and the Task of the Great Judge," 1 *Cardozo L. Rev.* 171 (1979). See generally B. Cardozo, *The Nature of the Judicial Process* (1921).

205. This account is an attempt to render more philosophically precise accounts with which I am morally sympathetic. See L. Tribe, *American Constitutional Law*, ch. 15 (1978); Craven, "Personhood: The Right to be Let Alone," 1976 *Duke L. J.* 699; Gerety, "Redefining Privacy," 12 *Harv. C.R.-C.L. L. Rev.* 233 (1977); Comment, "A Taxonomy of Privacy, Repose, Sanctuary, and Intimate Decision," 64 *Calif. L. Rev.* 1447 (1976).

206. Thus, Justice Douglas inferred the constitutional right to privacy as being in the "penumbra" formed by emanations of specific constitutional guarantees. *Griswold v. Connecticut* 38, U.S. 479, 484 (1965).

207. *Griswold v. Connecticut,* 381 U.S. 479, 486–99 (1965) (Goldberg, J., concurring); cf. Redlich, "Are There 'Certain Rights . . . Retained by the People'?," 37 *N.Y.U. L. Rev.* 787 (1962).

208. Due process of law should be explicated as the ultimate and most general requirement of constitutional reasonableness, requiring that all laws have reasons compatible with basic constitutional morality. Accordingly, any laws incompatible with such reasons should be subject to possible invalidations. Cf. Scanlon, "Due Process," in *Due Process: Nomos XVIII,* at 93 (J. R. Pennock & J. W. Chapman eds. 1977); see *Griswold v. Connecticut,* 381 U.S. 479, 499–502 (Harlan, J., concurring). See also *Poe v. Ullman,* 367 U. S. 497, 539–55 (1961) (Harlan, J., dissenting).

209. See note 42 & accompanying text supra.

210. These analogies may be stated in more compelling fashion. While the specific catalogue of rights guaranteed by the Bill of Rights is not involved in the right to privacy cases, the values underlying those rights are profoundly implicated in the conception of the liberty to love as a general good, so that the principles of justice, in light of modern knowledge, require that that liberty be acknowledged as a constitutional right. First, the idea of sexual love as a form of communication is a prominent feature of the modern conception of the experience. See, e.g., W. Masters & V. Johnson, *The Pleasure Bond* 30–311, 139, 228–29 (1975). On the general idea of nonverbal communication, see J. Benthall & T. Polhemus, *The Body as a Medium of Expression* (1975); S. Weitz, *Nonverbal Communication* (1974). On associated therapies, see B. Back, *Beyond Words* (1972). Surely, autonomy in controlling this form of communication is, to the modern mind, no less important to individual self-mastery and self-worth than the conventional forms of verbal communication protected by the free speech and free press clause of the first amendment. Second, the values of freedom of association, which protect the right of social clubs to engage in racial and religious discrimination (see Comment, "Discrimination in Private Social Clubs: Freedom of Association and Right to Privacy," 1970 *Duke L. J.* 1181), should apply *a fortiori* to the depth of human significance derived by lovers from this form of association. Cf. Karst, supra note 184. As we have noted, the decision on whom one shall love is a fundamental life choice, shaping one's entire self-conception and life plan. Third, the privacy interests, associated with third, fourth, and fifth amendments, are generally connected with forms of sexual intimacy. Human sexual love takes place in private and unobserved. See note 67, supra. Accordingly, privacy, conventionally understood as the control of personal information or experience, see note 42, supra, has one of its most valued uses in protecting sexual intimacy. Cf. Justice Douglas' opinion in *Griswold v. Connecticut,* 381 U. S. 479 (1965), which was particularly influenced by the forms of criminal enforcement there in question (e.g., searching the bedroom). 381 U.S. at 485. And fourth, privacy, thus involving the capacity to control information about oneself, is a crucial ingredient in the capacity for love, since loving relationships require as a prerequisite the possibility of selective disclosure of certain aspects of oneself to some but not others. See Charles Fried, supra note 165, ch. 9. Thus the values of privacy and love again converge.

211. See note 2, supra.

212. *Doe v. Commonwealth's Attorney for Richmond,* 425 U.S. 901 (1976).

3

Commercial Sex and the Rights of the Person

It is a remarkable fact, although usually not perceived as such, that the often eloquent literature calling for the decriminalization of "victimless crimes"[1] generally relies on efficiency-based arguments aimed at ending either the pointless or the positively counterproductive waste of valuable and scarce police resources expended in the enforcement of these laws. The literature omits entirely any critical discussion of the morality of the acts that have been criminalized. This absence of critical discussion of the focal issues that divide proponents and opponents of criminalization has made decriminalization arguments much less powerful than they can and should be. Indeed, as noted in Chapter 1,[2] such efficiency-based arguments have not been decisive in the retreat of the scope of "victimless crimes," whether by legislative penal code revision or by judicial invocation of the constitutional right to privacy.

This glaring lacuna in legal theory derives, I believe, from deeper philosophical presuppositions which the decriminalization literature appears often to assume: those of the utilitarian pragmatism associated with America's indigenous jurisprudence, legal realism.[3] American legal theory has been schizoid about the proper analysis of moral values in the law since the publication of Holmes's *The Common Law* in 1881.[4] On the one hand, traditional moral values underlying existing legal institutions have been "washed in cynical acid"[5] so that the legal institution may be analyzed without begging any questions about its moral propriety; on the other hand, the enlightened moral criticism of legal institutions has been conducted in terms of implicitly utilitarian calculations and has sought to maximize the greatest happiness of the greatest number.[6] In discussions propounding the virtues of decriminalization, this pattern of schizoid moral analysis is shown, first, by the dismissive concession of the traditional immorality of the acts in question, and second, by the discussion of moral reform exclusively in terms of efficiency-based considerations that lend themselves to implicit calculations of utility maximization. It is supposed that there cannot be any serious nonutilitarian critical analysis of the moral values thought to underlie "victimless crimes," simply because utilitarianism is presumed to be the only enlightened critical morality.[7]

Today, the pervasive utilitarian presuppositions of American legal theory are under attack both from within jurisprudence[8] and from external developments in normative and moral theory.[9] In moral theory, as we saw in Chapter 1, powerful philosophical objections have been made to the adequacy of utilitarianism as a normative theory, and plausible alternative theories have been proposed that better account for the moral point of view. In American legal theory, these general developments in moral theory are currently being harnessed to the examination of moral ideas in American law,[10] including, as we saw in the last chapter, controversial issues in constitutional law.

Anglo-American criminal-law theory has generally focused on certain pervasive structural features of the substantive criminal law,[11] but has not considered in any depth the question that is at the heart of much continental European criminal-law theory[12]—that of the role of moral wrongdoing in the definition of criminal offenses. Although general concessions are made that criminal sanctions properly apply to morally wrong acts,[13] little critical attention is given to how moral wrongdoing is to be interpreted as the necessary limiting predicate for the proper scope of the criminal penalty. In particular, advocates of decriminalization tend bizarrely to concede to opponents a conventionalistic definition of moral wrongdoing[14] and then to present, as we have seen, utilitarian arguments about special enforcement costs. To make such a concession, however, is unconditionally to surrender the war. It is a mark of the unhappy separation of legal and moral theory that legal theorists accept a definition of morality that is, for a moral theorist, as we already have seen,[15] transparently inadequate. The recent reintegration of antiutilitarian moral concepts into legal theory enables us to reconsider these questions in a new and inspiriting way. We may now critically investigate what should be the central issue in a sound theory of the criminal law: the concept of moral wrongdoing and its role in the just imposition of the criminal sanction.

This chapter will address this more general question as it arises in the context of arguments for the criminalization of prostitution. Prostitution is an interesting case for this kind of investigation because it represents the most striking example of a "victimless crime" with respect to which decriminalization advocates[16] have made no substantial progress[17] despite sound arguments of excessive and wasteful enforcement costs. This failure may be because, unlike the otherwise comparable areas of contraception,[18] abortion,[19] and noncommercial sex between or among adults,[20] there has been little serious critical moral argument[21] attacking the moral judgment of the per se immorality of commercial sex.[22] Yet there are forceful moral arguments to this effect that demonstrate that laws criminalizing commercial sex violate certain basic rights of the person. In order to justify these claims, however, we must consider foundational issues, such as the proper interpretation of the public morality that the criminal law expresses and the proper legal force that ideas of romantic love should have in this area. In particular, analysis of this question will disclose a uniquely American attitude to these matters that explains the remarkable fact that the United States is one of the few comparably developed countries that criminalizes prostitution.[23] When we have done the moral archeology[24] required to understand this historical development and why these American attitudes are an improper basis for the public morality of law, we will have stated a powerful moral argument why, at a minimum, prostitution must be decriminalized. We will then be in a position to inquire what alternative legal treatment of prostitution might be appropriate.

This chapter will have the following structure: first, a description of prostitution as an empirical phenomenon in historical and anthropological perspective; second, a consideration of the legal treatment of prostitution, reviewing the main arguments for criminalization in the United States; third, an application of the moral analysis of public morality developed in Chapter 1 and already elaborated in Chapter 2 to the critical examination of the moral and paternalistic arguments for criminalization of commercial sex; fourth, a statement of the case for a right to sexual autonomy that encompasses prostitution and the appropriate limits to such a right; and finally, a review of alternative approaches to the regulation of commercial sex.

I. PROSTITUTION: ANTHROPOLOGICAL AND HISTORICAL PERSPECTIVES

For contemporary purposes, prostitution is usually defined in terms of "an individual who indiscriminately provides sexual relations in return for money payments."[25] Older definitions strikingly omit the gender-neutral "individual" (or "person") and even the commercialism requirement. For example, one commentator defined it in 1951 as "the indiscriminate offer by a female of her body for the purpose of sexual intercourse or other lewdness."[26] These twin omissions suggest that the traditional concern for prostitution was peculiarly associated with female sexuality—more particularly, with attitudes toward promiscuous unchastity in women—apart from any commercial aspects.[27] Contemporary legal definitions attempt to modify the scope of prostitution.[28] On the one hand, they enlarge the class of persons who may be prostitutes to include men in order to square antiprostitution laws with emerging moral and constitutional norms of gender-neutral fairness in distributing governmental burdens and benefits.[29] On the other hand, the commercialism requirement narrows the class of prostitutional sexual activities to indiscriminate "sexual relations in return for money payments,"[30] thus excluding mere sexual promiscuity or unchastity per se.[31] Since enforcement patterns under even gender-neutral antiprostitution statutes indicate that the continuing concern is largely with female sexuality,[32] the total effect of the modern definitions has been to narrow the class of female sexual activities to which prostitution laws apply. A crucial concern has obviously been to exclude, from the concept of prostitution, forms of sexual relations that are not conventionally condemned today.[33] There may be a commercial element to some marital sexual relations, for example;[34] and there is not always a sharp line, perhaps, between the dinners and entertainment expenses in now conventional premarital sexual relations and the more formalized business transactions of the prostitute.[35] In consequence, in order to draw the desired distinctions between the conventional and the impermissible, contemporary definitions place great weight on money payments for indiscriminate sex. The mark of the contemporary prostitute is indiscriminate availability for sexual relations with any willing buyer, in contrast to other forms of now widespread pre- and extramarital sexual relations.[36]

The emergence of prostitution, within the terms of the modern definition, is generally associated with the development of urban civilization.[37] It is misleading to interpret the anthropological cross-cultural data of patterns of promiscuity among primitive peoples as forms of prostitution,[38] for such peoples often attached little value to virginity; furthermore, there is little evidence in this data of the existence of a class of women indiscriminately available to men for money.[39] Rather, the patterns of sexual promiscuity in primitive cultures represent highly selective choices, often spontaneous and mutually pleasurable, with no commercial elements other than gift giving.[40] The conditions of life in primitive society, with closely knit family and kin networks that regulate the behavior of the young in detail, do not lend themselves to the emergence of a rootless class of women who are available for anonymous indiscriminate sexual encounters for money. The phenomenon is historically associated with the emergence of large cities and the possibility of anonymity associated therewith.[41]

The emergence of commercial prostitution in the modern sense appears to have been a development from the institution of temple prostitution that was a feature of religious life in the first high civilizations.[42] Herodotus, for example, notes that women of ancient Babylonia, prior to marriage, were required to engage once in sexual intercourse as temple prostitutes with the first man who presented himself.[43] The religious significance of temple prostitution is remote from us, but it probably was an institutionalized expression of primitive orgiastic communion[44] with the divine forces of fertility, both sexual and agricultural. We know the appeasement and worship of these forces to have been at the core of the ancient Babylonian and Egyptian cosmological conceptions of the universal order.[45]

Forms of temple prostitution continued to exist in ancient Greece[46] but commercial prostitution emerged as an independent empirical phenomenon associated, for example, with the commercial life of Athens as a metropolitan seaport.[47] Both the ancient Greeks[48] and Romans[49] regulated prostitution, not merely permitting it but in some cases[50] establishing state brothels. Prostitutes appear to have been divided into distinct classes, not unlike the still familiar distinctions among streetwalkers, brothel prostitutes, and call girls.[51] In ancient Greece[52] and China,[53] the highest classes of prostitutes appear to have enjoyed extraordinary intellectual and artistic advantages that women of their periods were, in general, not permitted. Nonetheless, it is probably a mistake to romanticize the life of the typical prostitute of these periods.[54] Prostitutes were often slaves.[55] While their conduct was not criminal, their activities were highly regulated, and their status as prostitutes deprived them of rights that other women enjoyed.[56] Prostitutes were regarded as useful to the state in the context of two factors that appear empirically to be part of the standard causal background for the existence of prostitution: (1) toleration of male sexual experimentation but insistence on female virginity before marriage and fidelity in marriage, often combined with late marriage for men or lifelong bachelorhood,[57] and (2) a class of women freed from traditional familial and clan restraints.[58] The usefulness of prostitutes as an outlet for male sexual experimentation in such circumstances does not, of course, mean that they were esteemed[59] or, with certain narrow exceptions,[60] admired. On the contrary, we know that the ancient Greeks thought of women as of intrinsically inferior moral worth, their moral value deriving in large part from their role in nurturing the development of men, who were considered to have intrinsic moral worth.[61] Prostitutes were regarded as of worth instrumentally in satisfying certain male needs, much as Aristotle regarded slaves as valuable instruments and tools for their masters' uses.[62] For the Romans, with their higher esteem for respectable women as such, prostitutes were held in general contempt although, again, they were thought to be instrumentally useful.[63]

The history of prostitution under Christianity falls into two strikingly different periods: pre- and post-Reformation. In the pre-Reformation period, prostitution was perceived in the context of St. Augustine's classic conception that the only proper "genital commotion"[64] is that consciously aimed at the reproduction of the species in marriage.[65] Augustine argues that the only plausible explanation for the privacy associated with sexual experience is that humans experience sex as intrinsically degrading because it involves the radical loss of control over mental functions, experiences, sensations, and behavior. This perception of shame, in turn, is alleged to rest on the fact that the only proper form of sex is accompanied by the controlled marital intention to procreate. Augustine concludes that sexuality is intrinsically degrading because we tend to experience it without or independent of those intentions which alone can validate it.[66] It follows from this view not only that certain rigidly defined kinds of intercourse in conventional marriage alone are moral,[67] but that sexuality even within marriage is a natural object of continuing shame, for sexual drives generally operate quite independently of the will, let alone of the will to reproduce.[68] In the Augustinian view, prostitution, as a form of extramarital sex, is of course immoral. For Augustine, however, sexuality in general is problematic: asexuality is obviously the preferred state, and sex even in marriage is validated only by its procreational intentions. This unsentimental view of marriage and the desire to protect it realistically led both St. Augustine[69] and

St. Thomas[70] to argue for the toleration of prostitution on the ground that it best protected the marital procreational unit. Unmarried men, incapable of celibacy, would be tempted to seduce neither married women nor the virgins destined to be married, and married men, incapable of fidelity, would be tempted to seduce neither of the above nor to form more permanent liaisons that would threaten their dedication to the procreational unit. In the pre-Reformation period, as a consequence, prostitution, with a few notable exceptions, was tolerated.[71]

Reformation thinkers, such as Luther, perceived prostitution in the context of attacks on the Catholic idealization of celibacy as the religiously preferable state[72] and the corresponding greater emphasis on the status of companionate marriage, in which all one's sexual and emotional needs were to be satisfied.[73] Ideas of romantic love, which in the Middle Ages had been celebrated in secular literature in extramarital, often adulterous terms,[74] were here explicitly absorbed into religious thought and vested by Luther and other Reformation thinkers in the marital unit alone.[75] In consequence, Lutheran and Calvinist thought not only regarded prostitution as immoral but, unlike the Catholic thinkers, urged its absolute legal prohibition, because prostitution violated the moral norm that all one's emotional needs were to be satisfied in marriage alone.[76]

Calvinist thought, in the form of Puritanism, powerfully influenced popular attitudes toward and the legal treatment of prostitution in England and the United States. In England, Puritanism acted as a political force effectively prohibiting brothels for a short time.[77] As an empirical phenomenon, prostitution flourished in England due to the concurrence of the two standard, background causal factors noted earlier.[78] During the Victorian period, a combination of religious forces and the first wave of British feminists, led by the redoubtable Josephine Butler,[79] frontally attacked the toleration of prostitution and the double standard of sexual morality that they perceived to underlie it; men, like women, should be compelled to observe the same standards, which the reformers assumed to be chastity or sex in marriage alone.[80] Among other things, these reformers secured the end of the brief British attempt at government licensing of prostitution,[81] which was then common in Europe.[82] Consistent with the recommendations of the *Wolfenden Report*,[83] prostitution is not itself a crime in England today, although public solicitation on the streets is prohibited.[84] In consequence, commerce in sexual services in England is largely negotiated through discreet advertisements in certain familiar locations and publications.[85]

In the United States, Puritan ideas have had much deeper impact on the legal treatment of prostitution than in England.[86] Calvinist ideas of companionate marriage, secularized by the combined influence of Calvinist preachers and female popular novelists,[87] developed into a reigning theory of sentimental marriage in which the asexual and more intensely spiritual wife would purify and elevate the husband's coarser worldly nature.[88] Drawing on these ideas, the first wave of American feminists, including Susan B. Anthony,[89] viewed attaining the vote as a means to secure expression in American politics of the higher spiritual vision that was uniquely feminine. This vision took the form of "purity leagues" that frontally attacked slavery, and then alcoholism and prostitution.[90] The consequence of the latter attack was not merely the end of brief American experiments with licensing prostitution[91] and the decisive rejection of the sometimes eloquent arguments of American proponents of licensing,[92] but the criminalization throughout the nation of prostitution per se.[93] Of the American states today, only Nevada permits local communities to allow prostitution.[94]

In continental Europe, the pattern of broad state toleration of prostitution was set in the early 1800s by the Napoleonic licensing of brothels.[95] Licensing of prostitution continued throughout Europe into this century.[96] Growing concern for the alleged "white slave trade" in women and girls[97] led the League of Nations[98] and later the United Nations[99] to call for the abolition of licensed brothels, which were claimed to be the main sources of regular demand for the international commerce in women and girls. These international conventions, in conjunction with feminist arguments against the degree to which licensing unjustly regulated and stigmatized the lives of prostitutes,[100] led to the abolition of state licensing in Europe.[101] Although prostitution itself is not criminal in Europe, forms of solicitation and place of business are subject to various kinds of regulations.[102]

II. THE ARGUMENTS FOR THE CRIMINALIZATION OF PROSTITUTION

In order to understand the uniquely American practice of the criminal prohibition of prostitution per se, we must take seriously the four arguments familiarly offered in its defense: (1) criminogenesis; (2) the control of venereal disease; (3) the intrinsically immoral and degrading nature of commercial sex; and (4), cognate to (3), the self-destructive or debilitating nature of prostitution. Of these arguments, (1) and (2) do not justify absolute criminal prohibitions; therefore, the gravamen of the argument for criminalization turns, as we shall see, on the proper weight to be given to (3) and (4).

A. *Criminogenesis*

The argument has been made that the criminal prohibition of prostitution is justified because of the number of crimes, such as theft and assault of patrons, trafficking in heroin, and the enlarged scope of organized crime operations,[103] which are said to occur incident to prostitution and of which prostitution is alleged to be the genesis.[104] None of these considerations in fact justifies the criminalization of prostitution; indeed, to the contrary, criminalization itself fosters these evils by forcing prostitutional activities into the clandestine criminal underground, the covertness of which breeds incidental crime.[105] If prostitution were tolerated by the law in certain areas of the community as, for example, it is in West Germany and the Netherlands,[106] the public visibility of prostitution would enable the police to cope more effectively with whatever violence or fraud exists. Patrons would be more likely to complain candidly to the police, and, conversely, prostitutes themselves would be more likely to bring to police attention the violence or fraud sometimes directed against them by patrons or pimps.[107] Similarly, the connections between prostitution and heroin traffic[108] are probably fostered, not combatted, by criminalization of the former. The effects of the criminal stigma and enforced covertness probably encourage or at least reinforce dependencies on narcotics[109] and certainly make more difficult the detection and possible control of addiction among prostitutes.[110] The better detection of ancillary crimes that would result from decriminalization would also promote more rational handling of the heroin traffic. Finally, the association of prostitution with organized crime is clearly fostered, not combatted, by criminalization. Prostitutes naturally seek protection from the criminal law by whatever means they can. Certainly, with the American prohibition of brothels, prostitutes have been practically driven for self-protection into alternative arrangements, including those with pimps.[111] In fact, authoritative recent studies indicate that organized crime has little current role in prostitution.[112]

Arguments of criminogenesis are generally circular and question-begging: they argue for criminalization of prostitution on the basis of evils that criminalization, not prostitution, fosters. If there are crimes associated with prostitution, they are more rationally attacked by decriminalization and by criminal statutes directed at the evils themselves, not by overbroad statutes that actually encourage what they claim to combat.

B. *Venereal Disease*

Venereal disease is a significant contemporary health problem. In the 1970s, gonorrhea was first and syphilis third among reported communicable diseases in America.[113] The appearance of penicillin-resistant gonococcus presents new obstacles to the control of venereal disease.[114] Such control is rendered even more difficult by the absence of any simple, effective antibiotic prophylaxis for venereal disease[115] and by the fact that sufferers of this disease, unlike those of other diseases, do not develop an immunity from it for the future.[116]

Nevertheless, it is a mistake to infer from the extent of this problem that there is more pressing need now than ever before for criminal prohibitions of prostitution. Recent data show that prostitutes are responsible for no more than five percent of all venereal disease;[117] the great majority of prostitutes do not suffer from the disease, and most tend to take more precautionary measures than does the promiscuous amateur.[118] Those age groups in which the venereal disease rate is the highest are those in which patronage of prostitutes is the lowest.[119]The increase in venereal disease appears to be due to the increase in sexual activity among the young,[120] who are unaware of the causes of such infections and who fail to secure prompt treatment or to inform their sex partners about having contracted the disease.[121]

Arguments have been made in the past justifying criminalization on the ground that declines in venereal disease levels are causally associated with prohibitions of prostitution.[122] The cases adduced in support of the claim of causality are probably better explained by the general availability and widespread use of penicillin in its treatment.[123] In any event, the disappearance of prostitution today would still leave about ninety-five percent of the cases of venereal disease intact. In Sweden, for example, where there is virtually no prostitution,[124] venereal disease remains a serious problem.[125] Thus, in order to treat this problem, regulations or prohibitions would have to be directed against all sexual activity,[126] but absolute prohibitions in this area would clearly be rejected as unjustly overbroad. A regulatory program of compulsory examination of all sexually active people would be both impractical and unacceptable. The preferred course would appear to be massive public education concerning appropriate precautionary measures and safeguards to combat the incidence of the disease.[127] In any event, there is no defensible reason, premised on venereal disease prophylaxis alone, justifying the absolute prohibition of commercial sex.

We have seen that it is disingenuous to suppose that the basis for the American criminal prohibition of prostitution rests on secular concerns for criminogenesis and venereal disease control. Neither argument can justify such prohibitions; indeed, serious concern with the evils adduced by one of the arguments would require the opposite conclusion. These arguments are, at best, post hoc empirical makeweights for justifications of a quite different order, namely moralistic and paternalistic arguments of a peculiarly American provenance. In order to deal reasonably with the justifications for such criminal prohibitions, we must critically examine these arguments.

C. *Moral Arguments*

The moral argument for the criminal prohibition of prostitution was well summarized by the Supreme Court in 1908:

[Prostitution] refers to women who for hire or without hire offer their bodies to indiscriminate intercourse with men. The lives and example of such persons are in hostility to "the idea of the family, as consisting in and springing from the union for life of one man and one woman in the holy estate of matrimony; the sure foundation of all that is stable and noble in our civilization, the best guaranty of that reverent morality which is the source of all beneficent progress in social and political improvement."[128]

It is noteworthy that, consistent with the traditional definition of prostitution as female promiscuity,[129] the Supreme Court did not place weight on the element of commercialism per se; the gravamen of the moral evil, rather, is that a *woman* should engage in sex not only unchastely but *indiscriminately*, in complete isolation from sentimental attachments of a kind perfected in monogamous marriage. Prostitution is a moral evil because, in the Court's words, the "lives and example of such persons are in hostility" to a certain enormously powerful vision of women, their sexuality, and the role of marriage. We have sketched the origins of this vision already and will have cause to return to it in more detail below.

In contemporary circumstances, however, the force of this moral vision has been somewhat reinterpreted in line with the growing acceptability of noncommercial sex outside marriage.[130] For many, the objection to prostitution would today be based not on female promiscuity, but on the transformation of sex into an impersonal encounter with no emotional significance by means of commercialization.[131] This objection is sometimes put in Marx's terms, such that prostitution is said to be the *reductio ad nauseam* of capitalist commercialization of all personal relationships.[132] Some contemporary feminists generally reject the Victorian model of female asexuality but still perceive prostitution as the ultimate degradation of women into sexual objects or commodities.[133] Finally, the contemporary form of the moral objection has been put in terms of Kantian ethics: commercial sex is allegedly morally wrong per se because it involves the alienation of the body to the will of another, and thus undermines the ultimate roots of the integrity of moral personality.[134] Whatever the precise form of the argument, the sense of it rests on a vision of the necessary moral unity of sex and romantic love. This fact explains why many suppose that consensual adult noncommercial sex can no longer be regarded as immoral per se, but still condemn comparable forms of commercial sex.[135]

Even if no other moral judgment may appropriately be made about the probity of certain conduct, we may still believe that undertaking such conduct is sufficiently irrational that we have moral title to interfere on paternalistic grounds. Paternalistic arguments against prostitution have taken two forms: the first depicts prostitution as intrinsically degrading and is often a restatement of the moral arguments just discussed;[136] the second emphasizes various respects in which choosing to be or to patronize a prostitute is harmful in empirically ascertainable ways. With respect to the prostitute, various kinds of harms have been adduced, including a much-shortened life,[137] venereal disease,[138] mental deficiency or neurotic impairment,[139] incapacity for orgasm,[140] and vulnerability to exploitation by pimps.[141] With respect to patrons, alleged harms include venereal disease,[142] neurotic impairment,[143] and sexual dysfunction.[144] The criminal prohibition of prostitution has thus been justified on the basis of protecting people from these kinds of self-inflicted harms.

Obviously, the critical assessment of this argument, as well as the moral argument for the criminalization of prostitution, depends upon an assessment of many claimed matters of fact. But it is equally important to articulate the proper form of moral or paternalistic reasoning to which these arguments appeal, for only such a critical assessment will enable us to understand how facts are relevant at all. Accordingly, we must turn to moral and normative theory to be able critically to assess these arguments and the matters of fact to which they appeal. Such an assessment is crucial to the question of the justifiability of the criminalization of prostitution, for criminal prohibitions in this area rest on the normative arguments sketched above.

III. THE MORALITY OF PROSTITUTION AND THE RIGHTS OF THE PERSON

We argued in earlier chapters that constitutionally institutionalized conceptions of human rights may be reasonably elaborated to warrant a particular kind of scrutiny of criminal laws claimed to be justified by the "public morality." *One* of the alternative ways of such reasonable elaboration is that, recognizing the criminal law as a focal area for governmental abuse of human rights, the founders surrounded the criminal legal process with a number of procedural and substantive constitutional guarantees.[145] Fundamental among those guarantees is the idea of due process reasonableness—the insistence that government give reasons for its actions, particularly for deprivations of life, liberty, or property.[146] Because the moral reasonableness of the criminal law rests crucially on the soundness of the "public morality," constitutional values require critical examination of that morality in order to ensure that its claims are morally valid.[147]

Such criticism of the "public morality" on the basis of its due process reasonableness fully acccords with the moral point of view. The values of equal concern and respect for personal autonomy that we have unearthed as the foundations of American constitutionalism are the same values that recent moral theory, following Kant, has identified as fundamental to the moral point of view. In particular, contractarian theory, recognizing these values, affords a method for determining which beliefs can correctly be included in the "public morality" that may be enforced by law. Where public attitudes about morality are, in fact, demonstrably not justified by underlying moral principles, laws expressing such attitudes are morally arbitrary and should be found to violate minimal standards of constitutional due process.

It is important, however, not to be misunderstood as to the institutional significance of the foregoing argument. Although the moral constraints on the criminal law are of constitutional magnitude, their institutional relevance is not confined to constitutional interpretation and adjudication by courts. Specific reasons either of doctrinal principle or institutional competence may debar a court from extending a moral right to its full extent. For example, in the area of decriminalization, a court might limit its enforcement of underlying autonomy rights to more basic life choices or, even if it believes a claim to reflect such fundamental choices, not vindicate such a right if the decriminalization in question should reasonably be accompanied by alternative forms of regulation that a court is not institutionally equipped to mandate. Sometimes such judicial judgments are simply wrong, as I argued in Chapter 2 about the extension of constitutional privacy to consensual homosexuality; but sometimes such judgments are just. But even if the courts fail, for good or bad reasons, to recognize the full constitutional import of the requirement that its laws be morally justifiable, the requirement is nevertheless capable of implementation at the legislative level.[148] There being no defensible moral principle to sustain a given state interference, legislators should refrain from enacting laws that interfere in this way.[149]

Of course, in order to demonstrate an abuse of the "public morality" in a certain area, one must be prepared to offer a moral analysis of wherein the abuse consists: what kind of moral fallacy underlies the traditional arguments? Are the facts wrong? Has improper weight been given to certain kinds of personal ideals? Are there question-begging underlying assumptions about moral personality?

With respect to prostitution, which is our analytic concern here, the tradition of moral condemnation is ancient and surely entitled to a respectful hearing. I wish to take it very seriously and yet show with care how contractarian theory, of the kind here suggested, may enable us to understand why it is mistaken. In order to do this, we will appeal to moral theory and also to moral archeology. Ancient moral beliefs, like those surrounding prostitution, often rest on a residuum of primitive beliefs, which we self-consciously reject elsewhere in our social life but which, in certain circumscribed areas, unconsciously retain their force.[150] In order rationally to scrutinize these matters, we must exercise some historical and moral imagination in articulating and bringing to light these assumptions and in subjecting them to moral criticism. Let us begin with the grounds for the moral condemnation of prostitution per se, and then turn to the paternalistic grounds.

The moral condemnation of prostitution rests on a number of disparate grounds. Let us consider them *seriatim*.

A. *Prostitution as Nonprocreational Sex*

The model of procreational sexual love was given its classic formulation, as we have seen, in St. Augustine's conception that the only proper "genital commotion"[151] is that consciously aimed at the reproduction of the species in marriage.[152] Contraception, whether within or outside marriage, and extramarital (including prostitution) and homosexual intercourse are all forbidden as deviations from the only proper canonical form of legitimate sexuality—the intent to procreate within marriage. This marital procreational focus led Augustine[153] and St. Thomas,[154] on the one hand, to condemn prostitution morally and, on the other, to urge its toleration so as to keep wayward sexual appetites within bounds in a way least detrimental to the central procreational unit.

We discussed and criticized the Augustinian procreational model at length in an earlier chapter.[155] We may summarize those criticisms in the following ways. Augustine would blindly condemn as unnatural the use of sexuality as a way in which two people express mutual love as an end in itself, without procreational motives. At best, the procreational model is a plausible description of the animal, not the human, world.[156] For animals, sexual activity is rigidly bound to the period of female receptive fertility; natural human sexuality distinctively differs in that sexual propensities and readiness are not tied to the period of possible procreation. A more appropriate use of the "unnatural-natural" distinction would, therefore, be to call the exclusive use of sex for procreation unnatural for humans, though natural for animals.

Nor can the procreational model of human sexuality be sustained as intrinsic to the concept of love. Love is conceptually defined by its peculiar aims, beliefs, and experiences—for example, by the intensity of the experience, the desire to promote the good of the other, the identification of another's interests as one's own, and the desire for physical and psychological closeness.[157] The concept of love says nothing about the forms its physical expression must take. As a result, there is no ideal, exclusive, or proper physical expression of sexual love, for a large and indeterminate class of forms of sexual intercourse is compatible with the aims of love.

Consider an analogy of another great human appetite, hunger. Some people eat to live, but many others live to eat, elaborating food preparation into a highly sensual art and eating into an exquisite social ritual of friendship and even love. The class of utilitarian eaters, the Augustinians of gastronomy, might argue that eating must be regarded in bleakly utilitarian terms, and that all other forms of eating should be morally condemned and made criminal offenses. They would certainly have at hand some good arguments for adopting this attitude: keeping slim, maintaining dietary health, and conserving time and money for more socially significant enterprises. But such arguments are at best relevant to issues of personal prudence or personal ideals; they do not constitute a moral argument of the kind that justifies criminal enforcement of moral standards. There is an indeterminately large class of attitudes toward eating compatible with the neutrality toward visions of the good life that underlies equal concern and respect for autonomy. Food is, of course, a general good and should be distributed equitably. But to compel by law any one style of eating would evince contempt for the dignity of individual self-determination. Legal enforcement of a particular sexual ideal fails equally to accord due respect to individual autonomy.

Because the procreational model of sexuality can no longer be sustained by any good empirical or conceptual argument for the reasons just given, neither can it validly be legally enforced on the ground of public morality, for it fails to satisfy the ethical and constitutional requirement that legally enforceable moral ideas be grounded in equal concern and respect for autonomy and facts capable of interpersonal empirical validation. Recognition of this inadequacy of the procreational model underlies the decriminalization by constitutional decision of contraception,[158] abortion,[159] and pornography in the home,[160] and the gradual decriminalization of consensual noncommercial sexual relations between consenting adults.[161] In the same way, the procreational model cannot justify the criminalization of prostitution. Prostitution, that is, cannot appropriately be made criminal on the ground that it does not look toward procreation.

This does not mean, of course, that prostitution is necessarily superior to the procreational model as a personal moral ideal. Indeed, a number of the reasons adduced for rejecting the procreational model as a foundation for law would seem to apply equally to commercial sex. We spoke, for example, of sexual experience as the basis for longstanding and intense personal relationships, and as a way in which two people express mutual love. These descriptions do not apply in any obvious way to commercial sex. This fact in no way impairs the strength of our argument against using the procreational model as a ground for the criminalization of commercial sex, however. The model remains morally inadequate. But the apparent incompatibility of prostitution with love may be the basis for an independent argument for its criminalization. To this argument, then, we must turn.

B. *Prostitution and Romantic Love*

No argument supporting the moral condemnation of prostitution has a stronger hold on the American popular imagination than the argument for protecting romantic love. Even those who do not identify romantic love with the conventional family—indeed, who argue for freer extramarital expression of capacities for romantic love—sharply condemn prostitution.[162] In order to understand these claims, we must examine with care the idea and force of romantic love as a personal ideal and its peculiar associations in American intellectual and social history.

The history of the romantic love tradition in European thought is complex and much disputed.[163] Plato articulated the idea in the context of extramarital, male homosexual relationships.[164] The seminal works in medieval literature understandably did not identify romantic love with marriage,[165] because medieval marriages were commonly arranged by family and clan networks to serve larger economic, social, and procreational purposes.[166] According to some, the romantic love tradition is the offshoot of Christian heresy,[167] for it celebrates a form of intense human feeling outside of and indeed antagonistic to the then conventional marriage relationship. Certainly these ideas of romantic extramarital feeling are sharply opposed to the then current sorrowing Augustinian dismissal of sexuality as an unfortunate and spiritually empty concomitant of propagation.[168] The form of romantic love celebrated in the Middle Ages has left permanent marks on all later conceptions.[169] The emotional relationship between the lovers is intensely heightened by various frustrations, including a highly exacting code of chivalrous conduct,[170] continual tests of one's love, and sometimes the impossibility of sexual consummation.[171] In consequence, the beloved is often highly idealized in terms of inaccessible remoteness[172] and consummation is often associated with death,[173] the implicit just condemnation for indulging in spontaneous and natural feeling undisciplined by convention.

Reformation thinkers, however, gave to the theretofore secular and possibly heretical romantic love tradition religious respectabililty in the form of the Lutheran-Calvinist idea of companionate marriage.[174] The choice of marriage partner became increasingly invested with romantic feeling, and marriage took on a new psychological dimension as an expression of such feelings.[175] Accordingly, the choice of marriage partner was interpreted in the way of the medieval romantic lover; there was courting, testing, frustration, and idealization, but with the crucial difference that the process was ultimately consummated within marriage.[176] The subsequent history of the family is the history of the growing dominance of the psychological-romantic aspects of marriage over the economic aspect;[177] with contraception, even the procreational focus has receded.[178]

The Reformation absorption of the romantic love tradition into marriage had an especially telling impact on American intellectual and social history. The Calvinist-Puritan view of companionate marriage established romantic marital love not as one ideal among others, but as the exclusive form in which sexual and affectional feeling could legitimately be experienced. This new orthodoxy was secularized during the Victorian period by a confluence of supposed "[s]cience . . . with aesthetic and literary fashion to support the ideal of the delicate and frigid female"[179] in a powerful vision of sentimental marriage as the core of spiritual values. Such marriage was thought to protect the asexual and highly idealized woman from the pressures of a coarse, competitive, masculine world. In consequence, prostitution is morally condemned not so much because it is extramarital, but because it directly contravenes the model of romantic love, including the model of the allegedly proper role of women.

The gravamen of this moral objection is not the empirical claim that the toleration of prostitution makes marriage less stable. As the continental European and English experience shows,[180] there is no evidence whatsoever for this view; indeed, prostitution may have beneficial effects on the stability of marriage, as St. Augustine,[181] St. Thomas,[182] and many others[183] have shrewdly observed. The objection, rather, is a form of moral argument to the effect that prostitution blatantly violates the ideal of romantic love. The patron of the prostitute engages in sexual activity and experiences sexual release impersonally without the processes of courting, testing, frustration, and personal idealization of the beloved[184] that characterize romantic love. Many Americans today would no longer limit the scope of romantic love to marital relationships. Romantic love occurs maritally and extramaritally, homosexually and heterosexually. If there is a moral and human right to love, all of these relationships, within limits, invoke it.[185] But prostitution does not. Accordingly, the former loving relationships should be decriminalized, but not prostitution.

This argument represents a legitimate expression of personal ideals that one may urge upon others as desirable, but it is fallaciously misconceived as a valid moral argument to justify the application of criminal sanctions, as is made manifest by consideration of moral theory and the underlying values of equal concern and respect for autonomy. In order to preserve these values, the contractarian model deprives the contractors of knowledge of specific identity and requires that decisions on basic moral principles be based on empirical facts capable of interpersonal validation. The neutrality ensured by these constraints is incompatible with the invocation of the model of romantic love as the morally compulsory norm of sexual expression enforceable on society at large. First, the contractors, not knowing whether or not they have personal ideals of romantic love, would be reluctant to make it compulsory. Second, it is not justified to introduce the model of romantic love, under the guise of an empirical fact, as the only fulfilling form of sexual expression. This latter point raises the general question as to the appropriate form in which these questions would be raised in the original position. When we reject the procreational model of sexuality as the measure of legally enforceable sexual morality, we are able to understand the humane and fulfilling force of sexuality per se in human life, the scope of human autonomous self-control in regulating its expression, and the implications of these facts for the widening application of the concept of human rights to the sexual area.

Contemporary understanding of sexuality, building on Freud's insights,[186] has permanently transformed our view of the role of sexuality in human development and in the definition of the person. At the core of these insights lies Freud's perception that human sexuality serves complex imaginative and symbolic purposes that have important ramifications in a person's general orientation to the basic tasks of human life,[187] and that (in ways earlier described in Chapter 2)[188] understanding of unconscious processes of imaginative manipulations of sexual feelings (the defenses) is a step toward the deepening of the autonomy of the person. One is thereby able to see life as one's own, rather than as the result of the wishes of others. In view of these capacities and the powerful role of sexuality as an independent force in the imaginative life and development of the person, sexual autonomy appears to be a central aspect of moral personality through which we define our ideas of a free person who has taken responsibility for her or his life.

In this regard, it is a common but serious mistake to draw sharp dichotomous lines between the different ways that persons use sexuality in their lives, instead of recognizing the existence of a continuum. For example, people sometimes distinguish between sexual love and sexual lust, describing married couples as being "in love" or "falling in love," whereas others are, properly speaking, "in lust" with one another or have fallen "in lust."[189] Interestingly, however, we describe ourselves as "making love" to another person when we have sexual relations, even if we are clearly not "in love." Sexual attitudes are intrinsically evaluational: to desire to have sexual relations with a person is to perceive that person as desirable for certain reasons.[190] Thus, sexual attitudes can be enormously erratic when we discover that the other is not desirable in the way at first supposed. We discover that he or she is not gentle or sensitive or courageous in the way assumed, and our eros drily goes up in smoke. Sexual relations between lovers and those not in love share these evaluational significances and are often equally self-expressive. The relationships do differ, of course, but often the nature of the sexual experience does not.[191] In neither case is it correct to regard the sexual relations as blind or instinctive or spiritually insignificant, as is animal sexuality. This is no less true in the case of commercial sex than in noncommercial sex.[192]

It was argued earlier that the Augustinian model should not be legally enforced, precisely because it fails to take seriously this role of sexual self-determination as one focally important form of moral personality and thus deprives persons of autonomous choice regarding these fundamental experiences. Similarly, the invocation of romantic love as a compulsory moral standard must be criticized. Assume that the model of romantic love is the ideal of conducting personal sexual relationships in terms of a process of patient courting, including readiness to undergo frustrating testing of one's love in the interest of perfecting and cultivating sensitive response to the beloved, often aesthetically and sometimes religiously idealized. Assume also that this is an ideal of personal conduct to which many justly aspire, perhaps on the grounds of erotic chastity suggested by Havelock Ellis,[193] such that only by self-imposed frustrating restraints of the kind that pursuit of romantic love calls for do we realize the more exquisite sensual fulfillment of which our human nature is capable. Nonetheless, there is no reason to believe that this ideal is any more entitled to moral enforcement as the only legitimate model of sexual expression than is the Augustinian model of sexuality or, for that matter, the Augustinian model of gastronomy suggested earlier. It is simply dogmatic to say that romantic love can be the only means of human fulfillment. There are many other courses that may reasonably accommodate the diverse individuality of human competences, aspirations, and ends. What for one, is a reasonable, self-imposed ideal of deepened romantic sensuality may, for another, be a narrow and parochial narcissism, a waste of self in privatized obsession and broader social irresponsibility.[194] Consider, in this connection, the eloquent feminist literature that has urged self-criticism about the special force of the concept of love as used by and applied to women, which has allegedly blinded women to their real social and economic situation, sanctifying acquiescence in exploitative and masochistic personal relationships in the name of loving self-sacrifice.[195]

Surely, in matters of sexual choice, the range of reasonable personal ideals is wide, various, and acutely sensitive to personal context and individual idiosyncrasy. The law has no proper role in prejudging how these choices are to be made in general, and whether romantic love is to be chosen in particular.

Finally, it is particularly inappropriate to use an ideal such as romantic love to justify any form of compulsory moral norm.[196] This ideal, based on the cultivation of spontaneous romantic feeling, is the very antithesis to compulsory forms of sexual expression. Furthermore, loveless encounters are sometimes prerequisites for genuine love relationships; to forbid the former is, therefore, to inhibit the latter. Accordingly, the invocation of such ideals to justify such compulsory norms is a travesty of the spiritual meaning of these ideals.

C. *Prostitution and Degradation*

Another form of the moral argument for criminalization of prostitution focuses not on the character of the sexual relations, but on the alleged degradation of the prostitute. This argument takes at least three different forms: first, a moral argument based on female chastity; second, the immorality of treating a person as a commercial sex object; and third, alleged specific empirical harms to the prostitute or the patron. These arguments will be considered in the following three sections.

1. PROSTITUTION AS UNCHASTE SEX. To think of behavior as degraded rests on the twin assumptions that one's self-esteem is invested in the competent exercise of certain capacities of the person and that certain behavior fails to be competent in the required way. The degraded, thus, is the natural object of shame or self-disgust at personal failure to live up to standards of conduct that are valued as essential to the integrity of the self.[197] Accordingly, the understanding of the application of the concept of the degraded to prostitution requires an account of the valued forms of behavior from which it is alleged to deviate.

For this purpose, moral archeology is needed to unearth the ancient conceptions of female sexuality that underlie the view that prostitution degrades. The core of this view appears to be the definition of a woman's basic self-esteem in terms of her chastity—her control of sexual impulses for the marital obligations, which are her destiny in life.[198] The origin of these ideas is linked historically to the important function of women as means of exchange in the strengthening and widening of kinship networks and the consequent economic and social integration.[199] The virginity of one's daughter was a mark of her value for these exchange purposes, so that an unchaste woman was a waste of a family asset indispensable to social and economic well-being.[200] Primitive myths often explain these ideas in terms of female hypersexuality that must be controlled by rigidly enforced social and political sanctions, sometimes including quite barbaric physical disfigurements.[201] The idea of female vulnerability to concupiscent excesses is, in Western culture, associated with the seminal and pervasive Aristotelian vision of the morally inferior status of women,[202] the inferiority here taking the form of a lack of internal capacities for self-control.[203] In societies where these conceptions of rigid virginity prevail, female unchastity is conceived of as intrinsically degraded— as a disgusting failure to exercise self-control over appetites in the way required to perform one's mandated social role as wife and mother.[204] An important further presupposition of this way of thinking is that women are capable of only one kind of life, defined by procreation and child-rearing in the home.[205] Accordingly, in advanced urban societies with prostitution, occasional female unchastity was often regarded as morally equivalent to prostitution. This view, which seems to follow from the economic value placed upon a marriageable girl's chastity, was a self-fulfilling prophecy and tended so to stigmatize a girl who erred once "for love" that prostitution inexorably followed.[206]

In Victorian America, female chastity remained the ideal, but the ancient idea of female hypersexuality was radically denied and replaced by that of female asexuality. Remarkably,

despite internal dissension within the medical profession, for the first time in Western history there was a strong body of opinion which actually denied the existence of the sexual drive in the majority of women, and regarded the minority who experienced it to any marked degree as morally, mentally or physically diseased.[207]

A remarkable confluence of medical-scientific theory[208] and religio-sentimental literature[209] described women as having superior capacities for spiritual and moral inwardness that were properly insulated in the home from coarsely sensual, masculine, competitive concerns derived from the business and political worlds. It is this identification of women in the home with higher moral and spiritual sensibility that explains the striking and not at all self-evident association of the protection of this role with the preservation of the sources of morality. As one expression of this social perception, the first wave of British and American feminism proclaimed that women must carry this higher moral vision into the public world in the form of moral purification.[210] In particular, prostitution was the central focus of an attack by purity reformers,[211] who perceived it as a direct and outrageous offense to the Victorian higher moral "ideal of the delicate and frigid female,"[212] as prostitutes were sexual, aggressive, and commercial.

The idea that prostitution is morally degrading, resting on ideas of proper female chastity, can no longer be sustained, either as an empirical thesis about female sexuality or as an implication of women's social and economic role. As an empirical matter, contemporary studies of female sexuality make clear the ample natural sexual appetites of women, including substantial orgasmic capacity.[213] Ideas of natural female asexuality, on the one hand, and of the incapacity for sexual self-control, on the other, appear today to be not descriptions, but ideologies[214] by which women have been denied a basic self-conception acknowledging their moral right to sexual fulfillment. Correlative ideas of women's social and economic role as a necessary means of kinship exchange are, in their traditional form, obsolete today. Furthermore, in the compulsory and exploitative forms that they historically took, these ideas are repugnant to the equal concern and respect to which women, as persons, are entitled. Marriage no longer serves such economic and social purposes; contraception has mitigated many of the fears peculiar to female unchastity; and the general role of women, no longer limited to procreation and child-rearing, has been and continues to be transformed by the growing access of women to the formerly exclusive masculine realm of the public, competitive work, and politics.[215] From this perspective, arguments, such as those condemning prostitution that allegedly protected the spiritual, female sanctuary of the home from incursions from the sensual, competitive masculine world, appear to be malign ways in which women have been caged by an ideology that distorted and unrecognizably disfigured basic self-conceptions of natural capacity and responsible autonomy.[216]

Accordingly, the condemnation of prostitution as morally degraded appears not to rest on critically defensible moral arguments, but on an ideology that idealized female chastity and stigmatized as morally indecent any deviation from this ideal. The rejection of this ground for the criminalization of prostitution is, then, mandated by the deepest values of equal concern and respect for autonomy. Not only does it fail to respect female sexual autonomy; but, in addition, to permit this ideology to have the force of law today is inconsistently to accept a model of compulsory female chastity that we reject elsewhere in our social life.

Nevertheless, it may be objected that however sound the foregoing arguments against legal enforcement of a parochial view of female chastity may be, they do not really come to terms with the modern view that prostitution is degrading. Such an objection leads to what is, perhaps, the most interesting form of moral argument for the criminalization of prostitution from the point of view of moral theory.

2. COMMERCIAL SEX AND THE ALIENATION OF MORAL PERSONALITY. At the root of this argument is the idea of intrinsic moral limitations on the

range of human conduct that may be justly subjected to the economic laws of the marketplace. The argument, derived from the father of modern moral theory, Immanuel Kant,[217] is that commercial sex is immoral per se because it involves the sale of the body, which is the foundation of personal integrity, and thus the root of ethical relationships. Kant put the argument in Augustinian terms of objections to the intrinsically degraded nature of sexual appetite per se[218] as an appetite for another person's body. Kant's words are striking: "Sexual love makes of the loved person an Object of appetite; as soon as that appetite has been stilled, the person is cast aside as one casts away a lemon which has been sucked dry."[219] The only legitimate sexuality for Kant is in conventional marriage, where there is reciprocal equality, each party having full rights in the person and body of the other.[220] Commercial sex, in particular, is forbidden for the same reason that a person "is not entitled to sell a limb, not even one of his teeth."[221] Indeed:

to allow one's person for profit to be used by another for the satisfaction of sexual desire, to make of oneself an Object of demand, is to dispose over oneself as over a thing and to make of oneself a thing on which another satisfies his appetite, just as he satisfies his hunger upon a steak. But since the inclination is directed towards one's sex and not towards one's humanity, it is clear that one thus partially sacrifices one's humanity and thereby runs a moral risk. Human beings are, therefore, not entitled to offer themselves, for profit, as things for the use of others in the satisfaction of their sexual propensities. . . . To let one's person out on hire and to surrender it to another for the satisfaction of his sexual desire in return for money is the depth of infamy. The underlying moral principle is that man is not his own property and cannot do with his body what he will. The body is part of the self; in its togetherness with the self it constitutes the person; a man cannot make of his person a thing, and this is exactly what happens in *vaga libido*. This manner of satisfying sexual desire is, therefore, not permitted by the rules of morality.[222]

The integrity of the person rests on the integrity of the body; accordingly, the sale of the body is the alienation of moral personality, a kind of moral slavery. Charles Fried's recent references to prostitution in a discussion of the sale of body parts suggests a reintroduction of this argument, although without Kant's Augustinian view of sexual appetite as intrinsically degraded, nor Kant's view that only marital sex is legitimate.[223] Fried does seem to follow Kant in arguing that, in a society where distributive shares are just, the commercial sale of sex is intrinsically immoral for the same reason that the sale of body parts is shameful.[224]

This moral argument is sometimes put, in Marxist terms, that prostitution represents the ultimate capitalist degradation of personal relationships.[225] Since personal sexual love is conceived by Marx as the model for nonalienated personal relationships,[226] prostitution (degrading love into commerce) cuts to the heart of morality. In similar ways, some contemporary feminists regard prostitution as the ultimate symbol of woman as a degraded sex object, making sexuality a capital asset exploited in impersonal business terms.[227] These arguments seem to depend on the underlying Kantian argument about the alienation of moral personality.

Initially, it is important to see and be puzzled by the fact that the argument proves too much. Commercial sex is condemned as a sale of body parts, but this is, of course, not actually true. Commercial sex is no more the sale of sexual organs than is the sale of a mover's muscles or a model's beauty or a lawyer's legal talent. It is a gross misdescription to call commercial sex, on the one hand, a "sale," and, on the other, to denominate the latter as "services."[228] Both the one and the others are most accurately described as services. So construed, the condemnation of commercial sex as a service would surely require the condemnation of others as well. If it is argued, for example, that commercial sex in some way degrades the talents of the prostitute because the prostitute is emotionally alienated,[229] the same arguments could be made, perhaps more strongly, about other forms of service that our economy not merely tolerates but encourages.[230] Prostitutes clearly perform an important social service; many people find with them a kind of personal release and solace not otherwise available to them;[231] and many prostitutes perform complex supportive and even therapeutic roles for their patrons in addition to sexual services.[232] It is difficult to regard such services as intrinsically degraded: the work is no more emotionally detached than much other contemporary work, and may be less so.[233] It is often well and fairly paid,[234] and the needs served are deep and real. Many forms of factory work in the United States unnecessarily involve repetitive boring tasks that create an emotionally alienated work force and, in a plausible sense, degrade capacities for committed and engaged work.[235] Many people in highly remunerated service professions engage in boring, sometimes socially wasteful work that they know sacrifices their better talents and that leads to deep alienation and emotional detachment.[236] If prostitution is to be criminalized as degraded work, much other work in the United States, a fortiori, would have to be criminalized. We are not prepared to do so in the latter case because of considerations that apply to prostitution as well: in a society committed to equal concern and respect for autonomy, people are entitled to make choices for themselves as to trade-offs between alienation, social service, and remuneration. We certainly can criticize these decisions, but we do not regard criminalization as an appropriate expression of our condemnation.

It is impossible to see how sexual services can be distinguished from other cases. The suggestion, for example, that highly remunerated professional services require effort and training, but that prostitution does not,[237] obviously will not do. Many forms of service other than commercial sex call for comparably little effort and training; yet we do not criminalize them on that ground. In any event, why should years of training make any difference, if the work itself is empty, alienated, and socially unproductive?

However, let us assume *arguendo* that it is possible to distinguish commercial sex from other forms of service, and even to regard it as a kind of sale of the body like the sale of body parts. Kant's argument, nevertheless, rests on an indefensible interpretation of the relation of moral personality to the body. Kant identified the person with the body, and then argues roughly as follows:

1. It is always wrong to alienate moral personality.
2. Prostitution is the sale of the body.
3. The person and the body are the same.
4. It is always wrong to engage in prostitution.

The crucial assumption is the third, on the basis of which Kant associates prostitution with a kind of moral slavery.

Kant's identification of moral personality with the body in his discussion of sexual morality is remarkably inconsistent with what he says elsewhere about autonomy as the basis of moral personality. In his central statements of ethical theory, moral personality is described in terms of autonomous independence—the capacity to order and choose one's ends as a free and rational being.[238] By comparison, in his sexual morality discussion, the body acts as an absolute and inexplicable limit on autonomous freedom. It is impossible to square these views. Indeed, the deeper theory of autonomy, Kant's central contribution to ethical theory,[239] requires the rejection of the rather parochial and unimaginative views of moral personality applied in his consideration of sex. Autonomy, in the fullest sense, rests, as we have already seen,[240] on persons' self-critical capacities to assess their present wants and lives, to form and act on wants and projects, and to change them. Autonomy occurs in a certain body, occasioning a person self-critically to take into account that body and its capacities in deciding on the form of his or her life. The existence of certain capacities or physical traits, as opposed to others, will importantly shape basic decisions on work and love. But the embodiment of autonomy does not limit the exercise of autonomy in the way Kant supposes. Kant means to be making the valid point about autonomy-based ethics that it is immoral to abdicate one's autonomy, or one's capacity for self-critical choice about the form of one's life. All forms of slavery are thus forbidden because they involve such a surrender of basic autonomy and of the human rights that express and facilitate such autonomy. But Kant conflates this valid moral idea with the unrelated idea that one's body parts are not alienable. It is a flat non sequitur to assume that such alienations are alienations of moral personality. The self-critical capacities of autonomy may validly be exercised by the sale or donation of blood[241] or, within limits,[242] other body parts. The extension of the argument to commercial sex is equally mistaken. Voluntarily engaging in commercial sex cannot reasonably be supposed to be the same thing as the forbidden moral slavery of alienating moral personality. Indeed, there is something morally perverse in condemning commercial sex as intrinsic moral slavery when the very prohibition of it seems to be an arbitrary abridgement of sexual autonomy.

Kant's argument would be perceived as the non sequitur that it is if it were applied to other forms of commercial service. Certainly the form of Kant's argument renders dubious the whole idea of the marketplace and the role of personal services in it, as if there were some moral impediment to rendering services on equitable terms. There are moral limits on the range of activities to which the market properly applies; slavery and certain kinds of services are correctly forbidden.[243] But the market sensibly operates in making commercially available to willing buyers those willing to offer their services on terms equitable to both parties. Sexual services are not, in moral principle, any less worthy of being in the marketplace than are any other valued services. Rendering such services is no more harmful to the seller or buyer than many other personal services conventionally available and may, in some cases, be less so.[244]

In this connection, Kant, followed by Marxists[245] and recent feminists,[246] argues that in the sexual area there is a unique evil in treating another person as an object, and that commercial sex is the most degraded example of such objectification. Sexual relations of all kinds do, of course, involve making the sex partner the object of one's sexual interests, but it is a rather silly equivocation on the notion of sex object to conflate this uncontroversial truth with the moral claim that sex necessarily treats the partner as a nonperson. In many human relationships, we take other persons as the "objects" of our endeavors, but this grammatical truth says nothing about the morality of our endeavors, which may be highly humane and morally sensitive. In having sex, our partner is the object of our sexual interests, but the moral character of the intercouse will depend on many background factors. Among lovers, the morality of the intercourse may depend on exquisite issues of awareness of and sensitivity to giving and receiving reciprocal pleasure. Among nonlovers, the moral issues may center on issues of the nature of mutual understanding. In commercial sex, presumably a subcase of nonlovers, a crucial issue will be the fairness of the bargain, determined by the nature of the service and the money paid. There is no reason why the morality of a sexual relationship may not, like any other commercial service, be judged in this way. Kant argues that the only just reciprocity for sex can be marriage,[247] and Marx similarly suggests that the only just equivalence can be mutual love.[248] Kant's arguments, as we have seen, are mistaken; and Marx appears to invoke the model of romantic love, which we have seen to be an improper measure of legally enforceable morality. In general, commercial sex involves a valued service and may be given in a fair bargain. The buyer receives a kind of attention not secured elsewhere,[249] and the seller receives fair payment.[250] In neither case is there any evidence that the parties in question are disabled or rendered incapable of love elsewhere.[251] If one thinks of the prostitute as an unloved sex object, the alleged symbol of sexually exploited women carried to its immoral extreme, the crucial difference becomes clear: the prostitute demands and exacts a fair return, as an autonomous person should, for service rendered.

It is not difficult to understand how Kant, so powerful in his statement of abstract universalistic ethics, could be so time-bound in his casuistry of sex; he assumes, as the foundation of his discussion of sexual morality, the Augustinian model of sexuality. Thus, when Kant argues that we do not have a property right in our sexuality, he is not only making the confused argument about alienating moral personality just discussed, but he is echoing Augustine's quasi-theological argument that our sexuality is the property of God which we may employ only on His marital, procreational terms. Accordingly, Kant isolates sex from autonomy in the manner conventional for his period. But there is no reason to continue this mistake today. If the religious overtones of the subject caused Kant to miss the implications of his own ideas, there is no reason for us irrationally to isolate sex for ad hoc treatment. Such isolation blinds us to the reality of our sexual and social lives, encouraging us to see degradation in commercial sex when there may be better examples of the degradation of work elsewhere in our society, to see in prostitution loveless waste where, in fact, there may be fair service, and to support as national dogma romantic love which may be a sentimental mask for exploitative self-sacrifice.

3. PATERNALISTIC ARGUMENTS AGAINST PROSTITUTION. Even if no other moral argument on behalf of criminalization can be sustained, it may still be argued that undertaking particular conduct is sufficiently irrational for an agent that there is no moral title to interfere on paternalistic grounds. Such forms of argument in defense of prohibitions of commercial sex, however, are radically inappropriate.

Let us begin with a brief reminder of the proper scope of paternalistic considerations, which we already discussed in chapter 2.[252] We discussed the moral point of view in terms of a structure of reasons expressing mutual concern and respect, universalization, and minimization of natural fortuity, and have employed a contractarian model to articulate these ideas. This model would clearly justify a principle of paternalism and explain its proper scope and limits. From the point of view of the original position, the contractors would know that human beings would be subject to certain kinds of irrationalities with severe consequences, including death and the permanent impairment of health. They would, accordingly, agree on an insurance principle against certain of these more serious irrationalities in the event they might occur to them. There are two critical constaints on the scope of such a principle. First, the relevant idea of irrationality cannot itself violate the two constraints of morality imposed on moral contractors: ignorance of specific identity, and reliance only on facts capable of empirical validation. In particular, possibly idiosyncratic personal values cannot be smuggled into the content of "irrationality" that defines the scope of the principle. Rather, the notion of irrationality must be defined in terms of a neutral theory that can accommodate the many visions of the good life compatible with moral constaints. For this purpose, the idea of rationality must be defined relative to the agent's system of ends, which are, in turn, determined by the agent's appetites, desires, capacities, and aspirations. Principles of rational choice require the most coherent and satisfying plan for accommodating the agent's ends over time.[253] Accordingly, only those acts are irrational that frustrate the agent's own system of ends, whatever those ends are. Second, within the class of irrationalities so defined, paternalistic considerations would properly come into play only if the irrationality were severe and systematic (due to undeveloped or impaired capacities, or lack of opportunity to exercise such capacities) and a serious, pemanent impairment of interests were in prospect. Interference in irrationalities outside the scope of this second constraint would be forbidden, in large part because allowing people to make and learn from their own mistakes is a crucial part of the development of mature autonomy.[254]

When we consider the application of paternalistic considerations of these kinds to the choice of engaging in commercial sex, we face the question how to assess the rationality of this kind of choice. Again, the idea of rationality employed here takes as its fundamental datum the agent's ends. In this context, principles of rational choice call for the assessment of choices of occupation in terms of the degree to which each choice satisfies the agent's ends over time.[255] This is because choices of occupation determine a number of subchoices having effects throughout the agent's life, and indeed may determine the duration of that life.[256] Since the agent's ends over time are often complex and difficult to anticipate with exactitude, a number of such choices may be equally rational. Nonetheless, there is a coherent sense to the application of rationality criteria to such choices. Some such choices are clearly irrational if they frustrate every significant end that the agent has and available alternatives do not.[257] Such choices, if they satisfy the stringent constraints of the principle discussed above, may be the proper object of paternalistic interference.

No good argument can be made that paternalistic considerations would justify the kind of interferences, either in choices to render sexual services commercially or to use such services, that are involved in the criminalization of prostitution. Indeed, in many cases such choices seem all *too* rational. It is important, first, to understand that people are not always full-time prostitutes[258] or are full-time prostitutes only for certain periods of their lives, after which they lead more conventional lives.[259] For many, prostitution is engaged in for limited financial and social purposes and is abandoned when these purposes are achieved.[260] These purposes are not irrational. Prostitutes have been described as the highest paid professional women in America.[261] There is no evidence that prostitution itself is necessarily an unpleasant experience for the prostitutes,[262] or that, in general, it disables them from engaging in other loving relationships;[263] indeed, there is some evidence that prostitutes, as a class, are more sexually fulfilled than other American women.[264] Many women have traditionally found in prostitution a useful escape from limited, oppressive, and parochial family[265] and career lives.[266] Prostitution, for them, is not adopted exclusively for economic reasons but because its urban life style affords a kind of social and cultural variety, color, glamor, and range of possibilities[267] that would not have been available to them otherwise.[268] In periods when women had no substantial access to social and economic mobility and the jobs available to them were underpaid and servile, the case for prostitution was rationally powerful.[269] With greater social and economic opportunities for women today, presumably the case for adopting this life is no longer as strong, but that is not to say that it is not still one of the number of ways in which people may rationally advance their ends. At the least, there is no good case for its irrationality, let alone the kind of irrationality required to bring paternalistic considerations into play.

It is important to see that the traditional arguments for the irrationality of rendering commercial services are typically based on mistaken distortions of the facts. It is as if the extant moralistic condemnation of prostitution inexorably shaped the reading of the facts so as to confirm that the putatively immoral conduct was personally irrational as well. Older accounts of prostitutes, for example, claim that they are mentally deficient[270] and have much shortened life spans because of the horrors of their work.[271] Psychiatrists have commonly supplied a psychiatric makeweight to the moral condemnations by claims that the prostitute is mentally ill or, at least, neurotic.[272] None of these claims has been sustained by careful empirical research observing sound scientific methods.[273] The older claims generally rested on the limited sample of people whom the researcher mistakenly believed to be typical of the research population at large. For example, a psychiatrist might mistakenly infer from the class of prostitutes who seek therapeutic help that all prostitutes need therapeutic help. In fact, some recent studies indicate that classes of prostitutes may be happier and healthier than other women.[274] In any event, the class of prostitutes whose life is more harsh, the streetwalkers, is precisely the class affected most directly by criminalization.[275] There is reason to believe that much of the harshness of their lives would be ameliorated by decriminalization.[276]

I do not wish to romanticize the facts of the life of a prostitute. Many accounts forcefully show how difficult and costly an occupation it can be,[277] but many recent accounts of women's traditional role show how difficult and costly that life also can be.[278] It is as much a mistake to romanticize the life of the traditional woman as it is to romanticize the life of the prostitute. When we look at these lives unsentimentally, without the distorting myths that obscure American perception of these matters, we cannot regard either as necessarily rational or irrational. Rather, we must look with care and imagination at how people autonomously make such choices, often between lesser evils or lesser disadvantages. When we do so, we can see that there is no ground whatsoever to believe that prostitution is, for a mature adult, irrational in the way required to justify paternalistic interference.

In similar fashion, the conventional arguments about the intrinsic irrationality of using commercial sexual services are misplaced. Recent studies of patrons of prostitutes show that patrons thereby secure forms of sexual release, comfort, and even therapeutic understanding.[279] In a period where the most advanced sex therapy often employs paid third parties to help a couple solve their sexual problems,[280] the role of a prostitute as a kind of therapist is a natural one.[281] Certainly, some patrons are able to achieve with prostitutes the natural and fulfilling expression of sexual tastes and fantasies that they cannot indulge in their marriages or central personal relationship.[282] It is dogmatic to assert that these people do not in this way more rationally advance their ends; to the contrary, the use of prostitutes is all *too* rational. Of course, in using prostitutes, a person does not cultivate the higher capacities of sensitivity, taste, and testing that the romantic love tradition celebrates. But such ideals are not without internal critical flaws and, in any event, are not a just basis for legal morality. Even the initiate of the mysteries of romantic love may, on occasion, need a recreational respite from the rigors of his or her path. Commercial sex thus may facilitate the pursuit of this ideal. Compared to the rigors of the frustrations and idealizations of romantic love, prostitution has virtues of its own: the understanding is unsentimentally clear, the recriprocal bargain fair, and the terms are met. Some would say that the best of romantic love does not quixotically repudiate such virtues. Rather, the best in romantic love is realized when the relationship is most realistic, fair, and reciprocal, for then the idealization of the beloved is not a distorting fantastic myth[283] endowed with the egocentric expectations of one's childhood,[284] but the celebration of realistic virtues more intensely felt because they meet unique, totally individual needs of a kind that mutual love comfortably discloses.[285] If so, romantic love and commercial sex may, at their best, express common moral virtues.

The radical vision of autonomy and mutual concern and respect is a vision of persons, *as such,* having human rights to create their own personal lives on terms fair to all. To see people in this way is to affirm basic intrinsic limits on the degree to which, even benevolently, one person may control the life of another. Within ethical constraints expressive of mutual concern and respect for autonomy, people are free to adopt a number of disparate and irreconcilable visions of the good life. Indeed, the adoption of different kinds of life plans, within these constraints, affords the moral good of different experiments in living by which people can more rationally assess such basic life choices. The invocation of inadequate moral and paternalistic arguments of the kind we have discussed violates these considerations of human rights, confusing unreflective personal ideology with the moral reasoning that alone can justify the deprivations of liberty by criminal penalty. At the least, such arguments fail to take rights seriously, and thus fail to take seriously the separateness of other persons, their different situations, perspectives, interests, and ideals, and their right to build a life with integrity from such individual materials.

IV. COMMERCIAL SEX, HUMAN RIGHTS, AND MORAL IDEALS

So far, we have considered a number of negative arguments directed at showing why various moral arguments condemning commercial sex are mistaken. Let us now constructively consider the affirmative case for allowing commercial sex, that is, for the existence of rights of the person that include the right to engage in commercial sex. In this way, we can clarify the scope and limits of this right and address in more systematic fashion the relation of this right to the personal ideals, frequently invoked previously, that the state allegedly has no right to enforce.

Let us reconsider the view of sexual autonomy that emerged in our discussion of romantic love and its relation to the contractarian analysis of human rights. We argued that human sexuality is marked by its powerful role in the imaginative life and general development of the person, and that the neutral theory of the good, expressive of the values of equal concern and respect for autonomy, required toleration of a number of different visions of the role of sexuality in human life. In the contractarian model, we express these ideas by saying that the choice in the original position is choice under uncertainty: rational people in the original position have no ways of predicting that they may end up in any given situation of life, and they must decide only on the basis of facts capable of interpersonal empirical validation. By definition, none of the contractors knows his or her own age, sex, native talents, particular capacity for self-control, social or economic class or position, or the particular form of his or her personal desires. Each contractor will be concerned not to end up in a disadvantaged situation, with no appeal to moral principles to denounce deprivations that may render life prospects bitter and mean. To avoid such consequences, the rational strategy in choosing the basic principles of justice would be the "maximin" strategy.

As we have suggested, the contractors in the original position would regard self-respect as the primary good. Accordingly, their aim would be to adopt principles that would ensure that people have the maximum chance of attaining self-respect. Sexual autonomy, the capacity to choose whether or how or with whom or on what terms one will have sexual relations, would be one crucial ingredient of this self-respect; it is one of the forms of personal competence in terms of which people self-critically decide, as free and rational agents, what kinds of persons they will be. Because contractors in the original position are assumed to be ignorant of specific identity and to take into account only those facts subject to general empirical validation, they may not appeal to special religious duties to procreate in order to override sexual liberty; nor may they appeal to any taste or distaste for certain forms of the physical expression of sexuality in order to override the interest in sexual autonomy; nor may they appeal to concepts of love that illegitimately smuggle in covert premises or prejudices incompatible with respect for the myriad paths to sexual fulfillment. As we have seen, self-respect in the fulfillment and expression of one's sexuality is compatible with a number of modes. Sexual love is one of these modes; romantic love is one highly special form of it. But meaningful sexual fulfillment takes other forms as well. From the point of view of the original position and the values of equal concern and respect for autonomy that it expresses, there is no form of sexual expression that can be given preferred status, for a large and indeterminate class of forms of sexual intercourse is compatible with autonomous self-respect. Accordingly, subject to qualifying moral principles shortly to be discussed, the contractors would, in order to secure the values of sexual self-respect, agree to a principle of obligation and duty, defining correlative human rights, requiring that people be guaranteed the greatest equal liberty of autonomous sexual expression compatible with a like liberty for all.

The contractarian model would, of course, also yield qualifying moral principles relevant to understanding the limits of this human right. Thus, on contractarian grounds, one may easily derive principles forbidding killing or the infliction of harm or gratuitous cruelty.[286] These principles would be accepted because they protect basic interests. Such moral principles are relevant to sexual expression; sexual partners should not inflict serious and irreparable bodily harm on one another, even if such harm is consensual. On the other hand, these principles would not justify prohibition of forms of consensual sexual conduct, including commercial sex, which are not harmful. Similarly, moral principles of fidelity can be derived from the original position,[287] requiring that mutual undertakings, voluntarily and maturely entered into, be observed faithfully. Such principles, again, do not justify general prohibition of forms of consensual sexual conduct, or commercial sex in particular;[288] they justify, at most, only specific constraints on breaches of fidelity, such as breach of contract, or fraud and deception.[289] A principle of consideration can also be derived from the original position, requiring that persons not impose upon others unnecessary annoyance and disturbances.[290] This principle would justify time, place, and manner restrictions on prostitution and its solicitation, but certainly not a complete prohibition.

In addition, the contractarian model justifies, as we have seen, a moral principle of paternalism in certain carefully delimited circumstances. This principle does not justify an absolute prohibition on consensual sexual conduct in general or commercial sex in particular. However, it is important to notice here that the imperative of sexual autonomy would not apply to persons presumably lacking rational capacities—young children, for example—since the value of autonomous sexual expression turns on the existence of developed capacities of rational choice. Accordingly, the sexual commerce of quite young children may be forbidden, just as sexual intercourse with and by them may be limited in various ways. One would need, of course, to determine the appropriate age of majority for those purposes, based on available psychological data. The most that can be said here is that the principle of paternalism would not sustain an unrealistically old age at which sexual nonage is ended.[291]

Finally, principles of distributive justice would be agreed to in the original position that would require a certain form of the distribution of wealth, property, status, and opportunity.[292] Sometimes it is suggested that prostitution is appropriately criminalized in order to advance the more just distribution of the goods required by such principles of distributive justice, on the grounds that prostitution is mainly a temptation to the poor and a symptom of poverty.[293] Of course, on grounds of distributive justice, people should have more equal job opportunities than they currently have. Certainly better job opportunities should, for example, be available to racial minorities and women. But it does not follow that high-income job opportunities that currently exist for poor people[294] should, on grounds of justice, be ended. If one wishes responsibly to ameliorate the situation of racial minorities, who contribute a disproportionate number of the women arrested for prostitution,[295] decriminalization, not criminalization, is the just course. It would remove the moral stigma and the consequent unjustified self-contempt that they experience, the various ancillary evils that criminalization fosters,[296] and the uniquely degrading exposure to the American criminal justice system[297] that their more advantaged call-girl sisters[298] in large part avoid. In addition, responsible moral concern for whatever economic disadvantages streetwalkers suffer would take the form of regulations to ensure them economic fairness, including forms of union organization. Criminalization, in contrast, fosters the economic exploitation that it is fallaciously assumed to remedy.[299]

To summarize, the principle of sexual autonomy does not apply to persons presumably lacking rational capacities, such as young children, nor does it validate the infliction of serious bodily harm. In addition, the liberty of sexual expression comports with the liberty of others to choose to be sexual partners. It follows, therefore, that there should be no moral objection on grounds of sexual autonomy to the reasonable regulation of consensual adult sex as regards time, manner, and place. For example, there is no objection to the reasonable regulation of the obtrusive solicitation of sexual relations. But the moral principles qualifying the principles of sexual autonomy do not justify any absolute prohibition of sexual autonomy of the kind that the criminalization of prostitution involves. Such criminal prohibitions flatly violate the rights of the person. These rights may not be abridged by vague appeals to public distaste that, if given the force of law, would dilute their moral force and transform them from a powerful vindication of autonomy into the empty and vapid idea that people be allowed to do that which gives rise to no strong objection.[300] Majority attitudes by themselves, unsupported by defensible moral reasoning,[301] cannot justify the deprivations of liberty of the criminal law. They are merely intractable prejudices that the state should circumscribe where necessary to protect the system of human rights, rather than elevate into law.

It is important to see the scope and limits of an argument grounded in human rights of the kind here presented. To say that a person has a human right to do "x" is a claim of political and legal morality, which justifies the claim that certain conduct must be protected by the state from forms of coercive prohibition. But justifiably to assert the existence of such a right is not to conclude the question whether people should exercise these rights. This latter question is an issue of personal morality, the disposition of which may turn on considerations that have no proper place in questions of political and legal morality.

Consider, for example, the moral right to choose one's work. Often, we take highly critical attitudes to these choices, arguing, for example, that someone's choice is a waste of talent or a refusal to take risks with his or her life. Such arguments are often not simply prudential calculations of the best rational way to realize the agent's ends, nor are they purely morally supererogatory,[302] for we do not merely praise appropriate choices, but assign a species of moral blame for failing to act on these ideals or for acting on the wrong ideals.[303] We may criticize, for example, ideals of competitive excel-

lence on the grounds that they are elitist or in various ways inhumane, or we may challenge obsessive venality as crudely selfish.
Such moral arguments are a central focus of civilized life, for they
help us to cultivate our autonomy self-critically and to change our
lives with reasonable integrity and sensitivity. However, while such
arguments help us as individuals to decide how we should exercise
our rights, they are often not relevant to discussions of whether we
have these rights. We are frequently very clear that people
unqualifiedly have rights that they should not exercise; when they do
exercise these rights in ways we deem morally undesirable, we say or
think they had the right to do the wrong thing. How are we to
understand this important distinction, which we understand and apply throughout our everyday lives?

In order to explicate this distinction, we must note the fundamental
difference between the kinds of questions addressed by questions of
moral rights and issues of moral and human ideals. When we reflect
on questions of human rights, we consider the general conditions
that must be guaranteed to facilitate the exercise and development of
human capacities for autonomy. Such rights define minimum boundary conditions, assuring people personal integrity and independence
compatible with a like integrity and independence for all. Within the
constraints established by these rights, broad latitude is given to persons to decide on their own how they will choose to exercise the
independence that rights guarantee. When we consider how people
should make these choices, we invoke consideration of various kinds,
prudential and moral. One form of moral consideration is a moral
ideal, which defines the particular form in which a person dedicates
his or her self to lesser or greater service to others and on what terms.
Such ideals often bear metaphorical analogies to the principles that
define human rights, but they go well beyond them. Some of them
are the supererogatory ideals of saints and heroes, which justify special praise when they are acted upon, but no blame when they are
not.[304] Others, not requiring excessive sacrifice of personal self-
interest, define various ways in which one may render humane service beyond the rights owed others. Often we criticize and blame
people for not including such moral ideals among their narrow and
parochial ends and aspirations.[305]

Criticism of the actions of others, based on such moral ideals, is
importantly limited by two factors: first, mistakes are likely in the
judgments of one person about the circumstances and ends of
another; and second, the standards of value against which we judge
issues of these kinds are vague and indeterminate.[306] Issues of this
kind are uniquely sensitive to personal idiosyncrasy and individual
context. Often, one person's critical judgments of another in this area

betray failures of imagination to understand the other's special relation to his or her own life, to appreciate the sacrifices a certain choice would require, or to assess with sensitivity the trade-offs among humane values. Such factors explain why moral arguments of these kinds are so important to our lives and justify forms of critical blame, but, on the other hand, debar us from more extensive interference into the lives of others. Nothing can be more important than constantly cultivating and challenging our critical imaginations about whether we are living our lives as humanely as we can, but our respect for personal separateness and individuality restrains us from coercive interference.

To say, therefore, that people have a human right to engage in commercial sex is not to conclude the question whether everyone should exercise this right. For example, we have discussed certain ideals of romantic love that a person might justifiably invoke in refusing to engage in commercial sex. Certainly such ideals cannot justifiably be invoked to qualify our general rights of sexual autonomy, for sexual self-respect and fulfillment do not require conformity to this ideal. Even in the purely personal sphere, as a personal moral ideal, romantic love may be criticized as sentimental, unrealistic, and lacking reciprocity. Nonetheless, a person, after careful purification of the ideal by criticism, may justifiably espouse a form of it as a moral ideal, regulate his or her life accordingly, and criticize others for not observing it and thus being less humane in their sexual lives than they could be. Certainly, moral ideals like romantic love are of incalculable cultural and human importance. Indeed, in some views, the ideal of romantic love has humanely and pervasively tempered personal relationships of sexual partners and even more widely.[307] On the other hand, legal enforcement of such an ideal imposes a personal ideal upon persons who may find it unfulfilling or even oppressive and exploitative.

V. BEYOND DECRIMINALIZATION

I have tried to establish that there are no good moral arguments for criminalizing consensual adult commercial sex, and that its punishment is a violation of the rights of the individual. The criminalization of prostitution appears to be an illegitimate vindication of unjust social hatred and fear of autonomously sexual women, and their rights to define and pursue their own vision of the good. Having given such reasons for decriminalizing prostitution, we are able to take a much less confining view of the legal treatment of prostitution. Let us briefly consider three alternatives: licensing; regulations of place, time, and methods; and no regulations at all. I assume throughout that per se criminal prohibitions of prostitution are repealed or otherwise invalidated.

A. *Licensing*

The licensing of prostitutes is of ancient vintage[308] and was widespread in Europe until this century.[309] The idea of licensing is that, in order to engage in commercial sex, one must secure a permit from the state that entails having one's name entered in a public record, various regulations of dress, price, and place of business and solicitation, and, in the widespread European practice, regular medical inspections for venereal disease.[310] The European justification for licensing focused on alleged venereal disease prophylaxis.[311] When these considerations were urged in Great Britain and the United States, they were successfully resisted by a constellation of powerful political forces, including purity reformers and feminists.[312] The arguments of the feminists were of two kinds, the second of which is still made by contemporary feminists, who urge decriminalization but condemn licensing:[313] first, an attack on the double standard, urging that men be compelled to heed the same standards of chastity exacted from women;[314] and second, the degrading nature of European licensing to women, including public records that made it difficult to leave the profession, various arbitrary regulations and demeaning inspections, and general failure to regulate brothels on terms fair to the prostitutes.[315] Official European licensing schemes were ended, in large part, in response to international conventions that bound nations to end the "white slave trade" in women and girls, which was alleged to be due largely to the demand for prostitutes occasioned by licensed brothels.[316]

None of these arguments would be decisive against some form of licensing if there were good independent reasons for such licensing. First, the appeal to the double standard rests on an unexamined valuation of chastity that made sense in a sexually hypocritical era, but that makes little sense today when the answer to the double standard appears to be not equal chastity but equal sexual freedom.[317] Second, the form of European licensing was arbitrarily demeaning to women because it was clearly designed not for the realistic protection of the rights of prostitutes, but for the protection of their male customers at all costs.[318] However, the excesses of licensing in Europe give no indication of the merits of a licensing scheme that would accommodate the rights of the prostitutes. Such a scheme, for example, could ensure adequate and fair protection for their business dealings without making regulatory authorities the moralistic and often sadistically retributive police, and could keep records of prostitutes absolutely confidential, destroying them when the prostitute leaves the profession. Third, the "white slave trade" argument appears to have been a moralistic attack on commercial sex per se, overstating and distorting the facts. Often the trade consisted of consenting mature adults who wished to travel to a foreign country to be prostitutes, not of underage girls or bound-and-gagged women.[319] Of course, there are moral objections to international traffic in compulsory adult or voluntary underage prostitution, but there are moral objections to prostitution itself in these forms. If this was the object of the "white slave" opponents, it should have been addressed as such, not in the form of hysterically overbroad arguments that trenched on the rights of mature adults to determine where and how they would live.[320]

The problem with licensing is not that there are good arguments against it, but that there are no powerful arguments for it. The argument of prophylaxis of venereal disease appears to be weak, as there is no compelling evidence that licensing realistically advances this end.[321] Less restrictive alternatives are available that would more rationally do so. For example, cheap and noncoercive medical inspections that prostitutes would have strong incentives to use could be made available.[322] Adequate protection of the rights of prostitutes and customers would be secured by fair enforcement of existing criminal laws against force and fraud. Probably the best way to aid prostitutes to protect themselves from unfair business dealings with customers and pimps would be to provide legal facilities in the form of unions of prostitutes, which would bring the force of collective, organizational self-protection to this atomistic profession.[323]

In general, licensing is an appropriate prerequisite to valid exercise of a service profession when there is a long professional education and when incompetence in providing the service will disastrously affect the interests of customers.[324] Prostitution does not appear to satisfy either of these conditions, although arguably the development of specialized classes of prostitutes (for example, specialists in initiating virgin youth into sex or in certain kinds of sexual and psychological therapy)[325] might at some point reasonably be subject to some form of licensing, on the grounds that special training is needed and that important customer interests are thus furthered.

B. *Regulations of Place, Time, and Method*

In continental Europe and England, regulations of place, time, and method take two different forms. First, in England street solicitation for prostitution is forbidden, so solicitation takes place through ambiguously worded advertisements in various journals or in certain

well-known locations.[326] A likely motive for the English form of regulation may have been the desire not that prostitution cease to be
centered in the well-known London theater and shopping district,
where it has familiarly been located, but that it cease to take the form
of the obtrusive solicitation that was distressing to many theater-
goers and shoppers, who could not conveniently avoid exposure to
unwelcome solicitations. The English solution was to end such street
solicitations entirely, requiring customers and prostitutes to seek one
another out by more discreet means. In continental Europe, the form
of regulation appears to be some form of zoning whereby solicitation
is legal only in certain well-known districts of the urban centers.[327] In
West Germany, Hamburg's famous Eros Center was intended to cen-
tralize prostitutes in one building complex.[328] Such businesslike cen-
tralization appears to be unappealing to customers and prostitutes
alike,[329] but prostitutes do tend to cluster in certain parts of town.[330]

In the event of decriminalization in the United States, the English
solution would clearly be appropriate to a city like New York, where
prostitution tends to cluster in the theater district and where absolute
prohibitions on solicitation would obviate the problem of obtrusive
solicitation of people who cannot conveniently avoid being in the
district on other business. As in London, there might be an interest in
concentrating prostitution in this area while attacking the problem of
obtrusive solicitation. However, first amendment considerations in
the United States might make the English solution of absolute prohibitions on solicitation unconstitutional.[331] A more precise solicitation
statute would have to be drawn in order to accommodate the interests
of prostitutes and customers and at the same time secure the rights of
others not to be subject to obtrusive solicitations. Obviously, much
further study must be made of this matter.

Alternatively, the continental European solution could be explored.
Forms of regulatory zoning could limit solicitation to certain well-
known parts of town little frequented by people on other business, so
that the interests of customers and prostitutes could be accom-
modated and obtrusive solicitations minimized.[332]

In addition to appropriate forms of zoning and solicitation regulations, consideration should be given to a limitation of commercial sex
to brothels, as is currently the case in Nevada.[333] Such regulations,
which are another form of licensing, are problematic in the absence of
effective regulations protecting the economic and social rights of
prostitutes and forms of unionization which would assure some measure of equal bargaining power to prostitutes.[334] The European history of such regulated brothels is a sorry one.[335] Certainly, forms of
brothel are not, in principle, illegitimate.[336] But to require that

brothels be the only form of legitimate commercial sex seems unwarranted.

C. *Laissez-Faire*

Finally, one may suggest a regime of laissez-faire. After decriminalization, there would be no licensing, nor any regulation, but only the application of existing criminal laws against force and fraud. The argument against forms of time, place, and manner regulation might suggest that such regulations are unnecessary. For all practical purposes, solicitations for prostitution occur in familiar locations where no reasonable person can claim surprise.[337] Furthermore, the presence of prostitution is, on balance, one of the colorful amenities of life in large urban centers. It should not be hidden and isolated, but robustly accepted as what in fact it is: an inextricable part of urban life.[338] In this view, forms of regulation are hypocritical and moralistic subterfuges of irresponsible politicians, who seek to accomplish by isolation what they cannot legitimately achieve by prohibition.[339] While these arguments for laissez-faire do understate the sound reasons for regulation, they raise a central question that we should discuss in conclusion: what are the general advantages of the availability of commercial sexual services.

VI. CONCLUSION

We began with the general claim that the decriminalization literature is defective in its failure to take seriously the kinds of moral judgments that should underlie the criminal law. Without making a serious attempt critically to examine these judgments, decriminalization proponents make arguments of utilitarian-based efficiency that do not explain why such costs are readily borne in some areas and regarded as excessive in others. The answer, we have argued, is that the cases that decriminalization proponents emphasize tend to be those in which underlying traditional moral judgments cannot be critically sustained, whereas other cases, which no one attempts to decriminalize despite comparably great enforcement costs, are sustained by still valid moral judgments. Thus, I have tried to show that more powerful, precise, and predictive decriminalization arguments are available when we discard the sterile utilitarianism of decriminalization advocates and harness serious moral theory to the analysis of these questions.

The arguments here proposed are of general significance not only to the practical guidance and advocacy of decriminalization but to criminal-law theory in general. We are now in a position to take seriously the moral foundations of the criminal law in a critical and reasonable way.[340] We focused on prostitution because it is a striking area in which decriminalization has made negligible progress. This lack of progress was attributed to the failure to confront seriously the underlying moral arguments. Judgments of the immorality of prostitution are, we have argued, wrong; indeed, the right to engage in commercial sex is one of the rights of the person which the state may not transgress. In addition to these moral arguments centering on rights of prostitute and patron, we should also note the amenity that prostitution has traditionally been in the development of complex anonymous urban civilization.[341] People often critically discuss the anomic atomism of urban life[342] in contrast to the intimate solidarity of rural life. But fair social description requires that we also note the special goods that urban anonymity has fostered and made possible: release from onerous clan and family restraints, personal experimentation and competitive risk-taking, freedom and variety and the excitement of less-bound horizons.[343] Prostitution, inevitably, has been part of this complex and variegated urban civilization, for traditionally prostitution has been one of the unconventional ways that women were able to tap some of the energy and promise of urban life.[344] The critical moral arguments here presented should, I hope, help release us from the American moralistic myopia that fails to see prostitution realistically as continuous with the other things we value in urban life: its liberty, diversity, and potential for individual risk-taking.

I have tried to attack critically the widespread American Manichean vision of the prostitute as a degenerate affront to American moral values who must be made an example at all costs.[345] When we scrutinize these values with care, we discover a remarkable and specifically American vision that explains the unique American treatment of prostitution. The prostitute is branded as the Puritans branded their deviants, as an evil and willful outcast whose criminal stigma supportively demarcates the ideals of the saints from the inexplicable and satanic evils of the sinner.[346] We must disclose this cruel vision for what it is: not a critical moral judgment but a remnant of a sectarian ideology secularized into a moral ideal of sentimental marriage that the condemnation of prostitution sanctifies. There is no better description of the cruel and morally ambiguous character of this Puritan vision than Shakespeare's Angelo[347] who, not acknowledging the continuity of prostitution with reasonable human interests and aspirations, isolates and denies his common humanity, and thus exemplifies the ultimate image of the unethical: self-righteously demanding of others, as judge, what one cannot oneself conform to as the judged. The moral condemnation of the prostitute rests on and expresses such isolation and denial, disfiguring the reasonable perception of the forms sex takes in our lives,[348] drawing sharply moralistic distinctions between the decent and the indecent when, in fact, there is a continuum of varying personal modes of sexual expression and fulfillment.[349] It is striking how deep in Western moral thought is the example of the condemnation of the prostitute as the paradigm of moral bad faith, of people's lack of moral title to cast the first stone.[350] When we extend to prostitutes concern and respect for their equality as persons,[351] we can see the source of the previous misperception. The failure to see the moral and human dignity of the lives of prostitutes is a moral failure of imagination and critical self-assessment:

> . . . man, proud man,
> Most ignorant of what he's most assur'd,
> His glassy essence, like an angry ape,
> Plays such fantastic tricks before high heaven
> As make the angels weep.[352]

NOTES

1. Examples of illegal conduct sometimes described as "victimless crimes" are drug and alcohol abuse, gambling, prostitution, and homosexuality. See N. Morris & G. Hawkins, *The Honest Politician's Guide to Crime Control* 2–6 (1970); H. Packer, *The Limits of the Criminal Sanction* 266 (1968); Kadish, "The Crisis of Overcriminalization," 374 *Annals* 157 (1967). See also *Model Penal Code*, §§ 207.1-6, Comments (Tent. Draft No. 4, 1955); Comm. on Homosexual Offenses and Prostitution, *Report of the Committee on Homosexual Offenses and Prostitution*, Cmnd. No. 247 (1957) [hereinafter cited as *Wolfenden Report*].

2. See notes 38–44, Chapter 1, supra, and text accompanying.

3. See, e.g., G. Jacobsohn, *Pragmatism, Statesmanship, and the Supreme Court* (1977). It would be a mistake to regard legal realists as doctrinaire utilitarians when, in fact, they were antagonistic to Bentham's ahistorical approach to jurisprudence. See, e.g., M. White, "The Revolt Against Formalism in American Social Thought of the Twentieth Century," in *Pragmatism and the American Mind* 41 (1973). See generally W. Twining, *Karl Llewellyn and the Realist Movement* (1973). But the appeal to social policy considerations was, for them, implicitly utilitarian. See Richards, "Book Review," 24 *N.Y. L. Sch. L. Rev.* 310 (1978).

4. O. W. Holmes, *The Common Law* (M. Howe ed. 1963).

5. The famous appeal to wash the law in cynical acid derives from Holmes, "The Path of the Law," 10 *Harv. L. Rev.* 457, 462 (1897).

6. See generally O. W. Holmes, supra note 4.

7. H.L.A. Hart appears to acknowledge the existence of a critical morality that is not necessarily utilitarian, although he does not explore the content of this morality in his discussion of decriminalization. See H.L.A. Hart, *Law, Liberty, and Morality*, 45, 52, 67–68 (1963). But see H.L.A. Hart, *Punishment and Responsibility* (1968), where he repeatedly insists that principles of fairness and equal liberty, independent of utilitarian considerations, are needed to account for the principles of punishment, id. 72–73, and

the form of excuses in the criminal law, id. 17–24. For a striking attempt by Hart to construct a nonutilitarian theory of natural rights from Kantian premises, see Hart, "Are There Any Natural Rights," in *Society, Law, and Morality* 173 (F. Olafson ed. 1961).

8. See R. Dworkin, *Taking Rights Seriously* (1977); D. A. J. Richards, *The Moral Criticism of Law* (1977) [hereinafter cited as D. A. J. Richards, *Moral Criticism*]; Richards, "Taking 'Taking Rights Seriously' Seriously: Reflections on Dworkin and the American Revival of Natural Law," 52 *N.Y.U. L. Rev.* 1265, 1331–38 (1977).

9. See J. Rawls, *A Theory of Justice* (1971); D. A. J. Richards, *A Theory of Reasons for Action* (1971) [hereinafter cited as D.A.J. Richards, *Reasons*]; A. Gewirth, *Reason and Morality* (1978).

10. See note 8 supra. See also G. Fletcher, *Rethinking Criminal Law* (1978); C. Fried, *Right and Wrong* (1978); C. Fried, *Contract as Promise* (1981).

11. Primary emphasis is usually given to such questions as the nature and role of the requirements of mens rea and actus reus, the proper form of excusing conditions and justification defenses, and the appropriate relation between inchoate and consummated offenses. The classic text is G. Williams, *Criminal Law* (2d ed. 1961). See also J. Hall, *General Principles of Criminal Law* (2d ed. 1960); W. LaFave & A. Scott, *Handbook on Criminal Law* (1972).

12. For a comparison of continental and Anglo-American approaches to criminal law theory, with a focus on the role of Kantian moral theory in the former and utilitarianism in the latter, see G. Fletcher, supra note 10.

13. See, e.g., J. Hall, supra note 11, at 385: "It is pertinent to recall here that the criminal law represents an objective ethics which must sometimes oppose individual convictions of right."

14. For a striking conventionalistic definition of the morally wrong as that which an ordinary man chosen at random from the Clapham omnibus would intuitively find disgustingly immoral, see P. Devlin, *The Enforcement of Morals* 9–13 (1965).

15. See notes 106–16, and text accompanying, in Chapter 2.

16. See note 1 supra. For specific arguments for the decriminalization of prostitution per se, see Bode, "New Life for the Oldest Profession," *The New Republic,* July 8 & 15, 1978, at 21; Haft, "Hustling for Rights," 1 *Civ. Lib. Rev.*, winter/spring 1974, at 8; Jennings, "The Victim as Criminal: A Consideration of California's Prostitution Law," 64 *Calif. L. Rev.* 1235 (1976); Roby & Kerr, "The Politics of Prostitution," 1972 *The Nation* 463; Rosenbleet & Pariente," "The Prostitution of the Criminal Law," 11 *Am. Crim. L. Rev.* 373 (1973); Vorenberg & Vorenberg, " 'The Biggest Pimp of All': Prostitution and Some Facts of Life," *The Atlantic,* January, 1977, at 27; Wade, "Prostitution and the Law: Emerging Attacks on the 'Women's Crime,' " 43 *U. Mo. Kan. City L. Rev.* 413 (1975); Wandling, "Decriminalization of Prostitution: The Limits of the Criminal Law," 55 *Or. L. Rev.* 553 (1976); "Prostitution: A Non-Victim Crime?" 8 *Issues in Criminology No. 2,* at 137 (1973); Note, "The Principle of Harm and Its Application to Laws Criminalizing Prostitution," 51 *Den. L.J.* 235 (1974).

17. All American states except Nevada currently criminalize prostitution. For a review of the various forms of the prohibitions, see Rosenbleet & Pariente, supra note 16, at 422–27. There has been no substantial movement toward legislative decriminalization of the kind found in the area of consensual sodomy. See note 20 infra. In this connection, it should be noted that the *Model Penal Code,* which recommended the decriminalization of noncommercial consensual adult sexual relations, did not follow the *Wolfenden Report,* which recommended in addition that prostitution not be criminalized. Compare *Model Penal Code* § 207.51(1), Comment (Tent. Draft No. 4, 1955) (noncommercial sex recommendation) with *Model Penal Code* § 207.12, Comment (Tent. Draft No. 9, 1959) (commercial sex recommendation). Attacks on the constitutionality of antiprostitution statutes, unsurprisingly, have also failed. See *Morgan v. City of Detroit,* 389 F. Supp. 922 (E.D. Mich. 1975); *United States v. Moses,* 339 A.2d 46 (D.C. 1975), cert. denied, 426 U.S. 920 (1976). But cf. *in re P.,* 92 Misc. 2d 62, 400 N.Y.S.2d 455 (Fam. Ct. 1977) (successful attack on the New York prostitution statute as applied to a 14-year old), a decision, however, reversed on appeal.

18. See *Carey v. Population Servs. Int'l*, 431 U.S. 678 (1977); *Eisenstadt v. Baird*, 405 U.S. 438 (1972); *Griswold v. Connecticut*, 381 U.S. 479 (1965).

19. See *Roe v. Wade*, 410 U.S. 113 (1973).

20. The Supreme Court recently upheld the refusal to extend the constitutional right to privacy to consensual adult homosexuality. *Doe v. Commonwealth's Attorney for Richmond*, 425 U.S. 901 (1976), aff'g mem., 403 F. Supp. 1199 (E.D. Va. 1975) (three-judge court). However, there has been a gradual movement toward decriminalization of consensual sodomy by legislative repeal. As of 1976, at least 18 states had decriminalized sodomy. See Rizzo, "The Constitutionality of Sodomy Statutes," 45 *Fordham L. Rev.* 553, 570 n.93 (1976). A more recent overview indicates that 21 states have decriminalized. See Rivera, "Our Straight-Laced Judges: The Legal Position of Homosexual Persons in the United States," 30 *Hastings L.J.* 799, 950–51 (1979). For criticism of *Doe* and an argument that the constitutional right to privacy should encompass homosexuality, see Chapter 2.

21. For attempts to argue that various of these activities are not immoral, see R. Atkinson, *Sexual Morality* 132–79 (1965) (homosexuality and contraception); J. Wilson, *Logic and Sexual Morality* (1965); Margolis, "The Question of Homosexuality," in *Philosophy & Sex* 238 (R. Baker & F. Elliston eds. 1975). See also Wasserstrom, "Is Adultery Immoral?" in *Philosophy & Sex*, supra at 207–21.

22. For example, Bertrand Russell, who in general defended the much freer premarital and extramarital expression of romantic love, regarded prostitution as intrinsically morally degraded. See B. Russell, *Marriage and Morals* 150–53 (1929).

23. See A. Sion, *Prostitution and the Law* 43–50 (1977). For the treatment in other developed countries, see id. 33–43, 50–54. Sion's discussion of comparably developed countries is limited to the nations of Western Europe that are committed to forms of effective parliamentary constitutional democracy. Communist countries tend not to criminalize prostitution, but to engage in forms of aggressive rehabilitation. For the experience in the People's Republic of China, which claims to have no prostitution, see R. Sidel, *Women and Child Care in China* 50–51 (1972). The Soviets appear to have used not criminal penalties but forms of stigmatizing publicity directed against patrons, identified by name in a public bulletin as "Buyers of the Bodies of Women." L. Kanowitz, *Women and the Law* 17–18 (1969). A recent excellent study of British sex law regards the Marxist repression of prostitution as one of the crucial marks of these nations' failure to respect basic liberties of the person. See. T. Honore, *Sex Law* 116, 134, 165 (1978). One author alleges the United States is the only country in the world to criminalize prostitution as such. Sagarin, "Sexual Criminality," in *Current Perspectives on Criminal Behavior* 138, 150 (A. Blumberg ed. 1974).

24. For a similar methodology, see M. Foucault, *The Archaeology of Knowledge* (A. M. Sheridan Smith trans. 1972).

25. A. Kinsey, W. Pomeroy & C. Martin, *Sexual Behavior in the Human Male* 595 (1948). Other authors have offered the following definitions in current literature: "Prostitution is the act of a woman repeatedly and constantly practicing the sexual relationship with anybody, on demand without choosing or refusing any partner, for gain, freely and without force, her principal object being profit and not pleasure," J. Mancini, *Prostitutes and Their Parasites* 14 (1963); "Prostitution consists of any sexual acts, including those which do not actually involve copulation, habitually performed by individuals with other individuals of their own or the opposite sex, for a consideration which is non-sexual." 1 F. Henriques, *Prostitution and Society* 17 (1962); "Prostitution . . . [is] promiscuity—even transient promiscuity,—of sex relationship [sic] for pay, or its equivalent," A. Flexner, *Prostitution in Europe* 16 (1914); "Prostitution . . . [is] promiscuous unchastity for gain," W. East, *Society and the Criminal* 242 (1949); "Prostitution is the common lewdness of a woman for gain," R. Perkins, *Criminal Law* 392 (2d ed. 1969); "[P]rostitution exists when a woman (or a man) engages in sexual relations for other than sexual or amative motives," Benjamin, "Prostitution," in 2 *The Encyclopedia of Sexual Behavior* 869, 871 (A. Ellis & A. Abarbanel eds. 1961); "[I]t can generally be defined as the granting of nonmarital sexual access, establishᵔd by mutual agreement

of the woman, her client, and/or her employer, for remuneration which provides part or all of her livelihood," C. Winick & P. Kinsie, *The Lively Commerce* 3 (1971); "A prostitute is an individual, female or male, who for some kind of reward, monetary or otherwise, or for some form of personal satisfaction other than purely for the gratification of an awareness of love, and as a part-time or whole-time profession, engages in normal or abnormal sexual intercourse with a number of persons, who may be of the same sex as, or the opposite sex to, herself or himself," G. Scott, *Ladies of Vice* 13 (1968).

26. M. Ploscowe, *Sex and the Law* 226 (rev. ed. 1962) (emphasis deleted). Compare this definition with those of A. Flexner and Benjamin, supra note 25.

27. The *Model Penal Code* identifies sixteen states whose statutes define prostitution to include promiscuous intercourse without hire, *Model Penal Code* § 217.12, Comment at 175 n.24 (Tent. Draft No. 9, 1959). The tendency, reflected in such statutes, to assimilate the moral status of the lost virginity of the seduced and abandoned woman to that of the prostitute appears to have led, as a kind of self-fulfilling prophecy, to many of these women becoming prostitutes. See, e.g., K. Chesney, *The Victorian Underworld* 315 (1970); L. Stone, *The Family, Sex and Marriage in England* 1500–1800, at 601–2 (1977).

28. The influential definition of the *Model Penal Code* states:

A person who engages, or offers or agrees to engage in sexual activity for hire, or is an inmate of a house of prostitution, or enters this state or any political subdivision thereof to engage in prostitution, commits a petty misdemeanor. Such activity is hereinafter referred to as prostitution, and the actor is referred to as a prostitute.

Model Penal Code § 207.12(1) (Tent. Draft No. 9, 1959).

29. On the constitutional infirmities of more restrictive definitions of prostitution, see Rosenbleet & Pariente, supra note 16, at 381–403.

30. See note 25 supra.

31. The *Model Penal Code* commentary emphasizes that "only sexual activity 'for hire' is included" in the definition. *Model Penal Code* § 207.12(1), Comment at 174 (Tent. Draft No. 9, 1959). See also note 33 infra.

32. The *Uniform Crime Reports* issued by the Federal Bureau of Investigation indicate that 74% of the persons arrested for "prostitution and commercialized vice" in 1972 were women. See Federal Bureau of Investigation, *Crime in the United States—1972: Uniform Crime Reports* 130 (1973). As one author stated, "[p]rostitutes in the aggregate are primarily a one-sex, female group." Lemert, "Prostitution," in *Problems of Sex Behavior* 68, 69 (E. Sagarin & D. MacNamara eds. 1968). Indeed, prostitution appears to be the only sexual offense for which women are prosecuted to any significant extent. See H. Katchadourian & D. Linde, *Fundamentals of Human Sexuality* 517 (2d ed. 1975). Yet female prostitutes have male customers, who are equally legally culpable, and homosexual male prostitution exists. For discussions of homosexual prostitution, see H. Benjamin & R. Masters, *Prostitution and Morality* 286–337 (1964); D. Drew & J. Drake, *Boys for Sale: A Sociological Study of Boy Prostitution* (1969); R. Lloyd, *For Love or Money* (1976); C. Winick & P. Kinsie, supra note 25, at 89–96; Deisher, "Homosexual Prostitution," *Med. Aspects Human Sexuality*, Aug., 1975, at 85; Gandy & Deisher, "Young Male Prostitutes: The Physician's Role in Social Rehabilitation," 212 *J.A.M.A.* 1661, 1662 (1970). Male prostitutes are very seldom apprehended by the law because of a general lack of societal concern. See C. Winick & P. Kinsie, supra note 25, at 89. For example, out of 3,475 boys in a Philadelphia cohort who became recorded delinquents sometime by their seventeenth birthday, only one had been apprehended for prostitution. M. Wolfgang, R. Figlio, & T. Sellin, *Delinquency in a Birth Cohort* 68–69 (1972). Failure to prosecute male patrons has been rationalized by the *Model Penal Code* as follows: "Imposition of severe penalties is out of the question, since prosecutors, judges and juries would be likely to regard extramarital intercourse for males as a necessary evil or even as socially beneficial." *Model Penal Code* § 207.12(1), Comment at 180 (Tent. Draft No. 9, 1959). Failure to prosecute homosexual prostitution has been explained "because it is

fairly concentrated and offends relatively few people," C. Winick & P. Kinsie, supra note 25, at 89. If we ask ourselves why prostitution involving men is not regarded as culpable, we face issues of special concern for female sexuality. As one judge argued in justifying punishing the prostitute but not the customer, "a study of the history of prostitution from ancient times down to the present day leaves one with this underlying thought: Wherever suppressive or punitive measures were employed, they were directed against the female, not the male." *People v. Anonymous*, 161 Misc. 379, 383, 292 N.Y.S. 282, 286 (1936). For recent constitutional attacks on such enforcement patterns under anti-prostitution laws, see L. Kanowitz, supra note 23, at 15–18; Rosenbleet & Pariente, supra note 16, at 403–11.

33. The *Model Penal Code* explains its "for hire" requirement as follows: "It should be noted also that a law punishing promiscuous, but non-commercial, sex activity would reach all males who seek sexual gratification indiscriminately, whether with professional prostitutes or amateur partners. This would involve contradiction of our policies on illicit extramarital relations generally." *Model Penal Code* § 207.12(1), Comment at 175 (Tent. Draft No. 9, 1959).

34. The continuity of the motives of conventional women in marrying with those of a prostitute is one of Mrs. Warren's main points in her defense of her profession to her daughter. See G. B. Shaw, "Mrs. Warren's Profession," in *Plays Unpleasant* 249–50 (Penguin 1975). Of her defense, Shaw observes: "Mrs. Warren's defence of herself is not only bold and specious, but valid and unanswerable," id. 201.

35. On these problems of line-drawing, see H. Benjamin & R. Masters, supra note 32, at 21–32.

36. For evidence on the historical growth of pre-marital sexuality, see E. Shorter, *The Making of the Modern Family* 79–119 (1975). On contemporary extramarital patterns, see J. Smith & L. Smith, *Beyond Monogamy* (1974).

37. See, generally 4 H. Ellis, *Studies in the Psychology of Sex* 218–54 (1910).

38. See, e.g., V. Bullough, *The History of Prostitution* 9–15 (1964).

39. See H. Ellis, supra note 37, at 226–28; G. Scott, A *History of Prostitution from Antiquity to the Present Day* 53–58 (1936). Scott does, however, interpret many preurban sexual practices as almost equivalent to prostitution. Id.

40. This conclusion is reflected in the findings of a leading student of cross-cultural sexual practices, reviewing the cross-cultural data:

> Prostitution is not a problem in these societies. Nothing comparable to prostitution as it appears in civilized western societies today . . . is to be found in the societies of our sample. There are widespread customs of gift-giving as a prelude to or aftermath of sexual favors, oftentimes an exchange of gifts between the sex partners. But these customs can scarcely be thought of in the same light as prostitution, in which sexual favors are traded for a price. They are much more akin to the small favors a suitor in our society may bestow upon the girl of his choice in the form of candy or flowers.

Ford, "Sex Offenses: An Anthropological Perspective," 25 *Law & Contemp. Prob.* 225, 227 (1960). See also, C. Ford & F. Beach, *Patterns of Sexual Behavior* 98–99 (1951).

41. See H. Ellis, supra note 37, at 228.

42. V. Bullough, supra note 38, at 17–30; H. Ellis, supra note 37, at 228–38; W. Sanger, *The History of Prostitution* 35–42 (1897); G. R. Scott, supra note 39, at 59–66.

43. Herodotus, *Histories* Book 1, Ch. cxcix. The accuracy of this account, however, is questionable.

44. See H. Ellis, supra note 37, at 218–23.

45. See generally H. Frankfort, *Before Philosophy* (1961); H. Frankfort, *Kingship and the Gods* (1948).

46. See V. Bullough, supra note 38 at 36–37; H. Ellis, supra note 37, at 229–34; H. Licht [P. Brandt], *Sexual Life in Ancient Greece* 388–95 (J. Freese trans. 1932).

47. See V. Bullough, supra note 38, at 31–44; H. Ellis, supra note 37, at 234; H. Licht, supra note 46, at 329–63; S. Pomeroy, *Godesses, Whores, Wives, and Slaves* 88–92 (1975); W. Sanger, supra note 42, at 43–63; G. Scott, supra note 39, at 78–79.

48. Solon was reported to have established brothels as a state monopoly. The prostitutes in these brothels, called *dicteriades*, were typically foreigners, and were subject to a number of regulations, including strict segregation from reputable women, a special costume, forfeiture of any natal citizenship rights, and various legal disabilities for their children. See W. Sanger, supra note 42, at 43–44; G. Scott, supra note 39, at 78–79.

49. In Rome, prostitutes were required to register with the state and were subject to various regulations, including requirement of a special costume, certain prohibitions on marriage, and exclusion from certain temples. See V. Bullough, supra note 38, at 45–53; O. Kiefer, *Sexual Life in Ancient Rome* 55–63 (1934); W. Sanger, supra note 42, at 64–68; G. Scott, supra note 39, at 80–83.

50. See note 48 supra. Solon's Athenian brothels, a state monopoly, charged patrons a small set fee.

51. See V. Bullough, supra note, 38 at 31–53; H. Licht, supra note 46, at 332–63; W. Sanger, supra note 42, at 47–63, 68–70; G. Scott, supra note 39, at 76–80. On the contemporary distinctions, see H. Benjamin & R. Masters, supra note 32, at 119–91; C. Winick & P. Kinsie, supra note 25 at 131–84.

52. There was a remarkable class of women, the *hetairae*, who, unlike most Greek women, were permitted deep contact with masculine artistic and political culture. See V. Bullough, supra note 38 at 31–44; H. Licht, supra note 46 at 339–63.

53. See V. Bullough, supra note 38, at 91–103.

54. Sarah B. Pomeroy notes that "[t]he *hetaira* had access to the intellectual life of Athens, which we nowadays treasure, and a popular courtesan who was not a slave had the freedom to be with whoever pleased her," S. Pomeroy, supra note 47, at 92, but then carefully concludes that "the fact that we know of some courtesans who attempted to live as respectable wives, while we know of no citizen wives who wished to be courtesans, should make us reconsider the question of which was the preferable role in Classical Athens—companion or wife." Id. The entire classical Greek society regarded spending money on commercial sex as discreditable. See K. Dover, *Greek Popular Morality in the Time of Plato and Aristotle* 210 (1974). Thus, male homosexual relations, which were conventional and praised in ancient Athens, were discredited when done for money, the male prostitute losing his citizenship rights in perpetuity; apparently the male prostitute was viewed as degraded by his identification with the category of female prostitutes, who were non-citizens, largely of slave status. See id. 215–216.

The Romans appear to have had an even less romantic view of prostitution than the Greeks. See V. Bullough, supra note 38, at 45–53. Brothels were encouraged, but Cicero, for example, entered them "with covered head and face concealed in his cloak," H. Ellis, supra note 37, a 239.

55. See V. Bullough, supra note 38, at 48–49; S. Pomeroy, supra note 47, at 88–89. Comparable phenomena existed in China, V. Bullough, supra note 38, at 100–01, and in seventeenth century England, L. Stone, supra note 27, at 616–17.

56. See notes 48–49 supra.

57. In ancient Athens, for example, men did not usually marry until the age of 30, and respectable women were not available for premarital intercourse. See S. Pomeroy, supra note 47, at 91. In England, during the period when prostitution flourished, the age of marriage rose to 26 or older, and the younger sons often were not permitted to marry at all; respectable women were not available for premarital or extramarital intercourse. See L. Stone, supra note 27, at 615–20. In Italy, during the comparable period, promiscuity was more common among married women; consequently, prostitution was kept at a fairly low level. Id. 619.

In contemporry Sweden, there is reported to be little prostitution. See N. Elliott, *Sensuality in Scandinavia* 255 (1970); D. Jenkins, *Sweden and the Price of Progress* 203 (1968); B. Linner, *Sex and Society in Sweden* 90 (1967). This is generally attributed to liberal attitudes toward extramarital sex in Sweden. See N. Elliott, supra, at 255. In Sweden, 90% of the boys and 75% of the girls have had sexual intercourse by the age of seventeen. Id. 9.

58. See generally, H. Ellis, supra note 37, at 226–28. For an example of the form that

this rising class of urban poor woman historically took, see L. Stone, *supra* note 27, at 616–19. See also K. Chesney, *supra* note 27, at 314–15.

59. See note 54 *supra*.

60. See note 52 *supra*.

61. See e. g., K. Dover, *supra* note 54, at 95–102; S. Pomeroy, *supra* note 47, at 85.

62. See generally Aristotle, *Politics*, 1253b–1256a.

63. See V. Bullough, *supra* note 38, at 45–53; O. Kiefer, *supra* note 49, at 63.

64. This phrase appears in Catholic theological commentaries on the obscene and unnatural. See, e.g., Gardiner, "Moral Principles Toward a Definition of the Obscene," 20 *Law & Contemp. Prob.* 560, 567 (1955).

65. See Augustine, *The City of God* 577–94 (H. Bettenson trans. 1972) (1st ed. 413–426 A. D.). St. Thomas is in accord with Augustine's view. Of the emission of semen apart from procreation in marriage, he wrote: "[A]fter the sin of homicide whereby a human nature already in existence is destroyed, this type of sin appears to take next place, for by it the generation of human nature is precluded." 3 T. Aquinas, *On the Truth of the Catholic Faith: Summa Contra Gentiles* pt. 2, ch. 122 (9), at 146 (V. Bourke trans. 1946).

66. See the fuller discussion of Augustine's position at text accompanying notes 59–69, Chapter 2, *supra*.

67. One prominent account of the Catholic view notes that Catholic canon law "holds, as a basic and cardinal fact, that complete sexual activity and pleasure is licit and moral only in a naturally completed act in valid marrige. All acts which of their psychological and physical nature, are designed to be preparatory to the complete act, take their licitness and morality from the complete act. If, therefore, they are entirely divorced from the complete act, they are distorted, warped, meaningless, and hence immoral." Gardiner, *supra* note 64, at 564. See also T. Bouscaren, A. Ellis & F. Korth *Canon Law* 936 (1963); H. Gardiner, *Catholic Viewpoint on Censorship* 62–67 (1958). But see R. Haney, *Comstockery in America* (1960).

68. Thus, Augustine notes that not only is sexual impulse "totally opposed to the mind's control, it is quite often divided against itself," Augustine, *supra* note 65, at 577: that is, when we want to experience such feelings, we often cannot; and when we don't want to experience them, we do.

69. St. Augustine, commenting on prostitution asked:

What can be called more sordid, more void of modesty, more full of shame than prostitutes, brothels, and every evil of this kind? Yet remove prostitutes from human affairs, and you will pollute all things with lust; set them among honest matrons, and you will dishonor all things with disgrace and turpitude.

Augustine, *De Ordine*, II.4 (12).

70. St. Thomas observed that prostitution is "like the filth in the sea, or a sewer in a palace. Take away the sewer, and you will fill the palace with pollution; and likewise with the filth (in the sea). Take away prostitutes from the world, and you will fill it with sodomy." T. Aquinas, *Opuscula* XVI (IV in 1875 Paris ed.).

71. The most notable attempt during this period to extirpate prostitution was made by King and Saint Louis IX of France. For a general description of the medieval approach and of Louis' deviation from it, see V. Bullough, *supra* note 38, at 57–68, 107–26; H. Ellis, *supra* note 37, at 239–41; W. Sanger, *supra* note 42, at 86–131; G. Scott, *supra* note 39, at 89–94.

72. Luther attacked the hypocrisy of the Catholic religious who, although licentious themselves, demanded purity of women:

In order to attain the very summit of sanctity, a man is prohibited access to the priesthood if he has married a girl who was not a virgin, though he may have done so in ignorance, and by unfortunate mischance. But he may have had vile commerce with six hundred prostitutes, and seduced countless matrons and virgins, and kept many mistresses, yet nothing of this would be an impediment, and prevent his becoming a bishop, or a cardinal, or a pope.

M. Luther, *Selections from His Writings* 347 (J. Dillenberger ed. 1961).

73. See generally Luther, "The Natural Place of Women," in *Sexual Love and Western Morality* 134–43 (D. Verene ed. 1972).

74. The literature on the romantic love tradition is enormous. See e.g., H. Kelly, *Love and Marriage in the Age of Chaucer* (1975); C. S. Lewis, *The Allegory of Love* (1953); C. Morris, *The Discovery of the Individual 1050–1200 (1972);* D. Robertson, Jr., *A Preface to Chaucer* 391–503 (1962); J. Stevens, *Medieval Romance* (1973); M. Valency, *In Praise of Love* (1958). For a critique of the tradition, see D. de Rougemont, *Love in the Western World* (M. Belgion trans. 1956). For later developments, see M. Praz, *The Romantic Agony* (A. Davidson trans. 1933). For the relation of the tradition to the rise of the courtesan, see V. Bullough, supra note 38, at 117–26.

75. See note 73 supra; V. Bullough, supra note 38, at 128–31. Calvin's view of marriage, if anything, is more romantic than Luther's. Id. 129–30.

76. For Luther's violent attack on prostitution, see Luther, supra note 73, at 141–42. Correspondingly, Luther condemns homosexuality as "inhuman, satanic," id. 142–43. For the radical change this led to in attacking prostitution, see V. Bullough, supra note 38, at 130–31.

77. See W. Sanger, supra note 42, at 298.

78. See text accompanying notes 57–58 supra; L. Stone, supra note 27, at 615–20.

79. See generally E. Bristow, *Vice and Vigilance* (1977); M. Pearson, *The Age of Consent* (1972).

80. See Butler's attack on the double standard before a parliamentary commission, excerpted in M. Pearson, supra note 79, at 70. The moral justifiability of the double standard had been questioned by the Roman jurist Ulpian: "It seems to be very unjust that a man demands chastity of his wife while he himself shows no example of it." Ulpian, *Digest* XLVIII, 13, 5. Contemporary feminists note with regret that those aligned with Josephine Butler "did not take their understanding of every woman's fellowship with whores that bit further and investigate the potential of sexual expression for women rather than continence for men," Warner, "The Chastity Lobby," *Times Literary Supplement*, July 14, 1978, at 793.

81. See note 79 supra; G. Scott, supra note 39, at 97–103.

82. See generally A. Flexner, supra note 25.

83. *Wolfenden Report,* supra note 1.

84. See generally A. Sion, supra note 23, at 52.

85. Id. 64–72. Other forms of solicitation do occur in certain quasi-public places. Id. 54–64.

86. See V. Bullough, supra note 38., at 187–89.

87. See A. Douglas, *The Feminization of America Culture* (1977).

88. The underlying ideal appears to have been based on "stereotypes of ideal feminine virtue," id. 157, which ahistorically celebrated "the romance of domestic management," id. 185. In medical literature current in Victorian America, these ideas were expressed by the evolutionary purification of sexual feeling into asexual sentiment that women allegedly epitomized. See J. Haller & R. Haller, *The Physician and Sexuality in Victorian America* 126–27 (1974).

89. For Anthony's involvement with the aims of the purity leagues, see D. Pivar, *Purity Crusade* 51–52. (1973).

90. See generally id.

91. See G. Scott, supra note 39, at 103–07.

92. See generally W. Sanger, supra note 42.

93. For the history of this movement in the twentieth century, see C. Winick & P. Kinsie, supra note 25, at 211–43. For previous history, see V. Bullough, supra note 38, at 187–98.

94. See note 17 supra; C. Winick & P. Kinsie, supra note 25, at 221–23.

95. See W. Sanger, supra note 42, at 139–54; G. Scott, supra note 39, at 96–97.

96. See note 82 supra.

97. See V. Bullough, supra note 38, at 173–85.

98. See *International Agreement for the Suppression of the "White Slave Traffic,"* March 18, 1904, 35 Stat. 1979, T.S. No. 496, 1 L.N.T.S. 83; *International Convention for the Suppression of the Traffic in Women and Children,* Sept. 30, 1921, 116 B.F.S.P. 547, 9 L.N.T.S. 415.

99. See *Protocol Amending the International Agreements and Conventions on the White Slave Traffic*, May 4, 1949, 2 U.S.T. 1997, T.I.A.S. No. 2332, 30 U.N.T.S. 23; *Protocol to Amend the Convention for the Suppression of the Traffic in Women and Children* of Sept. 30, 1921, Nov. 12, 1947, 14 B.F.S.P. 871, 53 U.N.T.S. 13; *Convention for the Suppression of the Traffic in Persons and of the Exploitation of the Prostitution of Others*, March 21, 1959, 157 B.F.S.P. 482, 96 U.N.T.S. 271.

100. See M. Pearson, supra note 79, at 58–83.

101. See H. Benjamin & R. Masters, supra note 32, at 415–27; C. Winick & P. Kinsie, supra note 25, at 269–80.

102. Consider, for example, France, Netherlands, and West Germany. The French Penal Code contains provisions prohibiting procuring, pandering, and pimping, *The French Penal Code* art. 334 (G. Mueller ed. 1960), as well as keeping, or assisting one in keeping, a house of prostitution, id. art. 335; but the act of prostitution itself is not illegal. Solicitation is a simple misdemeanor punishable by no more than a small fine and a jail term of several days. J. Mancini, supra note 25, at 64–65. It is interesting to note that when the French Interior Minister ordered a nationwide crackdown on vice in 1975, which was followed by a brief crackdown on prostitutes in that country, the prostitutes went on strike and also commenced sit-in protests in various churches. *Time*, June 16, 1975, at 33. The prostitutes were demanding decriminalization of solicitation as well as social security and old age benefits. *Newsweek*, June 23, 1975, at 42. Interestingly, councilperson Marthe Richard, who sponsored the abolition of France's licensing of brothels, is now at the center of the movement to reinstitute houses of prostitution. See *International Herald Tribune*, Aug. 25–26, 1973, at 5; *N.Y. Times*, Aug. 16, 1970, at 13; *Time*, Nov. 9, 1970, at 30.

In Holland, any promotion of a brothel or habitual procuration of a person into prostitution is illegal, *Wetboek Van Strafrecht* [Code of Criminal Law of Holland] art. 250 (1973); and pimping is illegal, id. art. 432. Although the Code of Criminal Law of Holland contains no prohibition of prostitution per se, local government regulations do so. While most outlaw all prostitution, the large cities permit it in certain districts of the city; even in such areas, regulations are imposed. For example, an article of the *Regulations of Amsterdam* prohibits prostitution in certain enumerated areas of the city and solicitation for purposes of prostitution in all sections of the city, including the districts where prostitution is allowed. *Regulations of Amsterdam* art. 223 (1973). For a detailed description of the red-light district known as Zeedijk, located in one of the oldest centers of Amsterdam, see A. Mankoff, *Mankoff's Lusty Europe* 119–21 (1974). The effects of the national and local legislation are elimination, as in England, of the obtrusive solicitation aspects of prostitution by disallowing solicitation everywhere and prostitution in many areas, and protection of the prostitute from exploitation by pimps or the madams of traditional brothels.

In West Germany, there are controls on procuring and pandering, *German Penal Code of 1871*, ch. 13, §§ 180–181 (G. Mueller ed. 1961), and on pimping id. ch. 13, § 181a, but prostitution itself is not illegal. Those involved in the commission of prostitution are subject to various strictures, which include prohibitions of blatant annoyance to the public at large, id. ch. 13, § 183, and of various forms of obtrusive solicitation and acts of prostitution carried out near churches, schools, or children. They also include ordinances passed by municipalities aimed at repressing all prostitution within their boundaries. Id. ch. 29, § 361(6). The federal restrictions on houses of prostitution are complemented by state and local proscriptions which are more particular in nature. Houses of prostitution are allowed if they concentrate the prostitutes in such fashion as to make them controllable and if the community allows the houses to exist. The state governments of the federal republic have some degree of veto power over the existence of houses in its various communities, the extent of the veto power varying with the size of the community (in smaller communities prostitution may be prohibited entirely; in large communities, in parts of the community only). Art. 3 *Zehntes, Strafrechtsänderungsgesetz*, April 7, 1970, BGBl I 313. The local governmental unit generally imposes ordinances of its own on the prostitutes and the brothel, including regular visits by prostitutes to a venereal disease inspection center and provisions as to hours and days open for business. Accordingly, the modus operandi of the West German prostitute is dependent on the combination of laws in effect in the particular political subdivision in which the prostitute operates. In several areas of West Germany, notably Hamburg and West Berlin, various forms of sexual service are readily available. For a description of the Hamburg forms of regulated prostitution, see A. Sion, supra note 23, at 37–41.

For a useful general study of prostitution laws, including comparative law data, see J. F. Decker, *Prostitution: Regulation and Control* (1979).

103. See M. Ploscowe, supra note 26, at 247; G. Sheehy, *Hustling* 16 (1973).

104. See, e.g., B. Karpman, *The Sexual Offender and His Offenses*, 609 (1954).

105. See Esselstyn, "Prostitution in the United States," in *Sex and Society* 115 (J. Edwards ed. 1972).

106. See note 102 supra.

107. See Burstin & James, "Prostitution in Seattle," 6 *Wash. St. B. News* Aug./Sept., 1971, at 5, 28. To the extent that arguments for criminalization of prostitution are based on deterrence of violence, they are overinclusive in light of increasing evidence of violence within the marriage relationship. Clearly we would not consider a prohibition on marriage to combat this violence; similarly with prostitution, alternatives to criminalization could adequately protect both prostitute and client.

108. "Of the nondrug crimes, shoplifting, burglary, and prostitution account for the largest proportion of addict income used for drug purchases—perhaps 40 to 50 per cent," J. Wilson, *Thinking About Crime* 139 (1975) (footnote omitted).

109. See C. Winick & P. Kinsie, supra note 25, at 67–69. See also E. Schur, *Law and Society* 134 (1968).

110. See C. Winick & P. Kinsie, supra note 25, at 216.

111. "To the extent that decriminalization of prostitution would reduce the functional necessity of the pimp in the prostitute's livelihood, this casual association would be eliminated." Jennings, supra note 16, at 1244 (footnote omitted).

112. The President's Commission on Law Enforcement and Administration of Justice declared in 1967: "Prostitution . . . play[s] a small and declining role in organized crime's operations," President's Commission on Law Enforcement and Administration of Justice, *Task Force Report: Organized Crime* 4 (1967).

113. See American Social Health Association, *Today's VD Control Problem* 54 (1974). There are an estimated three to four million cases of gonorrheal infection per year in the United States. Williams, "Diagnosing Disseminated Gonorrhea," *Med. Aspects Human Sexuality*, May, 1977, at 57.

114. Siegel & Wiesner, "Pencillin-Resistant Gonococcus," *Med. Aspects Human Sexuality*, May, 1977, at 105.

115. Felman, "VD Prophylaxis via Drugs," *Med. Aspects Human Sexuality*, May, 1977, at 100.

116. See, e.g., Vance, "Immunological Factors in Gonorrhea," *Med. Aspects Human Sexuality*, May, 1977, at 106–07.

117. C. Winick & P. Kinsie, supra note 25, at 64; Note, supra note 16, at 254–55.

118. P. Wilson, *The Sexual Dilemma* 91 (1971). Most prostitutes examine their clients for signs of venereal disease and use prophylactics, safeguards rarely used by noncommercial sex partners. James, "Answers to the 20 Questions Most Frequently Asked About Prostitution," in *The Politics of Prostitution* 50 (J. James, J. Withers, M. Haft & S. Theiss eds. 1975). In addition, many streetwalkers, and virtually all "call girl" and brothel types, wash their customers' and their own genitals incident to their check for sores or discharge. M. Stein, *Lovers, Friends, Slaves . . . The Nine Male Sexual Types* 18 (1974).

119. While the 15- to 30-year old age group was found to be responsible for 84% of the reported cases of gonorrhea in the state of Washington, prostitutes interviewed in Seattle revealed that 70% of their customers are between 30 and 60 years of age. See Burstin & James, supra note 107, at 8 n. 22.

120. See L. Saxton, *The Individual, Marriage, and the Family* 86 n. 30 (1972); Chang, "Quiz: Gonorrhea and Sexual Behavior," *Med. Aspects Human Sexuality*, April, 1977, at 48, 50; Fouser, "Introduction" to Educational Broadcasting Corporation, *VD Blues* 11 (1972).

121. See Jennings, supra note 16, at 1243. Reticence when VD is contracted from a party outside the central relationship is a complicating factor. See "Viewpoints: How Do You Extend Treatment to the Spouse of a Patient with VD?" *Med. Aspects Human Sexuality,* June, 1977, at 89.

122. See, e.g., Turner, "The Suppression of Prostitution in Relation to Venereal Disease Control in the Army," 7 *Fed. Prob.,* April–June, 1943, at 8; Quisenberry, "Eight Years After the Houses Closed: Was "Controlled" Prostitution Good for Hawaii?" 39 *J. Soc. Hygiene* 312, 313–15 (1953); Williams, "The Suppression of Commercialized Prostitution in the City of Vancouver," 27 *J. Soc. Hygiene* 364, 369–71 (1941).

123. See A. Smith & H. Pollack, *Some Sins Are Not Crimes* 30 (1975).

124. See note 57 supra.

125. L. Bultena, *Deviant Behavior in Sweden* 154–55 (1966).

126. Clapp, "Social Treatment of Prostitutes and Promiscuous Women," 7 *Fed. Prob.,* April–June, 1943, at 23.

127. See Jennings, supra note 16, at 1243.

128. *United States v. Bitty,* 208 U. S. 393, 401 (1908) (construing an act of Congress prohibiting the importation of any woman or girl for the purposes of prostitution (quoting *Murphy v. Ramsey,* 114 U. S. 15, 45 (1885)), cited with approval in *Caminetti v. United States,* 242 U.S. 470, 486–87 (1917) (power of Congress under the commerce clause enables it to forbid interstate transportation for immoral purposes, even if unaccompanied by pecuniary gain).

129. See notes 25–27 supra & accompanying text.

130. See note 36 supra.

131. See note 22 supra.

132. See K. Marx, *Economic and Philosophic Manuscripts of 1844,* at 133 (M. Mulligan trans. 1964), where he describes prostitution as "only a *specific* expression of the *general* prostitution of the *labourer.*" Engels argues that only the abolition of private property will allow the development of romantic love. See F. Engels, *The Origin of the Family, Private Property, and the State* 75–89 (1972).

133. See S. Brownmiller, *Against Our Will* 390–92 (1975).

134. See C. Fried, *Right and Wrong* 142–43 (1978); I. Kant, *Lectures on Ethics* 162–71 (L. Infield trans. 1963) (first delivered 1780).

135. See note 22 supra. Troubling intermediate cases do exist, such as noncommercial acts of "pure" lust, but the extremes are generally the objects of settled moral judgment.

136. See A. Flexner, supra note 25, at 12–13. Cf. M. Ploscowe's invocation of the argument made in *United States v. Bitty,* 208 U. S. 393, 401 (1908) (quoted at text accompanying note 128 supra): "Men who frequent prostitutes can hardly obtain any elevated ideas as to the position of women in our culture from such contacts." M. Ploscowe, supra note 26, at 247.

137. Sanger claims that, on the average, prostitutes have a four-year life from the time they begin their careers. W. Sanger, supra note 42, at 455–56.

138. M. Ploscowe, supra note 26, at 245–46.

139. George, "Legal, Medical and Psychiatric Considerations in the Control of Prostitution," 60 *Mich. L. Rev.* 717, 746–52 (1962).

140. Id. 748.

141. M. Ploscowe, supra note 26, at 247.

142. A. Flexner, supra note 25, at 12.

143. George, supra note 139, at 758–60.

144. H. Greenwald, *The Elegant Prostitute* 221–37 (1970).

145. See, e. g., D. A. J. Richards, *Moral Criticism,* supra note 8, at 192–262.

146. Cf. Scanlon, "Due Process," in *Due Process: Nomos XVIII* 93–125 (J. Pennock & J. Chapman eds. 1977) (due process is grounded in principles of political right and the design of social institutions).

147. See generally Richards, "Human Rights and the Moral Foundations of the Substantive Criminal Law," 13 *Ga. L. Rev.* 1395 (1979). Cf. H. M. Hart, "The Aims of the Criminal Law," 23 *Law & Contemp. Prob.* 401, 401–06 (1958) (exploring the moral perspective of "constitution makers").

148. On the concept of judicially underenforced constitutional norms, see Sager, "Fair Measure: The Legal Status of Underenforced Constitutional Norms," 91 *Harv. L. Rev.* 1212 (1978).

149. See H. M. Hart, supra note 147.

150. My methodological procedure here is in line with that of O. W. Holmes, who believed that ancient residues in the law control behavior long after their rationale has ceased to exist. See O. W. Holmes, supra note 4, at 8–33. For a similar moral analysis of the assumptions underlying antiprostitution laws, published after the article from which this chapter is derived, see Lars O. Ericsson, "Charges against Prostitution: An Attempt at a Philosophical Assessment." 90 *Ethics* 335–66 (1980).

151. See note 64 supra.

152. See note 65 supra.

153. See note 69 supra.

154. See note 70 supra.

155. See notes 59–69, and text accompanying in Chapter 2, supra.

156. See generally C. Ford & F. Beach, supra note 40, at 199–267.

157. See D.A.J. Richards, *Reasons*, supra note 9, at 250–59. See also Aristotle, *Nicomachean Ethics* *1157b.

158. *Eisenstadt v. Baird*, 405 U.S. 438 (1972) (contraceptives and the unmarried); *Griswold v. Connecticut*, 381 U.S. 479 (1965) (contraceptives and the married).

159. *Roe v. Wade*, 410 U.S. 113 (1973).

160. *Stanley v. Georgia*, 394 U.S. 557 (1969).

161. See note 20 supra.

162. See note 22 supra.

163. See note 74 supra.

164. See Plato, *Phaedrus*, in *Collected Dialogues of Plato* 476 (E. Hamilton & H. Cairns eds. 1961); Plato, *Symposium*, in id. 527. Plato appears to have had a highly developed, idealized concept of romantic homosexual love which required that it rarely, if ever, be consummated. Plato, himself homosexual and a celebrant of aim-inhibited romantic homosexual love, appears to have condemned actual homosexual relations, introducing, for the first time anywhere, a philosophical argument for its unnaturalness. Plato, *Laws* (Book VIII) *835d–42a, in id. 1226, 1401–06; see note 76, Chapter 2, supra. For discussion of Plato's insistence that romantic love be aim-inhibited and of the question whether Plato believed consummated homosexual acts themselves to be unnatural, see G. Vlastos, "The Individual as an Object of Love in Plato," in *Platonic Studies* 3, 22–28 (1973). For a critique of Plato's arguments on the unnaturalness of homosexuality, see Richards, "Unnatural Acts and the Constitutional Right to Privacy: a Moral Theory," 45 *Ford. L. Rev.* 1281, 1308–9, 1323–27, 1328–33 (1977). See also Chapter 2, supra.

165. See C. S. Lewis, supra note 74, at 1–43; C. Morris, supra note 74, at 112–13; J. Stevens, supra note 74, at 37–38. Andreas Capellanus, for example, in his important treatise "De Arte Honeste Amandi," defines love as extramarital by nature:

> We declare and we hold as firmly established that love cannot exert its powers between two people who are married to each other. For lovers give each other something freely, under no compulsion of necessity, but married people are in duty bound to give in to each other's desires and deny themselves to each other in nothing.

A. Capellanus, *The Art of Courtly Love* 106–07 (J. Parry trans. 1941). See also id. 100:

> [E]verybody knows that love can have no place between husband and wife. They may be bound to each other by a great and immoderate affection, but their feeling cannot take the place of love, because it cannot fit under the true definition of love. For what is love but an inordinate desire to receive passionately a furtive and hidden embrace? But what embrace between husband and wife can be furtive, I ask you, since they may be said to belong to each other and may satisfy all of each other's desires without fear that anybody will object? Besides, that most excellent doctrine of princes shows that nobody can make furtive use of what belongs to him.

For commentary, see D. Robertson, Jr., supra note 74, at 391–448. For an argument that the tradition is not completely extramarital, see H. Kelly, *Love and Marriage in the Age of Chaucer* 31–48 (1975).

166. See C. S. Lewis, supra note 74, at 13; C. Morris, supra note 74, at 107–08; M. Valency, supra note 74, at 63–64.

167. The most famous statement of this critical viewpoint is that of D. de Rougemont, supra note 74, at 44–45, 283–87.

168. Indeed, a number of medieval theologians had condemned even sex in marriage if not for procreation. See D. Robertson, Jr., supra note 74, at 429–30. One commentator concluded, "Although the upholders of the dominant ascetical tradition carefully guarded themselves from the condemnation of marriage as such, they regarded passionate love as essentially sinful, and were apt to quote the ungenerous tag: 'every ardent lover is an adulterer with his own wife.'" C. Morris, supra note 74, at 107–08. The words quoted were those of St. Jerome, who was warning husbands that "nothing is more foul than to love a wife as though she were an adulteress." Augustine, *Enchiridion* 70.19, quoted in D. Robertson, Jr., supra note 74, at 429.

169. What, then, was the experience which is usually called "courtly love," and

> how can we know about it? We know about it in one sense, because, as romantic love, it still exists—the perennial theme of European literature, life, art, and our entertainment. From *Lancelot* to *Anna Karenina*, from *Les Deux Amants* to *Les Enfants du Paradis*, it is often quite literally the same story. In its domesticated, neo-Victorian form romantic love is the substance of the women's magazines and the radio serial. In its now equally admired but undomesticated form it is part of the "resistance movement" of youth—a spontaneous private unregulatable protest against the mediocrities of a middle-aged materialistic society. In George Orwell's *Nineteen Eighty-Four* it takes an overtly political twist.

J. Stevens, supra note 74, at 33.

170. The Capellanus text, supra note 45, describes the complex forms that aristocratic courting took.

171. The presence of such barriers created

> a heightening of sensuality, since it brought about the concentration of enormous libidinous energy upon such casual contacts as ordinarily have no special erotic significance. In this manner, a glance, a touch of the hand, a word of greeting could be transformed into an event of crucial character, so that the relations of lovers whose contacts were purely visual could be more deeply sensual than the physical coupling of husband and wife.

M. Valency, supra note 74, at 28.

172. An extreme example is Dante's religious idealization of Beatrice. Dante first met Beatrice when he was about nine and she eight; they met and spoke briefly only once again nine years later. Dante, *Vita Nuova* 3, 5 (M. Musa trans. 1973). Thereafter, Dante, by his own description, met with contempt from the lady, id. 17–18, and himself avoided her presence, id. 24–25. After her death, Beatrice appeared to Dante in a vision as a remote religious figure, demanding that he "be capable of writing about her in a noble way," Id. 68. She is, of course, the inspiring figure of *The Divine Comedy*, See also C. S. Lewis, supra note 74, at 21.

173. See D. de Rougemont, supra note 74, at 42–46. The connections between frustrated love, heightened sensuality, and death are central themes of later romanticism. See generally M. Praz, supra note 74.

174. See notes 72–76 supra & accompanying text.

175. See E. Shorter, supra note 36, at 79–107, 148–61; L. Stone, supra note 27, at 644–45.

176. See E. Shorter, supra note 36, at 148–61.

177. See id. 205–44.

178. See id. 245–54; L. Stone, supra note 27, at 680–81.

179. L. Stone, supra note 27, at 675–76.

180. There is no evidence that these countries, which do not criminalize prostitution, see note 102, supra, have less stable marriage relationships.

181. See note 69 supra.

182. See note 70 supra.

183. Lecky described the social functions of prostitution in protecting monogamous marriage as follows:

> [T]he supreme type of vice, she is ultimately the most efficient guardian of virtue. But for her, the unchallenged purity of countless happy homes would be polluted, and not a few who, in the price of their untempted chastity, think of her with an indignant shudder, would have known the agony of remorse and despair. On that one degraded and ignoble form are concentrated the passions that might have filled the world with shame. She remains, while creeds and civilisations rise and fall, the eternal priestess of humanity, blasted for the sins of the people.

2 W. Lecky, *History of European Morals* 283 (1921). Compare Schopenhauer's remark: "There are 80,000 prostitutes in London alone: and what are they if not sacrifices on the altar of monogamy?" A. Schopenhauer, "On Women," in *Essays and Aphorisms* 80, 88 (B. Hollingdale trans. 1970). Mandeville's view was similar:

> If Courtezans and Strumpets were to be prosecuted with as much Rigour as some silly People would have it, what Locks and Bars would be sufficient to preserve the Honour of our Wives and Daughters? . . . [I]t is manifest, that there is a Necessity of sacrificing one part of Womankind to preserve the other, and prevent a Filthinyss of a more heinous Nature. From whence I think I may justly conclude . . . that Chastity may be supported by Incontinence, and the best of Virtues want the Assistance of the worst of Vices.

B. Mandeville, "Remarks" to *The Fable of the Bees* 127, 130 (P. Harth ed. 1970) (1st ed. 1714).

184. Of course, patrons of prostitutes often engage in elaborate fantasies during sex with prostitutes.

> As far as his psychologic responses are concerned, the male in many instances may not be having coitus with the immediate sexual partner, but with all of the other girls with whom he has ever had coitus, and with the entire genus Female with which he would like to have coitus.

A. Kinsey, W. Pomeroy, C. Martin, & P. Gebhard, *Sexual Behavior in the Human Female* 684 (1953) [hereinafter cited as *Kinsey Report*]. But the personal idealization of the beloved that marks romantic love is not present. But see note 192 infra.

185. See Chapter 2, supra.

186. See generally S. Freud, *Introductory Lectures on Psycho-Analysis*, in 15 & 16 *Complete Psychological Works of Sigmund Freud* (Standard ed. 1958–1975) [hereinafter cited as *Standard Edition*]. See also S. Freud, *New Introductory Lectures on Psychoanalysis*, reprinted in 22 *Standard Edition* 5–182. For a useful general review of the empirical confirmation of Freud's major hypotheses, see S. Fisher & R. Greenberg, *The Scientific Credibility of Freud's Theories and Therapy* (1977).

187. The distinction between animal and human sexuality was a central postulate of Freud's emphasis on the distinctive role of sexuality in human personality:

> The sexual instinct . . . is probably more strongly developed in man than in most of the higher animals; it is certainly more constant, since it has almost entirely overcome the periodicity to which it is tied in animals. It places extraordinarily large amounts of force at the disposal of civilized activity, and it does this in virtue of its especially marked characteristic of being able to displace its aim without materially diminishing its intensity. This capacity to exchange its originally sexual aim for another one, which is no longer sexual but which is physically related to the first aim, is called the capacity for sublimation.

S. Freud, "Civilized Sexual Morality and Modern Nervous Illness," in 9 *Standard Edition*, supra note 186, at 181, 187. For a comparison of the animal and human data, see C. Ford & F. Beach, supra note 40, at 199–267. For a seminal development of Freud's ideas of the place of sexual defenses in understanding the personality or character structure of the person, see W. Reich, *Character Analysis* (V. Carfagno trans. 1972). For confirming data, see S. Fisher & P. Greenberg, supra note 186, at 80–169.

188. See notes 154–162 and accompanying text, Chapter 2, supra.

189. See Bertocci, "The Human Venture in Sex, Love and Marriage," in *Today's Moral Problems* 218, 227 (R. Wasserstrom ed. 1975).

190. See Diotima's speech, Plato, *Symposium* °201d–212c, wherein the object of erotic attraction is described as forms of desirable beauty, and thus forms of the good. Cf. Gabriele Taylor, "Love," in *Philosophy As It Is* 161–82 (T. Honderich & M. Burnyeat, eds. 1979).

191. The distinction between commercial and noncommercial sex is clearly not as sharp a line as many have believed. There are commercial, indeed dominantly economic, features in many traditional marriages, see, e.g., descriptions of traditional, premodern marriage in E. Shorter, supra note 36, at 22–78; and there are such features in sexual relations not regarded as commercial, see H. Benjamin & R. Masters, supra note 32, at 21–32. Further, the forms of commercial and noncommercial sex are not intrinsically different. For example, many conventional married women appear to engage in sex with their husbands without experiencing orgasm, presumably in order to retain their traditional role. See S. Fisher, *The Female Orgasm* 113–15 (1973); *Kinsey Report*, supra note 184, 373–76. Many traditional women experience prostitution fantasies. See 1 H. Deutsch, *The Psychology of Women* 265–69 (1944). And Freud suggests that masculine fantasies of sex with prostitutes are a relatively permanent feature of the masculine sexual imagination and sexual experience in general. See S. Freud, "A Special Type of Choice of Object Made by Men," in 11 *Standard Edition*, supra note 186, at 165–75; S. Freud, "On the Universal Tendency to Debasement in the Sphere of Love," in id. 178. Freud suggests a psychoanalytic explanation for the masculine tendency to divide affectionate feelings from sensual eroticism, expressed in asexual love for one's wife and sexual vigor with degraded prostitutes: the division between affection and sensuality derives from the Oedipal prohibition on sexual feelings with one's mother, so that in falling in love with a woman later in one's life, one idealizes her like one's asexual mother and thus experiences no sexual excitement, and one experiences eroticism with degraded women who least remind one of the idealized mother. For a recent striking investigation of the forms of sexual fantasy categorized by gender and sexual preference, see W. Masters and V. Johnson, *Homosexuality in Perspective* 174–92 (1979). The study indicates that such fantasies usually include, for men and women, heterosexual and homosexual, fantasies of sex with persons not of one's sexual preference.

192. For example, an in-depth and extensive study of the patrons of prostitutes indicates that the experience has complex and diverse meanings for the patrons. Fifty-two percent of the patrons in the sample imposed a thereapeutic role on the call girl that included ego support, crisis intervention, dealing with suppressed sexual material, and sexual counseling. M. Stein, supra note 118, at 91–92.

Stein summarizes the complex nature of the meaning of commercial sex for patrons as follows:

> Their behavior and needs in turn determined the call girl's role on call; to the Fraternizers—a party girl; to the Promoter—a businesswoman; to the Adventurer—a playmate. The Lover sought a romantic partner; the Friend, a confidante; the Slave, a dominatrix; the Guardian, a daughter-figure; the Juvenile, a mother-figure. The role playing became a kind of fantasy enactment for some of the Lovers, Friends, Slaves, Guardians, Juveniles. The part they assigned the call girl corresponded to an idealized image of woman which exerted great power over their erotic imagination, and the correspondence was a source of excitement and pleasure. The men's individual fantasies of the ideal partner can be seen as variations of female types idealized by our culture as a

whole; the Sexual superwoman; the Beloved; the Girlfriend; the Dominating Mistress; the Child-Woman; the Earth-Mother.

Id. 313–14. Other researchers studying patrons noted, "[e]motional, fantasy, cultural, or symbolic overtones of the situation may be more important to the clients than their desire for sex. The customer's relation to a prostitute is far more complex than has traditionally been believed." C. Winick & P. Kinsie, supra note 25, at 197.

193. See H. Ellis, supra note 37, at 143–77.

194. See, e.g., S. Peele, *Love and Addiction* 71–91 (1975). Cf. C. Lasch, *The Culture of Narcissism* (1979); R. Sennett, *The Fall of Public Man* (1974).

195. See S. de Beauvoir, *The Second Sex* 712–43 (H. Parsley trans. 1952); S. Firestone, *The Dialectic of Sex* 126–55 (1972).

196. See G. Gorer, *The Danger of Equality* 126–32 (1966). In some views, romantic love is peculiarly unsuspectible of generalization to people at large, for only a few "special souls" are authentically adequate to its demands. See id.

197. For a defense of this view of the concept of shame, see D. A. J. Richards, *Reasons*, supra note 9, at 250–67.

198. See H. Ellis, supra note 37, at 147–48.

199. The function of women as a means of kinship exchange and integration has been a prominent feature of the anthropology of Claude Lévi-Strauss. For the seminal works, see C. Lévi-Strauss, *Structural Anthropology* 83,309 (C. Jacobson & B. Schoepf trans. 1963); C. Lévi-Strauss, *The Elementary Structures of Kinship* 63–68, 381–85 (1969). For a useful general commentary, see J. Barnes, *Three Styles in the Study of Kinship* 139–55 (1973).

200. See H. Ellis, supra note 37, at 147–48; S. Weitz, *Sex Roles* 116–19 (1977).

201. In the Sudan, for example, Arab Moslem women undergo the genital mutilation of infibulation that is regarded as necessary in order to protect inherently oversexed women from unchastity. See S. Weitz, supra note 200, at 185–86. Another mutilation ritual is clitoridectomy, which removes the seat of female sexual feelings. Other forms of special control of female sexuality include sexual segregation, an extreme form of which is the Moslem custom of purdah (seclusion), and the double standard. Id.

202. See Aristotle, *Politics* bk. I, pt. V, *1259a40–1260b26.

203. Andreas Capellanus takes this view of female sexuality:

> Every woman in the world is likewise wanton, because no woman, no matter how famous and honored she is, will refuse her embraces to any man, even the most vile and abject, if she knows that he is good at the work of Venus; yet there is no man so good at the work that he can satisfy the desires of any woman . . . . in any way at all.

A. Capellanus, supra note 165, at 208. For other examples of this point of view, see T. Aquinas, *Summa Theologica* pt. II–II, question 149; M. Valency, supra note 74, at 67–68.

204. Havelock Ellis distinguishes the injustice of such "unnatural and empty forms of chastity," H. Ellis, supra note 37, at 144, "imposed by one sex on the opposite sex," id., from voluntary self-imposed chastity used to heighten one's romantic sensibilities. See generally id. 143–77.

205. See Chodorow, "Family Structure and Feminine Personality," in *Woman, Culture, and Society* 43 (M. Rosaldo & L. Lamphere eds. 1974); Ortner, "Is Female to Male as Nature is to Culture?," in *Woman, Culture, and Society*, supra, at 67; Rosaldo, "Woman, Culture, and Society: A Theoretical Overview," in *Woman, Culture, and Society*, supra, at 17. See also D. A. J. Richards, *Moral Criticism*, supra note 8, at 173–176.

206. Cf. *The Maimie Papers* xxxi (R. Rosen ed. 1977) (families stigmatize erring girls as "whores" and lock them out).

207. L. Stone, supra note 27, at 676. Stone continues:

> A marriage manual of 1839 stated as a fact that sterility was caused by any female who displayed "excessive ardour of desire," and advised that "tranquility, silence and secrecy are necessary for a prolific coition." It was very discouraging

advice, almost as discouraging as that offered to married women by Mrs. Ellis in 1845: "suffer and be still."

Id. Related medical advice was to limit the incidence of sex in marriage to moderate amounts. Id. 677. Similarly,

> the perils of masturbation developed into a major obsession not only of moralists but also of the medical profession . . . Inspired by fears of physical debilitation and even of insanity, some surgeons in the third quarter of the century, especially in England and America, were performing clitoridectomy on masturbating girls and deliberately painful circumcision on boys, while agitated parents were attaching toothed rings to the penis and locking adolescents into chastity belts or even in strait-jackets for the night.

Id. See also note 201 supra & accompanying text. For a detailed description of American medical views during this period, see J. Haller & R. Haller, supra note 88. For a discussion of the Victorian medical literature supporting female sexuality, see Degler, "What Ought to Be and What Was: Women's Sexuality in the Nineteenth Century," 79 *Am. Hist. Rev.* 1469 (1974).

208. One medical writer in Victorian America, for example, envisioned the evolutionary purification of mankind's sensuality, leading eventually to the removal of man's animal sensual pleasure entirely. See J. Haller & R. Haller, supra note 88, at 126–27. See generally id. 91–137.

209. See generally, A. Douglas, supra note 87. The sentimental literature of the period appears to have been based on "stereotypes of ideal feminine virtue," id. 157, flourishing in "the romance of domestic management," id. 185. For discussion of the comparable English phenomenon, see L. Stone, supra note 27, at 675–76.

210. The focal attack by feminists on the double standard was well summarized by Dr. Elizabeth Blackwell during this period:

> The great truth now to be recognized, is the fact, that male as well as female purity is a necessary foundation of progressive human society.
> This important subject must no longer be ignored. The time has come for its acceptance by all experienced men and women. The necessity of upholding one moral standard as the aim to be striven for, must become a fundamental article of religious faith.

R. Walters, *Primers for Prudery* 67–68 (1974). See also note 80, supra.

It is a notable historical paradox that the preeminent concerns of these first feminists should have been dominated by a moral vision born in the insulation and isolation of their traditional role, which was, accordingly, in many ways designed to confirm traditional stereotyped feminine roles. See Warner, supra note 80.

211. For the English experience, see note 79, supra. For the comparable American experience, influenced by British developments, see generally D. Pivar, supra note 89.

212. See L. Stone, supra note 27, at 676.

213. For a comprehensive general study, see S. Fisher, supra note 191. Other important studies include the *Kinsey Report*, supra note 184, at 346–408; W. Masters & V. Johnson, *Human Sexual Inadequacy* 214–315 (1970); W. Masters & V. Johnson, *Human Sexual Response* 27–168 (1966). A striking but somewhat speculative recent study suggests, in fact, that women have much greater natural orgasmic and sensual capacity than do men. M. Sherfey, *The Nature and Evolution of Female Sexuality* (1973).

214. Of the Victorian medical literature regarding the sexuality of women, Lawrence Stone observes: "On both sides of the argument much of the writing is clearly normative and moralistic rather than merely descriptive of proven biological facts." L. Stone, supra note 27, at 676.

215. See D. A. J. Richards, *Moral Criticism*, supra note 8, at 162–78.

216. Freud observed of the effects of the Victorian constraints on female sexuality:

> The harmful results which the strict demand for abstinence before marriage produces in women's natures are quite especially apparent. It is clear that educa-

tion is far from underestimating the task of suppressing a girl's sensuality till her marriage, for it makes use of the most drastic measures. Not only does it forbid sexual intercourse and set a high premium on the preservation of female chastity, but it also protects the young woman from temptation as she grows up, by keeping her ignorant of all the facts of the part she is to play and by not tolerating any impulse of love in her which cannot lead to marriage. The result is that when the girl's parental authorities suddenly allow her to fall in love, she is unequal to this psychical achievement and enters marriage uncertain of her own feelings. In consequence of this artificial retardation in her function of love, she has nothing but disappointments to offer the man who has saved up all his desire for her. In her mental feelings she is still attached to her parents, whose authority has brought about the suppression of her sexuality; and in her physical behaviour she shows herself frigid, which deprives the man of any high degree of sexual enjoyment.

S. Freud, " 'Civilized' Sexual Morality and Modern Nervous Illness," in 9 *Standard Edition,* supra note 186, at 181, 197–98. Of the effects on women themselves, Freud notes:

> Their upbringing forbids their concerning themselves intellectually with sexual problems though they nevertheless feel extremely curious about them, and frightens them by condemning such curiosity as unwomanly and a sign of a sinful disposition. In this way they are scared away from any form of thinking, and knowledge loses its value for them. The prohibition of thought extends beyond the sexual field, partly through unavoidable association, partly automatically, like the prohibition of thought about religion among men, or the prohibition of thought about loyalty among faithful subjects. . . . I think that the undoubted intellectual inferiority of so many women can . . . . be traced back to the inhibition of thought necessitated by sexual suppression.

Id. 198–99.

217. I. Kant, supra note 134, at 162–71.

218. Id. 163–64. Kant's words are deeply Augustinian: "Sexual desire is at the root of [sexual love]; and that is why we are ashamed of it, and why all strict moralists, and those who had pretensions to be regarded as saints, sought to suppress and extirpate it." Id.

219. Id. 163.

220. Id. 166–67.

221. Id. 165.

222. Id. 165–66.

223. C. Fried, supra note 134, at 140–43.

224. Id. 142. Fried's argument is specifically concerned with the question of the proper mode of distribution and contribution of valuable body parts, for example, kidneys, and is only concerned with prostitution and commercial sex by analogy. Indeed, Fried suggests that the sale of body parts in a just society would violate no one's rights, though there is something called "shame of selling one's body." Id. 142. In a note, Fried states that the sale of body parts is "though not wrong, . . . somehow shameful," id. 143, though the compulsion of donation of body parts is wrong. Fried's remark that there "may, after all, also be an absolute prohibition against engaging in sex for pay," id. 31, seems to indicate that the prohibition of commercial sex may in some sense be more wrongful than the sale of kidneys.

It is important to add that the criticism here made is only of a small part of Fried's larger scheme. Overall, that scheme is an admirable essay in moral and legal philosophy. See especially id. 81–163.

225. See K. Marx, supra note 132, at 133, where, in a footnote, Marx notes: "Prostitution is only a *specific* expression of the *general* prostitution of the *laborer,* and since it is a relationship in which falls not the prostitute alone, but also the one who prostitutes— and the latter's abomination is still greater—the capitalist, etc., also comes under this head." Cf. F. Engels, supra note 132, at 75–90 (prostitution as a product of monogamy). See also note 132 supra & accompanying text.

226. See K. Marx, supra note 132, at 134, where Marx expresses his model of the overcoming of alienation and the realization of species man in terms of the movement from "the infinite degradation" of sex with women as "the spoil and handmaid of communal lust" to romantic love.

> From this relationship one can therefore judge man's whole level of development. From the character of this relationship follows how much *man* as a *species being*, as *man*, has come to be himself and to comprehend himself; the relation of man to woman is *the most natural* relation of human being to human being. . . . In this relationship is revealed . . . the extent to which man's *need* has become a *human* need; the extent to which, therefore, the *other* person as a person has become for him a need—the extent to which he in his individual existence is at the same time a social being.

Id. Following this view, Engels argues that romantic love will fully emerge only with the coming of communism. See F. Engels, supra note 132, at 92–101.

227. See S. Brownmiller, supra note 132, at 438–54; Brownmiller, "Speaking Out on Prostitution," in *Notes from Third Year* 24–25 (1971); Kearon & Mehrhof, "Prostitution," in *Notes from Third Year*, supra, at 26–28. Even feminist authors who, unlike those just referred to, support decriminalization of prostitution often write of the woman's role in commercial sex in this way. See, e.g., S. de Beauvoir, supra note 195, at 631 ("I use the word hetaira to designate all women who treat not only their bodies but their entire personalities as capital to be exploited."); K. Millett, *The Prostitution Papers* 93–96, 111 (1973).

228. See H. Benjamin & R. Masters, supra note 32, at 435–74; H. Ellis, supra note 37, at 304–05.

229. One woman, reflecting on her life as a streetwalker, described her attitudes during commercial sex as follows: "I used to lie there with my hands behind my head and do mathematics equations in my head or memorize the keyboard typewriter." S. Terkel, *Working* 62 (1974).

230. The streetwalker, note 229 supra, compared her detached state of mind as a streetwalker to that of a person in a typing pool who receives work anonymously, in contrast to the more engaged call girl who is more like the executive secretary with a personal relationship to her employer. Id.

231. See H. Benjamin & R. Masters, supra note 32, at 435–74; note 282, infra.

232. See note 262 infra for the behavior of patrons and notes 281–282 infra for the complexity of services that a prostitute may render, including perception required in deciphering the needs of patrons.

233. See note 232 supra & accompanying text.

234. See note 294 infra.

235. See generally H. Braverman, *Labor and Monopoly Capital: The Degradation of Work in the Twentieth Century* (1974).

236. For a description of this state of mind, see R. Unger, *Knowledge and Politics* 145–90 (1975).

237. Fried attempts to use this distinction in order to distinguish the sale of the body from the sale of services. C. Fried, supra note 134, at 142.

238. See I. Kant, *Foundations of the Metaphysics of Morals* 65–71 (L. Beck trans. 1959) (1st ed. 1784). See, generally, discussions in Chapter 1.

239. Id.

240. See discussions in Chapter 1.

241. Of course, to say that the sale *or* donation of body parts is not morally forbidden is not to say that there may not be reasons to prefer donation over sale, other things being equal. For a suggestion of such reasons, see R. Titmuss, *The Gift Relationship* (1971). See also Arrow, "Gifts and Exchanges," 1 *Philosophy & Pub. Aff.* 343 (1972).

242. I assume some form of moral limit to exist on the donation of vital parts that would result in the death or severe impairment of the person donating or selling them.

243. Such services independently violate basic moral principles expressing equal concern and respect for autonomy. See generally text accompanying notes 286–299 infra. See also D. A. J. Richards, *Reasons*, supra note 9, at 75–211.

244. See notes 228–236 supra & accompanying text.
245. See notes 225–26 supra.
246. See note 227 supra.
247. See note 220 supra.
248. See notes 225–26 supra.
249. See note 231 supra.
250. If not, the concern of the law should be to secure payment on fair terms.
251. For example, despite the widespread speculation that a prostitute must be a basically immature person lacking the normal ability to respond with sexual excitement, when W. B. Pomeroy systematically interviewed 175 prostitutes, he found that they experienced orgasm and multiple orgasm more frequently in their personal, "noncommercial" intercourse than did the normal woman (as defined by Kinsey norms). Over 20% of the prostitutes even reported frequently experiencing orgasms while having intercourse with clients. See Pomeroy, "Some Aspects of Prostitution," 1 *J. Sex Research* 177–87 (1965).
252. See notes 185–200 and text accompanying, Chapter 2, supra.
253. See D. A. J. Richards, *Reasons,* supra note 9, at 27–48.
254. Id. 193.
255. Such a choice might involve a consideration of, for example, whether the exercise of competences that the agent can take pleasure in is called for, the degree to which human contacts satisfy one's desires for sociability, the level of remuneration in relation to other opportunities and trade-offs in the satisfaction of other wants, and the degree of leisure to pursue avocations.
256. See C. Fried, *An Anatomy of Values* 155–82 (1970).
257. In terms of rational choice theory, one plan would dominate another. See D. A. J. Richards, *Reasons,* supra note 9, at 28, 40–43.
258. About 10% of New York City prostitutes are estimated to be suburban housewives who engage in commercial sex part-time. See G. Sheehy, supra note 103, at 36–37, 189, 200–01. For the comparable British phenomenon, see A. Sion, supra note 23, at 67, 114–15.
259. See C. Winick & P. Kinsie, supra note 25, at 73–76; G. Sheehy, supra note 103, at 221–54. Compare Acton's well-informed remark in his study of London prostitution written in the middle of the last century that prostitution is "a transitory stage, through which an untold number of British women are ever on their passage." W. Acton, *Prostitution* 49 (1870). Similarly, Parent-Duchâtelet, the leading authority during this period on French prostitution, stated that "prostitution is for the majority only a transitory stage; it is quitted usually during the first year; very few prostitutes continue until extinction," quoted in H. Ellis, supra note 37, at 261–62.
260. Id.
261. See note 294 infra.
262. Stein's study shows that 92% of her sample of 1,230 clients expressed positive postorgasmic emotions and "behaved affectionately" toward the prostitutes. M. Stein, supra note 118, at 99–100. Another study found that no less than 66% of a sample of customers were willing to admit they could fall in love with the prostitute they frequented. C. Winick & P. Kinsie, supra note 25, at 197.
263. Of the much maligned relationship of the prostitute to her pimp, the *Wolfenden Report* notes that

> [s]uch evidence as we have been able to obtain on this matter suggests that the arrangement between the prostitute and the man she lives with is usually brought about at the instance of the woman, and it seems to stem from a need on the part of the prostitute for some element of stability in the background of her life.

Wolfenden Report, supra note 1, at 161–62, and then quotes approvingly the observation of one writer that the pimp is sometimes a coercive figure, but is often

> the only person in the world towards whom she feels affection and sense of possession; he is usually her champion in disputes and her protector in a skirmish. He is deeply despised by the police and by the public outside his trade;

> but he may be nevertheless the one humanizing element in the life of the woman on whom he lives.

Id. (quoting Hall, *Prostitution* (1933)). See also J. Murtagh & S. Harris, *Cast the First Stone* 147–68 (1957); T. Honoré, *Sex Law* 117 (1978). There is some evidence that prostitutes are less likely to have children than other women. See C. Winick & P. Kinsie, supra note 25, at 59–62. But of course this does not show that, if they do have children, they are not loving parents. If there were evidence that being a prostitute disabled one from being a minimally good parent, that would be a reason not to forbid prostitution but for some form of alternative parental care. But, in fact, there are many professions that one might regard as less than optimal in this regard, a fact hardly sufficient to warrant automatic deprivation of parental rights. That a person is a professional gambler may lead to a sad and socially wasteful life, but such an undesirable profession does not disentitle him or her per se from parenthood.

264. See note 251 supra.

265. Consider the remarkable collection of recently published letters of the Victorian ex-prostitute Maimie, which adds to the economic causes of prostitution the claim "that many of the young girls suffered from overly strict families who prevented them from enjoying a normal social life and who also refused them a few cents to fulfill necessary adolescent vanities and fantasies." *The Maimie Papers*, supra note 206, at xxxi.

266. Jennifer James found that of the approximately 135 prostitutes she studied, the occupations held by the 37 who were employed when they entered the profession were for the most part "low-paying, low-status, low-skilled service occupations." James, "Motivations for Entrance into Prostitution," in *The Female Offender* 177, 180, 201 (L. Crites ed. 1976). See also F. Adler, *Sisters in Crime* 76 (1975); C. Winick & P. Kinsie, supra note 25, at 35–38.

267. One older study of the causes of prostitution shrewdly observed:

> A very large constituent in what has been called the irresistible demand of natural instinct is nothing but suggestion and stimulation associated with alcohol, late hours, and sensuous amusements . . . Amid conditions as they exist in Paris, Berlin, and Vienna, and the smaller towns like Geneva which aspire to be world cities by being licentious, growing youth is characterized not by a normal, healthy, and natural sexual development, but by an overstimulated and premature sex activity—a purely artificial excitation of instinct.

A. Flexner, supra note 25, at 45–46.

268. See H. Ellis, supra note 37, at 287–302. See also P. Adler, *A House Is Not a Home* 128–29 (1953), where a woman who ran a house of prostitution for 25 years described this phenomenon:

> When a fifteen-year-old girl looks around her with the new awareness of adolescence and sees only poverty and ugliness, the groundwork is laid. She doesn't want to wind up like her mother, wornout from too much childbearing, slopping around in an old ragged dress, beaten up by a drunken stupid husband every Saturday night. She wants a chance at the kind of life she's seen in the movies, with becoming frocks to wear and handsome men to pay her court, a house on a pretty street, clean, smiling children . . . And suddenly she sees that she might not get all this, nor even any part of it, that in fact she does not even know how to go about getting it.

Id. 128. See also A. Flexner, supra note 25, at 84, 89; *The Maimie Papers*, supra note 206, at 156, 277. Cf. G. Sheehy, supra note 103, at 221–54.

269. See L. Stone, supra note 27, at 615–19, 645–47.

270. See G. Kneeland, *Commercialized Prostitution in New York City* 186–88. See also the review of the studies of Lombroso et al, H. Ellis, supra note 37, at 275–80. For more recent findings, see H. Greenwald, supra note 144, at 183; C. Winick & P. Kinsie, supra note 25, at 35–36.

271. See W. Sanger, supra note 42, at 455–56, who claims that the average prostitute lives only four years from the beginning of her career.

272. See M. Choisy, *Psychoanalysis of a Prostitute* 6, 62–63 (1961); O. Fenichel, *The*

Psychoanalytic Theory of Neurosis (1945); H. Greenwald, supra note 144, George, supra note 139, at 746–52.

273. Indeed, of prostitution

> some research sponsored by the British Social Biology Council suggests that in the majority of cases this way of life is chosen because it offers greater ease, freedom, and profit than available alternatives. There is no evidence that the incidence of neurosis or psychological abnormality is greater among prostitutes than among housewives.

N. Morris & G. Hawkins, supra note 1, at 21. On the existence of myths about the mental condition of prostitutes, as such, unconfirmed by any systematic empirical study, see James, supra note 266, at 188–92.

274. See "Happy and Healthy Harlots," in *Human Behavior*, August, 1978, at 66; note 251 supra.

275. See note 295 infra.

276. See notes 295–99 infra & accompanying text.

277. See A. Flexner, supra note 25; H. Greenwald, supra not 144; J. Murtagh & S. Harris, supra note 263; W. Sanger, supra note 42; G. Sheehy, supra note 103; C. Winick & P. Kinsie, supra note 25, at 23–96.

278. See S. de Beauvoir, supra note 195; S. Firestone, supra note 195; E. Janeway, *Man's World Woman's Place* (1971); K. Millet, *Sexual Politics* (1970); J. Mitchell, *Woman's Estate* (1971). For older accounts, see J.S. Mill, supra note 177; M. Wollstonecraft, *A Vindication of the Rights of Woman* (1794); V. Woolf, *A Room of One's Own* (1957).

279. See note 192 supra.

280. See E. Brecher, *The Sex Researchers* 295–96 (1969).

281. H. Benjamin & R. Masters, supra note 32, at 435–74; H. Greenwald, supra note 144, at xviii–xix; K. Millet, supra note 227, at 69; C. Winick & P. Kinsie, supra note 25, at 193–98. See note 192 supra. The therapeutic role of the call girl for ego support and for crisis intervention is operative in the frequent situations where the customer is relaxing from the tensions of work. M. Stein, supra note 118. In describing roughly 15% of her study sample, the so-called "lovers," Stein observes that they

> feel they must wear themselves out to maintain the upper-middle-class life style, just as they are beginning to question whether that life style has really brought the satisfactions they expected of it. At a time when they feel a great need for emotional support, many feel estranged from their wives and growing children; they no longer believe they are "communicating" in a rewarding way with the members of their family . . . They are aware that they are middle-aged in a society where youth is valued and they may believe the best moments of their lives have already passed. They are going through a middle-aged identity crisis and must find a way to deal with the feeling of being trapped by morality and circumstance, to overcome self-doubt and re-establish a sense of their own worth.

Id. 218. Many of the clients in Stein's sample spent as much time talking to the prostitutes as having sex, and for most this seemed as important as sex, if not more so. Id. 226. While some patrons merely used the call girl as a listener while they relieved tensions, others "really worked through problems and gained insights about themselves." Id. 237. For many in Stein's psycho-sexual study, the prostitute seemed to increase the patron's self-esteem—to help them reaffirm their battered self-worth. Id. 316–17. See also C. Winick & P. Kinsie, supra note 25, at 197 (61% of sample indicated prostitute refurbished battered ego).

282. The act most frequently requested of prostitutes is fellatio. H. Greenwald, supra note 144, at 223 ("between 75 and 90 per cent of all clients did not want normal intercourse but preferred oral sex"); D. Reuben, *Everything You Always Wanted to Know About Sex* 200 (1969) (75–85% of clients); M. Stein, supra note 118, at 95, 98 (83% of clients received fellatio; climax occured in association with coitus in only 51% of the cases and in association with fellatio in 29% of the cases); C. Winick & P. Kinsie, supra

note 25, at 207 ("Annual surveys conducted by the American Social Health Association suggests that as many as nine out of ten customers now want some form of oral satisfaction in contrast to the 10 per cent requesting it in the 1930's"). The fact that a large number of patrons take a "passive," rather than an "active," role in relationships with a prostitute, M. Stein, supra note 118, at 92 (48%), and that the majority of customers who were previously impotent are brought to climax during their contact with a prostitute, id. 97 (122 out of 237 patrons), indicates that patrons are able in prostitution comfortably to adopt sex roles they cannot easily adopt elsewhere. Other unsatisfied yearnings that very few nonprostitutes will consider relate to those tendencies about which customers have conflicts, such as masochism, homosexuality, sadism, fetishism, and transvestitism. Prostitution affords an outlet for these as well. See H. Benjamin & R. Masters, supra note 32, at 194–95; M. Stein, supra note 118, at 192, 243–65; C. Winick & P. Kinsie, supra note 25, at 206–09. Stein observed 156 clients' transactions with call girls in which masochistic tendencies were being acted out, and indicated that the focus of the transaction appeared to be "power, not pain." M. Stein, supra note 118, at 244. These transactions freed the clients to realize their desires without guilt or shame, and to act out impulses, normally expressed in more dangerous ways, "in a controlled context that channelled the impulses toward a pleasurable end." Id. 263. In general, prostitutes often evince great perception in deciphering the specialized needs of each client, id. 52–53. Stein observes: "I was continually surprised by the complexity of the transactions: each session involved an elaborated interplay of social, sexual, and psychological behavior . . . [C]omplicated desires and needs were not being satisfied in the ordinary fabric of men's lives." Id. 52.

283. The most extreme example of this in the courtly love tradition is Dante. See note 172 supra. Such forms of extreme idealization, which positively avoid any realistic knowledge of the beloved, evince the origins of the medieval romantic love tradition in aristocratic chivalry, where the point is observance of an aristocratic code of conduct, not deepening sensitivity to the realistic needs of the beloved. For the complex forms of the romantic love tradition, of which Dante's religious idealization is one subvariety, see notes 165–73 supra & accompanying text.

284. For the psychoanalytic distinctions between narcissistic primary love (derived from early parental attachments) and the development of the capacity for the mutualities of reciprocal genital love, see M. Balint, *Primary Love and Psychoanalytic Technique* 90–140 (1965).

285. See id. 109–20.

286. See D. A. J. Richards, *Reasons*, supra note 9, at 176–85.

287. Id. 148–75.

288. Kinsey and his associates concluded that 69% of the total white male population has had some experience with prostitutes. They noted, however, that no more than 15 to 20% have contacts with prostitutes "more often than a few times a year." In terms of the total outlet derived from contacts with prostitutes, they estimated that prostitutes accounted for somewhere between 3.5 and 4% of the total sexual outlet of the total male population. A. Kinsey, W. Pomeroy & C. Martin, supra note 25, at 597. Among single males, this research team found that prostitutes provided 3.7% of the total outlet for those in their late teens, nearly 10% for those who have reached their thirtieth birthday, and over 15% for those who are forty years age. Id. 250, 286. For married males, prostitutes were said to provide about 1% of the overall outlet. Id. 599.

The Kinsey data casts doubt on the assumption that commercial sex is necessarily linked to married men. They reported that single males of all ages had more contacts with prostitutes than married men; specifically, they concluded that the frequency of intercourse with prostitutes for singles between the ages of 16 and 25 was two to four times as high as for married men and that the frequency for singles between the ages of 46 and 50 was fifteen times greater than for married men. Id. 250.

289. It might be thought that these principles of fidelity would justify criminalization of prostitution on the theory that prostitution undermines marital fidelity. There seems to be no evidence that prostitution does undermine marriage, and some theorize that it actually strengthens marriage. See notes 181–83 supra & accompanying text. Even

assuming the doubtful proposition that commercial sex destabilizes marriage, the use of a prohibition on commercial sex as a means to preserve the institution of marriage is seriously underinclusive. Adulterous extramarital conduct probably has a more detrimental effect on marriage than commercial sex, but adultery is neither prohibited in all states, nor, where it is criminalized, is it prosecuted. See N. Morris & G. Hawkins, supra note 1, at 16. In addition, prohibitions of commercial sex are overinclusive, since patrons may not be married. See note 288, supra.

290. See D. A. J. Richards, *Reasons*, supra note 9, at 189–92.

291. Cf. R. Farson, *Birthrights* 129–53 (1974) (advocating sexual freedom for children).

292. See generally J. Rawls, supra note 9.

293. This was a familiar argument during the period when American purity reformers urged the wholesale criminalization of prostitution. See, e.g., Seligman, "The Social Evil With Special Reference to Conditions Existing in the City of New York," *Prostitution in America: Three Investigations, 1902–1914*, at 9–11 (1976).

294. Most prostitutes command an income that is substantially higher than they could expect in another job for which they might qualify. For full-timers the scale varies dramatically. "Call girls," according to reliable sources, make anywhere from $30,000, H. Greenwald, supra note 144 at 10, to $100,000 annually, J. Murtagh & S. Harris, supra note 263, at 2. See also F. Adler, supra note 363, at 65 (about $50,000); C. Winick & P. Kinsie, supra note 25 at 177 ($40,000). At the other extreme, the streetwalker will accumulate much less, perhaps in the neighborhood of $10,000. See F. Adler, supra note 266, at 64. Some streetwalkers may net no more than $5,000 per annum. G. Sheehy, supra note 103, at 12–13. Sheehy nonetheless observes of prostitutes in general: "These are the highest-paid 'professional' women in America." Id. 104.

295. Blacks represented 61.4% of the arrestees for prostitution and commercialized vice, while whites accounted for 37.2% of those arrests in 1972. *Uniform Crime Reports*, supra note 32, at 131. Cf. C. Winick & P. Kinsie, supra note 25, at 216–17. Arrested prostitutes are usually streetwalkers, who are more visible and easier to prosecute successfully than are brothel inmates or call girls. Id. 212–13.

296. See notes 103–134, supra & accompanying text.

297. For examples of police practices degrading to prostitutes, see J. Skolnick, *Justice Without Trial* 106–8 (1966).

298. See note 294, supra.

299. See notes 103–13, supra & accompanying text.

300. See H. L. A. Hart, supra note 7, at 46–47.

301. See generally R. Dworkin, supra note 8.

302. See Urmson, "Saints and Heroes," in *Essays in Moral Philosophy* 198–216 (A. Melden ed. 1958).

303. For the idea of supererogatory principles of blame, see D. A. J. Richards, *Reasons*, supra note 9, at 197–205.

304. See D. A. J. Richards, *Reasons*, supra note 9, at 205–08.

305. See note 303, supra.

306. The discussion here profited from conversations with Ronald Dworkin. See Dworkin, "Liberalism," in *Public and Private Morality* 113–43 (S. Hampshire ed. 1978). For a further exploration of the contrast between rights and ideals, see Richards, "Human Rights and Moral Ideals: An Essay on the Moral Theory of Liberalism," 5 *Social Theory & Prac.* 461 (1980).

307. On the civilizing effects of courtly love on the development of the "gentil" man, see J. Stevens, supra note 74, at 29–71.

308. See notes 48–56, supra & accompanying text.

309. See generally A. Flexner, supra note 25.

310. Id.

311. Id. 204–64.

312. See notes 79–93 supra & accompanying text.

313. See K. Millett, supra note 227, at 10–11, 30–31, 35–36, 72, 84–85, 121; "Prostitution: a Non-Victim Crime?" supra note 16.

314. See note 80 supra & accompanying text.

315. See note 79 supra. For a powerful American attack to similar effect, see A. Flexner, supra note 25. See also Seligman, supra note 293, at 112–113, who while noting the defects of European licensing, places the best American arguments against prostitution on moral grounds, id. 59–64, appealing, at the last, to "the Puritanical sentiment which prevails in this country," id. 147.

316. See notes 97–102, supra, and accompanying text. See also *Study on Traffic in Persons and Prostitution*, United Nations, Department of Economic and Social Affairs, New York, 1959. See pp. 10–12, id., where the report notes the tendency to abolitionist systems (eliminating licensing of prostitutes), but expressly disavows endorsement of prohibitionism (the American-style criminalization of prostitution *per se*).

317. See note 80 supra.

318. One critique notes: "According to this system of regulation, the police would treat her much as a chattel, and would keep her in good health for her clients' sake." Seligman, supra note 293, at 67.

319. It appears to have been a marked tendency of Victorian purity reformers to embroider the facts of often consensual prostitution in a picture of involuntary coercion. See M. Pearson, supra note 79, at 32–33, 49–50, 105–06. Today there is no evidence that prostitutes, except in remote instances, enter into or remain in the profession involuntarily. S. Janus, B. Bess & C. Saltus, *A Sexual Profile of Men in Power* 150 (1977); Lemert, "Prostitution," in *Prob. Sex Behavior* 68, 84 (E. Sagarin & D. MacNamara eds. 1968). Helene Deutsch suggests that many stories of white slavery are fantasy inventions of prostitutes used on their gullible patrons. See 1 H. Deutsch, supra note 191, at 262–63. Some older accounts of prostitution suggest the fantasy that prostitution is per se slavery, and thus must have a slave-holder. See A. Flexner, supra note 25, at 107.

320. See note 319 supra.

321. See A. Flexner, supra note 25, at 204–64; A. Sion, supra note 23, at 41–43; Seligman, supra note 293, at 98-113.

322. This is the English practice, in which the treatment of venereal disease is voluntary, free, and confidential and open to all, with the police taking no part in the detection or treatment of venereal disease. See A. Sion, supra note 23, at 53–54.

323. Consider the unionization attempts of Margo St. James in forming the prostitutes' union, COYOTE, an acronym for "Call Off Your Old Tired Ethics." See Haft, supra note 16, at 8–9.

324. See H. M. Hart & A. Sacks, *The Legal Process: Basic Problems in the Making and Application of Law* 873–76 (tentative draft 1958).

325. See notes 281–82.

326. See notes 83–85 supra & accompanying text.

327. See note 102 supra.

328. See A. Sion, supra notes 23, at 39–40. See also note 102, supra.

329. A. Sion, supra note 23, at 39.

330. Id. 39–41.

331. England has imposed an absolute prohibition on solicitation applicable to willing and unwilling buyers with the idea that the right of citizens against obtrusive solicitation "should be the prime consideration and should take precedence over the interests of the prostitute and her customers." *Wolfenden Report*, supra note 1, at 140. In the United states, assuming the legality of the transaction between the willing buyer and seller (through decriminalization, in the case of prostitution), it would seem that regardless of the commercial nature of the solicitation, recent case law would require first amendment protection. See *Bates v. State Bar of Ariz.*, 433 U.S. 350 (1977); *Virginia State Bd. of Pharmacy v. Virginia Citizens Consumer Council, Inc.*, 425 U.S. 748 (1976); *Bigelow v. Virginia*, 421 U.S. 809 (1975).

332. Zoning of the solicitation for prostitution may be an importantly different question from zoning of the prostitution itself. There may be no reasonable objections to the former; obtrusive solicitations are not protected by the rights of the prostitute or the customer, and zoning is one reasonable way to accommodate the rights of all con-

cerned without violating the rights of any. There may also be just grounds for zoning the business of prostitution itself, but the justification seems of a different kind. If the business of a prostitute involves no obtrusive solicitation (assume a quite discreet call girl), the business cannot be zoned to one area on the ground of protecting the rights of people not to be obtrusively solicited. The considerations that might justify such zoning are the same that justify barring certain businesses from residential neighborhoods, namely, avoiding certain kinds of business-associated noises and disturbances. Prostitution, as a form of commercial service, may be zoned on grounds applied in an even-handed way to other businesses: suppose a zoning provision allows certain kinds of commercial services in a neighborhood but forbids prostitution, although the prostitute in question has only occasional, very discreet customers who are in no way uncivil, noisy, or otherwise disturbing, and who are in fact more congenial than the customers of the permitted commercial services. Suppose in short, that the ground of the zoning prohibition on prostitution is derived solely from the thought that the neighbor is a prostitute engaged in commercial sex. If, as we have already seen, perceptions of such kinds, without any rational ground, cannot be a proper basis for the exercise of the public morality in defining acts as criminal, the question arises whether such perceptions can be permitted to be the just basis for the exercise of the zoning power. This raises large questions that we cannot pursue here but that should be pursued at some point: if we can understand why the criminal law cannot justly rest on such grounds, must similar scrutiny be extended to the zoning power? Of course, there are significant moral distinctions between the absolute prohibitions of the criminal law and the regulations of time, place, and order that underlie zoning. Cf. *Young v. American Mini Theatres*, 427 U.S. 50 (1976). Certainly, considerations are justly available for the exercise of the zoning power that are not available to the criminal law—for example, aesthetic considerations. But it seems wrong to suppose that these more extensive justifying considerations with respect to zoning justify anything and everything. There are limits on the invidious zoning out of the poor and racial minorities. See *Buchanan v. Warley*, 245 U.S. 60 (1917). There may also be limitations of analogous kinds on the proper zoning of commercial sex. For an opinion which seems strikingly unaware of such limitations, see *Village of Belle Terre v. Boraas*, 416 U.S. 1 (1974). But cf. *Moore v. City of East Cleveland* 413 U.S. 494 (1976).

333. See C. Winick & P. Kinsie, supra note 25, at 221–23. Nevada law prohibits prostitution in counties of over 200,000 inhabitants, meaning Las Vegas. Seven counties and two cities now license and regulate brothels; in five other counties there are no laws on the books either way, but bordello operators receive full police protection. Prostitutes are regulated in various ways under the Nevada system. First, they must register as prostitutes, and be fingerprinted, checked by health authorities, and licensed. These regulations assure that prostitutes leave behind in Nevada a record of participation in an activity illegal everywhere else. They must agree to stay in the brothel for specific periods of time, typically three-week stints. Some Nevada locales establish strict regulations governing hours when they may be in town, buildings where they are not permitted (bars, casinos, residential areas), and with whom they may associate (no boyfriends or husbands permitted). See Bode, supra note 16, at 24.

334. See notes 315–23 supra & accompanying text. Feminists have made these criticisms of the Nevada brothel scheme. See Bode, supra note 16, at 24–25.

335. See note 315 supra.

336. Brothels, when fairly run, have the virtue of giving steady work without the possibly exploitative pimp-prostitute relationship. See Bode, supra note 16, at 23–24.

337. See Haft, supra note 16, at 21. For an eloquent criticism by a British scholar of the English restrictions on solicitation, and related aspects of English law regarding commercial sex, see T. Honoré, *Sex Law* 137–142 (1978).

338. See H. Ellis, supra note 37, at 287–302.

339. On the general problem of political hypocrisy regarding prostitution in urban centers, see Roby & Kerr, supra note 16.

340. See, for a further development of this thought, Richards, "Human Rights and the Moral Foundations of the Substantive Criminal Law," note 147, supra.

341. See H. Ellis, supra note 37.

342. See, e.g., William Wordworth's *The Prelude,* Book VII, "Residence in London:"

> Oh, blank confusional true epitome
> Of what the mighty City is herself
> To thousands upon thousands of her sons,
> Living amid the same perpetual whirl
> Of trivial objects, melted and reduced
> To one identity, by differences
> That have no law, no meaning, and no end—

W. Wordsworth, *The Prelude* 113 (E. Reynolds ed. 1932) (II. 722-28).

343. See H. Ellis, supra note 37.

344. See notes 258–69 supra & accompanying text.

345. See note 128 supra & accompanying text.

346. For a fascinating general account of the Puritan way of handling deviants and its influence on later American institutions, which applies squarely to prostitution, see K. Erikson, *Wayward Puritans* (1966).

347. See W. Shakespeare, *Measure for Measure.*

348. This misperception blinds us to the reality of other more serious social problems. See, e.g., notes 231–36 supra & accompanying text.

349. See notes 189–90 supra & accompanying text.

350. See St. John 8:3–11 (King James).

351. See H. Ellis, supra note 37, at 312–18, 405–06, 409–19.

352. W. Shakespeare, *Measure for Measure,* Act II, sc. II, II. 117–22, reprinted in *The Oxford Shakespeare* 80 (W. Craig ed. 1966).

Part Two

DRUGS

4

Drug Use and the Rights of the Person

Laws criminalizing the use of certain drugs have been major targets of the general liberal critique of overcriminalization.[1] As in the case of commercial sex, advocates of decriminalization have had little success in opposing drug laws,[2] despite the sound arguments they have advanced that enforcement is costly and wasteful. It is not enough, however, to raise cost-benefit concerns;[3] it appears necessary to criticize independently the common assumption that drug use is immoral. There has been a dearth of serious argument on this point. Yet a forceful argument can be made, consistent with the pattern of our argument about commercial sex, that laws criminalizing many forms of drug use violate certain basic rights of the person.

This chapter will have a structure parallel to that of the previous chapter: first, a description of drug use as an empirical phenomenon in historical, anthropological, and medical perspective; second, a consideration of the main arguments for the criminalization of drug use in the United States; third, an application of the autonomy-based theory of morality, set out in Chapter 1 and elaborated in the previous chapters, to the critical examination of the main arguments for the criminalization of drug use; fourth, a statement of the case for a right to drug use, which would include the extension to drug use of the constitutional right to privacy; and finally, a review of alternative regulatory approaches to drug use.

I. DRUG USE: ANTHROPOLOGICAL, HISTORICAL, AND
   PHARMACOLOGICAL PERSPECTIVES

A drug may be broadly defined as "any chemical agent that affects living processes"[4] that may be ingested through the mouth, the rectum, by injection, or by inhalation.[5] Importantly, this standard definition is pharmacological: a substance is defined as a drug by its mechanism of chemical agency. Two significant conclusions follow. First, according to this definition, alcohol, caffeine, and nicotine are drugs, however ingested and in whatever circumstances, for they are chemical agents within its terms.[6] The reluctance of social convention to regard these agents as drugs requires explanation and investigation. The popular definition of drugs certainly cannot be accepted uncritically without begging a most important moral question.

Second, the scientific definition implies nothing about the purposes of drug use, which include therapeutic cure, [7] relief of symptoms, pain, or anxiety,[8] regulation of mood (by way either of depressants or stimulants),[9] stimulation and exploration of religious experience,[10] release of hallucinatory fantasy for a range of purposes,[11] and recreational pleasure.[12] A political or moral analysis of drug use must go beyond the pharmacological focus on the chemical agency common to all drugs and assess the propriety of various purposes of drug use.

Drug use appears to be very ancient, sometimes appearing in forms that mix inextricably several or all of the therapeutic, religious, and recreational elements. The very ancient tradition of the shaman[13] incorporated elements of drug use into rituals[14] in which the shaman experienced mystical and ecstatic states that appear to have brought comfort to the sick and afflicted.[15] In addition, the shaman through such rituals received prophetic and political messages for the society at large.[16] Anthropological research into cultures that retain this tradition reveals a complex and often highly stylized set of experiences, embedded in a cultural setting of religion, therapy, medicine, and even political protest, in which drugs derived from native plants play a prominent role.[17] In the ancient world, the drug soma, of uncertain identity,[18] appears to have been integral to the mystical experiences of the divine celebrated in the ancient hymns of the Hindu *RgVeda*.[19] Drug use in some form may have been central to the Greek mystery cults.[20] One historian controversially has identified drug use as contributing to the origins of Christianity.[21]

In the west, Christianity appears to have sharply repudiated the use of drugs as an organon of religious experience, finding it to be a form of Gnostic heresy.[22] Shamanic possession and ecstasy, at the heart of much earlier religion, becomes, from this perspective, one form of demonic or satanic witchcraft,[23] a charge that Catholic missionaries made against the shamanic practices they encountered in the New World.[24] The leading contemporary defender of this Judaeo-Christian repudiation, R. C. Zaehner, has argued that the technology of the self implicit in the orthodox western religions requires an unbridgeable gap between the human and the divine,[25] expressed in the submission of the self to ethical imperatives by which persons express their common humanity and a religious humility.[26] Accordingly, western, in contrast to nonwestern, mystical experience expresses the distance between the human and the divine. Drugs, including alcohol,[27] are ruled out as stimuli to religious experience because they bridge this distance, indulging the narcissistic perception that the user himself is divine and thus free of the constraints of ethical submission.

While drug use as an adjunct to religious experience was thus driven underground in the west, recreational uses continued in the secular sphere. Fermented alcoholic beverages were celebrated by Euripides,[28] and appear to have been part of the fabric of cultivated social intercourse in Plato's Athens.[29] Overindulgence, to the point of drunkenness, was certainly considered a vice,[30] but a well-regulated indulgence was not. On balance, the judicious Montaigne recommended the virtues of wine: "[W]e should make our daily drinking habits more expansive and vigorous."[31] When the use of caffeine and nicotine was introduced into western and other cultures, these drugs encountered cultural and some spirited political resistance,[32] but were in time integrated into new forms of social and personal life.

A striking political concern with alcohol use developed with the availability of distilled liquor.[33] Hogarth's classic engravings "Beer Street" and "Gin Lane" reflect the contrasting social perceptions of the benign effects of fermented beverages (wine and beer) and of the malign dissipation caused by use of distilled liquor (gin).[34] In Europe and England, this concern led to regulation aimed at controlling drunkenness as such. Neither Luther nor Calvin, both of whom followed Augustinian Catholicism in emphasizing original sin and salvation by faith,[35] appear to have seen any religious or moral benefit in the elimination of alcohol from social and personal life.[36] Religious support for prohibition of alcohol dates from the Radical Reformation,[37] which saw the rise of Anabaptist sects in Europe and of Quakers and Methodists in England.[38] These sects, stressing the inward spirituality of the imitation of Christ in a way in which Luther and Calvin did not, identified freedom from dependence on alcohol as part of the stewardship of the body in which the spirit of Christ might reside.[39]

The most powerful political expression of this religious perspective developed in the United States, where it thus shaped America's general perception of permissible drug use. An important expression of this emerging point of view was an influential book by a signatory to the Declaration of Independence, *An Inquiry into the Effects of Ardent Spirits upon the Human Body and Mind*,[40] by the Quaker physician Benjamin Rush. Rush focused on the malign effects of "ardent spirits" (distilled liquor), as opposed to the effects of fermented beverages which, with opium, he regarded as much less harmful alternatives.[41] His argument against hard liquor cited a litany of medical and social harms, including harms to physical well-being[42] and to social virtue.[43] Rush wrote mainly as a physician and social observer, but his medical and sociological perceptions clearly were colored by a religious morality that identified the immorality of distilled liquor with the wrongness of suicide.[44] In the conclusion of his argument, he described Quakers and Methodists as religious groups who comprehended their duty to renounce hard liquor,[45] and issued a call to American ministers of every denomination to join them as a moral force in combating this social evil.[46]

During the nineteenth and early twentieth century Rush's call was answered by the emergence of an explicitly religious argument. Such influential clergymen as Lyman Beecher found that the prohibition of liquor was required, not only to prevent the secular harms that Rush identified, but also by the terms of the Bible itself.[47] These often extravagant Biblical interpretations,[48] which defy any sound canons of Biblical scholarship,[49] fired an emerging American Protestant orthodoxy.[50] The political expression of this movement became increasingly intransigent, moving from voluntary associations concerned with helping people limit their use of hard liquor to absolute state prohibitions of all forms of liquor, whether distilled or fermented.[51] The prohibition of fermented beverages, which Rush would not have supported[52], derived from an increasingly popular argument found in the prohibition movement literature. It was maintained that fermented beverages were a steppingstone to distilled liquor[53] and, accordingly, that ending the "habit forming and brain perverting"[54] effects of hard liquor required the prohibition of fermented beverages as well.[55]

The religious ideals that fueled this movement became secularized into a dominant conception of "public morality," as articulated by purity reformers.[56] Identifying morality with the asexual and spiritual nature of women in the home,[57] these reformers perceived liquor use in the familiar masculine territory of the saloons as a threat to moral values,[58] calling men from the spiritual sanctuary of wife and children into the coarse, competitive, and sensual public worlds of work and politics.[59] Prohibition appears to have been associated, ideologically, with the purification of politics:[60] the evil of liquor was increasingly condemned as a form of slavery, which undermined "a citizen in his political capacity."[61] The culmination of this movement was, of course, Prohibition,[62] instituted via the eighteenth amendment to the United States Constitution in 1919, and repealed by the twenty-first amendment in 1933.[63]

This American moral perspective on the use of liquor played a significant role in the evolving legal treatment of opium and marijuana. Conceptions of proper drug use, developed in the liquor context, were applied, *mutatis mutandi,* to other drugs—to opium in the period of growing intransigence that culminated in Prohibition[64] and to marijuana in the frustrating period for purity reformers after Repeal.[65] The case of opium is particularly instructive. Opium, the use of which as an analgesic is ancient,[66] was brought to public notoriety in the early nineteenth century in the form of laudanum, an opium and wine mixture. Laudanum's capacity to spark imaginative exploration was both celebrated and deplored by such romantic poets as Coleridge[67] and Baudelaire,[68] and by the shrewd essayist De Quincey.[69] Its widespread use in America as an ingredient of the popular medicines used largely by women (who may have had religious scruples about alcohol)[70] went largely unnoticed until the end of the nineteenth century.[71] At that time, the acquisition by the United States of the Philippines brought their opium trade under American political responsibility. At issue was whether to reconstitute the Spanish licensing system whereby contractors paid the government for the right to grow and sell opium. The opium was, evidently, widely used by the Chinese population of the Philippines, largely for recreational purposes.[72] A central figure in shaping the American response was Bishop Brent, the Anglican bishop of the Philippines, who was one of three members appointed to the Philippine Opium Commission.[73] Brent argued:

The question is first and foremost a moral one. The use of the drug otherwise than medicinally is a vice. . . . The opium traffic stands in the category of crime except so far as it is imported for purely medicinal purposes. It cannot be ranked with the liquor trade, for, as every temperate man acknowledges, in this latter there is a legitimate consumption as a beverage, however much the liberty may be abused, whereas there is no unvicious use of opium or its immediate products as a foodstuff or beverage. The consumption of opium is not merely a personal weakness; it is a social vice, i.e. a crime.[74]

Brent's comparison of opium to liquor is striking in that it suggests a natural association of the two questions. Americans, who were gravitating to a more prohibitionary policy on liquor than Brent appeared to assume, understandably could tolerate no less for non-medicinal uses of opium.[75] The British assumption that use of opium, its benefits outweighing its harm, was as much a way of life in the east as use of liquor was in the west,[76] could take no hold on minds that increasingly questioned the propriety of liquor use itself. Brent's Commission not surprisingly, but prophetically for the future of American internal policies on drug use, recommended a government monopoly to effect the "control, repression and abolition of the use of opium and the traffic therein."[77] The United States thus became the first western nation to sponsor a respected study that advocated some form of prohibition.

The growing American concern with opium was fired by reports from Christian missionaries in China.[78] Opium was available to the Chinese either through a black market or after it had been subjected to a series of tariffs.[79] Although Chinese of all classes used opium, the poor inevitably suffered most from the high prices. Missionaries reported that men sold their businesses and families to satisfy their habits.[80] Apparently the missionaries did not perceive an appropriate solution in making opium available at lower prices. They associated opium use with a variety of physical and social harms,[81] similar to those Rush associated with alcohol. Missionaries thus perceived opium use as frustrating their own ambitions. To some extent, this was a consequence of history: the British success in the Opium Wars,[82] which opened China to the opium trade, opened China to Christianity as well.[83] While originally the Christian missionaries had welcomed this development, the association of Christianity with forcing opium on a recalcitrant people hardly endeared the teachings of the missionaries to the Chinese.[84] In light of this history, missionaries paradoxically identified the evils of Chinese social and political life (including opium) with its non-Christian religion and morality.[85] Indeed, the missionaries perceived the issue in terms of standard temperance doctrine long familiar in the United States. Opium was said to present a block to Christianity in China in the same way that alcohol presented a block to Christianity in the United States.[86] Both were forms of intemperance which were "enem[ies] of spirituality and . . . defiler[s] of the body."[87] Accordingly, Chinese converts were told they could not be both Christians and opium takers.[88]

These missionary attitudes reached the United States in a variety of ways.[89] For example, one lobbying group for the missionaries in the

United States, the International Reform Bureau, obtained a hearing before the State Department in 1905 to induce the Department to use its good offices to release China from its treaty obligations to tolerate opium traffic.[90] One of the missionaries, Bishop Brent, not only sat on the Philippine Opium Commission, but appears to have sent to President Roosevelt in 1906[91] the letter that led to the United State's organizing the 1909 Shanghai Opium Conference, thus beginning the international movement for the careful control of the opium trade.[92] When a study prepared for the Conference revealed widespread use of opium in the United States, [93] albeit under the guise of a medicinal agent, the government was already committed to an antiopium stance for complex economic, political, and ideological reasons.[94] The embarrassing gap in American domestic law,[95] in contrast to the United State's aggressively prohibitory international stance, [96] led to the Harrison Act of 1914, a regulatory and licensing statute for opium.[97]

The terms of the Harrison Act, while permitting the use of opium in the treatment of disease or injury, did not specify whether and to what extent physicians might prescribe opium for use in treating heroin addiction.[98] The administrative construction of the statute, which took form in the period of Prohibition, [99] decisively rejected any such use of opium.[100] The United States Supreme Court lent its imprimatur to this construction in several cases. The Court invoked in one such case the popular term "dope fiend";[101] in another it characterized the concept that heroin maintenance is sound medical practice as "so plain a perversion of meaning that no discussion of the subject is required."[102] In still another case, the Court spoke of heroin maintenance as "the gratification of a diseased appetite for these pernicious drugs."[103]

Although the Court later reversed itself,[104] its original decisions lent legitimacy to the construction of the Act by a small group of Washington administrators, [105] who condemned and prematurely ended experiments by several states in providing heroin maintenance clinics.[106] The medical profession in the United States, in contrast to the British profession, which strongly and successfully resisted similar measures in Britain,[107] was unable to prevent the prohibition of maintenance.[108] The American sense of proper drug use, formed in the battles over liquor, naturally reproduced itself in the perception of opium use with comparable social images of disease and disorder (the "drug fiend").[109] These dubious assumptions were never questioned. By the time of the first careful and impartial discussion of the facts,[110] the legal pattern was already cast. The United States was committed to the absolute prohibition of opium and its derivatives except for narrow medical purposes, while in England and Europe heroin maintenance dosages were available.[111]

In the wake of the repeal of Prohibition in 1933, social attitudes to drug use took on an independent significance in shaping legal developments. Arguably because of the failure of the attack on liquor, attitudes toward drugs became even more uncompromising.[112] The campaign leading to the passage of the Marihuana Tax Act of 1937,[113] for example, included remarkable distortions of the evidence of harm caused by marijuana,[114] ignoring the findings of empirical inquiries.[115] In later years, sanctions for the use of drugs, especially heroin, increased both at the federal and state levels.[116] California and New York experimented with hospitalization of addicts,[117] but in ways that may have been as objectionable as criminalization itself.[118] New York turned from its abortive experiment to some of the harshest criminal sanctions for drug use in the United States.[119]

Remarkable pharmacological advances in the past few centuries have been a mixed blessing; while many new kinds of relief are now available, some of them are simply purer and more powerful forms of the chemical agents of existing drugs. The dangers of abuse have increased correspondingly.[120] Among the hallucinogens, for example, mescaline[121] and LSD[122] induce more powerful experiences than previously known narcotic plants.[123] The chemical innovations of morphine[124] and heroin,[125] as well as the technological innovation of the hypodermic needle,[126] have increased both the strengths and the dangers of drug use beyond levels created by opium smoking and laudanum.

Contemporary drugs may be classified as: the narcotics (opium, morphine, heroin, methadone, and others),[127] caffeine,[128] nicotine,[129] the depressants (alcohol, barbiturates, tranquilizers, and other sedatives and hypnotics),[130] the stimulants (including coca leaves, cocaine, and amphetamines),[131] and the hallucinogens or phantasticants (mescaline, LSD, LSD-like drugs, marijuana, and hashish).[132]

The contemporary legal treatment of these drugs is summarized in the Comprehensive Drug Abuse Prevention and Control Act of 1970, a federal statute that has been the model for comparable state statutes.[133] Drugs are divided into five schedules, ranging from those with the highest potential for abuse, for which no use is permitted (Schedule I), to those for which medical use is permitted (Schedules II to V). For drugs in schedules III to V, control of production is removed; penalties for illegal use are decreased and are focused instead on manufacturing and distribution. Schedule I includes heroin, marijuana, LSD, mescaline, and others; Schedule II, morphine, cocaine, amphetamine-type stimulants, and others; Schedule III, nonamphetamine-type stimulants and barbiturates; Schedule IV, barbiturate and nonbarbiturate depressants, etc.; Schedule V, compounds with low amounts of narcotics, stimulants, and depressants. Of the drugs typologically described above, alcohol, caffeine, and nicotine are not within the schedules, and thus are unregulated by their strictures.[134]

II. THE ARGUMENTS FOR THE CRIMINALIZATION OF DRUG USE

In order to understand the American practice of criminal prohibition of certain forms of drug use, we must take seriously the arguments offered in its defense: (1) criminogenesis; (2) the control of ancillary forms of physical illness and injury; (3) the intrinsically immoral and degrading nature of drug use, either in and of itself or in its effects on other individuals and society in general; and (4) cognate to (3), the self-destructive or debilitating nature of drug use. Of these arguments, the first and second do not justify the current absolute criminal prohibitions of many forms of drug use; therefore, the gravamen of the argument for criminalization turns, as we shall see, on the proper weight to be given to the third and fourth arguments.

A. *Criminogenesis*

Criminal prohibition of the use of certain drugs, notably heroin and marijuana, has been justified as a means of suppressing other types of crime. It is said that drug users support their habits by theft and robbery; that drug use releases violence, induces illegal trafficking in drugs, and enlarges the scope of organized crime operations.[135] None of these considerations in fact justifies the criminalization of drug use; indeed, criminalization itself fosters these evils. It forces drug users into illegal conduct to obtain money for drugs and brings them into contact with the criminal underground, the covertness of which breeds incidental crime.

First, the association of drug use with illegal trafficking in drugs and the consequent enlarged scope of organized crime operations is a result of criminalization itself. Criminalization imposes a crime tariff on drugs, inflating prices and creating high profit margins that make the drug trade attractive to organized crime.[136] The organized crime argument begs the question, since it is criminalization, not drug use itself, that makes possible organized crime involvement.[137]

Second, to the extent that drug use is related to increases in other criminal activity, or diversion of criminal activity into certain forms,[138] that causal matrix depends on criminalization, not on drug use itself. In order to pay the crime tariff on drugs, users may engage in burglary, theft, or robbery, or in services with their own crime tariffs, such as prostitution, gambling, and drug trafficking itself. In addition, the criminal stigma and enforced covertness probably encourage,[139] or at least reinforce, dependence on narcotics, and certainly make detection and possible control of addition more difficult. Where heroin is made available to addicts in regulated contexts at low or minimal prices, as it is in Britain,[140] no causal nexus with ancillary crime exists,[141] and the level of drug addiction appears under control.[142] In the United states, prior to the Harrison Act, there was no link between drug use and ancillary crime. Indeed, the composition of the drug-using population in the United States has probably been decisively shaped by criminalization. The population of heroin addicts, which before criminalization included many middle-class women,[143] now includes a disproportionate number of poor urban minorities.[144] The moral implications of this shift, for which criminalization bears some responsibility,[145] are themselves an appropriate subject for further analysis.

Third, at least with respect to most drugs now criminalized, there is simply no factual support for the argument that drug use itself releases inhibitions or criminal tendencies. To the contrary, heroin and marijuana appear to diminish the aggressiveness which often expresses itself in violent crime.[146] No chapter of the history of American attitudes to drug use is more instructive than the dependence of advocates of criminalization on this argument. Often this argument was supported by selective citations from unreliable journalistic[147] or law enforcement reports,[148] self-serving confessions by criminals that their conduct was induced by drugs,[149] or unsubstantiated surmises of enforcement officials wholly lacking any critical impartiality on the question.[150]

This hystericalized social mythology may unwittingly aggravate the problem of violent crime that it obstensibly seeks to reduce. In deterring the use of the drugs that lessen violent propensities, criminalization may encourage the use of alcohol, which demonstrably heightens such violent tendencies.[151] In addition, upon discovering that certain illegal drugs do not cause violent crime, persons who use these drugs may fail to regulate appropriately their use in certain contexts—for example, prior to driving. This discovery may also lead them to conclude that all distinctions between legal and illegal drugs are irrational and hypocritical,[152] and may thereby encourage them to use other illegal drugs which might, in fact, stimulate illegal violence.

Wholesale criminalization, in contrast to fine-tuned regulation of drug dosages and uses, apparently creates or compounds the problem it is supposed to solve.

Arguments of criminogenesis are generally circular and question-begging; they argue for criminalization of drug use on the basis of the evils that criminalization, not drug use, fosters. If there are crimes associated with drug use, they are more rationally attacked by decriminalization and by criminal statutes directed narrowly at the evils themselves (for example, drug use before driving), not by overbroad statutes that actually encourage what they purport to combat.

B. *Control of Physical Injury and Other Harms*

Another argument supporting criminalization is that drug use may cause physical injury and even death. The image usually invoked is that of the contemporary, urban, ghetto heroin addict, whose addiction may be accompanied by hepatitis, tetanus, and abscesses at the site of injection. His practice of sharing needles may result in the communication of disease—for example, malaria. His addiction may also conceal the early symptoms of diseases, such as pneumonia, or lead to malnutrition, which increases susceptibility to disease. The varying strengths of doses may also increase the possibility of an overdose and sometimes death.[153]

This scenario fails to recognize that any drug that is used in sufficiently high dosages or in certain contexts (with other drugs, for example) will probably cause severe harm, including, sometimes, death. This is true of many drugs currently available without prescription.[154] Harm usually occurs when, intentionally or not, the instructions for proper use are not observed. In general, the composition and purity of legal drugs are carefully regulated, and the potential for harm is kept to a reasonable minimum by regulations, appropriate intructions, and warnings.

Many of the harms cited as the basis for criminalization could be avoided by the same forms of regulation that are applied to presently legal drugs. For example, because the Food and Drug Administration does not regulate the sale of heroin, the buyer is never sure of what he is getting and may accidentally give himself a fatal overdose.[155] The lack of appropriate medical supervision over the sterilization of hypodermic needles used to inject heroin accounts for the diseases found at the site of injection.[156] In addition, the illegality of drug use discourages the addict from seeing a physician. A physician, if consulted, might detect symptoms of illness that are masked by the addiction.[157] Malnutrition, for example, is common among addicts and is caused both by a lack of interest in food and by a lack of money due to the crime tariff. In short, the evils of heroin use that are alleged as a ground for criminalization are produced or fostered by such criminalization; all these dangers could be reduced appreciably if heroin use were legal and regulated, as it is in Britain.[158]

C. *Moral Arguments*

It is disingenuous to suppose that the American criminal prohibition of drug use is based on the secular concerns of criminogenesis and control of drug-related injuries. Neither argument can justify such prohibition; indeed, serious concern with the evils adduced by both arguments would require the opposite conclusion. These arguments are, at best, post hoc empirical makeweights for justifications of a different order, namely, moralistic and paternalistic arguments of a peculiarly American provenance. In order to deal effectively with the justifications for criminal prohibitions, we must examine these arguments critically.

Of course, in order to demonstrate that the concept of "public morality" has been abused, one must analyze the precise nature of the abuse. What moral fallacies underlie the traditional arguments? Are the facts wrong, or are they just unfairly assessed? Do the proponents of these traditional arguments give improper weight to certain personal ideals? Do they make question-begging assumptions about moral personality?

The tradition of moral condemnation of drug use is surely entitled to a respectful hearing. I wish to take it very seriously, and yet show how human rights theory of the kind earlier suggested demonstrates why such moral condemnation is mistaken. In order to do this, I will refer to moral theory and moral archaeology. Moral strictures such as those surrounding drug use often rest on beliefs which we consciously reject elsewhere in our social life but which, in certain circumscribed areas, retain their force. An historical and moral analysis reveals these unconscious assumptions and subjects them to moral assessment. Let us begin with the moral grounds for the condemnation of drug use per se, and then turn to the paternalistic grounds.

III. THE MORALITY OF DRUG USE AND THE RIGHTS OF THE PERSON

The moral condemnation of drug use rests on a number of disparate grounds. They will be considered *seriatim* as follows: (1) the intrinsically degraded character of drug use; (2) effects of drugs on particular third parties; (3) effects of drug use on society at large; (4) background issues of social and economic justice; and (5) paternalistic arguments about the self-destructive or debilitating nature of drug use.

A. *Drug Use and Degradation*

To think of behavior as degraded is to assume that one's self-esteem is invested in the competent exercise of certain personal abilities and that the behavior in question fails to be competent in the required way. The degraded one thus is the natural object of shame or self-disgust at his personal failure to live up to standards of conduct that are valued as essential to the integrity of the self.[159] Accordingly, the application of the notion of degradation to drug use requires an analysis of the valued behavior from which such use is alleged to deviate. This behavior apparently embodies certain general conceptions of self-control and also includes specific perfectionist ideals of such conceptions as well as notions of moral personality which drug use, especially drug addiction, alienates or enslaves in some fundamentally immoral way. Although these conceptions are interrelated, we may profitably discuss them separately.

1. GENERAL CONCEPTIONS OF SELF-CONTROL. One general conception of the person, which may underlie the claim that drug use is degrading, is the value of self-control. Before the value of self-control can be determined we must have some idea of the proper uses of this capacity. We should recall in this connection our earlier discussion of Saint Augustine's moral conception that sexual propensities not consistent with necessary procreational goals are a degrading loss of self-control.[160] Augustine's procreational model for sexuality was part of an emerging philosophy of self-mastery, marked by its concern to subordinate and, where necessary, to deny otherwise natural aspects of the self in the service of the stipulated moral conception. This philosophy appears to have encompassed, as well, the denial of religious drug use, since such use led to ecstatic experiences of personal divinity, which Augustine's theory condemned as heretical forms of possession.[161] From this perspective, there is an inner unity in the belief that both natural sexual impulses and drug experience are degraded. In this context they both are anarchic losses of self-control inconsistent with the proper aims of rational will: e.g., procreation and religious experience without drugs. This would explain the contemporary concern with those forms of drug use that most closely approximate earlier religious forms of drug use.[162]

The general Augustinian model of self-control is no more sustainable when applied to drug use than to sex:[163] drug use does not produce a drunken anarchy inconsistent with the aims of rational will as such. Humans use drugs for diverse purposes—for therapeutic care and cure, for relief of pain or anxiety, for stimulation or depression of moods, for exploration of imaginative experience (for creative, aesthetic, religious, therapeutic, or other reasons), for recreative pleasure, and the like.[164] Humans consciously choose among these purposes depending on the context and their individual aims. In so doing, they express self-respect by regulating the quality and versatility of their experiences in life to include greater control of mood[165] and, sometimes, increased freedom and flexibility of imagination.[166] For many, such drug use does not constitute fear-ridden anarchy, but promotes the rational self-control of those ingredients fundamental to the design of a fulfilled life. It is, of course, a banality of the literature of perceptive observers on drug experience that the quality of such experience varies according to the expectations, aims, and identity that the person brings to the experience.[167] This should confirm that drug experience is neither satanic damnation nor divine redemption of the self, but merely one means by which the already existing interests of the person may be explored or realized.

The Augustinian philosophy of the self, which disavows drug use as a mode of religious experience, might have some larger appeal if it were true that such drug experience prevented one from acting on the fundamental moral imperative of treating persons as equals. In the historical evolution of moral ideas, perhaps, the Augustinian philosophy played some benign role in the elaboration and practical efficacy of this moral imperative in social life. In any event, it is fallacious to assume that this hypothetical role now requires the conclusion that such drug experience is inconsistent with a life regulated by moral principles. There is no evidence whatsoever to support this proposition; indeed, there is some evidence (although hardly conclusive) that the contrary proposition is true.[168]

Because these models of sexuality and drug use can no longer be sustained, neither can they be legally enforced on the ground of public morality if, as I have argued in earlier chapters, to be legally enforceable moral ideas must be grounded in equal concern and respect for autonomy. Just as recognition of the inadequacy of the procreational model is a focus of argument critical of overcriminalization of consensual adult sexuality, the criminalization of drug use cannot be sustained on the comparable model of improper drug use.

This does not mean, of course, that drug use is necessarily a superior moral ideal. To the contrary, there is at least one particular moral conception of personal perfectionism which supposes all drug use is intrinsically degraded. To this we now turn.

2. PERFECTIONIST IDEALS OF THE PERSON. No argument supporting the moral condemnation of drug use has had a stronger and more pervasive hold on the American popular imagination than the argument for protecting the perfectionist ideal of the person.[169] This ideal should be distinguished from the earlier Augustinian conception, which condemned drug use as an organon of religious experience but did not object to drug use as such. Indeed, the western tradition outside the United States, in both Protestant and Catholic nations, tolerated many secular forms of drug use, notably liquor.[170] Excessive drug use, to the point of drunkenness, for example, was a vice,[171] but a well-regulated use was not.

The perfectionist ideal arose within the Radical Reformation and was carried to the United States by sects, such as the Quakers and Methodists, whose own moral conceptions appear to have decisively shaped the American conception of public morality.[172] This ideal is derived from the radical merger of the priesthood and laity that occurred in these sects, their tendency to downplay the doctrine of original sin, and their demand that all members spiritually imitate Christ.[173] The laity at large were thus expected to conform to a perfectionistic saintliness that earlier, more pessimistic attitudes would have required only of the clergy, or of certain of the laity whose lives were marked by extraordinary self-sacrifice and dedication. In addition, the Radical Reformation laid great emphasis on internal spirituality and expected its adherents to strive for perfectionistic saintliness in this sphere as well. It is as if the Augustinian concern to keep religious experience unpolluted by alien agents were generalized to subjective experience in general. For the radical sects and their offshoots, all personal experience was considered religious; therefore, the state and quality of such experience was properly the subject of religious concern. The use of drugs, in particular alcohol, for nonmedical purposes, was thus eventually condemned.[174]

This conception identifies virtue, including the virtues of citizenship, with personal imitation of Christ, and thus with a commitment to extraordinary self-sacrifice in the service of others, requiring the exercise of independent conscientiousness and self-control. Thus, Benjamin Rush, when analyzing liquor as a social problem,[175] focused not only on its alleged physical harmfulness, but also particularly on the resultant loss of control which was inconsistent with the required character of a life in service to others.[176] He strikingly defined the consumption of distilled liquor as a form of suicide,[177] a self-destructive impulse which ignores the constant call of service to others. The drug user, perceived through the lens of this moral conception, cultivates subjective experiences which lead to a similar self-indulgent loss of control. The use of drugs thus was naturally seen (in accordance with the Augustinian model of religious experience) as a radical evil, even as heresy or satanic possession,[178] with which there could be no compromise. This, in short, is the moral philosophy underlying America's unique experiment with prohibition of alcohol,[179] its remarkable generalization of this approach to opium and marijuana,[180] and its continuing prohibitions in other areas of drug use.[181]

One may legitimately urge this moral conception upon others as a guide for their conduct, but not as a valid justification of criminal sanctions. First, the autonomy-based concept of treating persons as equals rests on respect for the individual's ability to determine, evaluate, and revise the meaning of his or her own life. It was argued earlier that the Augustinian model of self-control should not be legally enforced precisely because it ignores this experience of responsible self-determination as an important aspect of moral personality. It thus deprives persons of autonomous choice regarding fundamental experiences. The invocation of the perfectionist ideal of self-control as a compulsory moral standard is open to similar objections. There is no reason to believe that it is the only legitimate model of responsible self-control, the only means of human fulfillment. Many other courses may reasonably and responsibly accommodate the diverse individuality of human competences, aspirations, and ends. What for one is a reasonable, self-imposed ideal of self-control and social service may be for another a self-defeating impoverishment of human experience and imagination, a rigid and inflexible willfulness without intelligent freedom or reasonable spontaneity, a masochistic denial of self and subjectivity in the service of uncritical and dubiously manipulative moral aims.

Second, the only moral principles that are properly enforceable by the criminal law are those that secure the higher-order rational interests at little cost.[182] These principles define a minimum morality of decency, which only requires such sacrifice of an individual's interests that may be reasonably and fairly expected. These principles do not require the kind of self-sacrifice that we may admire in saints and heroes.[183] Beyond this morality of decency there are standards of aspiration[184] which, without ethical demand, persons may individually adopt. It is, in fact, controversial whether the perfectionist ideal is a moral desideratum that should command the respect of all reasonable persons. Assuming it is, it is not properly enforceable through the criminal law because it requires a sacrifice of rational interests in the autonomous choice of fundamental experiences. Such a sacrifice cannot be compulsorily demanded, although it may be admired.

The religious conception that underlies the perfectionist ideal is centered on the cultivation of spontaneous religious experience by all persons. It is paradoxical that this emphasis was historically wedded to a rigid philosophy that excluded all alternative methods of achieving such religious experience. Surely, any such ideal of spontaneous feeling is the very antithesis of compulsory forms of experience. Indeed, the invocation of such ideals to justify compulsory norms is a travesty of the spiritual meaning of these ideals.

In any event, in such matters, the range of reasonable personal ideals is wide and acutely sensitive to personal context and individual idiosyncrasy. The law has no proper role in determining how these choices are to be made or in promoting the perfectionist ideal in particular.

3. THE ALIENATION OF MORAL PERSONALITY AND THE CONCEPT OF ADDIC-TION. Even if the argument that all drug use is degrading cannot be sustained on the basis of perfectionist ideals, there remains the intuition that certain forms of drug use degrade because they enslave moral personality, depriving the user of certain fundamental capacities. Immanuel Kant, the father of modern deontology, sketched a form of this argument when, after arguing that the drunk person "is simply like a beast, not to be treated as a human being,"[185] he observed:

The first of these debasements, which is even beneath the nature of an animal, is usually brought about by fermented liquors, but also by other stupefying agents such as opium and other products of the plant kingdom. These agents are misleading in that they produce for a while a dreamy euphoria and freedom from care, and even an imagined strength. But they are harmful in that afterwards depression and weakness follow and, worst of all, there results a need to take these stupefying agents again and again to increase the amount.[186]

Kant, like Rush,[187] apparently conceded that the moderate use of fermented beverages is moral because it may enliven the candor of social exchange.[188] Kant wrote, however, that "[t]he use of opium and distilled spirits for enjoyment is closer to baseness than the use of wine because the former, with the dreamy euphoria they produce, make one taciturn, withdrawn, and uncommunicative. Therefore, they are permitted only as medicines."[189] The gravamen of this argument today centers on the concept of addiction, those drugs, such as heroin which cause addiction, are said to be degrading, and thus may be morally condemned and legally prohibited.

Originally, the concept of addiction was not associated with drugs or chemical agents. When, in Shakespeare's *Twelfth Night*, Maria speaks of Olivia as "being addicted to a melancholy,"[190] she means that her mistress is subject to a dominant psychological propensity constituting a kind of devotion, which colors and organizes her other ends. Thus, Maria correctly observes that Malvolio's antics will be disfavorably interpreted in terms of Olivia's dominant psychological bent. In this sense, an addiction has a quasi-religious connotation; it has a devotional centrality in one's system of ends.[191]

When the concept of addiction is associated with certain drugs, at least four different strands of meaning are conflated: (1) tolerance (the progressive need for higher doses to secure the same effect),[192] (2) physical dependence (the incidence of withdrawal symptoms when drug use is stopped),[193] (3) psychological centrality of the drug in one's system of ends, and (4) a moral judgment of degradation (or, in the contemporary terminology, drug abuse).[194] Tolerance and physical dependence are often assumed to be inextricably linked to each other and to psychological devotion and drug abuse. None of these assumptions is, however, valid. Physical dependence does not invariably occur in every situation where tolerance develops. Tolerance and physical dependence, when linked, develop not only with narcotics, alcohol, and hypnotics, but also with medical administration of many other drugs in which neither psychological devotion nor drug abuse occurs.[195] Most strikingly, it is now clear that, even with respect to narcotics, alcohol, and hypnotics, tolerance and physical dependence are not sufficient causal conditions of psychological devotion or drug abuse. Many, perhaps most, persons who have developed tolerance for and physical dependence on a drug do not become psychologically devoted to it. Mere tolerance and physical dependence do not lead to psychological devotion or abuse unless the user is aware that the symptoms he may experience when the drug is stopped are symptoms of withdrawal,[196] which resumption of the drug would relieve. Even with such knowledge, psychological devotion or abuse does not always result. Most Vietnam War veterans who satisfied the requirements of tolerance, dependence, and knowledge, did not on return exhibit psychological dependence.[197] Conversely, it appears that neither psychological devotion nor abuse turns on tolerance or physical dependence in any direct way. Persons may become devoted to patterns of drug use even though their tolerance and physical dependence is low. Some assert that this is the condition of most American addicts.[198] Moreover, patterns of devotion or abuse may arise for drugs, such as the stimulants, which do not cause physical dependence.[199] Finally, psychological devotion and abuse do not appear to be permanent states: many persons give up drug use in a natural process of maturation.[200]

If physical dependence is neither necessary nor sufficient for psychological devotion or abuse, the popular belief that the use of certain drugs in itself leads to the enslavement of the user must be doubted.[201] In fact, careful empirical studies of the causes of drug devotion or abuse demonstrate the importance, not of physiological dependence, but of social and psychological factors.[202] As of 1968 a very large proportion of new heroin addicts in the United States, for example, were young, psychologically dependent in their personality structures, occupationally unskilled, socially deracinated, poor, and disadvantaged.[203] Many engaged in crime before they were addicted; after becoming addicted they turned to different kinds of crime more suited to maintain their habits.[204] Many perceptive social analysts have observed that such disadvantaged and alienated young people find in heroin a kind of socially confirmed identity.[205] Drug use may afford them an organizing focus. It generates its own social tasks and standards of successful achievement, its own forms of status and respect,[206] and its own larger meaning centering on the perceived qualities that the drug brings to the users' personal experiences, such as relief of anxiety and, sometimes, euphoric peace.[207] They may value the very danger of drug use, seeing it as a challenge to the dominant culture and an affirmation of their own values.

This perspective naturally leads one to question the conflation, implicit in the concept of drug abuse, of psychological devotion to drugs with a moral judgment of degradation. This conflation cannot, as we have seen, be sustained on some ground that the drug, in itself, immediately enslaves. There remains, however, the objection to drug use in its psychologically organizing and central role in the user's system of ends. The concept of addiction expresses, then, a form of moral criticism, couched in the obscuring language of "drug abuse," of such psychological centrality.[208]

The nature of this moral criticism may be clarified by extending it, by analogy, to other kinds of human behavior. Consider, for example, addiction to love[209] or to wealth.[210] In both cases, the analogy is exact: the concept of addiction does not, as we have seen, turn on physiological factors like tolerance and dependence, but on a certain kind of psychological centrality and some form of moral criticism thereof. Love then can be an addiction when a certain attachment has psychological centrality among the person's ends and when that centrality is subject to criticism. The lover may be said to have lost his capacity for "appreciation of and ability to deal with other things in his environment, or in himself, so that he had become increasingly dependent on that experience as his only source of gratification."[211] Wealth, correspondingly, is condemned as an addiction when the pursuit of it has such centrality at the inhumane cost of blinding the person to other fulfilling ends in his life and to ethical concern for the lives of others.[212]

Both arguments are intended as enlightened social criticism, pointing up defects in the rationality or humanity of the ways in which people structure their ends and lives. As long, however, as these defective life plans do not lead the agent directly to violate the moral rights of others—for example, by engaging in violence, robbery, or the like—no suggestion is made that these criticisms should be expressed through criminalization. In a constitutional democracy committed to equal concern and respect to autonomy, we honor the rights of persons to live their lives as they choose; we make our criticisms as part of a liberal culture offering pluralistic visions of the good life.

In similar fashion, the gravamen of the moral criticism implicit in the concept of drug abuse is the objection to the psychological centrality of drug use among a person's ends. Sometimes, the objection is put in terms of the propensity of addicts to commit violent crime and thus violate the rights of others, but this rests on false factual assumptions[213] or on causal connections that the criminalization of drug use, not drug use in itself, fosters.[214] We are left with the normative judgment that the psychological centrality of drugs in the user's life is unreasonable, because of the enormous risks or "unbelievable sacrifices"[215] that he undertakes or because of other values that he sacrifices. But it is difficult to see how this moral criticism can be given the normative weight that it is intended to bear, that is, to justify the criminalization of drug use, consistent with the autonomy-based interpretation of treating persons as equals. From this perspective, persons are to be guaranteed, on fair terms to all, the capacity to define with dignity and take responsibility for the meaning of their own lives, evaluated and revised in terms of standards and evidence which express higher-order interests in freedom and rationality. As we have seen,[216] the psychological centrality of drug use for many young addicts in the United States may, from the perspective of their own circumstances, not unreasonably organize their lives and ends. In contrast, the moral criticism implicit in the concept of drug abuse fails to take seriously the perspective and circumstances of the addict, often substituting competences and aspirations rooted in the critic's own background and personal aspirations to organize a self-respecting social identity, which might only exceptionally require drug use. Accordingly, the moral content of the concept of drug abuse appears deeply controversial. Certainly, it can bear no more just normative weight than the criticism of love or wealth as addictions. Society is not prepared to apply criminal sanctions in those cases because of considerations that should apply to drug use as well: in a society committed to equal concern and respect to autonomy, persons are entitled to make their own trade-offs among basic personal and social values. We certainly can criticize these decisions, but we do not regard criminalization as an appropriate expression of our condemnation.

From this perspective, Kant's identification of moral personality with freedom from drug use is remarkably inconsistent with what he wrote elsewhere about autonomy as the basis of moral personality.[217] In his central statements of ethical theory, moral personality is described in terms of autonomous independence—the capacity to order and choose one's ends as a free and rational being. By comparison, in his discussion of drug use, this autonomous freedom is isolated from any sovereignty over the qualities of one's experience. It is impossible to square these views. Indeed, the deeper theory of autonomy, Kant's central contribution to ethical theory, requires the rejection of this unimaginative view of moral personality. Kant meant to make the valid point that it is immoral to abdicate or alienate one's autonomy or one's capacity for self-critical choice about the form of one's life through consent to any form of slavery. But Kant was wrong in thinking that drug use involves a similar kind of alienation. Voluntary use of drugs cannot reasonably be supposed to be a slavery that alienates the moral personality, because even psychological devotion to drugs may express not a physiological bondage, but critical interests of the person. Indeed, there is something morally perverse in condemning drug use as intrinsic moral slavery when the very prohibition of it seems to be an arbitrary abridgement of personal freedom.

B. *Harms to Determinate Third Parties*

As we have seen, the autonomy-based interpretation of treating persons as equals yields a complex set of moral principles (those of obligation and duty) that may justly be enforced by the criminal law; these principles put constraints on the proper scope of criminalization defined in terms of preventing harms and interpreted in terms of higher-order rational interests of the person.[218] In general, these principles do not justify absolute prohibitions of drug use on the ground of preventing such harms to others, for, as we saw in our discussion of criminogenesis, there is no factual support for the proposition that many drugs currently criminalized lead to violent attacks on the interests of others; indeed, criminalization appears itself to foster, not combat, such links of drug use to attacks on others.

Although absolute prohibitions of drug use cannot be sustained on appropriate moral grounds, more limited and circumscribed moral arguments might justify forestalling drug use in specific circumstances. Decisions to use drugs do not occur in a vacuum: personal relationships may relevantly alter our moral evaluation of the situation. Consider, for example, moral obligations to third parties, which a person who uses drugs may not be able to discharge. The central class of such relevant relationships are those of a potential parent to an unborn child. Parenthood is a role embedded in social institutions of family and education and regulated by principles of justice that assess rights and duties, benefits and burdens, in terms of fairness and equity to parents, children, and society in general.[219] Voluntarily undertaking parenthood gives rise to, among other things, a social obligation to perform one's just parental role; in addition there are natural duties of parenthood that likewise require appropriate action.[220] It is a prima facie violation of such moral obligations to take drugs that impair the well-being of the unborn child.[221] To the extent that grave effects of such kinds may occur, drug taking by parents during the relevant period of risk may be appropriately regulated.[222]

Such moral obligations to determinate third parties, however, clearly do not justify any absolute prohibition on drug use. The requirements apply only to parents during the relevant periods of risk, and only to drugs which create risks of irreparable or serious harms. Such requirements might well apply to many drugs not currently subject to any form of criminal penalty.[223]

C. Harms to Society in General

A common argument for the criminalization of drug use centers on alleged harms to society.[224] It is said that drug users display an "amotivational syndrome" that deprives society of their performance for the public good, or that forms of drug experience are subversive of basic institutions.[225]

One natural form of this argument is to follow Benjamin Rush in describing drug use as a form of suicide,[226] and immoral for that reason. Both forms of self-destructive behavior, it is argued, violate the citizen's duty of service to the state, which has an interest akin to a property right in the lives and services of its citizens. This is a prominent feature of Aristotle's condemnation of suicide,[227] which was repeated with approval by Saint Thomas Aquinas[228] and read into the Anglo-American legal heritage by Blackstone.[229]

We shall investigate and criticize the underlying condemnation of self-willed death, which this argument assumes, in the next chapter's discussion of the right to die and the idea of one's life as the state's property. To anticipate that discussion, we may here note the conclusion of that argument: if the autonomy-based interpretation of treating persons as equals means anything, it means that the idea that other persons or institutions may have property rights in our lives is radically misplaced. If so, a general moral argument condemning drug use and suicide as self-destructive behavior that deprives the state of services cannot be sustained. There are means by which society may encourage performance for the public good. Money and status may be used as incentives. But as a free and rational being, a person has a right to choose a way of life in which such performance plays no central role, assuming minimal obligations of citizenship are met.[230] Certainly, criminalization of such conduct is profoundly unjust, tantamount to a violation of human rights.

If anything, criminalization probably exacerbates the self-destructiveness of the conduct it ostensibly aims to combat. When criminal penalties have not been used against heroin use, such as in the United States prior to the Harrison Act[231] and in Great Britain and European countries today,[232] heroin use could be appropriately regulated and supervised. Users could hold regular jobs and lead otherwise conventional lives.[233] By contrast, in the United States after criminalization, the now illegal and unsupervised forms of heroin use have become both more injurious[234] and more likely to be associated with a socially unproductive criminal underworld life.[235]

Sometimes the argument for criminalization is put more generally in terms of a right of existing institutions to protect themselves from subversion. The history of attacks on drug use is typified by arguments of this kind. The use of liquor in the United States was identified with the Catholic immigrants and their subversive (non-Protestant) values;[236] when heroin came under attack, it was identified with Chinese influences from which America, it was said, must be protected;[237] marijuana was associated with undesirable Hispanic influences on American values,[238] and cocaine with black influences.[239] It is difficult to see anything in these claims but familiar sociological manifestations of cultural hegemony.[240] From the perspective of fundamental moral theory, they certainly appear deeply question-begging: they assume what should be in dispute, the moral legitimacy of existing institutions. If existing institutions are illegitimate, their existence should not be rendered immune from change; change, rather, is precisely what is called for. Accordingly, this argument can fairly be credited only after we have evaluated positively the prior question of the legitimacy of existing institutions and their policies regarding drug use. In fact, however, only conclusory claims are ever offered, not critical argument.

In many cases, these claims are transparently baseless. Some forms of currently criminal drug use would, if decriminalized, probably have little effect on current American aims and aspirations; if anything, there might be benign shifts to these drugs from currently legal drugs such as alcohol.[241] In addition, the values invoked against certain forms of drug use are themselves subject to criticism. For example, the current division in American law between legal and illegal drugs distinguishes between drugs that influence levels of arousal (the stimulants and depressants) and those that affect the information-processing systems (the hallucinogens, LSD, mescaline, and hashish); the former class of drugs tends to be legal, the latter illegal.[242] Students of American culture have observed that this distinction reflects an underlying value of facilitating work at particular tasks, as illustrated by the illegality of drugs that introduce multiple realities of experience, which may disturb focus on discrete productive or technological tasks.[243] If one were prepared to construe American values in crudely utilitarian terms, with drug use evaluated solely in terms of its usefulness in maximizing production, this calculus might make some sense. But there are other fundamental values implicit in American constitutionalism, including a respect for human rights, that would subject any such arguments to fundamental moral criticism.

American arguments of institutional self-defense fail because they do not take seriously the deepest values of human rights, which American institutions express. Often, arguments of institutional subversion merely reflect majoritarian distaste for new values and ways of life which, on proper moral and constitutional analysis, enjoy or should enjoy protection from majoritarian incursions. Accordingly, to protect such new life styles from the cultural hegemony of the majority is not to subvert but rather to affirm and vindicate the most enduring and defensible values on which American institutions rest.

D. Social and Economic Justice

Consistent with the autonomy-based interpretation of treating persons as equals, principles of distributive justice that would require a certain distribution of wealth, property, status, and opportunity would be agreed to or universalized.[244] Sometimes it is suggested that certain forms of drug use are appropriately criminalized in order to advance the more just distribution of goods, on the ground that these forms of drug use are mainly a temptation to the poor and a symptom of poverty. Accordingly, decriminalization proposals are viewed skeptically: heroin, it may be suggested, is the true opiate of the people, whereby the anxieties and privations of their disadvantaged lives are temporarily alleviated, but at the expense of incapacitating them for the kind of political analysis and action required to attack the basic injustices from which they suffer.[245] Decriminalization, accordingly, is disfavored because it legitimates, by a misplaced ideology of tolerance, the passive vulnerability of the poor to exploitation.[246]

One is initially struck by the lack of historical and cross-cultural (including comparative law) perspective that this argument evinces. Countries that do not use the criminal penalty appear to have different patterns of drug use.[247] In the United States prior to the Harrison Act, opium addicts appear to have included many middle-class people, often women, for whom opium was a medicinal agent in various nostrums.[248] The composition of this drug-using population was probably decisively shaped by criminalization, resulting in a disproportionate number of addicts today among poor urban minorities.[249] That criminalization is responsible for these shifts is borne out by studies linking addiction to social and psychological factors.[250]

If the condition of members of racial minorities who are heroin addicts is to be ameliorated, decriminalization, not criminalization, is the proper course. To the extent that criminalization itself bears responsibility for the shifts in composition of drug users to more disadvantaged persons, a sound theory of justice should condemn, not endorse, a policy that appears to have worsened the circumstances of the most disadvantaged classes.[251] When it is observed that criminalization has clearly fostered injuries incident to drug use, including death, that regulation and supervision can lessen these dangers,[252] and that these injuries fall principally on the most disadvantaged classes, the case against criminalization becomes very strong indeed.

Of course, strong principles of justice, consistent with the autonomy-based interpretation of treating persons as equals, require that persons should have equal prospects for self-respect and well-being.[253] Certainly, more equal opportunities and conditions of life should be made available to racial minorities. Criminalization of drug use, however, does not advance these ends; indeed, it perversely aggravates injustice. Decriminalization would not, as critics of the ideology of tolerance urge, increase the vulnerability of the poor to exploitation;[254] rather, it would release them from a morally empty stigma and from the crime tariff industry which preys on them. Drugs would be cheaply and safely available, carefully regulated, and with enough information to fully inform persons of risks and benefits. The millenium of social justice would not be realized, but one form of unjust exploitation, one form (sanctified by unjust moralism) of blaming the victim, would be ended. Perhaps, in such circumstances, more poor persons would use certain drugs than more fortunate persons; perhaps not.[255] At least, however, the poor would be extended some measure of dignifying respect for their right to shape their own lives, undistorted by a false, sanctimonious, and class-biased moralism that ideologically distorts reality by underestimating the dangers in its own patterns of drug use and overestimating the dangers in the drug use of others.[256]

E. *Paternalistic Arguments Against Drug Use*

Even if no other moral argument on behalf of criminalization can be sustained, it may still be argued that drug use is sufficiently irrational conduct that there is moral title to interfere with it on paternalistic grounds. This is, however, an argument that is radically inappropriate to the defense of prohibitions of many forms of drug use.

A radically inappropriate form of paternalistic interference is grounded in the substitution of the interferer's own personal ends for the ends of the agent. This form of paternalism fails to recognize the fundamental principle that the agent's ends are given and that the agent acts irrationally only when his action frustrates them. This error is a frequent flaw in the paternalistic assessment of forms of drug use, for people find it all too natural facilely to substitute their own personal solutions for an imaginative understanding of the perspectives of others. The temptations to such paternalistic distortions are particularly strong in cases in which conventional moral judgments mistakenly condemn certain conduct, a fact which Mill dealt with by placing sharp limitations on the proper use of paternalistic reasoning in these contexts.[257] The idea of human rights may, in part, be understood as a prophylaxis against such abuses.

As we have seen in previous chapters, there is, however, a form of paternalistic argument that may legitimately be raised, namely, interference to preserve persons from certain serious irrationalities. There are two critical contraints on such a principle. First, the notion of irrationality must be defined in terms of a neutral theory than can accommodate the many visions of the good life compatible with moral constraints. For this purpose, rationality, for any individual, must be interpreted relative to his own system of ends, which is, in turn, determined by his appetites, desires, capacities, and aspirations. Second, even within the class of irrationalities so defined, paternalistic considerations would properly come into play only when the irrationality is severe and systematic, due to undeveloped or impaired capacities or lack of opportunity to exercise such capacities, *and* when a serious, permanent impairment of interests is in prospect.

It is initially important to distinguish two kinds of paternalism: interference on the basis of facts unknown to the agent, in order to save the agent from harms that he would wish to avoid, and interference on the basis of values that the agent does not himself share. Paternalism of the first kind, as applied in such laws as those securing the purity of drugs, is unobjectionable. Paternalism of the second kind, which underlies many laws currently criminalizing drug use, is not only objectionable, it is a violation of human rights.

On this basis, no good argument can be made that paternalistic considerations justify the kind of interference in choices to use drugs that is involved in the current criminalization of many forms of drug use. Indeed, in many cases, such choices seem all *too* rational.

Drug use serves many disparate purposes: therapeutic care and cure, the relief of pain or anxiety, the stimulation or depression of mood or levels of arousal, the exploration of imaginative experience for creative, aesthetic, religious, therapeutic, recreational, or other purposes, and sheer recreative pleasure.[258] These purposes are not irrational. To the contrary, the pursuit of them may enable the person better to achieve his ends in general, or to explore aspects of experience or attitudes to living which he may reasonably wish to incorporate into his theory of ends. There is almost no form of drug use which, in a suitably supportive context and setting, may not advance important human goods, including the capacity of some poor and deprived people to work more comfortably,[259] to endure adverse climactic and environmental circumstances,[260] and in general to meet more robustly and pleasurably the demands on their lives.[261] Some religions,[262] like some artists,[263] have centered themselves on drug use, finding in drugs a matrix of religious and imaginative experience in which to explore and sometimes realize their higher-order interests in giving life intelligible meaning and coherence.[264] Some persons today find in the triumph of technological society the *reductio ad absurdum* of certain dynamics of Western culture and identify drug use as one organon for cultivating a saner and more balanced metaphysical orientation that expresses their most authentic and reasonable interests.[265] Some find even in "addictive" drugs a way of life with more interest, challenge, and self-respect than the available alternatives.[266] It is dogmatic to assert that these and other people do not, through drug use, more rationally advance their ends.

Sometimes the paternalistic argument is made that certain forms of drug use, even if carefully regulated, may result in certain clear harms to the user. For example, heroin use may lead to addiction,[267] to impotence,[268] to certain organic disorders,[269] and sometimes, despite all proper precautions, to death.[270] As long as any such irreparable harm to the person is in prospect, it is argued, paternalistic interference is justified. Even if certain of these alleged harms, for example, addiction, are morally problematic and question-begging,[271] others, such as death, are not. The first requirement of just paternalism, however, is that judgments of irrationality must rest on a neutral theory of the good consistent with the agent's own higher-order interests in rationality and freedom. Even intentionally ending one's own life cannot, in all circumstances, be supposed irrational under this criterion. If intentional killing is not always irrational, neither, a fortiori, is drug use, in which the user makes trade-offs between valued forms of activity and higher risks of death that reasonable persons sometimes embrace. Certainly, the right of persons to engage in many high-risk occupations and activities is uncontroversial. Part of respect for human rights is the recognition of the right of persons, as free and rational beings, to determine the meanings of their own lives and projects, including the frame of such plans at the boundaries of life and death. The values that some persons place on drug use can be accorded no less respect. Certainly, drug use does not enable a person to realize more than is implicit in the interests and ambitions brought to the drug experience,[272] but that indicates not the frivolity or pointlessness of the experience, but its potential seriousness for the kinds of spiritual exploration and risk-taking by independent-minded and rational persons that should be centrally protected in a free society.

At most, paternalistic concern for forms of irreparable harm might dictate appropriate forms of regulation to insure that drugs are available only to mature persons who understand, critically evaluate and voluntarily accept the risks. To minimize pointless risks, such regulations might insure that certain drugs, LSD, for example, are taken only under appropriate supervision. In general, however, there is no ground of just paternalism for an absolute prohibition of such drugs.[273]

The radical vision of autonomy and mutual concern and respect is a vision of persons, as such, having human rights to create their own lives on terms fair to all. To view individuals in this way is to affirm basic intrinsic limits on the degree to which, even benevolently, one person may control the life of another. Within ethical constraints expressive of mutual concern and respect for autonomy, people are, in this conception, free to adopt a number of disparate and irreconcilable visions of the good life. Indeed, the adoption of different kinds of life plans, within these constraints, affords the moral good of different experiments in living by which people can more rationally assess such basic life choices.[274] The invocation of inadequate moral and paternalistic arguments of the kind discussed violates these considerations of human rights, confusing unreflective personal ideology with the moral reasoning that alone can justify the deprivation of liberty by criminal penalty.

IV. DRUG USE AND CONSTITUTIONAL PRIVACY

I have thus far set forth a number of negative arguments to show why various moral arguments condemning drug use are mistaken. The remainder of the chapter will consider the affirmative case for allowing forms of drug use, that is, for the existence of rights of the person that include the right to use drugs. In this way, the scope and limits of this right can be clarified, and its relation to the personal ideals secure from state intervention can be addressed.

As Chapter 2 argued, the constitutional right to privacy may be interpreted, consistent with the human rights perspective embodied in the Constitution, as subjecting the scope of the criminal law to constitutional assessment and criticism in terms of the autonomy-based interpretation of treating persons as equals. The United States is a constitutional democracy committed to the conception of human rights as an unwritten constitution, in terms of which the meaning of constitutional guaranties is to be construed. It is wholly natural and historically consistent with constitutional commitments to regard the autonomy-based interpretation of treating persons as equals as the regulative ideal in terms of which the public morality, which the criminal law expresses, is to be interpreted. Sometimes this thought has been expressed, as a rough first approximation, in terms of the harm principle, the principle that the state may impose criminal sanctions only on conduct which harms others. The present account has tried to reformulate the thought in terms of the autonomy-based interpretation of treating persons as equals, and has tried to show how this conception imposes specific constraints on the kinds of principles that may permissibly be enforced by the public morality. The traditional idea of "harm," for example, appears in the account, but is interpreted in terms of the rights of the person, in contrast to Mill's utilitarian reformulation.[275]

A corollary of this way of thinking is that, when the scope of the criminal law exceeds such moral constraints, it violates human rights. The constitutional right to privacy expresses a form of this moral criticism of unjust overcriminalization, and may be understood as a convergence of three viewpoints. These include, first, the view that the traditional moral argument for criminalization is critically deficient, and, indeed, demonstrably fails to respect human rights. A second element is an antipaternalistic feature. The still extant force of the invalid traditional moral arguments distorts the capacity to see that certain traditionally condemned life choices may be rationally undertaken. Paternalistic interference is tolerated and even encouraged, when, in fact, such interference cannot be justified. Third, there is a strong autonomy-based liberty interest in protecting human dignity from the invasions of moralism and paternalism.

In light of this convergence of factors, it is natural to expect that the constitutional right to privacy would have been aggressively invoked to invalidate prohibitions on drug use, as it was in sexual[276] and, more recently, right-to-die contexts.[277] In fact, aside from a free exercise of religion case not directly relevant to constitutional privacy issues, in only one notable case, *Ravin v. State*,[278] has a court unequivocally pursued such a privacy argument to strike down prohibitions of marijuana use in the home. Even the *Ravin* court, however, refused to attach the right to drug use in itself, finding the privacy right to arise out of the home context instead.[279] In short, American courts seem disinclined to pursue privacy arguments in contexts of drug use because they fail to identify drug use as a basic life choice.

In my view, this judgment cannot withstand critical examination. In order to understand why decisions to use drugs are embraced by the constitutional right to privacy, it is necessary to draw together earlier observations regarding the idea of human rights, the values of dignity and moral personality that it encompasses and should protect, the unjust moral argument that often underlies prohibitions of drug use, and the necessary implications of these ideas and values for the protection of certain forms of drug use. Even if decisions to use drugs were, in fact, rarely or never made or acted on, the right to so decide is, for reasons now to be explained, fundamental.

I have interpreted the human rights perspective in terms of the autonomy-based interpretation of treating persons as equals, which includes respect for the higher-order interests of persons in freedom and rationality. One central component must be respect for the capacity of persons—beings capable of critical self-consciousness—to regulate and interpret their experiences in terms of their own standards of reasonable argument and evidence. Thus, both historically and as a matter of moral principle, respect for independent religious conscience and for principles of religious toleration have been at the heart of evolving ideas of human rights. Historically, respect for religious belief has expressed what is today regarded as the deeper principle of respect for individual conscience, the right of persons independently to evaluate and control their own experience.[280]

Commitment to this basic moral principle requires a neutral respect for evaluative independence. But this principle is, as we have seen,[281] violated by the moral perfectionism that has dominated the American approach to drug control. Indeed, this moral perfectionism attacks the very foundations of evaluative independence; for it seeks to inculcate through law a kind and quality of subjective human experience modeled after a religious ideal of rigid self-control dedicated selflessly to the good of others. In the place of independent control over and evaluation of one's own experience, we have a reigning orthodoxy. Majoritarian legislatures seek to enforce a kind of secularized version of the religious technology of self-mastery.[282] The state, consistent with the autonomy-based interpretation of treating persons as equals, has no just role adjudicating among or preferring, let alone enforcing, one such technology over another. Such a use of state power is precisely the form of content-based control over ways of life, thought, and experience against which constitutional morality rebels.[283] Indeed, the enforcement of perfectionist ideals expresses precisely the contempt for autonomous evaluative independence and self-control that should trigger appropriate constitutional attack and remedy.

It may be objected that drug experience is not the kind of subjective experience protected by constitutional principles of toleration.[284] This is not an argument; rather it is an expression of the long American tradition of the public morality. This tradition cannot, as has been shown, be sustained. It is based on untenable forms of moral argument and is, on examination, inconsistent with deeper constitutional values to which all espouse fundamental allegiance. It fails to observe constitutional constraints on the kind of harm that may be the object of criminal penalties; indeed, ideologically, it seeks supremacy for its own model of self-mastery through the criminal law in the way that constitutional morality clearly forbids. In short, since this common sense of public morality cannot be sustained, higher-order interests in freedom and rationality would identify respect for choices to use drugs as an aspect of personal dignity that is worthy of protection under the constitutional right to privacy, and call for its implementation by courts and legislatures.[285]

A fair-minded respect for this right will assure respect for the pluralistic cultures and ways of life which different patterns of drug use embody and which have been heretofore lacking in America's cultural life. Patterns of drug use are implicitly ideological: alcohol use, for example, is often associated with cultural patterns in which aggressiveness plays a central role; use of marijuana, in contrast, is associated with more peaceful and inward ways of life.[286] Respect for the right of drug use would preserve individual and subcultural experience and experiment from a majoritarian cultural hegemony, rooted in a crude and callously manipulative utilitarianism. There is no good reason why this utilitarian ideology has been permitted to go unchallenged as the governing American ideal in matters of drug policy; it trivializes our vales into simplistic subservience to technological civilization[287] and fails to take seriously American ideals of human rights and their implications for a pluralism of spiritual perspectives.

We may summarize the implications of this right to use drugs in terms of the background moral principles, expressive of the autonomy-based interpretation of treating persons as equals, which define its limits. The principle of autonomy in matters of drugs does not apply to persons presumably lacking rational capacities, such as young children, nor does it validate the use of particular drugs in circumstances where they would lead to the infliction on others of serious bodily harm. There is no objection, for example, to the prohibition of drugs whose use demonstrably leads to violence,[288] or to limitations of drug use in certain contexts, such as before driving. In addition, the liberty of drug use includes the right of others to avoid involvement in the drug experience. There would be no objection, therefore, to reasonable regulations of the time, manner, and place of drug use, or of the obtrusive solicitation of drug use.

Finally, it is important to remind ourselves, yet again,[289] that there are limits to an argument grounded in human rights of the kind here presented. To say that a person has a human right to do an act is to make a political and legal claim that certain conduct must be protected by the state from forms of coercive prohibition. To assert the existence of such a right is not to assert that it should be exercised. The latter question is an issue of personal morality. Its disposition may turn on considerations that have no proper place in questions of political and legal morality.[290]

To say, therefore, that people have a human right to use drugs is not to conclude that everyone should exercise this right. For example, a person might justifiably invoke certain perfectionist ideals in declining to use drugs. These ideals might include religious dedications or purely secular conceptions that the control and cultivation of aspects of personal competence and subjectivity are inconsistent with drug use. Certainly, such ideals cannot justifiably be invoked to qualify our general rights of autonomy, for self-respect and fulfillment do not require conformity to such ideals. Even as personal moral ideas, however, perfectionist notions may be criticized as inhumanly rigid, masochistically manipulative, directed at questionable moral aims, and insensitive to the values of spontaneity and humanely varied experience. Nonetheless, an individual may justifiably espouse a moral ideal, regulate his or her life accordingly, and criticize others for not observing as humane an ideal in their personal lives. However, legal enforcement of such an ideal wrongly imposes a personal ideal upon persons who may find it unfulfilling or even oppressive and exploitative.

V. BEYOND DECRIMINALIZATION

This chapter has tried to establish that there are no good moral arguments for criminalizing many forms of drug use, and that their punishment is a violation of the rights of the person. A basis has thus been laid for a much less confining view of the range of regulatory alternatives for drug use. Five alternatives will briefly be considered: the vice model; licensing; regulations of place, time, and methods; no regulation at all; and forms of compulsory civil commitment for cure. It will be assumed throughout that per se criminal prohibitions of drug use have been repealed, otherwise invalidated, or sharply circumscribed.

A. *The Vice Model*

The vice model, to which some American jurisdictions appear to be moving in the area of the control of marijuana use,[291] would eliminate or reduce to the *de minimis* level any sanction for the use of drugs, but would continue criminal sanctions for commercial drug sales.[292] An analogy may be drawn to the control of other forms of commercialized vice, such as prostitution and gambling. These activities are, it is argued, vices, and although it may be desirable not to subject the buyer to criminal penalty, it would untowardly legitimate them if penalties for the seller were eliminated.[293]

Although one can understand the political attractions of the vice model as a kind of interim political strategy of decriminalization, it makes no sense as a matter of moral and constitutional principle. Certainly it cannot be regarded as a moral desideratum, for it begs the question at issue: the moral propriety of criminal penalties in this area. Furthermore, it perpetuates the crime tariff and its ancillary evils. Most decisively, it is inconsistent with the view of human rights here adduced. If there is a human right to some form of activity, which reasonably includes buyers and sellers within the scope of the right, the right must attach to both, unless there are convincing arguments to the contrary. Traditional arguments differentiating the legal treatent of user and seller are often themselves morally questionable, reflecting unjust, indeed immoral, assumptions that have no proper place in the enforcement of law. One example is the sexist assumption that prostitution is an evil for the female prostitute, but not for the male patron. If there are regulatory concerns appropriate to the sale of drugs, they can be pursued by appropriate regulatory measures tailored to meet these concerns, not by perpetuating uncritical moral assumptions that, in fact, are clearly violative of human rights.

B. *Licensing*

Proposals for the licensing of drugs take two forms: the licensing of sale and the licensing of use. The purpose of licensing is to collect the names of sellers or users on a public record, both to facilitate regulation of terms of sale—such as price, place of business, and solicitation or use—and to facilitate regular inspections to secure compliance with regulations or, in the case of use, for reasons of medical prophylaxis.[294] In general, licensing is an appropriate prerequisite to valid exercise of some form of service, sale, or use, when incompetence in the activity will disastrously affect human interests, and the licensing scheme might appropriately reduce such incompetence.[295]

Licensing schemes are familiar in the United States in the sale of legal drugs. New drugs must, for example, satisfy rigorous government tests before they may be marketed. Drug manufacturers in general must satisfy various requirements as to the purity and safety of their drugs and the integrity of their manufacturing and solicitation. Further, the local sale of some drugs, for example alcohol, is typically licensed.[296] In the event of the decriminalization of various forms of drug use, such licensing of sale would be appropriate to insure the purity and effectiveness of the drug for the purpose claimed. In some cases, the licensed seller could be required to withhold the drug from a buyer, as is presently appropriate with a person already drunk who is about to drive.

In addition, some forms of legal drugs require a medical prescription, which is a kind of license permitting the drug's sale and use in certain circumstances.[297] The licensing of the physician by the state as a competent medical professional empowers him or her in turn to license the sale and use of drugs, exercising proven medical competence to minimize and regulate the possibly disastrous effects of certain forms of drug use.

In the event of decriminalization, some form of the medical license would, most plausibly, be required for heroin use. Such forms of heroin maintenance have long existed in England and elsewhere in Europe,[298] providing heroin users with medical care and supervision to minimize the kinds of ills to which the American street addict is tragically subject.[299] More decisively, such licensing, whether in the form of prescriptions by individual physicians or special clinics (which may be more advisable),[300] would be consistent with the argument of human rights here offered. It has been argued above that even drugs with risks of dangers should, assuming reduction of pointless risks, be made available to persons who, as free and rational beings, want them.[301] Licensing of this kind would assure supervised availability of such drugs in a context of concerned rational dialogue. In contrast to the sadistic isolation that current law compels, the person desiring the drug could reasonably and voluntarily assess the risks and benefits of its use, and be accorded the respect of self-determination if he or she wished it.

A comparable licensing scheme, which would extend as well to supervision of the entire drug-taking process, may be appropriate for hallucinogens such as LSD and mescaline.[302] Such drugs, which may reasonably be taken for therapeutic, religious, creative, or recreational reasons,[303] appear to require concerned, intelligent, and experienced supervision in order to minimize untoward and undesired risks.[304] Such risks cannot be eliminated entirely; moreover, as was argued above, free and rational persons have a right to take them. A licensing scheme would ensure competent expertise to reduce pointless risks.

Some critics of existing American drug law have recommended a general form of licensing for the use of drugs such as marijuana, including a complex federal bureaucracy, record keeping, tests of adequate setting for receptivity to the drug, and the like.[305] If such a suggestion would be inappropriate in the cases of such drugs as alcohol or nicotine, it would seem, *a fortiori*, that it should be rejected in the case of marijuana. By almost every secular measure of harm, alcohol and nicotine are more harmful than marijuana,[306] and yet they are not subject to regulation in the form of licensing. In fact, the very predicate for any such intrusive licensing scheme, namely, the need to secure levels of competence that minimize irreparable harm, is quite absent in the case of marijuana, for there is no empirical support for the proposition that marijuana causes irreparable harm.[307]

The argument is conventionally made, in this connection, that although no such irreparable harm is now apparent, it may be so in the future, and that this possibility necessitates the present regulation of drugs like marijuana.[308] This argument is hypocritical, for it fails to face the already evident harm incident to use of alcohol, nicotine, and other legal drugs,[309] and more importantly, it fails to take seriously the autonomy-based foundation of constitutional morality. The principle that autonomous individuals should be treated as equals places the burden on the state to show harm as the predicate for just criminalization. In the clear absence of such a showing, the presumption must and should be for unregulated usage of the drug.

C. *Regulations of Place, Time, and Method*

In addition to the licensing proposals already discussed, regulations of place, time, and method of drug sale and use may take a number of forms. To minimize obtrusive solicitation of unwilling buyers, two strategies are suggested by the European regulation of commercial sex: one is the English prohibition of public street solicitation, so that solicitation must take place through ambiguously worded advertisements in various journals and in certain well-known locations.[310] Another is the continental European solution of zoning, whereby solicitation is permitted only in certain well-known districts of the urban centers.[311]

In addition to appropriate forms of solicitation regulation and zoning, and the licensing regulations already discussed (including the limitation of certain drug use to regulated contexts), consideration should be given to appropriate regulation of advertising and public education relating to drugs. While persons may have a right to take potentially harmful drugs, there is no duty on the state to encourage them to do so. To the contrary, to the extent that the state has a duty to insure that these risks are undertaken only by free and rationally informed persons, it may have a duty to regulate drug advertisement. Such regulation might require vivid reminders of possible harm[312] and insist that programs of public education, in the schools and elsewhere, continually communicate a fair and realistic picture of this harm to counter otherwise exploitative and manipulative commercial advertising campaigns. While such campaigns have been organized against nicotine,[313] it is strikingly anomalous that the real harms of liquor are not comparably recited and exposed.[314] In the event of decriminalization, a fair governmental regulation of drug advertising must insist that the comparative harms of drugs be fully revealed.

D. *Laissez-Faire*

It has been suggested that, after decriminalization, the state should neither license nor regulate the use of drugs, and instead enforce only the existing criminal laws against force and fraud.[315] Under this view, regulations are the hypocritical and moralistic subterfuges of those who seek to accomplish by regulation what they cannot legitimately achieve by prohibition. These arguments for laissez-faire understate the sound reasons for a properly framed regulatory program. They are also reminders that, in a nation like the United States with its long cultural history of prohibitory drug laws, it is necessary to guard against the distortion and disfigurement of the just aims of appropriate regulatory programs that unjust moralism might engender. The history of civil commitment for addicts provides a warning of such consequences.

E. *Compulsory Civil Commitment*

One alternative to decriminalization that has been tested in the United States is compulsory civil commitment both of addicts and alcoholics.[316] Such programs rest on the idea that addiction is a disease, for which the user is not morally culpable. Accordingly, just as criminal penalty for mental disease would be unjust and probably unconstitutional,[317] criminal sanctions are not the appropriate legal tool to handle addicts. Rather, a medical model of compulsory care and cure is in order, i.e., compulsory civil commitment.

This model for the treatment of drug use is based on an untenable attempt to interpret, as a medical problem of disease and defect, forms of drug use which, in the context of the agent's own interests and perspectives, are often not unreasonable.[318] To this extent, the medical conception of addiction as a disease is intrinsically ideological, reproducing in medical terms larger conventional moral judgments that condemn such forms of drug use.[319] Accordingly, to combine decriminalization with compulsory civil commitment would be simply to reproduce and reinforce the underlying violation of human rights caused by both these approaches.[320]

VI. CONCLUSION: AGAINST PROHIBITION

We have argued that judgments of the immorality of drug use are wrong; indeed, the right to use many drugs currently criminalized is one of the rights of the person which the state may not transgress. We have identified as the basis for these powerful moral judgments a formerly religious but now secular ideal of moral perfectionism, and have tried to show why this ideal cannot, consistent with human rights, be enforced through the criminal law.

In conclusion, we may take a more affirmative stance against the prohibitory force of this perfectionist ideal in the area of drug use, recognizing, first, the deep tension that exists between the enforcement of this ideal and a basic respect for the person and, second, the existence of a moral evil in enforcing a Manichean ideal through the medium of the law.

First, temperance has, since Plato,[321] been identified as a moral virtue, a desirable and appropriate character trait for every good person. The sense of temperance in Plato, however, is not that of the American temperance leagues. It is not the elimination from human life of all intoxicants, euphoriants, hallucinatory visions, or ecstasies of the transcendence of self, but the control of such experiences in the service of a balanced and humane life. Temperance, in this classical sense, assumes that ordinary people of good will have the capacity, when treated with decent respect, to regulate their own lives. When they fail, they do so as responsible beings who themselves ultimately bear the costs and degradation of their own disorder. When the perfectionist ideal in the United States took the form of compulsory prohibition of certain forms of drug use, it not only misinterpreted temperance, substituting an absolute prohibition for the Platonic balance and moderation, but it also deprived persons of the experience that makes virtuous action worthy of respect: namely, the self-mastery of appetite and temptation. In aspiring to create a New Jerusalem of saints, the moral perfectionists failed to observe the boundary conditions of minimal respect for human persons.

Second, the perfectionist ideal, implicit in America's prohibitory drug laws, is Manichean. Drug users are branded as the Puritans branded their deviants: evil and willful outcasts whose criminal stigma reflects the demarcation between the ideals of the saints and the inexplicable and satanic evils of the sinner.[322] We have disclosed this cruel vision for what it is: not a critical moral judgment, but a remnant of a sectarian ideology secularized into a moral ideal of emotional self-control. Such a conception fails to acknowledge the confluence of condemned forms of drug use and reasonable human interests and aspirations and isolates and denies both the common humanity underlying many disparate styles of life and the cultivation of experience they reflect. The moral condemnation of forms of drug use reflects such isolation and denial, disfiguring the reasonable perception of the forms and ways we cultivate experience. It draws sharply moralistic distinctions between the decent and the indecent, which reflect no consistent or defensible theory of harm, and which blinds social perception to the underlying moral reality of a continuum of personal modes of expression and fulfillment. The consequence is the remarkable spectacle of harmless conduct transmogrified by a perverse social imagination into a powerful stereotype of radical evil. Moreover, the balance of harm and good implicit in all patterns of drug use is dramatically shifted to the self-fulfilling prophecy of the worst possible consequences of drug use. We know that patterns of drug use fit into larger patterns of social intercourse, which often ameliorate the harms of the drugs and magnify their social and human benefits.[323] The American prohibitionist perfectionism, expressing a moral theory of extirpation and total denial, has not only failed to foster the kind of framework of legal regulation that could facilitate such social patterns, it has insured that its own vision of radical evil will produce the worst possible consequences for drug users and society at large.[324] This vision appears to feed on itself—immune to evidence, ferocious in the extent of penalties it is prepared to impose, and savage in its violations of basic human rights. We must, I believe, disencumber our conception of criminal justice of these perfectionist ideals, which pursue no aspiration that the state may justly compel and which work violence to basic human rights.

NOTES

1. See, e.g., E. Brecher, *Licit and Illicit Drugs* (1972); J. Kaplan, *Marijuana—The New Prohibition* (1970); T. Szasz, *Ceremonial Chemistry* (1974); N. Zinberg & J. Robertson, *Drugs and the Public* (1972).

2. The general pattern of legal treatment of drug use in the United States is set by the Comprehensive Drug Abuse Prevention and Control Act, 21 U.S.C. §§ 801–966 (1976). For discussion of its terms, see O. Ray, *Drugs, Society, and Human Behaviour* 24–28 (1972). State codes also prohibit drug use. See, e.g., *Uniform Controlled Substances Act*; N. Y. Pub. Health Law §§ 3300–3396 (McKinney 1980). There has been some change in the legal treatment of drug use only with respect to marijuana. The Comprehensive Drug Abuse Prevention and Control Act reduced federal penalties for marijuana possession. See E. Brecher, supra note 1, at 420. One state supreme court has invoked the right to privacy from its state constitution to invalidate criminal penalties on the use of marijuana in the privacy of one's home. See *Ravin v. State*, 537 P.2d 494 (Alaska 1975); cf. *People v. Sinclair*, 387 Mich. 91, 194 N.W.2d 878 (1972); (plurality opinion) (classification of marijuana as a narcotic held violative of equal protection). But cf. *State v. Kantner*, 53 Hawaii 327, 493 P.2d 306, cert denied, 409 U. S. 948 (1972) (classification of marijuana as a narcotic not violative of equal protection). In recent years, several states have decriminalized the possession or use of small quantities of marijuana. See *1976 Ann. Survey Am. L.* 343–57. For a recent update, see Sheinman, "The Latest Dope on Pot Laws," *High Times*, Apr. 1980, at 52–54. For various arguments in the legal literature supporting these and other developments, see Kurzman & Magell, "Decriminalizing Possession of All Controlled Substances: An Alternative Whose Time Has Come," 6 *Contemp. Drug Prob.* 245 (1977); Neier, "Public Boozers and Private Smokers," 2 *Civ. Lib. Rev.* 41 (Spr. 1975); Weiss & Wizner, "Pot, Prayer, Politics and Privacy: The Right to Cut Your Own Throat in Your Own Way," 54 *Iowa L. Rev.* 709 (1969); Comment, "State Interference with Personhood: The Privacy Right, Necessity Defense, and Proscribed Medical Therapies," 10 *Pac. L.J.* 773 (1979); Note, "Marijuana Prohibition and the Constitutional Right of Privacy: An Examination of *Ravin v. State*," 11 *Tulsa L.J.* 563 (1976).

3. For example, John Kaplan, author of the most notable attack on the criminaliza-

tion of marijuana use, focused on utilitarian, cost-benefit arguments. Although he briefly noted the moral argument, he quickly put it aside. J. Kaplan, supra note 1, at 292–93.

4. L. Goodman & A. Gilman, *The Pharmacological Basis of Therapeutics* 1 (6th ed. 1980).

5. R. Julien, *A Primer of Drug Action* 2–6 (2d ed. 1978).

6. This viewpoint is now commonplace in the serious literature on drug use. For general discussions of drug use that encompass alcohol, caffeine, and nicotine, see E. Brecher, supra note 1, at 193–266; L. Goodman & A. Gilman, supra note 4, at 135–50, 358–70, 588–92; R. Julien, supra note 5, at 60–70, 90–97; O. Ray, supra note 2, at 78–117.

7. See generally L. Goodman & A. Gilman, supra note 4.

8. Id. at 37–347.

9. See, e.g., O. Ray, supra note 2, at 157–77.

10. See, e.g., L. Grinspoon & J. Bakalar, *Psychedelic Drugs Reconsidered* 267–75 (1979); R. Masters & J. Houston, *The Varieties of Psychedelic Experience* 247–313 (1966). See also W. James, *The Varieties of Religious Experience* 299–336 (1961).

11. For descriptions of the range of uses to which psychedelic drug experience may be put, see L. Grinspoon & J. Bakalar, supra note 10; R. Masters & J. Houston, supra note 10. See also O. Ray, supra note 2, at 212–67; B. Wells, *Psychedelic Drugs* 112–49, 170–212 (1973).

12. See L. Grinspoon, *Marijuana Reconsidered* 202–06 (1971).

13. See R. Wasson, *Soma: Divine Mushroom of Immortality* (1968). Residues of shamanism persisted in the Old World, and flourished in the pre-Columbian era among the Indians of Central and South America. See generally I. Lewis, *Ecstatic Religion* (1971); see also L. Grinspoon & J. Bakalar, supra note 10, at 38–42.

14. See L. Grinspoon & J. Bakalar, supra note 10, at 38–55; M. Harner, *Hallucinogens and Shamanism* (1973); I. Lewis, supra note 13, at 39, 160. For discussion of the range of narcotic plants used for such purposes, see W. Emboden, *Narcotic Plants* (1979); R. Heffern, *Secrets of the Mind-Altering Plants of Mexico* (1974); Schultes, "Botanical Sources of The New World Narcotics," in G. Weil, R. Metzner, & T. Leary, *The Psychedelic Reader* 89–110 (1965). For a skeptical discussion of the religious role of psychoactive drugs in early human cultures, see R. Blum, 1 *Society and Drugs* 22–23 (1970).

15. See M. Harner, *The Way of the Shaman* (1980), in which a student of the healing properties of shamanic practices attempts to adapt them to western needs and practices.

16. For an excellent study of the complex functions of the shaman in these societies, see I. Lewis, supra note 13.

17. See id; G. Reichel-Dolmatoff, *The Shaman and the Jaguar* (1975).

18. For one suggested answer to this conundrum, see R. Wasson, supra note 13.

19. Id. at 3–66.

20. See R. Wasson, C. Ruck, & A. Hoffmann, *The Road to Eleusis* (1978).

21. J. Allegro, *The Sacred Mushroom and the Cross* (1970).

22. St. Augustine appears to have identified mushroom eating and its associated hallucinogenic effects as one of the condemned vices of the Manichean Gnostics. See R. Wasson, supra note 13, at 71, 191. The association of such experiences with heresy reveals a sharp distinction between Christianity and shamanic religions of ecstasy. See I. Lewis, supra note 13, at 39–40, 132, 174–75.

23. See M. Harner, "The Role of Hallucinogenic Plants in European Witchcraft," in *Hallucinogens and Shamanism* 124–50 (1973). But see N. Cohn, *Europe's Inner Demons* 219–24 (1975).

24. See W. La Barre, *The Peyote Cult* 23–24 (4th ed. 1975); G. Reichel-Dolmatoff, supra note 17, at 3–18; Schultes, supra note 14, at 99, 101.

25. R. C. Zaehner, *Mysticism Sacred and Profane* (1969).

26. Id. at 121–22.

27. Id. at 24–26. Zaehner argued that St. Paul's apparent condemnation of attending the divine service while intoxicated indicates that no form of drug-induced experience is to have any role in Christian religious experience proper. See also R. C. Zaehner, *Zen, Drugs and Mysticism* (1972).

28. In praise of Dionysus, god of wine, Euripides wrote:

The son of Semele, who when the gay-crowned feast is set
Is named among gods the chief;
Whose gifts are joy and union of soul in dancing,
Joy in music of flutes,
Joy when sparkling wine at feasts of the gods
Soothes the sore regret,
Banished every grief,
When the reveller rests, enfolded deep
In the cool shade of ivy-shoots,
On wine's soft pillow of sleep.

Euripides, *The Bacchae*, in *The Bacchae and Other Plays* 192–93 (P. Vellacott trans. 1954).

29. See Plato, "Symposium," in *The Collected Dialogues of Plato* 527–74 (E. Hamilton & H. Cairns eds. 1961). For a good history of alcohol use, see R. Blum, supra note 14, at 25–42.

30. Thus, Aristotle observed that the penalty for a crime was doubled if it was induced by drunkenness. Aristotle, *Nicomachean Ethics* 1113b30 at 65 (M. Ostwald trans. 1962).

31. See Montaigne, "Of Drunkenness," in *The Complete Essays of Montaigne* 247 (D. Frame trans. 1965).

32. Coffee drinking, for example, was the object of vigorous social criticism when introduced, and coffeehouses were sometimes outlawed as hotbeds of sedition. See O. Ray, supra note 2, at 108–10; cf. E. Brecher, supra note 1, at 195–98. For an example of the risqué connotations associated with coffee drinking, see Bach's "Coffee" Cantata, BWV. 211. Correspondingly, tobacco smoking, when introduced, was both condemned and legally outlawed, in one case on penalty of death. See E. Brecher, supra note 1, at 209–13. Cf. O. Ray, supra note 2, at 95–100. See generally R. Blum, supra note 14, at 87–114.

33. On the contrast between fermented and distilled alcohol products, see O. Ray, supra note 2, at 79–81.

34. See *Engravings by Hogarth* plates 75 and 76. (S. Shesgreen ed. 1975).

35. See G. Williams, *The Radical Reformation* 303 (1962).

36. See Bainton, "The Churches and Alcohol," *Alcohol, Science and Society* 287–98 (Quarterly Journal of Studies on Alcohol 1945).

37. See G. Williams, supra note 35, at 183, 191, 265; Bainton, supra note 36, at 287-98.

38. See C. Hill, *The World Turned Upside Down: Radical Ideas During the English Revolution* 198–203 (1975).

39. See G. Williams, supra note 37, at 303. George Fox, the Quaker leader, suggested that "the saints' bodies are the members of Christ and the temples of the living God," C. Hill, supra note 38, at 323.

40. See B. Rush, *An Inquiry into the Effects of Ardent Spirits upon the Human Body and Mind* (1814) reprinted in Y. Henderson, *A New Deal in Liquor* 185–221 (1935).

41. Id. at 208–09.

42. Examples of this type of harm given by Rush include liver obstruction, jaundice and dropsy, coughs, diabetes, belchings, epilepsy, gout, and madness. Id. at 193–94.

43. Such social harms include, wrote Rush, garrulity, captiousness, "uncommon good humour," profane swearing, disclosure of secrets, rudeness, immodesty, "clipping of words," fighting, and "extravagant" action. Id. at 190–91.

44. Id. at 197.

45. Id. at 213.

46. Id. at 211.

47. See, e.g., L. Beecher, *Six Sermons on the Nature, Occasions, Signs, Evils, and Remedy of Intemperance* (1827).

48. For standard examples of the kind of approach taken, see W. Hammaker, A. Ivy, E. Palmer, et al., *The Christian Case for Abstinence* (1955); *Temperance Selections* (J. Bechtel ed. (1970), first published 1893).

49. For discussions, by contrast, of serious Biblical studies, see F. Kermode, *The Genesis of Secrecy: On the Interpretation of Narrative* (1979); S. Neill, *The Interpretation of the New Testament* 1861–1961 (1966).

50. See note 236 infra.

51. For a history of this transition, see J. Kobler, *Ardent Spirits: The Rise and Fall of Prohibition* 23–218 (1973); P. Odegard, *Pressure Politics: The Story of the Anti-Saloon League* (1966).

52. See note 41, supra.

53. Thus one apologist for prohibition argued that because of the stepping stone effect (from fermented to distilled liquor), "the moderate drinker's personal liberty must yield to the superior right of the State to protect its interests." D. Colvin, *Prohibition in the United States* 588 (1926).

54. Id. at 587.

55. Id.

56. The definition of the feminine role as "expressive" and the ideology of the superior moral sensibility of women in nineteenth-century America and England grew, under the mutually reinforcing influences of Calvinist preachers, sentimental novelists, and pseudoscientists, into a politically powerful, sentimental ideology. See notes 77–102 and accompanying text, Chapter 3, supra; see also D. Pivar, "The New Abolitionism: The Quest for Social Purity, 1876–1900," (1965) (Ph.D. dissertation, available from University Microfilms, Ann Arbor, Mich.).

57. Delicate, asexual, and inward-looking, women were thought to need protection, found in the sanctuary of the home, from the polluting contagion of the "masculine" world. See generally N. Cott, *The Bonds of Womanhood* 64–98 (1977); C. Degler, *At Odds: Women and the Family in America from the Revolution to the Present* 249–327 (1980); A. Douglas, *The Feminization of American Culture* 44–79 (1977); L. Stone, *The Family, Sex and Marriage in England* 1500–1800, 666–80 (1977).

58. See note 51 supra.

59. See C. Degler, supra note 57. See also J. Kobler, supra note 51, at 131–65.

60. See note 55, supra.

61. D. Colvin, supra note 53, at 587; cf. C. Degler, supra note 57.

62. See note 236 infra.

63. For pertinent history, see J. Kobler, supra note 51, at 221–354.

64. See generally D. Musto, *The American Disease: Origins of Narcotic Control* 1–209 (1973).

65. See L. Grinspoon, *Marihuana Reconsidered* 15–29 (1971); D. Musto, supra note 64, at 210–29.

66. Opium use has been traced to ancient Sumeria, and it is mentioned in The Iliad. See C. Terry & M. Pellens, *The Opium Problem* 53–93 (1928). See also Macht, "The History of Opium and Some of its Preparations and Alkaloids," 64 *J. Am. Med. Ass'n* 477 (1915).

67. See A. Hayter, *Opium and the Romantic Imagination* 191–225 (1968); M. Lefebure, *Samuel Taylor Coleridge: A Bondage of Opium* (1974). For one of Coleridge's most remarkable expressions of despair, see "Dejection: An Ode," in L. Trilling, *The Experience of Literature* 1107–10 (1967).

68. See C. P. Baudelaire, "Les Paradis Artificels" (an analysis of the author's drug experience), in *The Drug Experience* 16–40 (D. Ebin ed. 1961). For commentary, see generally A. Hayter, supra note 67, at 151–61. See also L. Grinspoon, *Marihuana Reconsidered* 78–95 (1971). Cf. J. Cocteau, *Opium: The Diary of a Cure* (1958).

69. See T. DeQuincey, *Confessions of an English Opium Eater* (1885). For commentary, see A. Hayter, supra note 67, at 101–31, 226–54.

70. See C. Terry & M. Pellens, supra note 66, at 468–75.

71. To the extent it was noticed, it was associated with an abuse of medicinal remedies found in all classes. See Swatos, "Opiate Addiction in the Late Nineteenth Century: A Study of the Social Problem, Using Medical Journals of the Period," 7 *Int'l J. Addictions* 739–53 (1972). It is unclear whether the administering of morphine to soldiers during the Civil War was a significant factor in the increase of addiction in the United

States or whether it simply reinforced patterns already extant. See Quinones, "Drug Abuse During the Civil War," 10 *Int'l J. Addictions* 1007–20 (1975).

72. See. D. Musto, supra note 64, at 25–28.

73. See P. Lowes, *The Genesis of International Narcotics Control*, 102–07 (1966).

74. A. Zabriskie, *Bishop Brent: Crusader for Christian Unity* 98 (1948).   ·

75. On the connections between prohibitionist attitudes toward liquor and toward opium, see A. Lindesmith, *The Addict and the Law* 140–41 (1965); P. Lowes, supra note 73, at 13–14, 99–100; D. Musto, supra note 64, at 6, 65–68, 128–34, 156–57, 213–14.

76. On the contrasting British and American approaches, see P. Lowes, supra note 73, at 104, 142–43; A. Taylor, *American Diplomacy and the Narcotics Traffic, 1900–1939*, at 45, 68, 73, 191, 204–05, 217 (1969). Under international pressure from the United States and domestic pressure from its own temperance groups, Britain eventually acquiesced in the American prohibitionist approach, ending, for example, the export of opium from India to China. For a description of Britain's recalcitrant acquiescence, see P. Lowes, supra note 73, at 58–84, 102–89; A. Taylor, supra, at 47–122.

77. S. Doc. No. 265, 59th Cong., 1st Sess. (1906) (report of Committee appointed by the Philippine Commission).

78. See A. Taylor, supra note 76, at 11, 19, 21–22, 25–26, 29–30, 37–38.

79. Until 1858, the trade in British opium, imported to China from India, was illegal in China. In 1727, the Chinese Edict of Yung Cheng proscribed the importation and sale of opium for smoking. See D. Owen, *British Opium Policy in China and India* 51 (1934). Similar edicts followed, but all were unsuccessful. The Chinese government's serious attempt to bring the opium trade to a halt in 1839 led to the Opium War between China and Britain. China's defeat opened the nation to the opium trade. See P. Fay, *The Opium War* 1840–1842 (1975).

80. One such report stated that,

> the effect of the drug on the individual is to ruin him morally, mentally, physically, and financially. It first incapacitates him for business, then begins to eat up his capital, and does not halt until it robs him of all his property. He sells his house piece by piece, until only enough is left to shelter his family. Then the daughters are sold, next the sons, and last of all the wife, and then the man himself goes into the coffin. . . . When the habit is once fixed nothing but superhuman power can dislodge it.

S. Doc. No. 135, 58th Cong., 3d Sess. 14 (1905) (remarks by Rev. W. L. Beard).

81. Medical missionaries, attested "that the continual use of opium resulted in the loss of muscular power, bowel troubles, asthma, impotence and a total collapse of moral values." P. Barr, *To China with Love* 88 (1972).

82. See generally P. Lowes, supra note 73, at 36–57; A Taylor, supra note 76, at 3–19.

83. One commentator reported of the missionaries: "[T]hey thought that at last their prayers were to be answered and they received the news of the burning of the Summer Palace with the cry 'God has opened China to Christianity.' " Chao-Kwang Wu, *The International Aspect of the Missionary Movement in China* 231 (1960).

84. The missionaries were repeatedly asked, "If yours is a Christian people, why have they forced opium on us?" Merwin, "Drugging a Nation: The Story of China and the Opium Curse," *Success Magazine*, Dec. 1907, at 852.

85. One bitter Chinese observer reported: "It is repeatedly asserted—especially by Christian missionaries—that the evil features of Chinese political and social life are the result of our false religious and heathen ethics, and can be cured only by Christianity. . . . I have heard a missionary assert with dogmatic emphasis that the anti-opium campaign is foredoomed to failure unless China becomes Christian." Lin Shao-Yang, *A Chinese Appeal to Christendom, Concerning Christian Missions* (1911).

86. See J. Timberlake, *Prohibition and the Progressive Movement* 1900–1920, at 4 (1963).

87. Id.

88. Cooper, "Deliverance from the Opium Habit," in *Missionary Review of the World*, Dec. 1908, at 922. Missionaries opposed the English opium trade in China. Chao-Kwang Wu, supra note 83, at 231.

89. Missionaries carried on an extensive correspondence with church groups and parishioners, traveled and made speeches, had direct contact with government officials, and provided information to foreign correspondents. See Masland, "Missionary influence upon Far Eastern Policy," 5 *Pac. Hist. Rev.* 279–96 (1941).

90. See "Patriotic Studies," International Reform Federation, Inc.; "Report of Hearing at State Department on Petitions to the President to Use His Good Offices for the Release of China from Treaty Compulsion to Tolerate the Opium Traffic, with additional Papers," *S. Doc. No. 135*, 58th Cong., 3d Sess. 232–56 (1905).

91. P. Lowes, supra note 73, at 107–11.

92. Id. at 102–89. See also A. Taylor, supra note 76, at 47–81.

93. See P. Lowes, supra note 73, at 89–97, 122; A. Taylor, supra note 76, at 57–59. Results of studies of the period vary dramatically as to the extent of addiction; few of them are reliable. See, e.g., C. Terry & M. Pellens, supra note 66, at 1–52. Estimates of the number of addicts ranged from several thousand to several million. Id. at 1. One of the better studies estimated a reduction in addicts from 215,000 to 110,000 during the period 1915–1922. Id. at 42–43. It is estimated that, as of 1972, there were 250,000 to 315,000 heroin addicts. See E. Brecher, supra note 1, at 92.

94. In addition to the ideological input of the missionaries, the antiopium stance was supported by several aims of the United States: the reduction of Chinese resistance to American financial investments, the placating of Chinese resentment over the United States's law prohibiting the immigration of Chinese laborers to this country, and the satisfaction of domestic resentment against the Chinese immigrants here whose life style was associated with opium. See D. Musto, supra note 64, at 3–4.

95. The gap in American law was pointedly raised by the German delegates at the Hague opium conference in 1912. See A. Taylor, supra note 76, at 106–07.

96. Thus the United States at the 1912 Hague Convention urged other countries to establish internal control of narcotic drugs. See A. Lindesmith, supra note 75, at 4. The American prohibitionist stance on drugs appears to have had dramatic effect on the development of international conventions in this area. See generally P. Lowes, supra note 73; A. Taylor, supra note 76; see also J. Platt & C. Labate, *Heroin Addiction: Theory, Research, & Treatment* 3–13 (1976). Specifically it appears to have shaped the direction of drug policy in countries subject to American influence in the Far East. See A. Lindesmith, supra note 75, at 189–221. Nonetheless, many question the degree to which other nations or the international community generally share the American prohibitionist orientation. See e.g., Simmons & Gold, "The Myth of International Control: American Foreign Policy and the Heroin Traffic," 8 *Int'l J. Addictions* 779 (1973).

97. Pub. L. No. 63–223, 38 Stat. 785 (1914); see D. Musto, supra note 64, at 54–68.

98. See A. Lindesmith, supra note 75 at 3–5.

99. See id. at 140–41; D. Musto, supra note 64, at 183–89.

100. D. Musto, supra note 64, at 121–50.

101. *United States v. Doremus*, 249 U. S. 86, 90 (1919).

102. *Webb v. United States*, 249 U. S. 96, 99–100 (1918).

103. *United States v. Behrman*, 258 U. S. 280, 289 (1921).

104. See *Linder v. United States*, 268 U. S. 5 (1924).

105. See A. Lindesmith, supra note 75, at 140–41; D. Musto, supra note 64, at 183–89.

106. See D. Musto, supra note 64, at 91–209; A. Lindesmith, supra note 75, at 135–61.

107. H. Judson, *Heroin Addiction in Britain*, ;3–23 (1974). Indeed, in Britain, the evils of the American treatment of heroin are expressly kept in mind, to be consciously avoided. See P. Bean, *The Social Control of Drugs* 69, 171 (1974).

108. See D. Musto, supra note 64, at 56–58.

109. See C. Terry & M. Pellens, supra note 66, at 2.

110. See generally id.

111. For useful analyses of the British maintenance system, which is now carried out by clinics rather than individual doctors, see H. Judson, supra note 107; P. Bean, supra note 107. See also E. Schur, *Narcotic Addiction in Britain and America* (1962). For a discussion of the British and Western European system, see A. Lindesmith, supra note 75, at 162–88.

112. See A. Lindesmith, supra note 75, at 25–34, 222–42; D. Musto, supra note 64, at 210–29.

113. Pub. L. No. 75–238, 50 Stat. 551 (1937) (superseded 1939).

114. For an excellent analysis of some of these distortions, see J. Kaplan, supra note 1, 88–136.

115. See A. Lindesmith, supra note 75, at 25–34; J. Platt & C. Labate, supra note 96, at 24–43. For an example of a responsible study of marijuana available in the 1930s, see Indian Hemp Drugs Commission of 1893–94; for commentary thereon, see J. Kaplan, supra note 1, at 115–21. See also Siler et al., "Marijuana Smoking in Panama," 73 *Milit. Surg.* 269–80 (1933); "The Marijuana Problem in the City of New York: Mayor LaGuardia's Committee on Marijuana," in *The Marijuana Papers* 277–410 (D. Solomon ed. 1966).

116. See generally Quinn & McLaughlin, "The Evolution and Present Status of New York Drug Control Legislation," 22 *Buffalo L. Rev.* 705 (1972–73).

117. See N. Kittrie, *The Right to be Different* 210–60 (1971).

118. See id.

119. See N. Y. *Penal Law* § § 220.00–220.60 (McKinney 1980). See, for an overview, *The Nation's Toughest Drug Law: Evaluating the New York Experience* (1978); *Staff Working Papers of the Drug Law Evaluation project* (1978).

120. On the self-regulating features of natural drugs, see A. Weil, *The Natural Mind* 98–115 (1972).

121. For a discussion of mescaline, see L. Goodman & A. Gilman, supra note 4, at 195. Mescaline was isolated in 1896 and is the active principle of peyote. Id. The classic description of its unusual psychic and hallucinatory effects is contained in A. Huxley, *The Doors of Perception* (1954).

122. For a discussion of LSD, see L. Goodman & A. Gilman, supra note 4, at 195–97. The unusual psychological effects of LSD were discovered in 1943 by Albert Hofmann. See A. Hofmann, *LSD: My Problem Child* (J. Ott trans. 1980). The shattering effects of LSD and other psychedelic drugs are described in L. Grinspoon & J. Bakalar, supra note 10, at 89–156.

123. See A. Weil, supra note 120. Also see works cited at note 14, supra.

124. For a discussion of morphine, see L. Goodman & A. Gilman, supra note 4, at 237–55. Morphine, the alkaloid that gives opium its analgesic action, was isolated in 1803. By the middle of the nineteenth century the use of pure alkaloids replaced crude opium preparations throughout the medical world. Id. 237.

125. "Heroin does not occur naturally but is a semisynthetic derivative produced by a chemical modification of morphine that increases the potency. It takes only 3 mg of heroin to produce the same analgesic effect as 10 mg of morphine (heroin being three times as potent as morphine)." R. Julien, *A Primer of Drug Action* 108 (1975) (emphasis deleted).

126. See L. Goodman & A. Gilman, supra note 4, at 237.

127. For a discussion of narcotics, see id. at 237–313. Narcotic analgesics include any natural or synthetic drug that has morphine-like pharmacological actions, exerting effects on, *inter alia*, the central nervous system, including analgesia, drowsiness, changes in mood, and mental clouding.

128. For a discussion of caffeine, see O. Ray, supra note 2, at 86–99. Caffeine is one of the xanthines, the oldest stimulants known to man. For its effects, see id. at 95–98.

129. See O. Ray, supra note 2, at 162–85.

130. See id. at 124–61, 244–69, 290–94.

131. See id. at 270–88. Cocaine, the active ingredient in coca leaves, was isolated before 1860. Id. at 272. For a general discussion of the drug, see L. Grinspoon & J. Bakalar, *Cocaine: A Drug and Its Social Evolution* (1976) [hereinafter cited as L. Grinspoon & J. Bakalar, *Cocaine*]. Amphetamine, synthesized in 1932, is one of the most powerful drugs in stimulating the central nervous system. Methamphetamine is closely related to amphetamine chemically, but has somewhat different effects. See L. Goodman & A. Gilman, supra note 4, at 507–07. "Speed" is methamphetamine liquified for injection and used intravenously. It induces a state described as euphoric and orgasmic, but it frequently results in the development of paranoid psychosis and paranoia, accom-

panied characteristically by crawling sensations and repetitive and compulsive behavior. See O. Ray, supra note 2, at 285–88.

132. For a discussion of mescaline, see works cited at note 121, supra; on LSD, see note 122 supra. For a general discussion of the hallucinogens, see O. Ray, supra note 2, at 344–89. Marijuana and hashish are derivatives of the species *Cannabis sativa.* The psychoactive agent is concentrated in the resin of the plant, the concentration being greatest in the flowering tops and decreasing in the lower, more fibrous parts. Hashish, or "hash," consists of the flowering tops and is highly potent. Marijuana consists chiefly of leafy material and fine stems and is much less potent. See id. at 391–92. For a general discussion of marijuana and hashish, see L. Grinspoon, *Marihuana Reconsidered* (1971); O. Ray, supra note 2, at 250–268.

133. See O. Ray, supra note 2, at 39–43.

134. Legally available drugs can be divided into two categories: prescription drugs, which may be purchased only with a physicians's prescription, and over-the-counter drugs, which may be purchased at will. See O. Ray, supra note 2, at 48–54.

135. See, e.g., *Carmona v. Ward,* 576 F. 2d 405, 410–12 (2d cir. 1978), cert. denied, 439 U. S. 1091 (1979); *People v. Broadie,* 37 N. Y. 2d 100, 112–13, 332 N. E. 2d 338, 342–42, 371 N. Y. S. 2d 471, 476–77, cert. denied, 423 U. S. 950 (1975).

136. It is estimated that organized crime takes in about $2.2 billion a year from the illegal narcotics trade. Dilution of the drug is so great that a kilogram of heroin may sell on the streets for a quarter of a million dollars, some $300 of which may have been received by the farmer abroad (usually in Turkey) who originally sold the drug. See E. Brecher, supra note 1, at 99–100; O. Ray, supra note 2, at 327.

137. Official drug use statistics that are used to bolster the case for criminalization are often themselves distorted by the illegality of drugs. See Mandel, "Problems with Official Drug Statistics," 21 *Stan. L. Rev.* 991 (1969). The uncritical acceptance of this circularity is typical of the state of American understanding of drug use.

138. One of the better empirical studies of heroin addiction and crime among the young indicates that the cumulative amount of delinquent behavior is not a function of addiction, but rather that the kinds of delinquency change to reflect the special requirements of the addict—for example, changing to forms of criminal conduct that yield a profit, like robbery or burglary. See I. Chein, D. Gerard, R. Lee, & E. Rosenfield, *The Road to H* 57-65, 166–68 (1964) [hereinafter cited as I. Chein].

139. Perceptive commentators have long observed that the very publicity and notoriety associated with prohibitory drug laws may encourage persons with little else to undertake a life of drug use. Some analysts see the criminal prohibition of drugs as inciting "glamorous" risk taking, especially among the poor and disadvantaged. See I. Chein, supra note 138, at 6–7. See generally C. Terry & M. Pellens, supra note 66, at 134–36. Another commentator has hypothesized that the very scarcity of the drugs, which criminalization leads to, reinforces the obsession with addictive drugs. See A. Lindesmith, *Addiction and Opiates* 67 (2d ed. 1968). Criminalization may encourage the drug user to conceive of himself solely as an addict. See H. Becker, *Outsiders: Studies in the Sociology of Deviance* (1963); T. Duster, *The Legislation of Morality: Law, Drugs, and Moral Judgment* 88–96 (1970).

140. See note 111, supra.

141. See H. Judson, supra note 107, at 48–49.

142. See, e. g., A. Lindesmith, supra note 75, at 179–80. The contrast between the numbers of addicts in Britain and in the United States is striking. The United States had approximately 200,000 addicts in 1965, while Britain with one-third of the population had 1,000. See id. at 124–25. When a country like Britain speaks of an heroin epidemic, it has in mind an increase from 470 known addicts in 1961 to 753 in 1964. See P. Bean, supra note 107, at 78. The desire to bring this rise under control led Britain to change from its system of medical prescription of heroin maintenance (which evidently had been abused by a few physicians, leading to a rise in the number of addicts) to heroin maintenance through regulated clinics. See id. at 74–91; H. Judson, supra note 109, at 35–62. The reform appears to have stabilized the number of addicts in Britain. See id. at 127. On the varying practices of the British clinics, see id. at 63–122.

143. See text accompanying notes 70–71 supra.
144. See I. Chein, supra note 138, at 37–40, 55–56, 65–74; A. Lindesmith, supra note 75, at 132. In Britain, by contrast, there is no comparable pattern. See H. Judson, supra note 107, at 47–48.
145. See generally A. Lindesmith, supra note 75, at 131–34. See also sources cited at note 139 supra.
146. See L. Grinspoon, *Marihuana Reconsidered* 324–48 (1971); J. Kaplan, supra note 1, at 122–34 (1970). On the effects of opiates, see A. Lindesmith, *Addiction and Opiates* 23–45 (2d ed. 1968).
147. See J. Kaplan, supra note 1, at 94–98.
148. See id. at 90–94.
149. See id. at 94.
150. See id. at 106–12. Even then, empirical studies showed there was no support for this argument. See note 115 and accompanying text supra. Characteristically, such reports were not carefully analyzed but violently attacked, often by enforcement officials committed to the contrary position. See L. Grinspoon, *Marihuana Reconsidered* 27–29 (1971). Or when contrary evidence was acknowledged, it was interpreted in ways that showed no careful reading either of the methodology of the study or its conclusions. See the discussion of the campaign by Commissioner H. T. Anslinger of the Federal Bureau of Narcotics which led to the Marihuana Tax Act of 1937. Id. at 25–26. One critic offering such evidence was simply dismissed as "not cooperative." Id. at 26.
151. See J. Kaplan, supra note 1, 265–69.
152. This criticism has been extensively made by E. Brecher. See E. Brecher, supra note 1, at 185, 291–93, 331–32, 497–98.
153. See O. Ray, supra note 2, at 330–31.
154. Aspirin is an example. See id. at 211–12.
155. See generally E. Brecher, supra note 1, at 101–14.
156. See O. Ray, supra note 2, at 331.
157. Id. at 195–96.
158. See note 111 supra.
159. For a defense of this concept of shame, see D. Richards, *A Theory of Reasons for Action* 250–67 (1971).
160. See discussion at notes 59–71 and text accompanying, Chapter 2, supra.
161. See notes 22–27 and accompanying text supra. For a useful introduction to the Gnostic ideas against which Augustine (as a former Gnostic) was reacting, see H. Jonas, *The Gnostic Religion* (2d ed. 1963). For some later development, see N. Cohn, *The Pursuit of the Millennium* (2d ed. 1961); S. Runciman, *The Medieval Manichee* (1947).
162. Cf. O. Ray, supra note 2, at 16–17.
163. For an expanded explication of Augustine's view of sexuality, see discussion at notes 59–71 and text accompanying, Chapter 2, supra.
164. See notes 7–12 and accompanying text supra.
165. With respect to the phenothiazines, these properties have enabled many of the mentally ill to regain control of their mental lives in a way that would not otherwise be possible. See O. Ray, supra note 2, at 136–55.
166. In this connection, it is important to distinguish the effects of the following different drugs: (1) narcotic analgesics, (2) marijuana, (3) mescaline, and (4) LSD. Writers who have taken opium have both praised its virtues in stimulating preexisting imaginative powers (dream imagery, for example), and criticized its perceived debilitating effects. See generally A. Hayter, supra note 67. For praise, see. C. P. Baudelaire, supra note 68, at 19–28 (although Baudelaire expressly wrote of hashish, he probably had more experience with opium; see L. Grinspoon, *Marijuana Reconsidered* 91–94; A. Hayter, supra, at 151–152); T. DeQuincey, supra note 69, at 15–18. See also J. Cocteau, *Opium: The Diary of a Cure* 70–71 (M. Crosland & S. Road trans. 1958) ("To say of an addict who is in a continual state of euphoria that he is degrading himself is like saying of marble that it is spoilt by Michaelangelo, of canvas that it is stained by Raphael, of paper that it is soiled by Shakespeare, of silence that it is broken by Bach.")

One of Coleridge's more remarkable poems, "Kubla Khan," may have been inspired by one of his opium reveries. See A. Hayter, supra at 214–25. For the poem, see L. Trilling, *The Experience of Literature* 870–71 (1967). For criticism of opiates, see C. P. Baudelaire, supra, at 28–40; T. DeQuincey, supra at 83–127. For reference to Coleridge's poem of despair, see "Dejection: An Ode," supra note 67.

For the uses of marijuana as an imaginative stimulant, see A. Ginsberg, "First Manifesto to End the Bringdown," in *The Marihuana Papers* 230–48 (D. Solomon ed. 1966). See generally L. Grinspoon, *Marihuana Reconsidered* 123–30, 150–55 (1971); C. Winick, "The Use of Drugs by Jazz Musicians," 7 *Soc. Prob.* 140–53 (1960).

For a remarkable statement of the imaginative uses of mescaline, see A. Huxley, *The Doors of Perception* (1954).

For the imaginative uses of LSD, see L. Grinspoon & J. Bakalar, supra note 10, at 261–73; B. Wells, *Psychedelic Drugs* 170–212 (1973). See generally R. Masters & J. Houston, *The Varieties of Psychedelic Experience* (1966).

167. DeQuincey observed: "If a man 'whose talk is of oxen' should become an opium-eater, the probability is, that (if he is not too dull to dream at all) he will dream about oxen: whereas, in the case before him, the reader will find that the opium-eater boasteth himself to be a philosopher." T. DeQuincey, supra note 69, at 16. And Baudelaire observed of the intoxicated person: "He remains, despite the adventitious force of his sensations, merely the same man increased, the same number raised to a very high power." C. P. Baudelaire, supra note 68, at 20. On the importance of atmosphere to the drug experience, see H. Becker, *Outsiders: Studies in the Sociology of Deviance* 41–58 (1963); L. Grinspoon, *Marihuana Reconsidered* 6, 136, 137, 181, 185, 206–07 (1971); L. Grinspoon & J. Bakalar, supra note 10 at 14, 89–90, 105–06, 125 ff; A. Weil, *The Natural Mind* 29 (1972); N. Zinberg & J. Robertson, *Drugs and the Public* 78–86 (1972).

168. Using Lawrence Kohlberg's theory of moral development, one may argue that the students who protested at Berkeley in the name of free speech were on a high stage of moral development. They appealed to principles of independent conscience and sought to vindicate them against an unjust society. See L. Kohlberg, "Education for Justice: A Modern Statement of the Platonic View," in *Moral Education* 78–79 (T. Sizer ed. 1970). If certain forms of drug use support such a critical moral culture, such use may also reflect similar moral independence.

169. For a history of American attitudes toward drug use, see text accompanying notes 30–119 supra.

170. See text accompanying notes 28–36 supra.

171. See notes 30–31 and accompanying text supra.

172. On the contrast between the Magisterial Reformation of Luther and Calvin and the Radical Reformation, see G. Williams, *The Radical Reformation* xxiii–xxxi (1962).

173. See text accompanying notes 37–40 supra.

174. See text accompanying notes 40–57 supra.

175. See B. Rush supra note 40.

176. See id. at 190–91.

177. See id. at 197.

178. See text accompanying notes 21–22 supra.

179. See text accompanying notes 50–57 supra.

180. See text accompanying notes 58–119 supra.

181. On the legal status of psychedelic drugs, see L. Grinspoon & J. Bakalar, supra note 10, at 309–12.

182. See Chapter 1, supra.

183. See Urmson, "Saints and Heroes," in *Essays in Moral Philosophy* 198–216 (A. Melden ed. 1958).

184. See D. Richards, *Reasons for Action* supra note 159, at 205–8.

185. I. Kant, *The Metaphysical Principles of Virtue* 88 (J. Ellington trans. 1964).

186. Id.

187. B. Rush, supra note 40, at 208–9.

188. I. Kant, supra note 185, at 89.

189. Id.

190. W. Shakespeare, *Twelfth Night,* Act II, Scene V, *The Oxford Shakespeare* 310 (W. J. Craig ed. 1966); cf. W. Shakespeare, *Othello,* Act II, Scene II, id. at 953, where a herald announces to a crowd that "each man to what sport and revels his addiction leads him."

191. Strikingly, DeQuincey invoked religious metaphors in characterizing his addiction to opium:

[T]he opium-eater . . . feels that the diviner part of his nature is paramount; that is, the moral affections are in a state of cloudless serenity; and over all is the great light of the majestic intellect.

This is the doctrine of the true church on the subject of opium: of which church I acknowledge myself to be the only member,—the alpha and omega. . . .

T. DeQuincey, supra note 69, at 71.

Using similar vocabulary but to different effect, Baudelaire spoke of the power of the drug as that of the "Prince of Darkness." C. P. Baudelaire, supra note 68. See also id. at 35, 38. Similarly, the drug user is his own "godhead." Id. at 31. In consequence, drug taking is "obscene heresy." Id. at 34.

192. See L. Goodman & A. Gilman, supra note 4, at 537–38.

193. See id.

194. See id. at 535.

195. Some such drugs are anticholingergics, chlorpomazine, imipramine, and cyclazocine. See id. at 537.

196. See L. Goodman & A. Gilman, supra note 4, at 309; A. Lindesmith, *Addiction and Opiates* 69–127 (1968).

197. See, e.g., B. Johnson, "Once an Addict, Seldom an Addict," 1978 *Contemp. Drug Prob.* 35–53; Robins, Davis, & Goodwin, "Drug Use by U.S. Army Enlisted Men in Vietnam: A Follow-Up on their Return Home," 99 *Am. J. Epidemiology,* 235–49 (1974).

198. See Fingarette, "Addiction and Criminal Responsibility," 84 *Yale L.J.* 413, 431 (1975) (pointing out the low potency of the heroin available to American addicts). By contrast, the heroin available to American soldiers in Vietnam was of high potency, yet they exhibit low continuing commitment to the drug. See works cited at note 197 supra. The natural inference is that levels of addiction are not related solely to chemical or physiological factors.

199. See L. Goodman & A. Gilman, supra note 4, at 279–83, 293–98; O. Ray, supra note 2, at 64–65.

200. See C. Winick, "Maturing Out of Narcotic Addiction," 14 *Bull. Narcotics* 1–7 (1962). The rate of relapse in programs of compulsory rehabilitation for addiction appears to be high. See E. Brecher, supra note 1, at 64–78. Voluntary therapeutic communities, however, appear to have more success at least where the patient continues to live in the community. Id. at 78–83. One perceptive commentator has noted that in view of the dominant importance of psycho-social factors in explaining psychological devotion to drugs, "curing a person of addiction might, in this sense, be compared with curing a person of a college education." A. Lindesmith, *Addiction and Opiates* 204 (1968).

201. Correlatively, we should question the popular idea of the moral degeneracy of the addict. See, for trenchant comments on the conventional wisdom, C. Terry & M. Pellens, supra note 66, at 513–16.

202. See generally I. Chein, supra note 138, L. Goodman & A. Gilman, supra note 4, at 535–37, 542–44; A. Lindesmith, *Addiction and Opiates* (1968); J. Platt & C. Labate, supra note 96; C. Terry & M. Pellens, supra note 66; Salmon & Salmon, "The Causes of Heroin Addiction—A Review of the Literature" (pts. 1 & 2), *Int'l J. Addictions* 679–96, 937–51 (1977).

203. See generally I. Chein, supra note 138.

204. Id. at 57–65, 166–68.

205. R. Ashley, *Heroin—The Myths and The Facts* 73 (1972); I. Chein, supra note 259; A. Lindesmith, supra note 195, at 131–34; Preble & Casey, "Taking Care of Business: The Heroin User's Life in the Street," in *It's So Good, Don't Even Try It Once* 116 (D. Smith &

G. Gay, eds. 1972). See generally E. Brecher, supra note 3, at 42–46; Chein, "Psychological Functions of Drug Use," in *Scientific Basis of Drug Dependence* 14–15 (H. Steinberg ed. 1969); Vaillant, "The Natural History of Urban Narcotic Drug Addiction—Some Determinants," id. at 351.

206. J. Douglas, *Youth in Turmoil* 52 (1970); Feldman, "Ideological Supports to Becoming and Remaining a Heroin Addict," *Drug Dependence,* Mar. 1970, at 10.

207. I. Chein supra note 138, at 248 (withdrawal experiences "become integrated in their self-images as a valid, interesting, and necessary aspect of themselves").

208. For a similar analysis of the abuse of the concept of addiction and related concepts, see L. Grinspoon & J. Bakalar, *Cocaine: A Drug and Its Social Evolution* 177–207 (1976); cf. T. Szasz, *Ceremonial Chemistry* 6, 56, 85, 99–101, 164–65 (1974).

209. S. Peele, *Love and Addiction* (1975).

210. P. Slater, *Wealth Addiction* (1980). Large numbers of Americans describe themselves as "addicts" to some substance or activity. See *N.Y. Times,* Jan. 27, 1981, § C., at 1.

211. See S. Peele, supra note 209 at 61.

212. P. Slater, supra note 210, at 33–64.

213. See text accompanying notes 146–50, supra.

214. See text accompanying notes 135–45, supra.

215. A. Lindesmith, *Addiction and Opiates* 49 (1968).

216. See text accompanying notes 205–07, supra.

217. I. Kant, *Foundations of the Metaphysics of Morals* 51–52 (L. W. Beck trans. 1959).

218. See Chapter 1, supra.

219. See Richards, "The Individual, the Family, and the Constitution: A Jurisprudential Perspective," 55 *N.Y.U. L. Rev.* 1 (1980).

220. The moral idea here is that, quite apart from background institutional roles, merely giving birth to a vulnerable child, other things being equal, gives rise to duties of care and nurturance. See J. Locke, *Second Treatise* in *Two Treatises of Government* (P. Laslett ed. 1960), §§ 56–58.

221. Among the drugs that may have effects on newborns are the hypnotics, see R. Julien, supra note 5, at 59; alcohol, see id. at 62; caffeine, see id. at 93; nicotine via lactation, see id. at 94; nicotine, on the fetus, see id, at 96–97; heroin, see id. at 104; and marijuana, see id. at 180. In some cases, the effects can be avoided by not ingesting the drug during pregnancy. See id. at 180. Allegations that the use of LSD causes chromosomal damage are not well supported. See L. Grinspoon & J. Bakalar, supra note 10, at 188–90; O. Ray, supra note 2, at 247.

222. As long as parents so regulate their drug use as not to violate their basic moral duties of care and nurture of their children, there can be no moral objection to it. It appears likely, in this connection, that forms of regulation of drug use, such as heroin maintenance, are more likely to render drug use consistent with parental duties than a prohibitory scheme like that of the United States. See H. Judson, supra note 107, at 83–84, 88, 120; cf. L. Goodman & A. Gilman, supra note 4, at 1670.

223. See note 221 supra.

224. For judicial use of this argument, see Soler, "Of Cannabis and the Courts: A Critical Examination of Constitutional Challenges to Statutory Marijuana Prohibitions," 6 *Conn. L. Rev.* 601, 649–55 (1974). Cf. L. Grinspoon, *Marihuana Reconsidered* (1971), at 302–3, 307–8 (use of cannabis not per se criminogenic, but by aggravating psychopathic disorders may lead to increased criminal activity).

225. For the politically manipulative uses of this kind of argument, see E. Epstein, *Agency of Fear: Opiates and Political Power in America* (1977); G. Hamburger, *The Peking Bomb* (1975).

226. See B. Rush, supra note 40, at 197.

227. See Aristotle, *Nicomachean Ethics* 1138a4–1138b14 (M. Ostwald trans. 1962).

228. Saint Thomas Aquinas, *Summa Theologica* Part 2-2, Q. 64, Art. 5 (Blackfriars ed. 1975).

229. See 4 W. Blackstone, *Commentaries on the Laws of England* 189.

230. Such a person is perhaps not a very socially productive citizen but can meet

minimal obligations of compliance with law, bearing a fair share of the burdens of social life, taxes, and the like. See L. Goodman & A. Gilman, supra note 4.

231. See A. Lindesmith, supra note 75, at 130–31; Swatos, supra note 71.

232. See note 142 supra.

233. See E. Brecher, supra note 1, at 17–20; H. Judson, supra note 107, at 83–84, 88, 120; Swatos, supra note 71.

234. See text accompanying notes 155–57.

235. See text accompanying notes 135–45.

236. See Gusfield, *Symbolic Crusade: Status Politics and the American Temperance Movement* (1963).

237. D. Musto, *The American Disease* 5–6 (1973).

238. Id. at 219–21.

239. Id. at 7–8.

240. See J. Gusfield, supra note 236; cf. T. Duster, *The Legislation of Morality: Law, Drugs, and Moral Judgment* (1970) (moral stigma of addiction is based upon middle class perspective and depends upon social obedience of users of the drug—not upon its physiological effects.)

241. One recent study of the relative hazards of various forms of drug use concluded that alcohol use is potentially more hazardous to the individual and society than are cocaine, cannabinoids, and opiates. See Irwin, "A Rational Approach to Drug Abuse Prevention," 2 *Contemp. Drug. Prob.* 3, 15–26 (1973).

242. See O. Ray, supra note 2, at 273–74; cf. G. Stent, *The Coming of the Golden Age* 131–36 (1969) (since this technological civilization is now at an end, we will turn to drugs more suited to our increasingly nonproductive orientation).

243. See works cited at note 242 supra.

244. See, generally, J. Rawls, *A Theory of Justice* (1971).

245. For versions of this argument over the use of coca leaves in Latin America, see L. Grinspoon & J. Bakalar, *Cocaine: A Drug and Its Social Evolution* 218–22 (1976).

246. See Bayer, "Heroin Decriminalization and the Ideology of Tolerance: A Critical View," 12 *Law & Soc'y Rev.* 301, 314 (1978). In the political forum, such arguments sometimes take the form of assertions that heroin maintenance would be "genocide" against blacks, sedating ghetto protest. See H. Judson, supra note 107, at 110.

247. See A. Lindesmith, supra note 75, at 162–221; cf. P. Bean, supra note 107, at 95–129 (legislative changes in British drug laws as response to altered composition of addict population). But cf. H. Judson, supra note 107, at 81–84, 88, 120 (various patterns of drug use in absence of criminal sanction determined by sociological factors); E. Schur, supra note 111, at 86–146 (various patterns of drug use in absence of criminal sanction determined by sociological factors).

248. See E. Brecher, supra note 1, at 17–20; C. Terry & M. Pellens, supra note 66, at 469–75; Swatos, supra note 71.

249. See E. Brecher, supra note 1, at 18–19; A. Lindesmith, supra note 75, at 131–34.

250. See notes 138–45, 205–07, and accompanying text supra.

251. For the focal significance, in a theory of justice, of improving the condition of the most disadvantaged classes, see J. Rawls, supra note 244.

252. See text accompanying notes 153–58, supra.

253. See J. Rawls, supra note 244.

254. Indeed, the notion of exploitation here is problematic. One becomes an addict as a result of social processes within one's peer group, not principally because of the blandishments of the stereotypical aggressive pusher preying on the young. See I. Chein, supra note 138, at 149–53. Criminalization is crucial to the social and economic context of this natural process of experimentation. Accordingly, decriminalization would be the proper course to alter the structure of social incentives in order to make drug use a less desirable choice for a young person. Indeed, it seems that the morally sound account of exploitation is that criminalization itself unjustly exploits the vulnerabilities of the exposed social and economic position of the poor. This theory of criminalization bespeaks contempt for the poor, imputing to them a basic lack of dignity because of the high rate of addiction among them, when this may reflect a not

unreasonable and undignified response to a social context which criminalization itself created.

255. On the lower rates of addiction in countries which regulate, but do not prohibit, heroin, see note 142, supra. Attempts to deny the relevance of the experience of these countries, particularly Britain, have been characterized as racist. See N. Zinberg & J. Robertson, *Drugs and the Public* 161–63 (1972). Certainly, these attempts have been ill-informed, often guided by American enforcement officials who refused to recognize the distinctive features of foreign regulatory treatment of drugs. See A. Lindesmith, supra note 75, at 183–84; E. Schur, supra note 111, at 173–85. Sometimes, a rise in British rates of heroin addiction is interpreted as a general failure of the British approach when, in fact, by any reasonable measure of comparison with the United States, the British have the problem well under control. For the British experience, see note 142, supra. For the American misinterpretation, see H. Judson, supra not 107, at 123–41.

256. For a realistic study of the relative dangers of drugs, which are monumentally distorted by American drug treatment policy, see Irwin, supra note 241. See generally E. Brecher, supra note 1.

257. See note 13, Chapter 1, supra.

258. See text accompanying notes 7–12, supra.

259. See V. Rubin & L. Comitas, *Ganja in Jamaica: A Medical Anthropological Study of Chronic Marihuana Use* 55–57 (1975). On the medical uses of illegal drugs, see Korcok, "The Medical Applications of Marijuana and Heroin: High Time the Laws Were Changed," 119 *Can. Med. Ass'n. J.* 374 (1978).

260. See L. Grinspoon & J. Bakalar, *Cocaine,* supra note 245, at 9–16, 87–94, 103, 108, 120–29, 155–56; Berridge, "Fenland Opium Eating in the Nineteenth Century," 72 *Brit. J. Addiction* 275–84 (1977); Berridge, "Opium and the Historical Perspective," *The Lancet,* July 9, 1977, at 78–80; Berridge, "Opium Eating and the Working Class in the Nineteenth Century: The Public and Official Reaction," 73 *Brit. J. Addiction* 107–12 (1978); Berridge, "Working-Class Opium Eating in the Nineteenth Century: Establishing the Facts," 73 *Brit. J. Addiction* 363–74 (1978).

261. If this is so, the task of a just drug policy should be to facilitate a fair cultural setting in which the goods of drug use may be reasonably pursued, rather than punitively frustrated. See L. Grinspoon & J. Bakalar, *Cocaine,* supra note 245, at 238–67; cf. N. Zinberg & J. Robertson, *Drugs and the Public* 78–86 (1972) (hostile social attitudes toward drugs cause personality disorganization).

262. See text accompanying notes 13–21 supra.

263. See note 166 supra.

264. Of opium, De Quincey wrote: "O just, subtle, and mighty opium! . . . thou hast the keys of Paradise." T. De Quincey, supra note 69, at 83–84.

265. See generally A. Weil, *The Natural Mind* (1972). See also L. Grinspoon & J. Bakalar, supra note 10, 238–308; A. Hoffman, supra note 122, at 195–209; A. Huxley, *The Doors of Perception* 62–79 (1954); T. Leary, *The Politics of Ectasy* (1968); G. Weil, R. Metzner, & T. Leary, *The Psychedelic Reader* (1965).

266. See text accompanying notes 205–07, supra. Cf. E. Brecher, supra note 1, at 33–41 (examples of American addicts not from the ghettoes).

267. For a discussion of the concept of addiction, see text accompanying notes 190–216, supra.

268. See J. Platt & C. Labate, supra note 96, at 95–96.

269. See generally id. at 86–96.

270. See L. Goodman & A. Gilman, supra note 4, at 286.

271. See text accompanying notes 190–216, supra.

272. See note 167, supra.

273. One class of drugs that might plausibly be prohibited is that of methamphetamines or "speed". See note 131 supra. See also E. Brecher, supra note 1, at 281–93. One commentator has noted that the sometimes violent and uncontrolled hyperactivity that "speed" causes approximates the stereotype of the "dope fiend" that is

improperly applied to heroin addiction. L. Goodman & A. Gilman, *supra* note 4, at 302–05.

It is important to see that the traditional arguments for the irrationality of criminalized forms of drug use are typically based on distortions of the facts. It is as if the extant moralistic condemnation of drug use inexorably shaped the reading of the facts so as to confirm that the putatively immoral conduct was personally irrational as well. Older accounts of drug use in the United States, for example, claimed such use leads to insanity and much shortened life spans, to the release of violent aggression, to sexual rapine, to political irresponsibility and personal decline. Psychiatrists have commonly supplied a psychiatric makeweight to the moral condemnations by claiming that the drug users are mentally ill or, at least, have some form of neurotic personality. Few of these claims are supported by careful empirical research observing sound scientific methods. See, e.g., E. Glover, *On the Early Development of the Human Mind* 187–215 (1956). Often such studies rest on a limited sample of people, which the researcher mistakenly believes to be typical of the research population a large. For example, a researcher or observer might mistakenly infer from the class of drug users who come to the attention of the criminal law or seek therapeutic help that all drug users are intrinsically criminal or in need of therapeutic help. See C. Terry & M. Pellens, *supra* note 66, at 513–14. In addition, as Terry and Pellens perceptively observed in their pathbreaking study:

> In addition to the foregoing possible misinterpretations on the part of the writers quoted, is it not possible that where individual writers have accorded to certain types a tendency to the use of this drug, effect has been mistaken for cause? Have not these patients, possibly as a result of the situation in which they find themselves—the toxic effect of the drug, disturbed metabolism, fear of discovery and realization that unaided they cannot regain their health—presented temporarily characteristics that were not constitutional with them? . . . In other words, the pre-addict has not been studied, and traits of character, ethical standards, and intellectual capacities based on *post hoc* findings may or may not have a *propter hoc* significance.

Id., 514–15.

Thus it may be argued that, in the United States, such studies record effects not intrinsic to taking the drugs, but related to a context of criminalization and its effects on patterns of drug use. See, e.g., E. Brecher, *supra* note 1, at 33–41, E. Schur, *supra* note 111, at 86–146; which suggest that quite different forms of personality, some highly competent and productive, emerge when users have regular access to drugs they desire. One study suggests that addicts may be more intelligent and educated than their peers. See J. Platt & C. Labate, *supra* note 96, at 175. More recently, arguments have focused on the "addictive personality," marked by a certain pattern of family life, for example, a dominant mother and an absent father in the case of men, resulting in an allegedly passive and dependent personality. See, e.g., id. at 126–75; Salmon & Salmon, "The Causes of Heroin Addiction—A Review of the Literature" (pts. 1 & 2), 12 *Int'l Addictions* 679–96, 937–51 (1977). The empirical grounds for these studies have been questioned; J. Platt & C. Labate, *supra* note 96, at 146–54, 312. Assuming, arguendo, their validity as a matter of aetiological explanation, it is irrelevant to public policy that a certain pattern of behavior has a certain aetiology unless there are independent normative grounds to question the behavior. In fact, these studies assume what must be shown, that drug-taking is itself objectionable. See Fingarette, "Addiction and Criminal Responsibility," 84 *Yale L. J.* 413, 439–43 (1975). See also notes 190–216 and accompanying text supra.

In fact, the history of American prohibitory legislation regarding drug use is a remarkable spectacle marked, among other things, by its dependence either on the moralistic perceptions by persons such as Christian missionaries in China, ill-suited to assess empirical questions regarding drug use in the United States, or on quite distorted factual interpretations made available by enforcement officials—in blatant disregard of the accumulating empirical literature of dispassionate and scientific merit which reveals the emptiness of the factual assumptions on which the prohibitions rested. See generally text accompanying notes 58–119 supra. For a useful analysis of the social irrationality surrounding anti marijuana laws, in particular, see R. Bonnie & C. White-bread, "The Forbidden Fruit and the Tree of Knowledge: An Inquiry into the Legal History of American Marijuana Prohibition," 56 Va. L. Rev. 971 (1970).

274. For some sense of the cultural experiment which drug use introduced into patterns of American culture, see T. Wolfe, The Electric Kool-Aid Acid Test (1968). On new forms of music, see id. at 212–13, 230–52; on life styles, see id. at 354–55; on religious feelings, see id. at 125–49, 182–85, 192.

275. See Chapter 1, supra.

276. See notes 26–31, and note 38, Chapter 1, supra.

277. See note 32, Chapter 1, supra.

278. 537 P. 2d 494 (Alaska 1975).

279. In explanation, the court observed that "[f]ew would believe they have been deprived of something of critical importance if deprived of marijuana." Id. at 502. But cf. Justice Levinson's dissent in State v. Kantner, 53 Hawaii 327, 339, 493 P. 2d 306, 313 (1972). Courts have, however, invoked privacy arguments in support of mental patients' right to refuse drugs. See e.g., Rennie v. Klein, 462 F. Supp. 1131 (1978); Rogers v. Okin, 478 F. Supp. 1342 (1979); In re K. K. B., 609 P. 2d 747 (1980). These cases, in their vindication of the right to control one's mental state, suggest a larger privacy right relevant to drug use.

280. See generally L. Tribe, American Constitutional Law 812–990 (1978).

281. See text accompanying notes 169–84 supra.

282. See notes 160–68 and accompanying text supra.

283. For further discussion, see Richards, "Free Speech and Obscenity Law: Toward a Moral Theory of the First Amendment," 123 U. Pa. L. Rev. 45, 59–83 (1974).

284. In American constitutional theory, this claim is made in the form of a denial that forms of drug use are entitled to protection under the free exercise of religion clause of the first amendment. See Giannella, "Religious Liberty, Nonestablishment, and Doctrinal Development: Part I, The Religious Liberty Guarantee," 80 Harv. L. Rev. 1381, 1426–31 (1967). Giannella has made this claim on two grounds: first, that prohibition of drug use poses no threat of "alienation from one's Maker, frustration of one's ultimate mission in life, and violation of the religious person's integrity," id. at 1427; and second, that certain forms of drug use are "as subversive of the existing secular order as conduct made criminal because it is offensive to public morality." id. Neither claim can withstand scrutiny under the analysis offered in this chapter. The first argument begs the point at issue, adopting a conception of religious experience that assumes the technology of religious self-mastery that is in dispute. The second assumes precisely the conception of public morality that this chapter has shown to be inconsistent with the deepest foundations of constitutional conceptions of human rights.

285. It may be that there should be an appropriate division of labor in this area between courts and legislatures. Courts might move more aggressively in cases like marijuana use, where the case for decriminalization seems very clear and the case for extensive regulatory schemes (for example, licensing) is weak, while legislatures might have more proper competence where, in addition to decriminalization, extensive regulation will clearly be required (for example, in heroin maintenance). On the concept of judicially underenforced constitutional norms, see Sager, "Fair Measure: The Legal Status of Underenforced Constitutional Norms," 91 Harv. L. Rev. 1212 (1978).

286. See L. Grinspoon, Marihuana Reconsidered 331–34 (1971); K. Singer, "The Choice of Intoxicants Among the Chinese," 69 Brit. J. Addiction 257–68 (1974). For the contrasting cultural interpretations of heroin in India and China, see R. Blum, supra note 14, at 48–51.

287. See note 242, supra.

288. See note 273, supra.

289. See the more extensive discussion of these distinctions at notes 302–07 and accompanying text, Chapter 3, supra.

290. See generally Richards, "Human Rights and Moral Ideals: An Essay on the Moral Theory of Liberalism," 5 Soc. Theory & Prac. 461 (1980).

291. See note 2 supra.
292. See J. Kaplan, supra note 1, at 315–21.
293. Id. at 322–23.
294. See e.g., J. Kaplan, supra note 1, at 332–47; N. Zinberg & J. Robertson, *Drugs and the Public* 259–63 (1972).
295. See H. Hart & A. Sacks, *The Legal Process: Basic Problems in the Making and Application of Law* 873–76 (tentative draft 1958).
296. See generally O. Ray, supra note 2, at 2–34.
297. Id. at 12–13.
298. See works cited at note 111, supra.
299. See notes 153–58 and accompany text supra.
300. For a useful study of Britain's use of a clinic system and its advantages, see H. Judson, supra note 107.
301. There are, for example, certain advantages in substituting a methadone addiction for a heroin addiction: methadone may be taken by mouth (avoiding infections from injection needles); it is longer acting that heroin, which requires several shots a day and produces mood bounces between each; it does not produce a tendency toward increases in dosage that some heroin addicts experience; and it staves off heroin withdrawal symptoms. See E. Brecher, supra note 1, at 161–62. While heroin maintenance is impermissible in the United States, methadone maintenance is not, and there have been notable experiments with it. See id. at 135–82. For criticisms of methadone maintenance see Bayer, "Methadone Under Attack: An Analysis of Popular Literature," *Contemp. Drug. Prob.* 367–400, Fall 1978. For a recent defense, see Dole, "Addictive Behavior," *Sci. Am.,* Dec. 1980, at 138–54. If a heroin addict wishes to substitute another form of addiction, that is, of course, his or her right; perhaps clinics should even encourage heroin addicts to do so, pointing out the advantages. On the other hand, if a heroin addict wishes, on reflection, to continue the addiction, that is also his or her right. Heroin maintenance as an available option is, therefore, the just course.
Indeed, as one group of peceptive analysts observed, it follows from the basic moral postulate of human rights that persons "are morally entitled to the best help that can be offered." See I. Chein, supra note 138, at 380. The addict, it is argued, should not be limited to a minimal maintenance dose:

> especially if giving him his "high" would keep him off the illegal market and provide the "high" under conditions of maximum safety to him and others. In fact, we see nothing wrong, under the conditions stated, with having the physician help such an addict plan his drug-taking strategy—switching drugs from time to time, helping him with planned and optimally spaced withdrawals, mixing drugs, or whatever it takes.

Id. at 378.
For the forms of social service that this model may involve, see H. Judson, supra note 107, at 63–122. In addition, such licensing—consistent with appropriate guarantees of privacy and confidentiality—would assure something irrationally lacking in America and strikingly present in Britain, namely, good and reliable records of persons who take heroin. For the vagaries of American drug statistics, see note 137; for the British system, see H. Judson, supra note 107, at 23–27.
302. Cf. L. Grinspoon & J. Bakalar, supra note 10, at 291–308 (suggesting psychedelic drugs should be neither condemned nor worshipped).
303. See generally id at 89–156, 192–290; see generally R. Masters & J. Houston, supra note 10; B. Wells, supra note 11, at 57–82, 112–49, 170–213.
304. See generally L. Grinspoon & J. Bakalar, supra note 10, at 157–91.
305. See N. Zinberg & J. Robertson, supra note 1, at 242–63.
306. See e. g., Irwin, supra note 241, at 15–26. In Irwin's careful comparison of drug hazards, distilled alcohol received the highest hazard rating (81/79), cigarettes an intermediate hazard rating (37/0), and marijuana a lower rating (25/29).
307. See generally, L. Grinspoon, *Marihuana Reconsidered* (1971); J. Kaplan, supra note 1, at 141–98. In contrast, the greater dangers from alcohol or nicotine might justify some form of licensing.

308. See, e.g., Brody, "The Evidence Builds Against Marijuana," *N. Y. Times*, May 21, 1980, at C1, Col. 1. The argument is made that one drug should be forbidden, not because of its intrinsic dangers, but because it may lead to the use of other, more harmful drugs. The argument is a familiar move in American prohibitionist literature, having been used to defend the absolute prohibition of liquor. See text accompanying notes 51 and 52, supra. In fact, there is little empirical support for such casual theses. See generally L. Grinspoon, *Marihuana Reconsidered* 231–52 (1971); J. Kaplan, supra note 1, at 199–262. To the contrary, the best way to prevent such steps from one drug to another is to permit one and forbid the other, rather than hypocritically confusing all drugs in one global and undiscriminating way. On the evils of such confusions, see E. Brecher, supra note 1, at 291–93, 331–32, 497–98. Brecher argues that once drug users peceive one drug is not harmful at all, they conclude that all illegal drugs are harmless, losing faith in the rationality of the law-making process.

309. See generally Irwin, supra note 241. See also E. Brecher, supra note 1.

310. See text accompanying note 326, Chapter 3, supra.

311. See text accompanying note 327, Chapter 3, supra.

312. It is assumed that such regulation could satisfy constitutional constraints. See *Bigelow v. Virginia*, 421 U. S. 809, 825 n. 10 (1975); *Banzhaf v. FCC*, 405 F. 2d 1082, 1099–1103 (D. C. Cir. 1968), cert. denied sub nom. *Tobacco Inst., Inc. v. FCC*, 396 U. S. 842 (1969).

313. See E. Brecher, supra note 1, at 229–44; O. Ray, supra note 2, at 75–78.

314. See generally Irwin, supra note 241. Cf. J. Kaplan, supra note 1, at 263–310.

315. See generally T. Szasz, supra note 1.

316. See generally N. Kittrie, supra note 117, at 210–96.

317. See *Robinson v. California*, 370 U. S. 660, 666–67 (1962).

318. See Fingarette, supra note 198, at 431–32.

319. See generally T. Szasz, supra note 1, at 153–74.

320. See N. Kittrie, supra note 117, at 247–58. Of course, civil commitment may properly be available for short periods in cases of severe debilitation.

321. See Plato, *Charmides*, in *The Collected Dialogues of Plato* supra note 154, at 100–22.

322. See also K. Erikson, *Wayward Puritans* (1966). For an incisive application of this conception to American views of drug users, see R. Blum, supra note 14, at 323–41.

323. The extremes of harms that a drug may work are thus domesticated by a social context of use; for example, caffeine is ingested in forms so diluted as to make excessive doses unlikely, wine is taken with meals, and liquor drunk in controlled social contexts of mutual regulation. See, E. Brecher, supra note 1, at 205–06. See generally N. Zinberg & J. Robertson, supra note 1, at 12; R. Blum, supra note 14.

324. This theme was importantly sounded in the debates that led the British to resist the American example of prohibition of heroin use. See H. Judson, supra nore 107, at 17–18.

Part Three

DEATH AND THE
MEANING OF LIFE

5

Constitutional Privacy, the Right to Die, and the Meaning of Life

In previous chapters, moral theory was used to clarify the proper form of decriminalization argument, whether used in a sound conception of the substantive criminal law or of developments in constitutional law premised on the constitutional right to privacy. Here, I propose to address these general questions through an examination of the moral basis for the decriminalization of certain decisions to die. In terms of the general legal literature on decriminalization, such arguments were classically stated by Glanville Williams in *The Sanctity of Life and the Criminal Law*,[1] using the terms characteristic of decriminalization advocates, namely, utilitarianism. For Williams, the only available moral contrast is between utilitarian humanism, which would dictate the decriminalization of certain acts of euthanasia and suicide, and a religious ethics, which requires such criminalization.[2] Correspondingly, legal critics of Williams' arguments, like Yale Kamisar,[3] do not question his utilitarian arguments of principle but raise practical problems of abuse, which should caution us against institutionalizing such arguments. It is doubtful whether this sterile contrast between utilitarianism and religious ethics exhausted the alternatives of ethical analysis even at the time Williams first wrote. The Protestant theologian Joseph Fletcher[4] supported his arguments for the legitimacy of euthanasia not on solely utilitarian grounds, but in terms of arguments grounded in dignity and personhood. There is good reason to believe that the utilitarian form of William's classic arguments for decriminalization in this area rendered such arguments less ethically powerful than they were and could be; for if the gravamen of the utilitarian's argument for a right to die is the simple presence of a balance of pain over pleasure in a person and surrounding persons, the inference is natural and was logically drawn[5] that the argument applied in full force not only to consenting and terminally ill adults (voluntary euthanasia), but to all cases of persons suffering from a balance of pain over pleasure, including those who do not and would not consent to die (involuntary euthanasia).[6] In light of recent antiutilitarian moral theory, we may reconceive the fundamental arguments for the decriminalization of certain decisions to die in terms of the rights of the person, which expressly disavow the manipulative utilitarianism that Williams's account assumes.

Such an account should enable us concurrently to address the issue of whether or to what extent the constitutional right to privacy should encompass certain decisions to die. In three striking recent cases, *In re Quinlan*,[7] *Superintendent of Belchertown State School v. Saikewicz*,[8] and *In re Eichner*,[9] state courts in New Jersey, Massachusetts, and New York, respectively, have invoked the constitutional right to privacy as the basis for vindicating the right to refuse certain kinds of medical treatment in extreme cases of terminal life or illness when death was the likely consequence. While the Supreme Court has carefully avoided the task of clarifying the degree to which, if at all, its conception of constitutional privacy encompasses a right to die in these or other contexts,[10] it must eventually—consistent with its constitutional duty reasonably to elaborate constitutional values—articulate a principled conception of the relationship of constitutional privacy and the right to die.[11] To the extent that recent antiutilitarian moral theory starts from the premise of the basic rights of the person on whose protection American constitutionalism importantly builds, it should enable us to grapple with these issues.

In order to deal with these matters sensibly, this chapter will have the following organization: first, an application of the autonomy-based interpretation of treating persons as equals to the explication of the moral principles that define the structure of the right to life; second, a critical examination of the traditional moral and paternalistic arguments for the criminalization of all decisions to die; third, a statement of the case for the right to die, its limits, and its proper effectuation as a form of the constitutional right to privacy; and fourth, a discussion of possible limits on the degree to which the full scope of the right to die may be enforced by constitutional privacy.

I. THE MORALITY OF DECISIONS TO DIE AND THE RIGHTS OF THE PERSON

In order to assess critically the arguments for the criminalization of all decisions to die, we must carefully examine the moral structure of the idea of the right to life that underlies such criminalization. The concept of the right to life, like any complex moral and legal concept, such as the right to property, appears to consist of several distinguishable elements,[12] each having different implications and requiring separate analysis. First, let us examine the cluster of moral principles of obligation and duty, sketched in general terms in Chapter 1, which are constitutive of the right to life; then, we may critically examine the proper force of various common arguments for the criminalization of all decisions to die.

A. *Moral Principles Constitutive of the Right to Life*

For purposes of the present analysis of the moral right to life, let us stipulate a common denominator of the idea of rights as such, whether moral rights or legal rights—those enforceable by the civil or criminal law. Having a right implies at least the justifiability of coercion, in some form, in protecting certain kinds of choice from incursion by others, whether the individual has the additional liberty of choosing whether these rights shall be enforced, for example, contracts in the civil law, or whether he does not have that choice, for example, rights to personal safety in the criminal law.[13] In the moral sphere, such justifiability of coercion would be crucially defined by moral principles of obligation and duty, which by definition justify coercion in their enforcement. Accordingly, the delineation of the moral structure of the right to life requires analysis of the pertinent moral principles of obligation and duty that justify coercion in the protection of life. We shall focus here on the relevant aspects of three such principles: nonmaleficence, mutual aid, and paternalism.

In general, these principles define natural duties that apply to personal relationships, whether within or outside common institutions.[14] These principles do not exhaust the moral principles of obligation and duty relevant to the full assessment of the morality of acts in general and killing in particular. To be specific, personal relationships within institutions and between institutions are governed by principles of justice and fairness, which regulate the distribution of benefits and burdens of such institutions.[15] In particular, certain of these principles of justice will bear on questions of the morality of inflicting harms. Principles of just punishment, for example, will justify certain kinds of infliction of evil in order to uphold the just aims of the criminal law,[16] including the enforcement of the natural duties,[17] and the principles of just war may, in appropriate circumstances and within defined limits, justify the infliction of harms consistent with measured aims of justice.[18] In some cases such principles may justify forms of killing. For present purposes, let us assume that some reasonable set of such principles of justice has been formulated and that we have confidence that some forms of the infliction of harms justified by such principles are circumscribed within sharp limits of proportionality and effectiveness. With such principles in the background and assuming the justifiability of forms of harm infliction justified by such principles, we may turn to the principles of natural duty which establish and define a general moral right to life.

1.   THE PRINCIPLE OF NONMALEFICENCE. The principles of natural duty are those principles, justifying coercion in their enforcement, that would be agreed to or universalized, consistent with the autonomy-based interpretation of treating persons as equals, as an effective public morality governing the relations of persons *simpliciter*, whatever their institutional relations to one another. Foremost among these principles is the principle of nonmaleficence,[19] which, for our present purposes, we may construe in terms of the requirement not intentionally, knowingly, or negligently to inflict harms on other persons except in cases of necessary and proportional self-defense[20] or in certain extreme cases of just necessity[21] or extreme duress.[22] Since our present concern is with the broad implications of this principle for the right to life, which it in part defines, let us focus here on the moral basis of the prohibition of harm.

Let us begin with the idea of personhood, or rational autonomy, in terms of which treatment as equals, from the human rights perspective, is defined.[23] As we have seen, personhood is defined in terms of certain higher-order capacities, developed or undeveloped, that enable persons critically to reflect on and revise the form of their lives in terms of arguments and evidence to which they freely and rationally assent. The exercise of these capacities is shown when people adopt plans of living in terms of various forms of evaluative criteria—: sometimes principles of rational choice whereby they define and pursue their system of ends in a way designed to satisfy all or a great number of them in an harmonious and complementary way over their life cycle,[24] sometimes personal ideals of excellence in which they invest their rational self-esteem,[25] and sometimes in terms of ethical principles either of minimal decency[26] or superogatory heroism or beneficence.[27] From the perspective of an autonomy-based ethics, divergent and quite disparate plans of life may be reasonably affirmed and pursued on such terms;[28] the notion of rationality, in terms of which persons often evaluate and revise their lives, yields a neutral theory of the good which is compatible with enormous diversity and idiosyncrasy of life design. Consistent with this diversity and idiosyncrasy, however, are certain things which we may assume all rational persons want as typical conditions of whatever else they want. For purposes of his theory of distributive justice, Rawls calls these "general goods"[29] and focuses on wealth, status, property, etc., as examples. For purposes of our present focus on the natural duties, we may identify as such goods the typical rational interest of persons,[30] as conditions of pursuing whatever else they want, in basic integrity and control of their bodies, persons, and lives and thus in security from forms of interference with this integrity, including injury, pointless cruelty, and most forms of killing.[31]

The principle of nonmaleficence would be agreed to or universalized, consistent with the autonomy-based interpretation of treating persons as equals, because it secures the fundamental interest of personal integrity in terms of a prohibition that does not typically require persons to sacrifice substantial interests. Substantial interests are not sacrificed because the pursuit of persons' substantial interests does not indispensably require acts forbidden by the principle,[32] or at least does not typically do so. Forms of self-defense and the like are expressly exempt from the principle because they do not clearly observe this or similar conditions.[33]

The principle of nonmaleficence, consistent with its moral basis in protecting personal integrity on fair terms to all persons who both benefit from the principle and bear the burden of observing it, is defined in terms of the prohibition of harms, which is in turn defined in terms of the frustration of the rational interests of persons as conditions of whatever else they want. It is important to see and give weight to the place that *harm*, so understood, plays in properly interpreting its requirements. Not all forms of pain are forbidden by the principle, for some kinds of pain infliction do not violate the rational interests of persons and thus are not harms. Consider, for example, the pain of self-knowledge that good education or therapy may indispensably involve. The infliction of such pain, guided by wise experience, is no harm; indeed it is often among the greater benefits one person can do for another.[34]

Correspondingly, the principle does not forbid killing as such, but forbids those killings which are harms.[35] Clearly, most killings of persons are harms in the sense to which we can give a sensible interpretation,[36] namely that persons typically have a rational interest in living which killing frustrates. Epicurus, in a famous conundrum, challenged the intuition that one's death could be an evil:

So death, the most terrifying of ills, is nothing to us, since so long as we exist, death is not with us; but when death comes, then we do not exist. It does not then concern either the living or the dead, since for the former it is not, and the latter are no more.[37]

Surely this paradox falsely supposes that the evil of death must, to be sensible, be contemporal with life as such, which would render the concept senseless and incoherent,[38] but it is a mistake to identify the evil of death with some absence of good in living.[39] The rational self-interest of persons in life is not in life as such, but in the kinds of plans and aspirations of the person which life makes possible. Such plans and aspirations are independent of our actually living, for their success or failure may be known only long after our deaths.[40] And during our lives, such plans and aspirations are our reasons for living; indeed, death is an evil, where it is an evil, because it cuts off those still vital plans in which we have centered our selves.[41]

It must follow that there are some cases in which killing or ending one's life will not be a harm, namely, where a person has a rational interest in dying.[42] We can illustrate this idea not merely in terms of specific examples, such as the terminally ill cancer patient, in terrible pain and demanding death, but in terms of a general characterization of cases, namely, those in which the person's plans, assessed and subject to revision in terms of standards and arguments to which he or she gives free and rational assent, are better satisfied by death than by continued life.[43] From the point of view of the neutral theory of the good, fundamental to the autonomy-based interpretation of treating persons as equals, these matters must be assessed in terms of the individual person's coherent system of rational ends, plans, and projects. From this perspective, there are cases of both altruistic and egoistic motivation in which certain persons more reasonably secure their rational ends by death than by continued life. We have no difficulty in understanding the reasonableness of such actions in cases of heroism or saintly beneficence, when death is embraced as the necessary means to do great goods for others and death thus realizes a personal vision of fulfillment whose ideals cannot be met better. Comparable cases exist in which, for persons with certain coherent and rationally affirmed plans of life in certain circumstances, death may be reasonably justified in terms of better realizing the ends of their life plan. For example, a person for whom the pain of terminal illness has no redemptive meaning, for whom the illness frustrates all the projects of life in which the person centers life's meaning, for whom death is, in any event, highly probable, and for whom pointless pain and physical decline affirmatively violate ideals of personal integrity and control, may find in present death more rationality and meaning than in prolonged life.[44] Even outside such contexts as terminal illness, present death may be a reasonable course for persons who find in continued life the frustration of all the significant aims and projects in which, as persons with freedom and full rationality, they define themselves and in which the choice of death may, as an expression of dignified self-determination, better realize their ideals of living than a senseless life of self-contempt. In Ibsen's *Ghosts*, when Mrs. Alving is asked by her son Oswald to kill him when his incurable idiocy comes on him again, Oswald's voluntary choice appears rational in terms of his preference for death rather than a life spent in dependent idiocy and childishness.[45] The sense in which Oswald rationally wishes death must be interpreted in terms of his individual desire for personal competence and autonomy which is, for him, the sine qua non of satisfying all other desires he may have. His rational ends are better secured by being killed intentionally by another, and thus ending all desire, rather than by continuing life with the frustration of his basic personal ideals of competence.[46] Perhaps, as Seneca argued,[47] for some persons such a course would be similarly reasonable when facing the prospect of senility.[48]

If death in such cases cannot be regarded as harmful, such forms of killing cannot be properly regarded as within the scope of the principle of nonmaleficence. But, consistent with our discussion of these cases, we must underline the limited nature of the exemption of these cases from the principle of nonmaleficence, namely, that the infliction of death is not a case of harm when the individual person voluntarily requests such death, or can reasonably be shown would request it, *and* the request appears rational in terms of the system of rational ends that the person would, with full freedom and rationality, affirm.[49] Fundamental to the autonomy-based interpretation of treating persons as equals is the idea that the rational self-determination of the person is ethically fundamental and cannot be parsed in terms of some more basic moral element like pleasure or pain. A main objection of this perspective to utilitarianism is that utilitarianism, in its obsessive focus on pleasure as such, dissolves moral personality into utilitarian aggregates ignoring the *ethically* crucial fact that *persons* experience pleasure and that pleasure has significance and weight only in the context of the life that a person chooses to lead.[50] Accordingly, the human rights perspective, which focuses on treating *persons* as equals, gives no fundamental weight to pleasure or pain as such; rather, it secures to persons, on fair terms to all, respect for higher-order capacities of personal dignity, whereby persons may define for themselves the weight that pleasure will play in their design of life. In the context of the present discussion of nonmaleficence, we see the dramatic implications of this perspective in concrete terms: forms of killing are not exempt from nomaleficence on any basis of a net of pain over pleasure or evil over good, however measured, in the life of the person, let alone the surrounding persons. Many people whose lives contain more misery and pain than pleasure find in such lives robust and sustaining meaning[51] and find death wholly irrational, certainly nothing they would voluntarily request. From the perspective of human rights, killing them is as violative of nonmaleficence as killing the most flourishing hedonist. Properly exempt from nonmaleficence are only those cases of killing that express the underlying values of human rights—voluntary choice *and* rational self-definition.[52]

It is important to understand the significant constraints that this account imposes on exempt forms of killing: if a person is capable of voluntary consent, such consent must always be secured; if such consent is impossible, it must be determined reasonably that it would be given in such circumstances. Even voluntary consent, however, does not suffice. In addition, it must be clear that the form of death is one that appears rational in terms of the system of ends that the person would, with full freedom and rationality, affirm. We shall return to this point when we examine the principle of paternalism.

Again in contrast to utilitarianism,[53] this account puts sharp constraints on killing in cases where persons are incapable of consent, for example, young children and the defective.[54] We begin with the thought that all creatures are persons who have the capacities, developed or undeveloped, to be persons with some capacity for self-critical reflection on their lives.[55] Aside from certain extreme cases,[56] most young children and defectives are persons in this sense: they have these capacities in some form.[57] It is difficult to see how killing them could be justified as an exemption from nonmaleficence. In the case of those who have been mature adults, but who are now incapable of consent, for example, the comatose, we may reasonably infer the nature of their consent from those who have known them intimately.[58] But in the case of those who have been incapable of consent, it appears difficult to give a defensible sense to either imputed consent on their behalf or to the idea that they would rationally consent to die. The point is not merely the obvious one of just suspicion of the independent judgment of those who consent on their behalf, who may have strong interests to free themselves from such dependents; but at a deeper level, how can a person who has lived as a mature adult justly enter into the personal world of a child or defective who has never been a mature adult?[59] There is no injustice in asking the intimate of a mature adult now incapable of consent what that person, if still capable of consent, would wish to be done if he knew he would be in his present situation; we regard the reasonably ascertained wishes of a mature adult as authoritative in such cases. But there is no moral symmetry between this case and that of a person who has never been capable of rational consent. A person, while capable of rational consent, certainly has authority to determine what shall happen to her or him when lacking such capacity, but there is no comparable moral authority—at least over decisions to die—of mature adults for those who have never been capable of consent. To permit this inference would allow persons to decide this issue on irrelevant grounds, supposing the choice to be what they— with the ideals of personal independence of a mature adult—would want if they knew they would become a child or defective, like Ibsen's Oswald. But of course the child or defective lacks these ideals, and justly may center her or his life in other sensible ways, which the adult cannot conceive.[60] Without reasonable access to the consent of these persons or insight into their system of ends,[61] there is little reason to infer an exemption from nomaleficence.[62]

2. THE PRINCIPLE OF MUTUAL AID. Another set of facts, relevant to the formulation of another principle of natural duty that bears on the right to life, relates to forms of assistance and aid which, at only slight cost to oneself, one person may render to another in saving the other from grave forms of harm.[63] Consistent with the autonomy-based interpretation of treating persons as equals, persons would agree to or universalize this principle, enforceable by coercion if necessary, because in this way they will guard against the possibility that they themselves may end up in such a position of requiring assistance from other persons, where they would wish such assistance to be given.

It is important to see that the agreement on the principle of mutual aid arises from the consideration of a certain circumscribed set of circumstances and not all possible circumstances of aid. In other words, the principle is concerned only with aid, given at slight personal cost, that secures a great good to the person aided. The distinction of mutual aid from different sorts of circumstances in which persons may do good to other persons must be contrasted usefully with the traditional and contemporary failure of philosophers to draw this distinction. Consider Kant's argument in the *Foundations of the Metaphysics of Morals* as to why it is a moral *duty* to give aid to others in great distress—the argument involving basically the sort of reasoning just sketched.[64] When Kant, however, in the *Metaphysical Principles of Virtue* explicitly discusses duties of this sort, we learn that they are part of the general category of duties of beneficence, which include taking the morally permissible ends of others as one's own. Thus Kant, on the one hand, wishes to insist that these requirements are *duties*, and, on the other, to indicate that they are forms of imperfect duty which, unlike the imperfect duties of respect, are meritorious, not owed to other persons.[65] In similar fashion, Price discusses the duty of beneficence, which covers both a person's doing "all the good he can to his fellow-creatures" generally and doing good to "distressed persons he ought to relieve."[66] And Sidgwick clearly describes both nonmaleficence and mutual aid as a "somewhat indefinite limit of Duty" beyond which "extends the virtue of Benevolence without limit," but he sees these as only relative distinctions within the wider principle of beneficence, in reference to which he grants that the "distinction between Excellence and Strict Duty does not seem properly admissible in Utilitarianism."[67] What is common to these traditional philosophers is the assimilation of the circumstances of mutual aid to those of general beneficence and the consequent failure to distinguish and explain the different sorts of moral principles that are relevant to those different sorts of circumstances.[68]

Mutual aid, in contrast to beneficence, requires aid only where rendering the aid is of little cost to the person who aids: a person may save another from drowning by merely putting out her hand or throwing out a lifebelt. This feature explains how the principle could be agreed to as one of duty, justifying coercion and defining correlative rights: persons would only agree to or universalize such a principle, as one of duty, if they knew it did not require a person to sacrifice life and limb to save another. Of course, acts of heroism, saving persons at such risks, are morally admirable on the ground of the principle of beneficence.[69] But we are here concerned not with the moral ideals of saints and heroes, but with the human rights that are properly enforceable by law. The principle of mutual aid defines a natural duty which, properly understood and limited, imposes such enforceable rights.[70]

For purposes of our present analysis, we should note that the operative concept in the principle of mutual aid, as in that of nonmaleficence, is harm—here, relieving likely harms. Again consistent with the underlying values of equal concern and respect for autonomy, harm must be interpreted in terms of the rational interests of the person. Thus, in line with our previous discussion of death as harm, in the absence of reason to believe that a person both wants death and such death is reasonable in terms of a rational life plan, the opportunity to save from death would be governed by the principle of mutual aid.

In order to assess the concrete implications of this principle, consider that mutual aid appears to be a fundamental ethical principle underlying medical care.[71] Medical professionals, by training and self-conception, are in a position to render forms of life-saving aid. In addition, because they are well paid and define their lives in terms of rendering such aid, often it will be of little cost for them to render aid. Indeed, there may be some gain. In consequence, the requirements of mutual aid apply to such professionals more extensively than they do to ordinary people.[72] If this is so, it appears that different moral principles relevant to the right to life have different scopes of application. Whereas the principle of nonmaleficence appears broadly to apply to all persons equally, the principle of mutual aid appears to have more extensive applications to some persons than to others.[73] Most cases of mutual aid involve saving from harms which no one, including the person aided, would dispute were harms calling for relief; but some cases are disputed.

3. THE PRINCIPLE OF JUST PATERNALISM. As we have already seen,[74] the autonomy-based interpretation of treating persons as equals would clearly justify a natural duty defined by a principle of paternalism and explain its proper scope and limits. From the point of view of agreement to or universalization of basic principles of natural duty consistent with this perspective, persons would be concerned with the fact that human beings are subject to certain kinds of irrationalities with severe consequences, including irreparable harms. They accordingly would agree to an insurance principle requiring interference, if at little cost to the agent, to preserve persons from certain serious irrationalities in the event they might occur to them. There are two critical constraints on the scope of such a principle.

First, the relevant idea of irrationality itself cannot violate basic constraints of the autonomy-based interpretations of treating persons as equals: the neutral theory of the good, expressed by Rawls as ignorance of specific identity, and reliance only on facts capable of empirical validation. For this purpose, the idea of rationality must be defined relative to the person's system of ends which, in turn, are determined by the person's appetites, desires, capacities, and aspirations. Principles of rational choice require the most coherent and satisfying plan for accommodating the person's projects over time.[75] Accordingly, only those acts are irrational that frustrate the person's own system of ends.

Second, within the class of irrationalities so defined, paternalistic considerations would properly come into play only when the irrationality was severe and systematic, that is, due to undeveloped or impaired capacities or lack of opportunity to exercise such capacities, *and* a serious, permanent impairment of interests was in prospect.

When we consider the application of these paternalistic considerations to decisions to die, we immediately see that the second constraint is satisfied: death is, typically, an irreparable harm, indeed the most irreparable of harms. Accordingly, decisions to die are a natural object of paternalistic concern. Indeed, in the absence of any specific knowledge of the situation or life history of a person about to inflict death on himself, the general presumption that death is a harm would appear to warrant paternalistic interference. In such contexts, one's possibly mistaken interference may only lead to postponement, which is certainly preferable to not interfering and discovering that the death in question was clearly irrational.[76]

On the other hand, as we earlier observed, there are surely some deaths that are not harms that are both voluntarily embraced and consonant with a rational plan of life, which is, with freedom and rationality, affirmed. In such cases, the first constraint of just paternalism is not satisfied, and assuming a potential interferer has knowledge that a person's prospective death is of such a kind, one would lack any moral title to interfere.

If medical care often is governed by mutual aid, in some cases paternalism as well comes into play. Consider a case where the medical professional's conception of the good of the patient is inconsistent with the patient's conception, so that we do not have a clear case of proper mutual aid. In such controversies, arguments of paternalism naturally come into play: may the professional interfere for the patient's own good?[77] Surely the conditions of just paternalism are, at least arguably, present: the interference is often at little cost to the professional, and the patient appears irrationally to decline medical services that may alone save his life. If the state of the law is that patients in all such cases have an absolute right to decline medical treatment,[78] the law cannot be justified by the principles here articulated, for such rejection may be clearly irrational in terms of the patient's own rational life plan and thus the proper object of paternalistic interference.[79]

On the other hand, it would be grotesquely wrong for the state to compel any person, other things being equal, to have medical treatment, even if necessary to save life, when the person conscientiously rejects such treatment as inconsistent with a life plan that he rationally and freely affirms. To defend such interference on the ground of the universal value of life is the essence of unjust paternalism, smuggling into the content of irrationality, which defines the scope of just paternalism, majoritarian ideologies which are no more neutral than the religious ideologies they despise—for example, that of a Jehovah's Witness.[80] Complications are introduced when dependent children and the like are introduced into the picture, either in the form of dependents of the person who prefers death[81] or as the person who allegedly prefers death.[82] These are cases in which other factors are relevant. Absent such factors, however, paternalism is clearly unjust.

4. THE STRUCTURE OF THE RIGHT TO LIFE. The interlocking requirements of these three principles of natural duty—nonmaleficence, mutual aid, and paternalism—establish the moral structure of the right to life. On this account, that right is to be understood in terms of the choices protected by the requirements (justifying coercion) of these principles: namely, that harm not be inflicted (nonmaleficence), that persons be saved from harms if at little cost (mutual aid), and that persons be saved from the irreparable harms likely to be worked on themselves by their own irrational folly (paternalism). The moral complexity of this right is seen in the fact that its constitutive principles seem to have different scopes of application; nonmaleficence applies to everyone, whereas mutual aid and paternalism[83] may have special application to service professionals. This difference may have important consequences in later defining the morality of various kinds of decisions leading to death. In general, it cannot be supposed plausibly that these principles forbid the infliction of death in all circumstances. What then are the arguments supposed to justify such an absolute prohibition?

B. *Moral Arguments for the Prohibition of All Acts Inflicting Death*

The criminal law in the United States appears to express the moral judgment that, with certain narrow exceptions—the defenses—all forms of killing are wrong. While suicide itself is no longer criminal in many states,[84] aiding and abetting suicide is, in general, criminal.[85] In the United States forms of euthanasia, which in European countries are often grounds for mitigation and even exculpation,[86] are officially regarded as equally criminal as pure murder.[87] The underlying moral condemnation of all acts inflicting death appears to rest on a number of disparate grounds including: (1) life as God's property, (2) life as the property of the state, (3) the immorality of despair, (4) life as the inalienable basis of moral personality, (5) harms to determinate third parties, (6) paternalistic arguments about the irrationality of all decisions to die, and (7) wedge arguments.

1. LIFE AS GOD'S PROPERTY. The most ancient philosophical argument for the immorality of self-willed death, which echoes through the history of all later reflection in western thought on this question, is Socrates' brief argument in Plato's *Phaedo* to the effect that release from life must take place only at God's will, for "the gods are our keepers, and we men are one of their possessions."[88] Plato appears to use this argument metaphorically as a way of expressing moral conclusions arrived at on other grounds. Clearly, in the *Phaedo*, Socrates's death, which is regarded as self-willed, is supposed to be one in which "God sends some compulsion,"[89] in the sense that death here is "my country's orders";[90] and elsewhere, Plato extends this category to include forms of stress, calamity, and disgrace, which compel self-willed death.[91] To this extent, Plato's metaphor of divine compulsion is not inconsistent with, and indeed may be a way of giving expression to, the idea of appropriate death in extreme circumstances of disease or degradation; certainly, the Roman Stoics and other ancients interpreted Plato in this sense.[92]

The idea of life as God's property, originating as a metaphor in Plato, is rigidified into an absolute prohibition on all forms of self-willed death only by St. Augustine,[93] whose complex argument St. Thomas rather summarily adopts;[94] this summary prohibition, in turn, appears to be the basis, clearly present in Blackstone,[95] of the English heritage of grisly punishment of self-willed death, in particular, for suicide.[96] Augustine's argument is complex with many strands, some of which we shall later examine; its conclusion is an absolute prohibition, except in those mysterious cases—here, a faint echo of Plato[97]—where "the Spirit . . . secretly ordered" self-willed death.[98] For present purposes, we may focus on Augustine's argument that in all cases our life is the property of God that *we* may not surrender.

The heart of Augustine's argument appears to be a theological interpretation, in fact highly controversial,[99] of "You shall not kill" in the Decalogue.[100] On the basis of this interpretation, Augustine seems prepared to question even the justifiability of self-defense,[101] let alone forms of self-willed death. Such a theological argument may compel the assent of those who share Augustine's perceptions and interpretations; certainly, they have the right to govern their lives in accord with its mandates. But of course it is not a moral argument of the form that may be an acceptable basis for the public morality of persons of differing religious and philosophical perceptions, for—on the model of constitutional morality here deployed—a theological argument of this form would be given no decisive weight in determining public morality by persons lacking knowledge of specific identity, whose agreements depend on facts capable of interpersonal validation. Indeed, from the perspective of the autonomy-based interpretation of treating persons as equals, the idea that our lives are the property of anyone but ourselves appears to compromise the basic dignity of moral personality.

Perhaps Augustine's argument may be given an appealing moral interpretation as a way of saying that the basic equality of all persons means that no person may judge the worth of other persons and that forms of killing, if permitted at all, would compromise this basic value.[102] Certainly, this kind of argument has appeal when directed against certain kinds of utilitarian defenses of killing, which suppose that the net of pain over pleasure talismanically identifies those who may live and those, including young infants and the defective, who must die.[103] But then, it is a general objection to utilitarianism that it fails to take seriously treating *persons* as equals. Defects in its account of permissible killing evince this larger mistake. It is not true, however, as this interpretation of Augustine supposes, that all justifications of killing must commit this error, for there is one person who may, within limits, justly assess the rational meaning of life or death to a person, namely, the individual himself. Indeed, to deprive the person of this right, in the cases to which it properly applies, is to deprive him of the dignity of constituting the meaning of his life.

2. LIFE AS THE PROPERTY OF THE STATE. That self-willed death immorally violates our duties to the state is a prominent feature of Aristotle's condemnation,[104] which St. Thomas repeats with approval,[105] and Blackstone reads into the Anglo-American legal heritage.[106] Aristotle's argument is certainly consistent with his general perfectionist ethics of heroic and creative display and performance: the highest exemplars of ethical conduct are persons of heroic capacity and intellectual and creative talent who devote their lives to public service through the achievement of works of excellence, whether in war, politics, the arts, or the life of theory.[107] Since the self-willed death of such a person, except in some heroic exploit, deprives society of a

perfectionist asset, it is paradigmatically immoral or, as Aristotle prefers to put it, unjust.[108]

Aristotle's ethics, like Plato's, is remote from the autonomy-based interpretation of treating persons as equals, which introduces concepts of human and natural rights unknown in the thought of ancient Greece.[109] Certainly the Aristotelian assumption that one's life is a collective asset, which the state may exploit on whatever terms redound to its perfectionist glory, is at war with the contractarian metaphors of human rights, which require, as conditions of just obedience, reciprocal respect of individual well-being and dignity. From this perspective, the absolute prohibition on self-willed death in circumstances reasonably perceived by the person as perpetuating pointless and degraded life must appear to be, as Montesquieu put it, "the unjust sharing of their utility and my despair."[110]

The state certainly has a just interest, defined in terms of background principles of justice incumbent on it, not only to protect the right to life of its citizens and persons subject to its protection, but to guarantee fair conditions of life that enable persons to live well with self-respect.[111] When the state reasonably meets its duties of justice in such respects, persons who benefit therefrom may be under moral obligations of fairness and natural duties of justice to obey the law.[112] Sometimes, for example, in a just war regulated by principles of proportionality and effectiveness,[113] citizens may even be under moral duties to risk their lives in defense of the just institutions from which they have benefited; sometimes, where such obligations have been fairly and freely undertaken and have yielded the person countervailing and reciprocal benefits in the past, persons may have obligations to put aside private despair in order to afford some great social good to society that cannot otherwise be supplied.[114] But such reciprocities of benefit and obligation apply only in certain circumstances and to limited extents; they do not yield any general duty of the kind that Aristotle and his tradition suppose. Indeed, such a general duty appears clearly unjust: it ignores the basic contractarian implications of human rights, giving no weight to the intrinsic limits on state power that the rights of the person require. The state may not require anything and everything of persons, as Aristotle's idea of life as the property of the state mistakenly supposes. If the autonomy-based interpretation of treating persons as equals means anything, it means that the whole idea of property rights in our lives—whether title lies in God, other persons, or the state—is radically misplaced, denying, as it does, the basic dignity of the person in shaping a life, as a free and rational agent and demanding, as a condition of any just demand on one for contribution or obedience, respect for this dignity.

Aristotle's idea of unconditional demand indulges the kind of fantasy of total control and subordination which the ideal of a free person, expressed in the human rights perspective, repudiates and should repudiate. It is a kind of demand that a just state or a just God[115] would not make, at least in the form of an enforceable legal duty.

3. THE IMMORALITY OF DESPAIR. Both Plato[116] and Aristotle[117] evince concern with forms of self-willed death that involve moral defects of character, in particular, the courage that a person of reasonable firmness would display in the face of certain kinds of fear and disappointment and consequent temptations to end it all. Neither philosopher appears to be thinking of all forms of self-willed death. Aristotle appears clearly to regard certain forms of altruistic, self-willed death as both moral and admirable,[118] and Plato regards self-willed death as justified in certain extreme circumstances.[119] In Augustine,[120] followed by St. Thomas,[121] this form of argument has evolved into a general moral objection to all forms of self-willed killing, including even acts of heroism or martyrdom—except for the mysterious cases which "the Spirit . . . secretly ordered"[122]—on the ground that they involve the immorality of despair. The immorality of such deaths for Augustine is illustrated by Judas's suicide, for "he despaired of God's mercy and in a fit of self-destructive remorse left himself no chance of a saving repentance."[123]

One specific application of Augustine's argument suggests what may have been the primary intention of his thesis. In discussing cases where reasonable people may suppose self-willed death to be justified, Augustine clearly considers the hardest case to be when a Christian in order to protect herself from violent sexual violation might kill herself rather than submit.[124] Augustine, often suggestively Freudian, argues that this moral calculation is defective, resting on the indefensible—we would say sexist—assumption that the woman attacked bears some moral responsibility for having been raped.[125] But this assumption, Augustine insists, is deeply wrong; the woman has done no wrong, but would do wrong in acquiescing in the false and sexist condemnation by killing herself.[126] In an era of rampant Christian martyrdom,[127] Augustine appears concerned to expose the irrationalities and sometimes immoral assumptions that underlie certain forms of self-willed death. The point of the argument appears to be to purify Christian ideals of self-sacrifice from a false romanticism of martyrdom.

This form of Augustine's argument is interesting, forceful, and valid: the romantic idealization[128] of self-willed death, which in fact is irrationally inconsistent with the very ideals that the person claims to express in this death, should be exposed for the false and pathetic thing it is. But Augustine's total prohibition goes well beyond these cases; clearly, he appeals here to the independent theological argument earlier sketched:[129] it is because our lives are God's property that *we* may not will our deaths and that the despair that motivates such will is wrong.

But how, from the perspective of the autonomy-based interpretation of treating persons as equals, can all cases of self-willed death be regarded as despairing, and why—in those cases that are despairing—is such despair always ruled out? Certainly altruistic forms of self-willed death not only may be free from despair, but may be affirmative of our most admirable values and aspirations,[130] and even egoistic forms of such death, if undertaken with certain styles and within certain constraints, may be in some circumstances more expressive of ideals of dignified invention and unrepining self-mastery than continued life would be.[131] In any event, there is no reason to believe that the neutral theory of the good, fundamental to ideas of human rights, rules out despair as one possibly appropriate response of persons to certain prospects of pain and degradation. Augustine invokes, in this connection, a particular ideal, highly controversial and disputable, of the redemptive value of suffering;[132] he assumes, *sub specie aeternitatis*, that any suffering or degradation now, like the suffering of Jesus, will be redeemed, indeed that our patient endurance of such suffering may be the test of our Christian mettle. Nonetheless, there is no reason to believe that this ideal is any more entitled to moral enforcement, as the only legitimate attitude to suffering, than any other conception. To say that Christian patience is the only attitude to suffering consistent with rational personhood is dogmatic.[133] Many other courses may reasonably accommodate the diverse individuality of human competences, aspirations, and ends. What for one is a reasonable, self-imposed ideal of the sanctity of holy and redemptive suffering is,[134] for another, pointless degradation, a waste of dignity in obsequious decline.[135]

The Augustinian picture here is like the utilitarian's idea of the simple meanings of pleasure and pain, by which we may analyze all hard and controversial questions; only here, the elements are not pleasure and pain as such, but a particular form of pain—despair—that we are told can have only *one* tolerable moral interpretation, namely, being wrong and forbidden. But just as utilitarians are wrong about the unambiguous meanings of pleasure and pain, Augustine is wrong about despair. For some persons, with visions of life that they rationally and freely affirm and revise, certain kinds of suffering and degradation are the natural objects of despair, and they have a right to respond to this interpretation, in appropriate circumstances, by ending their lives. It would be outrageous from the perspective of the autonomy-based interpretation of treating persons as equals to stay their hand *solely* on the basis of an Augustinian interpretation of despair, which they do not reasonably share and which has, in any event, no superior moral claim to enforcement by law. Surely, in such matters, the range of reasonable personal ideals is wide, various, and acutely sensitive to personal context and individual idiosyncrasy. The law has no proper role in prejudging the method of choosing, in general, and the proper attitude to suffering, in particular.

4. LIFE AS THE INALIENABLE BASIS OF MORAL PERSONALITY. Perhaps the most interesting of the arguments regarding the wrongness of self-willed death are those that center on moral personality. St. Thomas puts this argument in terms of the natural law of self-preservation, which self-willed killing unnaturally violates.[136] Immanuel Kant, the father of modern deontological moral theory, adapts this argument in the form of the claim that ending one's life is, in some way, inconsistent with the foundations of one's moral duty to his own personality, and thus is morally wrong. Kant thus appears to suppose that to "destroy the subject of morality in his own person is tantamount to obliterating . . . the very existence of morality itself"[137] and appears to think of self-mutilation as wrong, that is, as a kind of "partial self-murder," for the same reason."[138] Kant's sense of the horror of suicide is striking:

We are . . . horrified at the very thought of suicide; by it man sinks lower than the beasts; we look upon a suicide as carrion . . .
   Humanity in one's own person is something inviolable; it is a holy trust; man is master of all else, but he must not lay hands upon himself. . . . Man can only dispose over things; beasts are things in this sense; but man is not a thing, not a beast. If he disposes over himself, he treats his value as that of a beast. He who so behaves, who has no respect for human nature and makes a thing of himself, becomes for everyone an Object of freewill.[139]

Initially, it is important to be puzzled by the imputation to persons of the natural end of self-preservation, which self-willed killing unnaturally violates, when it is conceded that the capacity for self-willed killing appears to be a distinctive mark of persons. Accordingly, why does Kant regard this as a sign of our sinking lower than the beasts, when, in fact, it may be a feature of the critical self-consciousness that sets persons apart from other creatures?[140] Donne surely is correct when he argues against the Thomist argument that what is fundamental to persons is not the preservation of life but the pursuit of their rational good, as they define it, which may or may not mean continued life.[141] If anything, a purely naturalistic description of animals and persons might indicate that self-preservation is a fair description of the animal world but not of the world of persons, for whom continued life is only one value among others and not always the dominant one.[142] Kant appears to concede this description when he grants the morality of forms of altruistic, self-willed death,[143] but he appears to draw the line at egoistic, self-willed deaths, supposing them inconsistent with the constraints of morality.

At one point, Kant puts this latter argument in terms of universalization: persons could not consistently universalize a principle of egoistic self-willed killing, for humankind would come to an end, which is inconsistent with the aims of self-love.[144] Kant's argument is question-begging: it assumes what must be shown, that persons' rational good always involves continued life. The argument also grossly travesties the kind of limited exemption from nonmaleficence, mutual aid, and paternalism that is consistent with the autonomy-based interpretation of treating persons as equals. Instead of the circumscribed exemption that we have described, Kant supposes a kind of moody and open-ended weariness with life, which, like Shakespeare's Hamlet, any loosening of the "canon 'gainst self-slaughter"[145] would unleash in a rash of mass suicides. Kant underestimates the degree to which persons' rational good flourishes only in continued life, making the remarkable and quite indefensible assumption that only an absolute moral prohibition on egoistic self-willed death could bind us, in general, to life—a rather striking failure of imagination that the pre-Christian era does not support.[146] In any event, if life were so desperate and impoverished as to make this assumption reasonable, why *should* a Kantian morality of decent respect for dignity bind us to a life which our conscience finds empty of rational meaning?

We are now at the heart of Kant's argument: the assumption that ending one's life on egoistic grounds is to repudiate moral personality, like the sale of one's body or alienation of body parts. Kant's argument here, as elsewhere in his discussion of traditional Augustinian offenses against morality,[147] rests on an indefensible interpretation of the relation of moral personality to the body.[148] Kant identifies the person with the living body, and then argues roughly as follows: (1) it is always wrong to alienate moral personality; (2) the living body and the person are the same; (3) egoistic self-willed death is a kind of alienation of the living body; and (4) it is always wrong to engage in egoistic self-willed death. The crucial assumption is the second, on the basis of which Kant associates self-willed death with the surrender or alienation of moral personality and thus labels it a forbidden alienation of the morally inalienable.

Kant's identification of moral personality with the body in this discussion is inconsistent with what he says elsewhere about autonomy as the basis of moral personality.[149] These views are impossible to square. Indeed, Kant himself appears to sense the strain that his absolute condemnation of egoistic suicide works on his deeper ideals. He characterizes proponents of such a right of self-willed death in ways that betray respect: "[I]f man is capable of removing himself from the world at his own will, he need not submit to any one; he can retain his independence and tell the rudest truths to the cruellest of tyrants."[150] And suddenly, Kant draws back from such admiration with a non sequitur.

> Let us imagine a state in which men held as a general opinion that they were entitled to commit suicide, and that there was even merit and honor in so doing. How dreadful everyone would find them. For he who does not respect his life even in principle cannot be restrained from the most dreadful vices; he recks neither king nor torments.[151]

But the defense of such a right, properly interpreted, is not only consistent with an autonomy-based interpretation of treating persons as equals; it appears to be justified on such a basis.

Kant means to be making the valid point about autonomy-based ethics that it is immoral to abdicate or alienate one's autonomy or one's capacity for self-critical choice about the form of one's life. Kant fuses this valid moral idea with the unrelated idea that self-willed death is a similar kind of alienation. For an autonomy-based theory, this fusion is conceptual nonsense, darkly obscuring what Kant dimly senses but cannot acknowledge: that what is ethically ultimate is the capacity of persons independently to interpret and to evaluate the rational meaning of the projects and aims that constitute their lives, and that this dignity, properly understood, may embrace a decision to die. There is no slavery here, but only the deeper realization of autonomous independence, which must extend, if it extends to any profound level at all, to evaluations of the meaning of the boundaries of one's life with death.

It is not difficult to understand how Kant, so powerful in his statement of abstract universalistic ethics, could be so time-bound in his casuistry of decisions to die; he assumes, as the foundation of his discussion, the Augustinian assumptions regarding death that he also unquestioningly accepts regarding sex.[152] Thus when Kant argues that we have no right to control our dying, he is not only making the confused and indefensible argument about alienating moral personality just discussed, but he is echoing, as the texts make clear,[153] Augustine's quasi-theological argument about our lives as the property of God, which *we* may not alienate. Kant accordingly isolates death from autonomy in the way conventional for his period. There is no reason to continue this mistake today. Indeed, we may note the ultimate intellectual and moral paradox of Kant's argument: that the submerged reason for denying *our* right to control decisions about death is to place such authority in another, God. An argument thus couched in the rhetoric of repudiating moral slavery in fact disfigures and denies our moral freedom in the name of a hidden master.

5. HARMS TO DETERMINATE THIRD PARTIES. Earlier arguments for the immorality of all self-willed deaths premised on the idea of our life as property of the state suggested that absolute prohibitions resting on this conception could not be sustained, but that more circumscribed moral arguments might be available forestalling such deaths in specific circumstances of fairly undertaken moral obligations of fairness—for example, military service in a just war or completing some project that affords an indispensable good to society before one takes one's leave. We regarded such arguments as resting on the background of institutional principles of justice and fairness, which qualify the scope of application of the principles of natural duty directly relevant to the moral structure of the right to life—nonmaleficence, mutual aid, and paternalism. Such moral obligations to society are the most that can be critically sustained of the absolute prohibitions resting on the idea of life as the property of the state. But of course they are not absolute, applying only in limited contexts and circumstances. If, for example, a person has completed any services or projects which society on grounds of reciprocal fairness may demand of him, there is no just claim that society may make demanding that she or he remain.[154]

A similar analysis applies to moral obligations to determinate third parties, which a person's decision to die may call into question. Decisions to die do not occur in a vacuum: perons who express such wishes reasonably may be embedded in personal relationships that may relevantly alter our moral evaluation of the situation. Certainly the central relevant relationships are those of parent to still young and vulnerable children. Parenthood is a role embedded in social institutions of family and education, clearly regulated by principles of justice which assess rights and duties as well as benefits and burdens in terms of fairness and equity to parents, children, and society in general.[155] Voluntarily undertaking parenthood gives rise to moral obligations of fairness to perform one's just role as the kind of nurturing and sustaining parent which the well-being of children requires; in addition, natural duties of parenthood appear, in such circumstances, convergently to require appropriate forms of care and commitment.[156] A *prima facie* violation of such moral obligations and duties is abandonment, which may involve two independent wrongs: first, breaking the bond of psychological parenthood in early childhood, which may harm the child developmentally;[157] and second, failing to insure that the child receives alternative care of the ethically required kind—individualized attention, stable affection, stimulation, and concern.[158] Now such wrongs are *prima facie;* countervailing considerations may outweigh such wrongs. For example, military service and the like may require prolonged parental absence and may even lead to death, but in some circumstances may be the conduct which may be ethically justified. Self-willed death of a young parent, however, appears deeply problematic: in most cases, such abandonment appears clearly wrong. Perhaps we should distinguish the case of the terminally ill parent from the case of the parent who could continue living quite ably but who, in terms of her or his good, rationally and freely affirmed, prefers death—for example, the Jehovah's Witness who on religious grounds declines medical treatment, but who could survive with treatment. The prolongation of life of the terminally ill parent may do little good for the child and, indeed, may do ill in some cases; perhaps here the ethical requirement would be that the parent must insure that some alternative parental care will be afforded the child before the parent takes her or his leave. The parent who could easily survive may do wrong, in abandoning the child in such circumstances.[159] But perhaps some justification may be present in those cases where the parent can demonstrate that the child already identified with a network of stable and living persons, that the network will continue after the parent's death, and that the care has been so generalized that the parent's absence will not be felt appreciably by the child.[160]

Such moral obligations to determinate third parties do not justify an absolute prohibition of self-willed death in all cases. Not all persons who reasonably contemplate self-willed death are parents. Even with respect to those who are parents, it would be unacceptably onerous to generalize the arguments sketched above to restrict the liberty of parents in all stages of their life cycle.[161] Children grow up, develop lives and relationships of their own, and become autonomous. It is as wrong, as violative of the rights of the person, to suppose that parents' lives are forever the property of their children as to suppose that lives are property of God or of the state. Parents have lives of their own, shaped by aspirations, ends, and projects of which being a parent is only one part, and not necessarily the most important part. If, in terms of the meaning of life which a person reasonably and freely affirms, death is the preferred and projected course, the existence of adult children cannot morally qualify their right to act so.[162] If a parent faces the realistic prospect of terminal illness and reasonably decides that self-willed death is the better course, how can the grief of those who do not share the pain or the vision of degradation stay their hand? Why, ethically, is the grief over this form of death any worse than the grief over the possibly prolonged and terrible death that would otherwise take place?[163] The death of parents is, in any circumstances, difficult for children who are prone to experience therein unconscious fears, guilt, and remorse.[164] If the self-willed death of parents holds special terrors for their adult children, that may be because of the long tradition of moralistic condemnation of it which, since Augustine, has dominated the west. But this tradition appears to be wrong and indefensible, indeed to violate the rights of the person. When we disencumber ourselves of these false demons, we may enable parents to explain such choices with lucid rationality to their children, to dissolve their unjust fears or guilt, and to explain the meaning of this act as an expression of the person they are.[165] Unlike the Stoics and others,[166] we do not have such rituals of self-willed dying: a way of speaking one's own death, of sharing the moment with those one loves and respects, of mutual solace and support, all of which may better affirm the meaning of one's life than a more isolated and pain-wracked death.[167] But that lack of ritual is our problem, our impoverishment, our failure of social imagination;[168] it is no justification for our failure to respect the possible dignity of self-willed death and to establish rituals adequate to our moral needs.

6. PATERNALISTIC ARGUMENTS. Even if no other moral argument on behalf of condemnation can be sustained, it may still be argued that undertaking particular conduct is sufficiently irrational so that there is moral title to interfere on paternalistic grounds. We have already examined the proper scope of paternalistic considerations, consistent with the autonomy-based interpretation of treating persons as equals, and their application to self-willed death. Our conclusion was that self-willed death was a natural object of just paternalistic concern, death typically being irreparable harm, but that such concern, on balance, was unjustified in cases where the person voluntarily and rationally embraced death. There is one case—children—where these

considerations clearly dictate just intervention. On the other hand, these considerations, sometimes mistakenly, are supposed to render suspect all forms of self-willed killing. Let us first examine the issue of children and then turn to the abuses of paternalism in this area.

If there is one category of persons whose capacity to undertake death voluntarily appears justly suspect, it is young children. The issue arises dramatically when parents, who on religious grounds would will death for themselves, extend such treatment to their young children.[169] While children in such cases typically ratify the parental view, we justly question the rational independence of mind underlying the ratification. Since the child's view is not the expression of the freedom and rationality that exempts from paternalism, and since the conduct does involve irreparable harm to the child, state interference is justified, on the grounds of just paternalism, in the cases to which the above considerations apply. Also justified is state insistence on the medical treatment which, in the case of a mature adult, it could not, consistently with human rights, order.[170]

Sometimes, however, paternalistic considerations are supposed to justify intervention well beyond this limited case. In this connection we must observe the temptation to employ certain radically inappropriate forms of paternalistic arguments, and query the force of this temptation in the condemnation of decisions to die.

When we consider the application of paternalistic considerations to choices of self-willed death, we face the question how to assess the rationality of this kind of choice. The idea of rationality employed here takes as its fundamental datum the agent's ends and aspirations, which the agent organizes, evaluates, and revises dispassionately in terms of standards and arguments to which she or he assents as a free and rational being. In this context, principles of rational choice are those standards which call for the assessment of choices in terms of the degree to which alternative choices better satisfy the person's ends and aspirations over time.[171] Since the agent's ends and aspirations over time are often complex and difficult to anticipate with exactitude, a number of such choices in a particular case may be equally rational. Nonetheless, there is a coherent sense to the application of rationality criteria to these choices. Some such choices are clearly irrational if they frustrate every significant end which the agent has, and available alternatives do not.[172] Such irrational choices, if they also are likely to lead to irreparable harms, may be the proper object of paternalistic interference.

No good argument can be made that paternalistic considerations would justify the kind of intervention that is involved in the traditional condemnation of all decisions to die. In some cases, such choices seem quite rational. For example, a person has a coherent vision of the good of his life, rationally and freely affirmed and revised, and faces the prospect of painful death or deterioration in which all significant projects of his life will be frustrated, a frustration which for him has no redemptive meaning, and indeed in which continued life would betray the central ideals around which he centers his conception of a meaningful life. For him, self-willed death better meets his significant ends than the alternative. Indeed, the alternative—continued life—which frustrates all his significant ends in a way death would not, may be, by comparison, irrational.[173] If he voluntarily embraces such death, affirming therein the considered and reasonably reflective values of his integrity as a person, there is no ground of paternalism which could justly stay him.

In such cases, we may suspect the views of the persons who would make paternalistic claims for intervention. Some of the arguments for the irrationality of all such decisions may be based on mistaken distortions of the facts. It is as if the extant moralistic condemnation of decisions to die inexorably shaped the reading of the facts so as to confirm that the putatively immoral conduct was personally irrational as well. Accounts of suicides, for example, claim that they are mentally disturbed[174] or socially maladapted.[175] Psychiatrists sometimes supply a psychiatric makeweight to the moral condemnations by claims that suicides are mentally ill or at least neurotic.[176] None of these claims has been sustained by careful empirical research, observing sound scientific methods.[177] Typically, such claims rest on the limited sample of people whom the researcher mistakenly believes to be typical of the research population at large.[178]

The empirical literature on suicide, for example, makes clear that the phenomenon is complex and divides it into different kinds of phenomena, which should not be confused.[179] One class, those who "attempt" suicide, tend to be young, disproportionately female, not undertaking suicide in a way clearly calculated to succeed, and ambivalently hoping for help.[180] The other class of more typically successful suicides is older, more likely to be male, and designs suicide with a reasonable expectation of success, often in contexts of realistic deprivation.[181] Nothing is to be gained in confusing the differing moral realities of these two kinds of persons. The former are persons who, if not mentally ill in any clinical sense, are subject to moods of depression, which disable them from assessing alternatives in a reasonably flexible and free way; the project of suicide is not, for them, the expression of a critically evaluated rational life plan, as is shown by the ambivalent nature of their planning.[182] Such persons are the just subjects of continuing social concern on the ground of just paternalism, for their conduct, the product of mood and depression, perhaps of youth, and not of a critically reflective life plan realistically assessed, is the kind of irrationality which, in the presence of irreparable harm, should trigger intervention. Just concern for such persons has given rise in England to the Samaritans[183] and in the United States to suicide prevention centers,[184] which seek to provide institutional facilities where such persons can discuss their problems, develop needed perspective on them, and seek the help which they appear ambivalently to want. Such facilities are part of the kind of intervention that just paternalism appears to support, for such intervention is not an absolute prohibition but, at the most, voluntary postponement to encourage processes of reasonable reflection and dialogue that may better secure society's ethical interest in ensuring that such conduct is undertaken rationally.[185] Thus there is no inconsistency; rather there is mutually complementary support between the ethical grounds for such programs, in the cases to which they properly apply, and respect for the right of rational self-willed death, in the cases to which this right properly applies.[186] Both conceptions rest on support and encouragement and respect for capacities of rational dignity; in the one case, we insure their existence; in the other, we respect their exercise.

In general, since the ground for programs of suicide intervention is concern for forms of irrationality, it would be perverse to enforce such aims through the use of the criminal sanction, which generally requires, as a condition of just punishment, the presence of capacities of rational choice and deliberation.[187] Even if intervention, including stopping the act if possible, may be justified in *some* cases of self-willed death,[188] criminalization appears wholly inappropriate to accomplish even such limited aims.

Finally we should remind ourselves that, outside this circumscribed area of just paternalistic concern in decisions to die, there is no ground whatsoever for interference. Paternalistic interest in such cases represents the kind of unjust influence of moralistic judgments condemning all such cases, which cannot be critically defended consistent with respect for human rights. Special reason to be suspicious of the motives for such distortions exists in the case of self-willed death, for it is all too easy to substitute, in the place of genuine concern for the rational perspective of others on their own lives and deaths, one's fears of one's own death[189] or one's egoistic desires to hold those we love in the world as long as we can.[190] Dialogue with those who propose death, urging our point of view and our needs as factors in their deliberations, is one of several ways to deal with such impulses. But there is no ground on which we can justly express these impulses through absolute prohibitions on all forms of self-willed death. We must recognize these impulses, however understandable and natural, for what they are: the desire to control those we love, to remain the omnipotent and loved child,[191] to not be left alone. We should acknowledge these impulses as needs and try to deal with them honestly; but we, consistent with human rights, cannot dignify them in terms of a moral imperative forbidding self-willed death. The justice of our desires to control even those we love has limits.[192] Those limits are established by respect for human rights in terms of which we express our respect for personal dignity, including the possible dignity of self-willed death.

7. WEDGE ARGUMENTS. The nature of wedge arguments for the absolute prohibition of all decisions to die is to concede, *arguendo*, the moral force of the critical arguments discussed above and to grant that *some* cases of self-willed death may be morally right, but then to argue that there is no way to express in law or conventional morality this judgment, for the validation or legitimation of *any* such conduct inexorably will be the entering wedge of arguments for killing that are clearly unethical.[193] This argument takes two common forms: first, that any legitimation of voluntary euthanasia will also validate the horrors of Nazi genocide; and second, that even if voluntary euthanasia could be validated without this implication, forms of voluntary euthanasia would be abused in terms of putting pressure on people to die. Neither argument can be sustained.

The former argument is classically stated by Yale Kamisar[194] in response to Glanville Williams,[195] in a way which brings out the fallacy in the objection. Kamisar claims to agree with Williams that the scope of the criminal law should be critically assessed and reformed in the light of utilitarian objectives.[196] He then claims, however, that such utilitarian assessment—which would legalize voluntary euthanasia of the consenting terminally ill on the ground that, because such persons experience more pain than pleasure in themselves and cause more pain than pleasure in others, voluntary euthanasia would maximize pleasure over all—inevitably must ignore the voluntary consent requirement and thus would validate massive forms of involuntary euthanasia of the defective, whose elimination might maximize utility over all, which is the rationale for the racial genocide of Naziism.[197] Kamisar's argument contains two distinct objections: first, that the voluntary consent requirement cannot be made effective;[198] and second, that utilitarianism justifies euthanasia in other cases besides those of voluntary consent.[199] Kamisar's objection to an effective institutional embodiment for voluntary consent is technical: how, he argues, can one be certain that what a terminally ill patient in pain now requests is what he or she would want if his or her mind were not clouded by pain, and how can one be sure that what a person says she or he would want prior to being in such pain is decisive of what they want when now in pain and unable voluntarily to consent? The answer, sensibly made by Williams,[200] is that optimally we should seek both: voluntary consent prior to illness and consent, if possible, when ill. But clearly, if consent when ill is not possible—for example, when the person is comatose and unlikely to regain consciousness—the voluntary consent of a person of the requisite form in certain circumstances, given prior to the nonconsenting state, might be ethically determinative. As we have seen, other things being equal, the two conditions of a self-willed death that is not violative of the natural duties are voluntary consent *and* reasonableness in terms of the person's own life plan, rationally and freely adopted and assessed by the person. Surely some kind of formal consent given under precisely defined legal conditions prior to illness, like the "living wills" which have already been adopted in several states,[201] would be highly probative on both these questions; in addition, there must be assurance that there is no overreaching in securing the consent and—independent of consent—that the illness in question is one which the person reasonably might escape by death, that is, a painful terminal illness which the person has little probability of surviving in any event.[202]

Kamisar appears to sense the weakness of this technical objection and moves quickly to a more profound problem in Williams's argument: the general thrust of Williams's utilitarian argument extends beyond voluntary euthanasia, narrowly defined in terms of consent and reasonableness in the circumstances, to involuntary euthanasia of the defective or the eugenically unfit, and such euthanasia leads to the horrors of Nazi genocide.[203] It hardly seems fair to impute to a utilitarian like Williams, who writes in the tradition of liberal utilitarian reform of John Stuart Mill[204] and H. L. A. Hart,[205] the false and vicious racial theories which were the actual moral basis for the Nazi programs.[206] If utilitarian arguments would legitimate forms of involuntary euthanasia at all, this legitimization would apply in sharply circumscribed circumstances that bear not the slightest resemblance to either the Nazi theory or practice.[207] Thus, to the extent that Kamisar uses utilitarianism as his operative critical morality, he cannot give expression to the kind of objection he intends.

The objection is true and important; but once we see its moral basis for what it is, we cannot draw the implications that Kamisar confusedly does. The objection is that utilitarianism is a manipulative moral theory that does not take seriously treating *persons* as equals; one mark of this failure is the theory's tendency to legitimate involuntary euthanasia of persons if they appear to be suffering more pain than pleasure and occasioning more pain than pleasure in the others who must care for them.[208] Indeed, from the viewpoint of pure utilitarian ethics, the elimination of a person has no ethical negative significance if pleasure overall is thus advanced,[209] as it might be not only by ending the net pain produced by a defective but replacing him or her by a nondefective person who produces a net pleasure.[210] The proper answer to this objection is not to retain one's utilitarianism and disavow one's beliefs about the propriety of voluntary euthanasia and impropriety of involuntary euthanasia, but to question one's intuitive commitment to utilitarianism and seek a moral theory more adequate to one's considered moral judgments. We have already suggested one form of such a theory that expresses an autonomy-based interpretation of treating persons as equals, the substantive moral conclusions of which are clearly antiutilitarian. The consequence of this theory is that voluntary self-willed death in certain circumstances is not morally wrong, but involuntary forms of killing of persons cannot be ethically justified. Thus we may disavow Williams's and Kamisar's utilitarianism, disavow entirely any legitimation of involuntary euthanasia of persons, and place voluntary forms of self-willed death on solid antiutilitarian ethical foundations with no malign tendency *at all.*

One form of the wedge argument remains that we should consider briefly: even if we limit permissible killing to circumscribed forms of voluntary euthanasia, the legitimation of voluntary euthanasia by law or social convention will lead to abusive manipulation of persons to encourage them, when old and dependent, to avail themselves of this option[211]—freeing their children, for example, of the burdens of care and passing on the estate that the children regard as their due. Now, of course, it is a mark of rights that they can be abused;[212] but before we permit the possibility of abuse to compromise our definition of rights, we must make sure that the forms of such abuse are not unfairly probable and cannot be minimized by ways of conditioning the exercise of such rights. Certainly, manipulative enticement of such kinds, in contemporary circumstances of affluence and longevity, would be abusively wrong.[213] But in contemporary life, forms of social security, pension benefits, and the like make the life of older people, in contrast to previous historical periods,[214] sufficiently independent that they cannot be regarded, in general, as unfairly manipulable by the young. If we are concerned about abuse of the old, surely we should be concerned not to compromise their rights, but as a just society to further guarantee the independent well-being of older citizens[215] so that they retain in old age an autonomous dignity that does not make them easy prey to the callousness of the young. In addition, we may minimize the incidence of this kind of abuse by conditioning the exercise of the right in certain ways, by requiring, for example, a showing that no form of overreaching has occurred before the requirement of voluntariness can be met, or by imposing a stringent requirement that the action be reasonable in terms of the independently assessed life plan of the person, as, for example, with a painful terminal illness. If such conditions are met, we must respect the dignity of choice of older persons, whatever the altruistic or egoistic ingredients of their deliberations.[216]

II. CONSTITUTIONAL PRIVACY AND THE RIGHT TO DIE

So far the argument has been pointedly negative: we have explicated the moral right to life in terms of the intersecting requirements of three principles of natural duty—nonmaleficence, mutual aid, and paternalism—and shown that the moral right to life does *not* include all cases of self-willed death; and we have analyzed the various traditional and contemporary arguments to justify absolute prohibitions of all decisions to die and shown that they do *not* work. We must now put these analyses to a constructive use in defining an affirmative right, the right to die, and show why this right is embraced by the constitutional right to privacy.

We should recall, at this point, our interpretation of the constitutional right to privacy as a natural consequence of the implications of the autonomy-based interpretation of treating persons as equals:[217] when the scope of the criminal law exceeds the moral constraints mandated by this conception, the criminal law violates human rights; it limits the scope of liberty and dignified life choice in ways that fail to respect the neutral theory of the good and the capacity of persons to define their own lives. Introduced into the criminal law are idiosyncratic and parochial ideologies that do not rise to the level of the moral reasoning which alone may be enforced by the criminal law. The constitutional right to privacy expresses a form of this moral criticism of unjust overcriminalization and may be explicated in terms of the intersection of three variables: (1) the antimoralistic strain that the forms of traditional moral argument, supposed to justify a certain form of criminalization, are critically deficient and demonstrably fail to take the proper form required by respect for human rights; (2) the antipaternalistic feature that the extant force of the valid traditional moral arguments, in popular or conventional morality, distorts person's capacity to see that certain traditionally condemned life choices may be rationally undertaken and encourages them to justify paternalistic interference therein; and (3) a strong autonomy-based interest in protecting human dignity from (1) and (2), since the liberty in question relates to a basic life choice around which people may organize their personhood.

The previously stated negative arguments—both regarding the moral structure of the right to life not extending to all forms of self-willed death and the criticisms of the traditional moral arguments supposed to condemn all such acts—make clear that both the antimoralistic and antipaternalistic strains of the constitutional right to privacy apply to certain decisions to die. While our legal system no longer tends to criminalize suicide as such,[218] it does forbid aiding and abetting suicide[219] and all forms of euthanasia[220] whether voluntary or involuntary. As we have seen, no good moral argument to sustain such absolute prohibitions exists. Because of the force of the traditional moral condemnation in the conventional morality which the law supports, persons abusively are tempted to suppose that persons cannot rationally wish and undertake their deaths and that, therefore, paternalistic interference is always justified.

It is natural that the application of the constitutional right to privacy has surfaced in cases like *In re Quinlan*,[221] *Superintendent of Belchertown State School v. Saikewicz*,[222] and *In Re Eichner*.[223] In both *Quinlan* and *Eichner* we have irreversibly comatose and essentially vegetative patients and reason to believe that each, in such circumstances, would want to be allowed to die; in *Saikewicz*, we have the prospect of painful treatments of a terminally ill person who, being mentally incompetent, lacks rational capacity to consent. Let us focus here on *Quinlan* and *Eichner*, in which the underlying moral argument, interpreted in terms of the theory here proposed, appears strongest.[224] In these cases, we may pose the issue in terms of the natural duty of mutual aid: does the principle of relieving harm, when accomplished at little cost to oneself, bind the medical professional to continue these persons on life-sustaining equipment? There is clearly no background duty or obligation which here might require continued life, for there is no general obligation of social service, fairly and reciprocally incurred, and no special moral obligation to determinate third parties—neither being parents—which either person had still to render or, the comatose state being irreversible,[225] could render. While the voluntary consent of Ms. Quinlan appears not to have been as considered and rationally given as that of Brother Joseph Fox in *Eichner*,[226] a good case for such consent can be made, and in both cases, continued life appears to be something neither would reasonably want. Thus both the stipulated conditions of proper forms of self-willed death are here satisfied: voluntary consent *and* reasonableness in terms of the person's life plan. Accordingly to save either would not be relieving harm, as contemplated by the principle of mutual aid, and there would be no breach of mutual aid by not prolonging life. Indeed, to insist in such cases that life be prolonged would appear to rest on the kind of paternalistic distortion which we have earlier noted.

Since in such cases both antimoralistic and antipaternalistic features of the constitutional right to privacy are in play, we have a putative candidate for the application of the right. But, how can death be regarded as a basic *life* choice?

III.   THE RIGHT TO DIE AND THE MEANING OF LIFE

In order to understand why certain decisions to die must be embraced within the constitutional right to privacy, we should draw together earlier disparate observations regarding the idea of human rights, the values of dignity and moral personality that it protects, and the necessary implications of this idea and these values for the protection of certain decisions to die. Even if such decisions to die in fact were never exercised or exercised only rarely, the right to so decide is, for reasons now to be explained, fundamental.

A common feature of serious critical reflection on one's life, indeed the kind of critical reflection fundamental to our being persons with what I have called autonomy, is that ordinary people of good will pose the issues in terms of the query: what is the meaning of life? The weightiness of this question is caused, I believe, by our human capacity for self-examination and by the consequent and inexorable realization of our eventual death. If personhood gives us the capacity of higher-order reflection on and evaluation of our system of ends and how they cohere in life, the terms of that reflection and evaluation are posed by the thought of our death, the formal constraint which circumscribes the design of our life, and by the need to make sense of death.

When traditional methods of rationalizing death no longer appear true or valid, people naturally express this loss of faith in terms of the meaninglessness of life or the associated thought that, without such meaning, suicide is called for. Dostoevsky's Kirillov argues that if God is dead, man is God, and he, the first man-God, shows his Godhead by suicide.[227] Camus, finding life absurd because empty of providential redemptive meaning, poses, as the first question of philosophy, why—in the face of meaninglessness—not commit suicide?[228]

Why should this be so? Why should the fact that one's death is final and without personal immorality, as Kirillov and Camus and many other moderns assume, imply or be taken to imply that one's *life* is meaningless? The naturalness of the inference is based, I believe, on this: that because we, as persons, are critically self-conscious of our lives as a whole, including death which defeats and frustrates the projects on which we center our lives, making sense of death appears to be an inexorable part of making sense of life. If death is senseless, life may be senseless too.

Of course there is a nonsequitur in this inference: the fallacy of supposing that because one system of beliefs, which places death in the framework of personal immortality and interprets one's life in terms of this framework, is no longer accepted as true or valid, then all alternative systems of belief and value must be similarly hollow. This supposition is flatly false: it expresses a failure of imagining and constructing new systems of belief and value in terms of a self-fulfilling romantic desperation about the task of giving meaning to life *at all*.[229]

The idea, the meaning of life, is ambiguous, and this romantic desperation plays on the ambiguity.[230] On the one hand, the idea of life's meaning may be interpreted in terms of teleological purpose externally defined and specified, like books which have the purpose of being read or buildings of affording shelter; this interpretation is externally defined in terms of the purposes of the creator or user of the artifact in question, which may be God or Nature.[231] On the other hand, life's meaning may be interpreted in terms of the structure of evaluations which the person imposes on and expresses through the structure of her or his existence; in this sense, the meaning of life is not interpreted in terms of teleological purpose externally defined, but in terms of the purposes of the person[232]—the idea, close to the core of linguistic or language meaning, that an expression is meaningful in virtue of the intentions which it is known and purposed to communicate.[233] The romantic desperation of Kirillov and Camus and others[234] uses the defeat of teleological purpose as a way of defining life's meaning (because of disbelief in a personal God or in personal immortality) in an argument that the meaning of life, in the form of personal evaluation, is empty. But the argument is a non sequitur. Indeed it may be precisely because life *is* meaningless in the teleological sense that there is such weight to be placed on personal meaning, as the proper task of a human life.[235]

This personal sense of the meaning of life is at one with the ideas of personal autonomy and rational personhood which, I have argued, are the central values in terms of which human rights are to be interpreted. On this view, it is an open question, consistent with the neutral theory of the good, how persons with freedom and rationality will define the meaning of their lives, and no externally defined tele-ological script is entitled to any special authority or weight in such personal self-definition. Once we see the issue in this way, we can see that the fact of one's own death frames the meaning one gives one's life in widely differing ways.

Sometimes psychologists[236] and philosophers[237] claim that the thought of one's death is in some way impossible for us, a claim that may rest on the startling confusion between the content of the thought of one's death, which has nothing to do with one's continued life, and one's having this thought, which requires one to be alive.[238] Surely the claim is not true; indeed, the mark of personhood is that one frames the issue of how to live one's life by death and one plans accordingly, as any estate lawyer will attest. The meaning of one's life is defined by one's projects, by the evaluative organization of one's ends and aspirations in a plan of life that express one's sense of self-respect in the competences, contributions, and relationships in which one centers one's person, one's sense of a life well and humanely lived. One's death plays innumerable roles in this process: it pro-vides, for example, the sense of a mortal life plan, so that hard choices must be made about the use of time, about the life cycle and tasks appropriate thereto, about the developmental subordination and complementarity of tasks;[239] it suggests the need to consider the proj-ects that one wishes to survive one, and how this need will best fulfill one's sense of values that should endure—for example, the belief in education, charity, or artistic cultivation; it raises the whole question of dying and the issue of dying in a way one finds meaningful.[240]

Since persons have broad latitude to define the dignified meaning of their lives, they must have, consistent therewith, the corollary right to define the meaning of their deaths, including forms of self-willed death that are consistent with treating persons as equals. In-deed, I believe, a natural feature of the striking normative attitude that human rights take to the person is that reflection on one's death may, ethically and appropriately, cultivate the kind of evaluative scrutiny of and responsibility for the living of one's life that person-hood calls for,[241] in the same way that Tolstoy's Ivan Ilych sees the emptiness of his successful and complaisant conventionalism in the prospect of his death.[242] Consistent with such considerations, the concern for personal responsibility, fundamental to human rights, appears to support an *affirmative* moral interest in encouraging per-sons to reflect on the kinds of considerations, if any, that would lead them reasonably to depart life. When the cultivation of critical self-consciousness as an end in itself entered human thought with the rise of philosophy in ancient Athens, one finds concomitantly an elaboration on the vocabulary and concepts of self-willed death[243] as a natural subject of critical reflection. How could it be otherwise? Through such critical reflection, even if most people would rarely find such departure reasonable, they would affirm and express, as reflective persons with responsibility for ordering the projects of their life, the meaning, the uncompromisable values, on which they center their integrity.

Certainly, consistent with the neutral theory of the good,[244] persons will meet this task in widely disparate ways. Some persons who adopt the Augustinian script would thus affirm the values of the sanctity of suffering, on which they center their lives,[245] for they would see the right to die as one they could not exercise consistent with their integrity. Others, however, would better understand and articulate the values of their rational dignity by seeing that holding to life in such cases would be the shallowest fetishism since their dignity would be more reasonably achieved by death than continued life in certain circumstances.

Through acknowledging the right to die, in cases to which it properly applies, we secure to persons the fundamental human right upon which they may call their life their own, guaranteeing to them the kind of independent responsibility in ordering and revising their ends, as free and rational beings, that enables them to affirm both in life and death the meanings of their integrity. Perhaps because our law does not acknowledge this right, we have lost the capacity for serene lucidity before death, the kind of moving affirmation of the integrity of one's values that one often finds in those who accept this right, for example, the Stoics[246] and David Hume.[247] Instead we isolate death from life, rendering unspeakable and unspoken the personal meaning that a person has a right to bring to death[248] as she or he does to life.[249]

Kant, the greatest philosopher of human rights, senses this point, from which he inexplicably draws back when he notes the remarkable independence of mind which the Stoic doctrine of self-willed death reflects: "he recks neither king nor torments";[250] and Rousseau, consistent in the face of a conventional wisdom which even Kant could not resist, senses that if there is not this right "there is no human action which might not be made a crime."[251] The right is, within limits described earlier, the right to decide to die when this decision more rationally fulfills one's projects, reasonably and freely affirmed, in a coherent and considered plan of life.

In contrast to the Thomist and Kantian claim that self-willed death places man beneath the animals,[252] I would argue that it is the mark of our dignity as persons and our capacity to build a meaningful life, and to depart it when it cannot realistically meet our reasonable demands.[253] In this, we show ourselves neither the property of God, nor the state, nor our children, but as persons who may best express, as ends in themselves, as an expression of rational self-mastery and dignity, the meaning we give our lives by ending them.

IV. THE LIMITS OF CONSTITUTIONAL PRIVACY IN EFFECTUATING THE RIGHT TO DIE

We have now completed our argument for the existence of a moral and human right to die and for the proper place of the constitutional right to privacy in effectuating it. Constitutional privacy rests on the three variables: (1) antimoralistic critique of existing laws as not resting on moral judgments that can be sustained reasonably in terms of the constitutionally authoritative mandate of the autonomy-based interpretation of treating persons as equals; (2) antipaternalistic distortions, which tend—because of the conventional moral judgments still widely held and enforce by law[254]—to make people interfere in conduct that is assumed to be irrational; and (3) an area of life choice in which the protection of autonomy from the incursions of (1) and (2) defends centrally important forms of dignity. Constitutional privacy is the right deployed as a prophylaxis against the injustices of (1) and (2) in the protection of (3). Since both (1) and (2) apply in the case of certain decisions to die, and since such decisions appear to effectuate a central dignity in life choice (3), constitutional privacy, correctly understood, embraces the right to die.

But, to what extent may the full scope of this right to die properly be enforced by the constitutional right to privacy? Certainly as we have observed, the right was properly invoked in *In re Quinlan*[255] and *In re Eichner*.[256] While both cases may be justified forms of voluntary euthanasia, they involve forms of so-called "passive" euthanasia—letting die through withdrawal of life-support systems of "extraordinary" kinds—which have the approval even of religions that claim to rest on Augustinian doctrine.[257] What is the proper procedure in these "passive" euthanasia cases, and to what extent should constitutional privacy embrace even more controversial cases of voluntary active euthanasia (killing) and exemption in some cases from criminal liability for aiding and abetting suicide? Even if we grant the existence of the moral right to die in certain cases beyond voluntary passive euthanasia, is the constitutional right to privacy the way to effectuate this right?

On the view here proposed, these issues would be assessed in terms of the relevant moral principles of natural duty—

nonmaleficence, mutual aid, and paternalism—and background moral obligations that qualify the scope of these principles. Cases like *Quinlan* and *Eichner* are appropriate because voluntary consent *and* reasonableness for the person, as grounds for exemption from mutual aid, are reasonably established, and in those cases there are no relevant background moral obligations. It is important to see that the ethical justification for such cases here turns on mutual aid, a moral principle with special relevance to determining the moral duties of health care professionals and hospitals.[258] Since such persons and institutions are in the business of mutual aid, it appears important that institutional schemes be designed so that they may meet their duties and understand clearly when voluntary passive euthanasia is called for. Accordingly, the *Quinlan* scheme seems appropriate if we interpret it this way: both consent *and* reasonableness may be inferred from written consent of intimates who know the patient, and the hospital committee is to make clear that the patient is irretrievably comatose (on the issue of reasonableness). The presence of a court order, as in *Eichner*,[259] appears cumbersome and pointless. Of course, if the *Quinlan* conditions are not met, criminal liability would occur.

One must understand that voluntary passive euthanasia cases of this kind rest ethically on mutual aid and on the exemption conditions from mutual aid. Ethically, mutual aid happens to be of direct relevance to cases of letting die, although the idea of letting die is stretched, in a Pickwickian way, to denominate taking off a respirator as a form of letting die.[260] Whether we interpret taking off the respirator as an act or omission, it is ethically right in such circumstances because there is an exemption from the requirements of mutual aid.

Voluntary active euthanasia poses a different moral issue not because it calls for an act versus an omission, but because, in contrast to passive euthanasia, it rests on the prohibitions of the natural duty of nonmaleficence, which has a broader application than mutual aid to all persons rather than, as with mutual aid, mainly to health professionals. For this reason, it seems to me morally mistaken to regard cases of voluntary active euthanasia as, in any sense, the special responsibility of health care professionals. Voluntary active euthanasia is an ethical issue that any legal reformation would wisely remove from medical execution, as opposed to pertinent medical advice.

Sometimes, the distinction between voluntary active and voluntary passive euthanasia is expressed in terms of the supposedly operative moral distinction between killing, which is always wrong, and letting die, which sometimes is right.[261] There are in some cases moral distinctions between killing and letting die;[262] but the proper moral force

of the distinction is expressed not in terms of an absolute moral prohibition in the one case and a sometime permission in the other,[263] but
in terms of the different requirements and applications of the principles of nonmaleficence and mutual aid.[264] Sometimes it does make a
moral difference that one has killed, rather than let die;[265] but sometimes there is no moral difference at all.[266] In particular, on the issue
of voluntary euthanasia, there are cases in which, given the requisite
conditions of voluntary consent *and* reasonableness to the person and
no pertinent background moral obligations, it would be no more
wrong to kill the person than to let the person die, for in both cases
there would be an exemption from the pertinent scope of the relevant
principles of natural duty—nonmaleficence, mutual aid, and paternalism.

Sometimes it is argued that although there is no controlling ethical
distinction in certain cases of voluntary active and passive
euthanasia, passive euthanasia is consistent with the proper medical
ethic of care and concern for the dying, in a way in which active
euthanasia is not.[267] While, as an abstractly conceived ethical matter,
it may be no more caring for the person to let them die rather than
acquiesce in their request to end their lives—and in some cases it may
be much less caring if the criterion is, as it should be, the reasonably
expressed wishes of the person[268]—there is no good ethical reason
why the exemption from nonmaleficence should be enforced by
medical professionals, whose whole ethical orientation is defined by
mutual aid and its requirements.[269] Certainly in cases of terminally ill
persons who request death, medical advice would be appropriate on
the issue of the reasonable probability of death and the unlikelihood
of cure, which is relevant to exemption from nonmaleficence (on the
issue of the reasonableness of the request). But once such advice is
given and painless ways of ending life suggested, it would be more
consistent with the ethics of medicine if the infliction of death were
left to others.[270]

But if this is so, if indeed persons in such cases have a clear moral
and human right to die, should the constitutional right to privacy
protect both the active and passive forms of voluntary euthanasia?
There is reason to doubt whether the constitutional right to privacy
would be the appropriate way to enforce the right to die in all the
cases to which it applies. Constitutional privacy is, after all, the creature of judicial reasoning and enforcement, and it is doubtful whether
judicial enforcement would be a reasonable way to effectuate the
right to die in all cases.

If, as I have suggested, voluntary active euthanasia is not an appropriate demand to make of medical professionals, there is obviously a

need for some alternative procedure to effectuate the right in a suitably circumscribed way: some system of "living wills" that extends to active euthanasia,[271] consultation with intimates to make sure that death is what the person reasonably wants, some facility or training for how to administer death painlessly, perhaps some showing that, in the patient's context, there is no way for her or him to inflict death on her or his own,[272] and the like. Many such alternative schemes could be imagined, but they all seem more appropriately the objects of a legislative scheme than some judicial innovation. In the absence of such schemes, courts would have to rest content with enunciating, in some clear cases of voluntary active euthanasia consistent with ethical principles, a constitutional defense to criminal liability predicated on a very clear showing that all the requisite moral constraints are satisfied.[273]

The constitutional right to privacy rests, I have argued, on certain ethical principles of respect for personhood, and the court has the appropriate role of elaborating the underlying moral right consistent with its judicial capacities. But the court should not strain its resources beyond its reasonable capacities, looking instead to legislative reforms that better effectuate certain aspects of the underlying right.[274] I do not suggest that the court should remain supine in the area of voluntary active euthanasia or certain cases of aiding and abetting suicide.[275] The state of American law on these questions is deeply wrong, remitting ultimate moral questions to the discretion of prosecutors, judges, and juries, and producing a pattern of erratic and unjust results inconsistent with any defensible moral principle.[276] The court should intervene in egregiously clear cases and make it clear that deep constitutional principles are flouted by the state of our law; but once it has done so, it should make clear that legislatures bear responsibility as well to effectuate the underlying rights.

NOTES

1. G. Williams, *The Sanctity of Life and the Criminal Law* 248–350 (1957).

2. This way of drawing the distinction implicit in Williams's book was emphasized and applauded by Bertrand Russell in a review of it. See Russell, "Book Review," 10 *Stan. L. Rev.* 382 (1958).

3. Kamisar, "Some Non-Religious Views Against Proposed 'Mercy-Killing' Legislation," 42 *Minn. L. Rev.* 969 (1958).

4. See J. Fletcher, *Morals and Medicine*, 3–34, 172–225 (1954).

5. Kamisar, supra note 3, at 1014–41.

6. For recent forms of utilitarian arguments that appear to justify forms of infanticide on such grounds, see J. Glover, *Causing Death and Saving Lives* 150–69 (1977) and P. Singer, *Practical Ethics* 122–26, 130–39 (1979). Both theorists sharply distinguish euthanasia of a person who could consent and does not, which is not permissible, from

the case of a person who cannot or is not capable of consent, which sometimes is permissible. J. Glover, supra, at 190–202; P. Singer, supra, at 146–47. In the case of Glover, this idea rests on a principle of respect for autonomy, which he employs as an important constraint on just killing, J. Glover, supra, at 74–85, but never fully explains in terms of his general utilitarian approach. Importantly, the principle does not apply to those incapable of consent, for example, young infants.

7. *In re Quinlan*, 70 N.J. 10, 355 A.2d 647, cert. denied, 429 U.S. 922 (1976).

8. *Superintendent of Belchertown State School v. Saikewicz*, 373 Mass. 728, 370 N.E.2d 417 (1977).

9. *In re Eichner*, 102 Misc. 2d 184, 423 N.Y.S.2d 580 (1979), modified and aff'd sub nom. *Eichner v. Dillon*, 73 A.D.2d 431, 426 N.Y.S.2d 517 (1980). This case was recently affirmed and modified on appeal to New York's highest state court, the New York Court of Appeals. See *"Eichner v. Dillon," N.Y.L.J.*, April 2, 1981, at 1, col. 2 (March 31, 1981). The Court of Appeals chose to premise the decision on common law principles rather than the constitutional right to privacy. Since the argument of the court so closely tracks arguments based on the constitutional right to privacy, I have chosen to regard the decision as one of constitutional privacy, thus following the reasoning of the lower courts in this case.

10. Certiorari has been denied in *Quinlan* and in a number of other cases where the Court might have clarified the constitutional status of the right to die. See *Anderson v. Raleigh Fitkin-Paul Morgan Memorial Hosp.*, 377 U.S. 985 (1964); *Jones v. President & Directors of Georgetown College, Inc.*, 377 U.S. 978 (1964); *Perricone v. New Jersey*, 371 U.S. 890 (1962); *Labrenz III ex rel. Wallace*, 344 U.S. 824 (1952).

11. For an argument that constitutional privacy does embrace a right to die, see Delgado, "Euthanasia Reconsidered—The Choice of Death as an Aspect of the Right of Privacy," 17 *Ariz. L. Rev.* 474 (1975). See also Orbon, "The Living Will"—An Individual's Exercise of His Rights of Privacy and Self-Determination," 7 *Loyola U.L.J.* 714 (1976); Scher, "Legal Aspects of Euthanasia," 36 *Alb. L. Rev.* 674 (1972); Strand, "The 'Living Will': The Right to Death with Dignity?" 26 *Case W. Res. L. Rev.* 485 (1976); Survey: "Euthanasia: Criminal, Tort, Constitutional and Legislative Considerations," 48 *Notre Dame Law.* 1202 (1973); Comment, "The Right To Die," 10 *Cal. W.L. Rev.* 613 (1974); Comment, "Proposed State Euthanasia Statutes: A Philosophical and Legal Analysis," 3 *Hofstra L. Rev.* 115 (1975).

12. Hart, "Bentham on Legal Rights," in *Oxford Essays in Jurisprudence*, 2d Ser. 170–201 (A. Simpson ed. 1973).

13. See D. Richards, *A Theory of Reasons for Action* 99–106 (1971).

14. See id. at 92–95, 176–95.

15. See id. at 107–75.

16. See, e.g., Richards, "Human Rights and the Moral Foundations of the Substantive Criminal Law," 13 *Ga. L. Rev.* 1395, 1416–20 (1979).

17. The natural duties, by definition, apply to personal relationships, whether or not persons are in an institutional relationship to one another. Persons, for example, would be bound in their relationships in some state of nature to observe the principle of nonmaleficence and the like. However, since the principles of natural duty are the justifiable object of coercive enforcement when a just form of coercive enforcement exists—for example, a nation-state with a just legal system—the natural duties are the subject of coercive enforcement, for example, through the criminal law. See generally Richards, "Human Rights," supra note 16, *at 1414–20.*

18. See D. Richards, *Reasons for Action*, supra note 13, at 137–41. See also C. Beitz, *Political Theory and International Relations* (1979); M. Walzer, *Just and Unjust Wars* (1977).

19. For a general discussion of this principle, see D. Richards, *Reasons for Action*, supra note 13 at 176–85. See also T. Beauchamp & J. Childress, *Principles of Biomedical Ethics* 97–134 (1979).

20. On self-defense, see D. Richards, *Reasons for Action*, supra note 13, at 181; Richards, "Human Rights," supra note 16, at 1435–36. See also C. Fried, *Right and Wrong* 42–53 (1978).

21. See Richards, "Human Rights," supra note 16, at 1437–39.

22. See id. at 1431–32.

23. See Chapter 1, supra.

24. For an account of rational choice and its principles in such contexts, see D. Richards, *Reasons for Action,* supra note 13, at 27–48.

25. See id. at 264–67.

26. See id. at 107–95.

27. See id. at 205–11.

28. See Dworkin, "Liberalism," in *Public and Private Morality* 113–43 (S. Hampshire ed. 1978).

30. I omit here any discussion of the possible interest of persons in constraining forms of cruelty to animals. For some discussion, see D. Richards, *Reasons For Action,* supra note 13 at 182–83.

31. For a similar formulation, see Brandt, "A Moral Principle About Killing," in *Beneficent Euthanasia* 106–14 (M. Kohl ed. 1975).

32. The requirement that actions required by a principle do not call for substantial sacrifices of personal interests—for example, death, ill health, penury—is a central reason why the principle is one that defines duties or obligations which may be coercively enforced; otherwise, justifiable coercion would never be agreed to. D. Richards, *Reasons for Action,* supra note 13 at 277.

33. In self-defense contexts, the agent would be harmed unless harm were used in defense. See authorities cited note 20, supra. In cases of just necessity, harm is inflicted only as a way of fairly avoiding greater harm. See Richards, "Human Rights," supra note 16, at 1437–39. In duress, the agent is threatened with harm which a reasonable person cannot resist. See id. at 1431–32.

34. Even masochistic pleasure in some cases may be regarded as a good not forbidden by nonmaleficence. See D. Richards, *Reasons for Action,* supra note 13, at 178.

35. Brandt, supra note 21, at 106–14. See also Brandt, "The Morality and Rationality of Suicide," in *Ethical Issues in Death and Dying* 123–33 (T. Beauchamp & S. Perlin eds. 1978).

36. Joel Feinberg has noted the oddity of asking whether a murderer has harmed his victim. See Feinberg, "Harm and Self-Interest," in *Law, Morality and Society* 299 (P. Hacker & J. Raz eds. 1977), Nonetheless, on reflection, he can give a sense to the idea. Id. at 299–308.

37. Epicurus, "Letter to Monoeceus," in *The Stoic and Epicurean Philosophers* 31 (W. Oates ed. 1940). For the comparable passages in Lucretius, see III *de Rerum Natura* 11.830–1091. For commentary, see Silverstein, "The Evil of Death," 77 *J. Phil.* 401–24 (1980).

38. See generally Silverstein, supra note 37.

39. See id. at 405–10.

40. See Feinberg, supra note 36, at 299–308, where the point is made in terms of posthumous harms to one's interests, for example, the frustration of altruistic aims in which one centered one's life or defamation to one's reputation. In Nagel, "Death," in *Moral Problems* 361–70 (J. Rachels ed. 1971), Nagel notes the existence of harms of which a person is not and cannot be aware, for example, "the misfortunes of being deceived, despised, or betrayed." Id. at 366. Nagel includes in this idea that breaking a deathbed promise is "an injury to the dead man." Id.

41. See Nagel, supra note 40, at 361–70. See also B. Williams, "The Makropulos Case: Reflections of the Tedium of Immortality," in *Problems of the Self* 82–100 (1973). Williams's argument rests on the thought that the boredom that immortality would introduce into our appetite for plans and aspirations would be so extreme that life might become an evil.

42. See authorities cited note 35, supra. See also D. Richards, *Reasons for Action,* supra note 13 at 177–79, 193–95.

43. See Brandt, "The Morality and Rationality of Suicide," supra note 35, at 123–33.

44. D. Richards, *Reasons for Action,* supra note 13, at 177–79, 193–95. See also M. Kohl, *The Morality of Killing* 71–110 (1974); Barrington, "Apologia for Suicide," in *Euthanasia and the Right to Death* (A. Downing ed. 1969); Flew, "The Principle of Euthanasia," in *Euthanasia and the Right to Death* 30–48 (A. Downing ed. 1969).

45. The example is taken from D. Richards, *Reasons for Action*, supra note 13, at 178–79.

46. Id.

47. Seneca observes:

I will not relinquish old age if it leaves my better part intact. But if it begins to shake my mind, if it destroys its faculties one by one, if it leaves me not life but breath, I will depart from the putrid or tottering edifice. I will not escape by death from disease so long as it may be healed, and leaves my mind unimpaired. I will not raise my hand against myself on account of pain, for so to die is to be conquered. But if I know that I must suffer without hope of relief, I will depart, not through fear of pain itself, but because it prevents all for which I would live.

H. Fedden, *Suicide: A Social and Historical Study* 178 (1938) (quoting Seneca). The same passage is excerpted in Gillion, "Suicide and Voluntary Euthanasia: Historical Perspective," in *Euthanasia and the Right to Death* 174–75 (A. Downing ed. 1969). For an extended general treatment by Seneca of suicide, see *The Stoic Philosophy of Seneca* 202–7 (M. Hadas trans. 1965). See also Seneca *Letters from a Stoic*, 124–30 (R. Campbell trans. 1969).

48. D. Portwood, *Common-Sense Suicide: The Final Right* (1978).

49. D. Richards, *Reasons for Action*, supra note 13, at 178–79.

50. See notes 63–67 & accompanying text, supra, Chapter 1.

51. For a starkly dramatic statement of this position, derived from the experience of Jews in Nazi camps, see V. Frankl, *Man's Search for Meaning* (1959). For a good statement of this point by a philosopher, see Foot, "Euthanasia," in *Ethical Issues Relating to Life and Death* 14–40 (J. Ladd ed. 1979).

52. The infliction of pain, as opposed to killing, may be justified in certain cases without a voluntary consent requirement. See D. Richards, *Reasons for Action*, supra note 13, at 180.

53. For recent forms of utilitarian argument to this effect, see note 6 supra.

54. In this, I disagree with Marvin Kohl, who extends his notion of voluntary euthanasia, with which the account here given is sympathetic, to encompass the consent of parents on behalf of infants. See Kohl, "Voluntary Beneficent Euthanasia," in *Beneficent Euthanasia* 134 (M. Kohl ed. 1975). Kohl's insensitivity to this problem arises, I believe, from the emphasis of his account on the quasi-utilitarian concept of "kindness," rather than the rights of the person. See generally M. Kohl, *The Morality of Killing* 77–91, 96, 106 (1974). For a similar query about this move in Kohl's argument, see P. Devine, *The Ethics of Homicide* 174–75 (1978).

55. See D. Richards, *Reasons for Action*, supra note 13, at 81, 182–83. See also - E. Kluge, *The Practice of Death* 88–95 (1975).

56. An example of such extremes is human creatures born without brains, a condition characterized medically as anencephaly. See J. Warkany, *Congenital Malformations* 189–99 (1971).

57. There are two distinct positions in the recent philosophical literature on what makes a creature a person and thus gives rise to moral claims of rights. First, there is the position that personhood rests not on capacities for self-critical rationality, but on actual exercise of such capacities in forms of actual self-consciousness. This position appears to have been adopted because it makes sharply clear that unborn fetuses are not persons in any sense, but it also has the consequence that young infants are not persons either since infants lack the requisite exercise of higher-order self-consciousness. See Tooley, "A Defense of Abortion and Infanticide," in *The Problem of Abortion* 91 (J. Feinberg ed. 1973); Feinberg, "Abortion," in *Matters of Life and Death* 183–217 (T. Regan ed. 1980). Recent utilitarian theories appear to deploy something like this argument, introducing nonutilitarian considerations of autonomy or personhood as strong, indeed conclusive, reasons against killing when a person has developed self-consciousness, but, when developed self-consciousness does not yet exist, supposing the moral issue to depend on utilitarian consequences. With this view, infanticide of young infants and involuntary euthanasia of defectives may be justified. See J. Glover, supra note 6, at 150–69, 190–202; P. Singer, supra note 6, at 122–26, 130–39. Nonutilita-

rian theorists, who adopt Tooley's conception of the person, concur with the utilitarian theorists about the justifiability of involuntary euthanasia of newborn infants. See, e.g., Engelhardt, "Ethical Issues in Aiding the Death of Young Children," in *Killing and Letting Die* 81–91 (B. Steinbock ed. 1980) (even voluntary euthanasia of defective infants may be morally justified, but, on grounds of prudence, passive euthanasia is to be preferred).

Second, there is the position, here adopted, that personhood turns not on actual self-consciousness, but on the capacity, whether developed or undeveloped, for self-consciousness. On this view, personhood turns on the presence in a creature of the capacity, in some form, for the functions of personhood, even though these capacities are not and cannot be now fully exercised. For humans, the mark of this, empirically, is the presence of the brain and higher-brain function in some form. There are two views of when the capacity exists: (1) that it exists in any organism that will develop this capacity, though it does not now have it; (2) that it exists only in a creature that has the capacity. For a defense of (1), see P. Devine, supra note 54, at 74–105, a view which has the consequence that abortion at virtually all stages of pregnancy is equivalent to or is the killing of an innocent person. The view here adopted is (2), which has the consequence that abortion only in the latter stages of pregnancy raises issues of killing persons. See, e.g., E. Kluge, supra note 55, at 1–100. On this view, the thesis of (1) confuses capacities with potentialities. See id. at 15–18, 180.

58. For the contrary view, see Bandman & Bandman, "Rights, Justice, and Euthanasia," in *Beneficent Euthanasia* 91–99 (M. Kohl ed. 1975).

59. For an eloquent statement of this view, see Robertson, "Involuntary Euthanasia of Defective Newborns: A Legal Analysis," 27 *Stan. L. Rev.* 213 (1975).

60. The supposition appears to be that the child or defective is a former mature adult now in the child's or defective's body and tortured by the perception of present degradation of previous talents and competence. But, of course, in this case, unlike the case of Oswald and the like, there is no such previous person against whom the perception may be ethically checked.

61. For a moving and illuminating account of the world of a handicapped person from within, see Metzler, "Human and Handicapped," in *Moral Problems in Medicine* 358–63 (S. Gorovitz et al., eds. 1976). If this account surprises one in ways one could not have anticipated, the discontinuities between the worlds of even more handicapped persons and our own may be, *a fortiori*, even more severe.

62. For similar skepticism about medical practices of passive euthanasia of defective newborns, see Gustafson, "Mongolism, Parental Desires, and the Right to Life," in *Ethical Issues in Death and Dying* 145–72 (R. Weir ed. 1977). See also McCormick, "To Save or Let Die: The Dilemma of Modern Medicine," in *Ethical Issues in Death and Dying* 173–84 (R. Weir ed. 1977). Consider, in this connection, that adequate care could alleviate much of the suffering of spina bifida children. See Zachary, "Ethical and Social Aspects of Treatment of Spina Bifida," in *Moral Problems in Medicine* 342–48 (S. Gorovitz et al., eds. 1976). For recent philosophical argument in support of the position here taken, see E. Kluge, supra note 55, at 131–209. See also P. Devine, supra note 54, at 167–80. One caveat: one should distinguish, in the discussion of these matters, the moral issue of involuntary euthanasia or infanticide, namely that either violates nonmaleficence, from the issue of who bears the just burden of rearing such children. Certainly, it seems unfair for parents to be regarded as the just persons to bear such a burden, when they bear no special responsibility for it and did not fairly anticipate it. Certainly, a just society would give a high priority to relieving parents of this unfair burden, seeking alternative forms of care—including other parental figures with substantial state input—consistent with the rights of the children.

63. See D. Richards, *Reasons for Action*, supra note 13, at 185–89.

64. Specifically, the argument asserts that a requirement of mutual aid is a minimum requirement that one would be willing to agree to obey oneself, since it would secure a great good to oneself, if one were distressed and others obeyed, and that others would also agree to obey, from an original position of equal liberty. I. Kant, *Foundations of the Metaphysics of Morals* (L. W. Beck trans.) at 41; see, e.g., I. Kant, *Critique of Practical Reason* 34–35 (L. Beck trans. 1956); L. Kant, *Metaphysical Principles of Virtue* 52, 115, 117

(J. Ellington trans. 1964). For comments on Kant's argument, see Eisenberg, "From the Forbidden to the Supererogatory: The Basic Ethical Categories in Kant's Tugendlehre," 3 *Am. Phil. Q.* 255–69 (1966).

65. I. Kant, *Metaphysical Principles of Virtue*, supra note 64, at 112.

66. R. Price, *A Review of the Principal Questions in Morals* 120–21 (D. Raphael ed. 1948).

67. H. Sidgwick, *The Methods of Ethics* 253, 492 (7th ed. 1963).

68. This unfortunate confusion continues in philosophical work today. Philippa Foot, for example, who aptly describes the relevance of different kinds of moral principles to the justifiability of euthanasia, insists on characterizing what is here called nonmaleficence as a stringent duty of justice; whereas, mutual aid is said to involve charity. The result is that the contrast between nonmaleficence and mutual aid, which, properly understood, are two natural duties, is made into a contrast between duty and supererogation. Foot, supra note 51, at 25–32. Beauchamp and Childress present an even more systematic account of the range of moral principles relevant to these issues. T. Beauchamp & J. Childress, supra note 19, at 56–96 (autonomy and paternalism); id. at 97–134 (nonmaleficence); id. at 135–167 (beneficence and paternalism); id. at 168–200 (justice). Yet again, Beauchamp and Childress, by describing mutual aid as the principle of beneficence, obscure the fundamental moral distinction between mutual aid as a natural duty and beneficence as a principle of supererogation.

69. See D. Richards, *Reasons for Action*, supra note 13, at 205–11.

70. See Richards, "Human Rights," supra note 16, at 1429–30, and D. Richards, *The Moral Criticism of Law* (1977) at 209–16, for moral criticism of the failure of Anglo-American law to recognize such enforceable legal duties commensurate with mutual aid.

71. Foot, supra note 51, at 25–32; See also T. Beauchamp & J. Childress, supra note 19, at 135–67.

72. See Foot, supra note 51, at 25–34.

73. See id. See also T. Beauchamp & J. Childress, supra note 19, at 96–134 (nonmaleficence); id. at 135–67 (beneficence).

74. See notes 185–200 and text accompanying, Chapter 2, supra. Cf. T. Beauchamp & J. Childress, supra note 19, at 153–64.

75. See D. Richards, *Reasons for Action*, supra note 13, at 27–48.

76. J. Glover, supra note 6, at 176–79.

77. See T. Beauchamp & J. Childress, supra note 19, at 82–94, 153–64.

78. For a sense of the complexity of the case law, see Byrn, "Compulsory Lifesaving Treatment for the Competent Adult," 44 *Fordham L. Rev.* 1 (1975). For a broad defense of such a right, see R. Veatch, *Death, Dying and the Biological Revolution* 116–63 (1976); Cantor, "A Patient's Decision to Decline Life-Saving Medical Treatment: Bodily Integrity Versus the Preservation of Life," 26 *Rut. L. Rev.* 228 (1973). For criticism of such a right, see Comment, "Unauthorized Rendition of Lifesaving Medical Treatment," 53 *Calif. L. Rev.* 860 (1965).

79. It may be, however, the intention of defenders of such a right that the idea of "informed consent," on which it turns, requires the kind of rational deliberation and capacity which would exempt the case from just paternalism. See Cantor, supra note 78, at 236–54.

80. For a case that may be attacked on such grounds, though the issue of competency is not in fact clear, see *John F. Kennedy Memorial Hosp. v. Heston*, 58 N. J. 576, 279 A.2d 670 (1970) (blood transfusion ordered for severely injured 22-year old, unmarried woman who had been a Johovah's Witness for some time even though her mother refused to authorize the transfusion). Other courts have upheld the right to refuse a transfusion on religious free exercise grounds. *In re Brooks' Estate*, 32 Ill. 2d 361, 205 N.E.2d 435 (1965) (adult Jehovah's Witness, with spouse and adult children who did not oppose her express refusal); *Erickson v. Dilgard*, 44 Misc. 2d 27, 252 N.Y.S.2d 705 (Sup. Ct. 1962) (on general grounds of self-determination).

81. See, e.g., *Application of the President and Directors of Georgetown College, Inc.*, 331 F.2d 1000 (D.C. Cir.) (mother of seven-month old child), cert. denied, 377 U. S. 978 (1964).

82. See, e.g., *State v. Perricone*, 37 N. J. 463, 181 A.2d 751 (parental religious objection

to blood transfusion for baby with congenital malformation overruled), cert. denied, 371 U. S. 890 (1962). For a general discussion of the complexities of the case law, see R. Veatch, supra note 78, at 124–36.

83. Paternalism and mutual aid have special application to service professionals for the same reasons, special training and aspirations.

84. W. LaFave & A. Scott, Jr., *Handbook on Criminal Law* 568–70 (1972).

85. Id. at 570–71.

86. See generally Silving, "Euthanasia: A Study in Comparative Criminal Law," 103 *U. Pa. L. Rev.* 350 (1954). In Switzerland, for example, physician assistance in a patient's suicide, for reasons of mercy, is not punishable at all. Id. at 376–77. In Uruguay, homicide motivated by compassion and performed at request is totally exculpated. Id. at 368–69. In Germany and Switzerland, euthanasia for mercy mitigates. Id. at 360–68.

87. W. LaFave & A. Scott, Jr., supra note 84, at 408–13. However, the actual history of litigation relating to cases of euthanasia reveals strikingly erratic patterns of either no prosecution, acquittals, convictions for lesser crimes, and the like. See, e.g., Sanders, "Euthanasia: None Dare Call It Murder," 60 *J. Crim. L.C. & P.S.* 351 (1969); "Survey: Euthanasia: Criminal, Tort, Constitutional and Legislative Considerations," 48 *Notre Dame Law.* 1201, 1213–15 (1973); Comment, "The Right to Die," 10 *Cal. W.L. Rev.* 613 (1974); 34 *Notre Dame Law.* 460 (1959).

88. Plato, "Phaedo" 62b, in *The Collected Dialogues of Plato* 45 (E. Hamilton & H. Cairns eds. 1961).

89. Id. at 45.

90. Id. at 44.

91. In "Laws," Plato discusses the punishment for "self-slaughter though no sentence of the state has required this of him, no stress of cruel and inevitable calamity driven him to the act, and he has been involved in no desperate and intolerable disgrace, the man who thus gives unrighteous sentence against himself from mere poltroonery and unmanly cowardice." Plato, Book IX "Laws," 873c-d, at 1432, in *The Collected Dialogues of Plato* (E. Hamilton & H. Cairns eds. 1961).

92. The most notable example of this in the ancient world was the widely admired suicide of Cato, which took place after reading the "Phaedo." See H. Fedden, supra note 47, at 95–101. For a general description of attitudes to suicide in the ancient Greek and Roman world, see id. at 49–106. See also, J. Choron, *Suicide* 15–24 (1972). For examples of the sentiments of Roman Stoics, see the Seneca excerpts in note 47, supra. On the pervasive influence of the Socratic model, see J. Rist, *Stoic Philosophy* 233–55 (1969).

93. See Augustine, *Concerning the City of God-Against the Pagans* 26–39 (1972).

94. T. Aquinas, *Summa Theologica*, Part. II-II, q. 64, art. 5.

95. Blackstone's justification for the grisly penalties for suicide is clearly theological and statist. "[T]he suicide is guilty of a double offence; one spiritual, in invading the prerogative of the Almighty, and rushing into his immediate presence uncalled for; the other temporal, against the king, who hath an interest in the preservation of all his subjects." 4 W. Blackstone, *Commentaries* 189. The strong theological base for the English prohibition was expressly acknowledged by English judges. Suicide was criminal as

> an offence against nature, against God, and against the King. Against nature, because it is contrary to the rules of self-preservation . . . to destroy one's self is contrary to nature, and a thing most horrible. Against God, in that it is a breach of His commandment, thou shalt not kill. . . . Against the King in that hereby he . . . has lost one of his mystical members.

Hales v. Petit, 1 Plowden 253, 262, 75 Eng. Rep. 387, 400 (1562).

96. This heritage included dishonoring the corpse of the suicide—inherited from Christian practices—and forfeiture of estate of the suicide. See G. Williams, supra note 1, at 257–64.

97. See note 90 & accompanying text supra.

98. Augustine, supra note 93, at 32. Augustine uses this explanation to account for Samson's suicide. Id. at 37.

99. There is little evidence that the Old Testament was concerned with suicide as such; the suicides mentioned there go without comment. Even the New Testament nowhere condemns suicide; the Church only develops concern with it in the third century. See J. Choron, supra note 92 at 13–15, 24; H. Fedden, supra note 42, at 30–31. One scholar has observed linguistic evidence of Old Testament unconcern with suicide as such. Daube, "The Linguistics of Suicide," 1 *Phil. & Pub. Aff.* 387, 394–99 (1972). Daube also notes the lack of any authoritative evidence in Jewish doctrine of the appropriate period for the Augustinian subsumption of suicide under the Sixth Commandment's prohibition of "murder," the Hebrew word never being used for self-willed death. Id. at 414–15 n. 166. For an argument by a Christian theologian that the Augustinian interpretation is clearly wrong, see J. Fletcher, supra note 4, at 195–96. For current Jewish views, see Sherwin, "Jewish Views of Euthanasia" in *Beneficent Euthanasia* 3–11 (M. Kohl ed. 1975).

100. Augustine, supra note 93, at 31–32.

101. Id. at 36.

102. See e.g., Sullivan, "The Immorality of Euthanasia" in *Beneficent Euthanasia*, 12–33 (M. Kohl ed. 1975). Specifically, Sullivan argues that man does not have full dominion over his life, that he has even less dominion over the lives of others, and that God has dominion over the lives of all. Id. at 14. This is the typical Christian argument that man has no absolute control over his life: he has the use of it but may not destroy it. See N. St. John-Stevas, *Law and Morals* 51 (1964). See also P. Devine, supra note 54, 167–80.

103. See notes 53–62 & accompanying text supra.

104. Aristotle, *Nicomachean Ethics* 1138a4–1138b14, at 143–44 (M. Ostwald trans. 1962).

105. T. Aquinas, *Summa Theologica*, Part. II-II. q. 64, art. 5.

106. See note 95, supra.

107. The whole of Aristotle, *Nicomachean Ethics* (M. Ostwald trans. 1962), is an attempt to describe the human excellences, which morality requires us to maximize. See Book 10 for a characterization of the special weight Aristotle gave to the human excellence of theoretical wisdom.

108. See Aristotle, supra note 104.

109. See Richards, "Rights and Autonomy," *Ethics*, October, 1981.

110. C. Montesquieu, *The Persian Letters* 157 (1961). David Hume similarly remarks:

> All our obligations to do good to society seem to imply something reciprocal. I receive the benefits of society, and therefore ought to promote its interests; but when I withdraw myself altogether from society, can I be bound any longer? But allowing that our obligations to do good were perpetual, they have certainly some bounds: I am not obliged to do a small good to society at the expense of a great harm to myself: why then should I prolong a miserable existence, because of some frivolous advantage which the public may perhaps receive from me?

D. Hume, "On Suicide," in *Essays Moral Political and Literary* 593–94 (1963) (1st ed. Edinburgh 1741).

111. See D. Richards, *Reasons for Action*, supra note 13, at 107–47; J. Rawls, *A Theory of Justice* (1971).

112. D. Richards, *Reasons for Action*, supra note 13, at 148–75.

113. See note 18 & accompanying text supra.

114. See D. Richards, *Reasons for Action*, supra note 13, at 150–51.

115. See Brandt, "The Morality and Rationality of Suicide," supra note 35, at 123–33.

116. See note 91 supra.

117. See Aristotle, supra note 104. See also id. 1116a10–1116a15, at 71–72.

118. See id. 1115a23–1115b6, at 69–70.

119. See note 91, supra.

120. See Augustine, supra note 93, at 26–39.

121. See T. Aquinas, supra note 94.

122. Augustine, supra note 93, at 32.

123. Id. at 27.

124. Id. at 26–31, 36, 38–40.

125. Id. at 26–28.

126. Id. at 26–31.

127. For historical background of the rampant martyrdom, notably the Donatists, against which Augustine was writing, see H. Fedden, supra note 47, at 118–33.

128. On suicide as an expression of romantic idealization in literature, see A. Alvarez, *The Savage God* 139–213 (1972).

129. See notes 93–103 & accompanying text supra.

130. See Aristotle, *Nicomachean Ethics* 1115a3–1115b6, at 69–70 at note 104 supra.

131. This is a prominent feature of Stoic reflection on suicide. See note 47 supra. See generally J. Rist, *Stoic Philosophy* 233–55 (1969).

132. This endurance of suffering is, for Augustine, a mark of true greatness of soul. See Augustine, supra note 93, at 32–34. For frank acknowledgement that suffering "for the Christian is not an absolute evil but has redeeming features," see N. St. John-Stevas, supra note 102, at 51.

133. The attempt to articulate intuition as an argument inevitably falters and ends up resting on the question-begging affirmation of the preeminent value of life. See, e.g., P. Devine, supra note 54, at 201–02. Devine first argues that the Stoic attitude to suicide is inconsistent because it fails to follow its own principle of altering attitudes to the world rather than the world itself, that is, learning better to endure suffering, rather than commiting suicide. Id. In fact, the description fails to take seriously the Stoic idea of dignity, trivializing it into a kind of passive adjustment without inner ideals rationally affirmed. Devine does not pursue that point and begs the question by merely affirming the value of life.

134. For at least one model of Christian spirituality, St. Ignatius, overcoming suicidal despair on the ground that it was forbidden by God was part of his journey to sanctity. See *St. Ignatius' Own Story* 17–20 (W. Young trans. 1956). A similar journey is expressed by the poet Gerard Manley Hopkins in his "(Carrion Comfort)". See *Poems and Prose of Gerard Manley Hopkins* 60–63 (W. Gardner ed. 1953). For Hopkins, the resistance to "Despair" is expressed in "I can; . . . not choose not to be." Id. at 60.

135. See notes 42–62 & accompanying text supra.

136. See T. Aquinas, supra note 94.

137. I. Kant, *The Metaphysical Principles of Virtue* 83–84 (1964).

138. Id. at 84.

139. I. Kant, *Lectures on Ethics* 151 (1963).

140. H. Fedden, supra note 47, at 312.

141. J. Donne, *Biathanatos* 49 (1930). In Donne's view then, the principle of self-preservation ceases to be of force when life either ceases or, in the individual's determination, appears to cease to be a good. David Hume's argument, in response to the Thomistic natural law conception, is more speculative in scope, but to similar effect: all nature, Hume argues, is subject to causal laws according to which God rules, and man's nature is also so governed. But since man has reason to achieve his purposes, man uses these laws to achieve his purposes; it is no more contrary to nature for a man to achieve his rational purposes of ending pain and shame by death than it is for man to alter the natural order in order better to achieve other rational ends, for example, using medicine to fight disease. See D. Hume, supra note 110, at 587–93. For the English debates on these matters, see S. Sprott, *The English Debate on Suicide from Donne to Hume* (1961).

142. To say that person is by definition a self-maintaining system, as in P. Devine, supra note 54, at 20, either reintroduces the unacceptable Thomistic assumption or uninformatively fails to characterize the nature of the self in which persons have rational interests.

143. See I. Kant, supra note 137, at 84–85; I. Kant, supra note 139, at 150. Kant refuses to characterize altruistic self-sacrifice as "suicide" in any sense. Id. On the vagaries of characterizing certain behavior as "suicide," see J. Margolis, *Negativities* 23–35 (1975). See also Beauchamp, "What Is Suicide?" in *Ethical Issues in Death and Dying* 97–102 (T. Beauchamp & S. Perlin eds. 1978).

144. See I. Kant, *Foundations*, supra note 65, at 39–40.

145. See W. Shakespeare, *Hamlet*, act I, scene ii, ll. 131–32.

146. See J. Choron, supra note 92, at 15–24; H. Fedden, supra note 47, at 95–101; J. Rist, supra note 131, at 233–55.

147. See notes 217–51 and text accompanying, Chapter 3, supra, for a discussion of Kant's arguments against commercial sex; see also notes 185–217 and text accompanying, Chapter 4, supra, for comparable condemnation by Kant of drug use.

148. See e.g., I. Kant, supra note 13, at 148–54.

149. See I. Kant, supra note 64, at 51–52.

150. I. Kant, supra note 139, at 153.

151. Id.

152. See note 147, supra.

153. While Kant insists that suicide is immoral on ethical grounds independent of putative condemnation by God's will, he concludes his discussion of its immorality with the telling Augustinian remark, echoing Plato: "[A] suicide opposes the purpose of his Creator, he arrives in the other world as one who has deserted his post; he must be looked upon as a rebel against God." I. Kant, supra note 139, a 153–54.

154. Compare the remarks of Montesquieu at text accompanying note 110 supra with the remarks of Hume at note 110 supra.

155. See Richards, "The Individual, the Family and the Constitution: A Jurisprudential Perspective," 55 *N.Y.U.L. Rev.* 1 (1980).

156. The moral idea here is that, quite apart from background institutional roles, merely giving birth to a vulnerable child, other things being equal, gives rise to duties of care and nurturance. See Locke, "The Second Treatise," in *J. Locke's Two Treatises of Government* 323–25 (P. Laslett ed. 1960).

157. See generally J. Bowlby, *Attachment and Loss*, [3 vols.: *Attachment* (1971); *Separation: Anxiety and Anger* (1975); *Loss: Sadness and Depression* (1980)]; J. Bowlby, *Child Care and the Growth of Love* (1953); J. Goldstein, A. Freud & A. Solnit, *Beyond the Best Interests of the Child* (1973); M. Rutter, *Maternal Deprivation Reassessed* (1972).

158. See authorities cited note 157 supra. See also A. Clarke-Stewart, *Child Care in the Family: A Review of Research and Some Propositions for Policy* (1977).

159. Even if there is no moral justification for such conduct, there may be mitigating circumstances and even forms of excuse—mental disturbance, for example—which would qualify and sometimes exculpate from moral blame.

160. See *In re Osborne*, 294 A.2d 372 (D.C. 1972), in which the decision of a Jehovah's Witness to refuse blood transfusions on religious grounds was upheld though the man had two young children. The man's wife had testified about continuing care for the children:

> My husband has a business and it will be turned over to me. And his brothers work for him, so it will be carried on. That is no problem. In fact, they are working on it right now. Business goes on.
> As far as money-wise, everbody is all right. We have money saved up. Everything will be all right. If anything ever happens, I have a big enough family and the family is prepared to care for the children.

Id. at 374 (quoting testimony). The record also indicated a close family relationship extending beyond the parents. Id. For commentary, see R. Veatch, supra note 78, at 158–59.

161. For the idea of a parental life cycle, see R. Rapoport, R. Rapoport & Z. Strelitz, *Fathers, Mothers and Society: Towards New Alliances* (1977). See also R. Rapoport & R. Rapoport, *Leisure and the Family Cycle* (1975).

162. D. Portwood, supra note 48, at 93–106.

163. Certainly, in the circumstances where death is morally permissible, for example, terminal illness, it is uncertain that one who considered effects of his dying on those he loves would prefer prolonged death and deterioration over available suicidal alternatives, if one assumes appropriate explanation. For one form of such explanation, see Johnston, "Artist's Death: A Last Statement in a Thesis on 'Self-Termination,'" *N.Y. Times*, June 17, 1979, at 1, col. 1.

164. For a classic study of the pathology of grieving, see S. Freud, "Mourning and Melancolia," in 14 *The Standard Edition of the Complete Psychological Works of Sigmund*

Freud 243–58 (J. Strachey trans. 1957) [hereinafter cited as Standard Edition]. See generally J. Bowlby, *Attachment and Loss,* supra note 157. For the larger social implications of unresolved grief, see A. Mitscherlich & M. Mitscherlich, *The Inability to Mourn* (1975).

165. See note 163 supra.

166. For descriptions of these moving ceremonies of self-willed death, see the description of the suicide of Cato, H. Fedden, supra not 47, at 95–101. For Tacitus's account of Seneca's similar death, see *The Stoic Philosophy of Seneca,* supra note 47, at 243–44. For the suggestion by Enlightenment thinkers of the need for the revival of such rituals, see T. More, *Utopia* 108–09 (E. Surtz ed. 1964); M. Montaigne, "A Custom of the Island of Cea," in *The Complete Works of Montaigne* 251–62 (1948); F. Nietzsche, *Human All-Too-Human* 85–86, 88, 286–87 (1964). See also Montesquieu, "The Grandeur and Declension of the Roman Empire," in III *Complete Works* 86–87 (London 1777); F. Nietzsche, *The Twilight of the Idols* 88–90 (1964); F. Nietzsche, "Thus Spoke Zarathustra," in *The Portable Nietzsche* 183–86 (W. Kaufman trans. 1954); A. Schopenhauer, *Essays and Aphorisms* 77–79 (1970); Voltaire, "Of Suicide," in 17 *Works* 165 (4th ed. 1772).

167. Recent social historians have brought home the dramatic point that the impersonal isolation of contemporary dying in hospitals has occasioned the loss of the comforting rituals of public dying at home, which characterized previous eras, where the dying person would bid farewell to family and friends in a ceremony of mutual comfort. See generally P. Aries, *Western Attitudes Toward Death: From the Middle Ages to the Present* (P. Ranum trans. 1974); P. Aries, *The Hour of Our Death* (H. Weaver trans. 1981); E. Kubler-Ross, *On Death and Dying* 1–33 (1969); D. Standard, *The Puritan Way of Death* 188–94 (1977). The humane need for such rituals would apply to both ordinary dying and self-willed death. Of course, it is possible that with more humane concern for the dying some would not request death. See id. at 122–38. Others, however, might avail themselves of such rituals reasonably to will an earlier death.

168. See note 167 supra.

169. See note 82 supra.

170. See the discussion of this problem in Richards, supra note 155, at 50–52.

171. C. Fried, *An Anatomy of Values* 155–82, (1970).

172. In terms of rational choice theory, one plan would dominate another. See D. Richards, *Reasons for Action,* supra note 13, at 28, 40–43.

173. See notes 42–62 & accompanying text supra.

174. See, e.g., K. Menninger, *Man Against Himself* (1938).

175. The classic statement of this position is E. Durkheim, *Suicide: A Study in Sociology* (1951). Durkheim appears to assume the Kantian moral view, see notes 136–153 & accompanying text supra, to the effect that suicide, as such, immorally violates the foundations of moral personality. See E. Durkheim, supra, at 333–38. For an alternative attempt by a sociologist to account for the moral and social complexities of suicide, see J. Douglas, *The Social Meanings of Suicide* (1967). See also J. Baechler, *Suicides* (1979).

176. See K. Minninger, supra note 174.

177. See, e.g., J. Choron, supra note 92, at 74–78; E. Stengel, *Suicide and Attempted Suicide* 58–59 (1975).

178. More judicious commentators, like Stengel, who see the fallacy of this inference, nonetheless remain skeptical about the commonness of rational suicide, largely on the basis of their work with suicide prevention, which benefits often largely confused and desperate people who do not rationally contemplate suicide. See E. Stengel, supra note 177, at 125, 132–34. Here, Stengel appears himself fallaciously to reason from an admittedly skewed sample. His argument that persons who face the same misfortune, for example, terminal cancer, have different responses—some contemplating suicide, others never doing so—does not show, as he mistakenly infers, that some uniform response must be rational. It only shows that persons have very different conceptions of their ends, which may justify different judgments of rationality on similar facts. See id. at 133. The implicit judgments here of normality, id. at 58, thus appear to suppress the kinds of fundamental moral distinctions regarding human individuality which an ethical medical practice should here observe.

179. See id. On successful suicides, see id. at 19–73. On attempted suicides, see id. at 77–117.

180. See id. at 77–117.

181. Id. at 19–73.

182. For the importance of ambivalence in the psyciatric assessment of the rationality of suicide behavior, see Motto, "The Right to Suicide: A Psychiatrist's View," 3 *Life-Threatening Behavior* 183–88 (1972).

183. See E. Stengel, supra note 177, at 137–49.

184. For the kinds of evaluations and procedures typical of such centers, see generally E. Schneidman, N. Farberow & R. Litman, *The Psychology of Suicide* (1970).

185. See note 76 & accompanying text supra.

186. J. Choron, supra note 92, at 79–82, 96–106, 152–56.

187. See Richards, "Human Rights," supra note 16, at 1417, 1428–34.

188. See notes 74–82 & accompanying text supra.

189. One study, for example, indicates that physicians are significantly more afraid of death than either the healthy or sick lay people. This was the case even though 63% of the physicians said they were less afraid of death now than they had been heretofore. See Feifel et al., "Physicians Consider Death," *Proc. Am. Psych. Assoc.* 201–02 (1967).

190. On forms of love bond that disable the lover from realistically perceiving the needs of the beloved, see M. Balint, *Primary Love and Psychoanalytic Technique* 90–140 (1965).

191. Id.

192. These limits importantly govern and regulate the justice of relations of parents to children, and the converse. See Richards, supra note 155.

193. For a classic statement of this form of argument, see Kamisar, supra note 3.

194. See id.

195. See notes 1–2 & accompanying text supra.

196. See Kamisar, supra note 3, at 974.

197. Id. at 1014–41.

198. Id. at 978–1013.

199. Id. at 1014–41.

200. See G. Williams, supra note 1, at 339–46. See also Williams, "Euthanasia Legislation: A Rejoinder to the Non-Religious Objections," in *Euthanasia and the Right to Death* 134–47 (A. Downing ed. 1969).

201. At least eight states have adopted a "Natural Death Act" whereby an individual executes a so-called "living will." Comment, "North Carolina's Natural Death Act: Confronting Death with Dignity," 14 *Wake Forest L. Rev.* 771, 774–77 (1978). The seminal statement in support of the "living will" was Kutner, "Due Process of Euthanasia: The Living Will, a Proposal," 44 *Ind. L.J.* 539 (1969). See generally Kutner, "The Living Will: Coping with the Historical Event of Death," 27 *Baylor L. Rev.* 39 (1975). For commentary, see the articles on the "living will" cited at note 11 supra. See also Kaplan, "Euthanasia Legislation: A Survey and a Model Act," 2 *Am. J. Law & Med.* 41–99 (1976); Raible, "The Right to Refuse Treatment and Natural Death Legislation," 5 *Medicolegal News* 6 (1977); Note, "The Legal Aspects of the Right to Die Before and After the Quinlan Decision," 65 *Ky. L.J.* 823 (1976–77); Note, "The Tragic Choice: Termination of Care for Patients in a Permanent Vegetative State," 51 *N.Y.U. L. Rev.* 285 (1976); Comment, "The Living Will: Already a Practical Alternative," 55 *Tex. L. Rev.* 665 (1977).

202. In this connection, Yale Kamisar argues that medical judgments about terminal illness and incurability are fallible and that the death of patients should not be a hazard of medical fallibility. Kamisar, supra note 3, at 993–1013. But surely, the issue is one of reasonable assessment of prognosis on all the available facts. If the person perceives that a highly probable evil should and will be escaped by death, then there can be no moral objection to the person's decision to die. Part of such reasonable assessment is, of course, the possibility of medical fallibility. But once the person is thus apprised and the assessment is not unreasonable, the relative weight of the probabilities must be left to the person. Williams, supra note 200, at 134–47. Kamisar's use of the objective mode

would here deprive the person of the right of reasonable judgment that is her or his right.

203. See Kamisar, supra note 3, at 1014–41.
204. See J. Mill, *On Liberty* (1957).
205. See H. Hart, *Law, Liberty, and Morality* (1963).
206. M. Kohl, supra note 44, at 96–100.
207. See discussion of J. Glover and P. Singer at notes 6, 57 supra.
208. See discussion of J. Glover and P. Singer at notes 6, 57 supra.
209. This intuitively harsh consequences of pure utilitarianism is avoided by both Jonathan Glover and Peter Singer by somewhat ad hoc and anti-utilitarian devices. For Glover, this takes the form of his principle of autonomy, whereby creatures with developed self-consciousness who can and do express wishes to live are given enormous weight, which, for him, outweighs countervailing utilitarian consequences which might, absent the enormous normative weight given autonomy, require death. J. Glover, supra note 6, at 74–85. In similar fashion, Peter Singer claims that "persons" with self-consciousness have a kind of overwhelming normative weight that gives them, should they want continued life, a kind of right to it. P. Singer, supra note 6 at 72–92. For both theorists, since young infants, for example, lack such self-consciousness, they have no such weight, for their lives are thus subject to utilitarian calculations of the normal kinds. For commentary, see notes 6, 57 supra.
210. For the idea of replacement, see J. Glover, supra note 6, at 72–73, 159–60, 163. See also P. Singer, supra note 6, at 122–26, 130–39.
211. See Kamisar, supra note 3, at 990–93. See also Foot, supra note 51, at 38–39.
212. See Richards, "Human Rights and Moral Ideals: An Essay on the Moral Theory of Liberalism," 5 *Social Theory & Prac.* 461–88 (1980).
213. Philippa Foot suggests that such forms of enticement might have a quite different moral status in "an extremely poverty stricken community where the children genuinely suffered from lack of food." Foot, supra note 51, at 39.
214. In preindustrial society, parental dependence on children in old age was extreme, for the child provided parents with "a form of social security, unemployment insurance, and yearly support." J. Kett, *Rites of Passage: Adolescence in America, 1790 to the Present* 23 (1977).
215. One aspect of such concern would be to relieve impersonality in the process of dying, a contemporary inhumanity of some magnitude. See note 167, supra. Perhaps such concern would lead some reasonably to put aside willing their own death. Perhaps others would, with appropriate understanding, more reasonably embrace self-willed death. In any event, on grounds of justice, persons should have such support in their moments of dying, no matter what influence it has on the exercise of their rights.
216. Williams observes in this connection:

> If a patient, suffering pain in a terminal illness, wishes for euthanasia partly because of his pain and partly because he sees his beloved ones breaking under the strain of caring for him, I do not see how this decision on his part, agonizing though it may be, is necessarily a matter of discredit either to the patient himself or to his relatives.

Williams, supra note 200, at 138.
217. See Chapter 2, supra.
218. W. LaFave & A. Scott, Jr., supra note 87, at 568–70.
219. Id. at 570–71.
220. See note 87, supra.
221. 137 N.J. Super. 227, 348 A.2d 801 (Ch. Div.), rev'd, 70 N.J. 10, 355 A.2d 647, cert. denied, 429 U.S. 922 (1976).
222. 373 Mass. 728, 370 N.E.2d 417 (1977).
223. 102 Misc. 2d 184, 423 N.Y.S.2d 580 (1979), modified and aff'd sub nom. *Eichner v. Dillon*, 73 A.D.2d 431, 426 N.Y.S.2d 517 (1980). See note 9, supra.
224. *Saikewicz* involves a 67-year-old profoundly retarded ward of the State of Massachusetts, who was terminally ill with leukemia. Chemotherapy, which statistically

caused remission in 30–50% of the cases for periods ranging from 2 to 13 months, was medically indicated, though it would cause Saikewicz adverse side effects and discomfort. Based upon the patient's inability to provide informed consent for the chemotherapy treatment and his inability to understand the treatment, a guardian was appointed who recommended his not being treated on the grounds that it was in his best interests. 373 Mass. at ____, 370 N.E.2d at 419. The court in *Saikewicz* upheld the guardian's recommendations on the ground of the constitutional right to privacy if the declining of the life-prolonging treatment was in his actual interests. Id. at ____, 370 N.E.2d at 435. On the view here proposed, this result is morally problematic since there is not actual consent nor was anyone reasonably apprised of what a reasonable person's consent would here have been, since Saikewicz never had the capacity for informed consent. Saikewicz's lack of understanding of the effects and discomfort does not, in these circumstances, wholly rebut one's moral doubts about here not giving treatment that would, absent the retardation, have been medically indicated. On what ground, ethically, are we, the nonretarded, entitled to impute consent to Saikewicz when, in the case of a comparable nonretarded person, chemotherapy would normally be indicated?

225. Neither Quinlan nor Brother Joseph Fox were dead by the brain death criterion of the Ad Hoc Committee of the Harvard Medical School, which requires no discernible central nervous system activity. Ad Hoc Committee of the Harvard Medical School to Examine the Definition of Brain Death, "A Definition of Irreversible Coma," in *Ethical Issues in Death and Dying* 11–18 (T. Beauchamp & S. Perlin eds. 1978). The criterion arose from advances in medical technology, which could sustain respiratory and heart function—the traditional indicia of life—even in the absence of capacity for brain function. Previously, the cessation of breathing and heart function had been correlated with lack of brain function. See Black, "Definitions of Brain Death," in *Ethical Issues in Death and Dying* 5–10 (T. Beauchamp & S. Perlin eds. 1978). The Harvard criterion has been criticized both for not being permissive enough and for being too permissive. The former criticism focuses on the fact that the Harvard criterion allows total brain death to mark "death" when there has been irreversible loss of the cerebral neocortex's function on which the capacities of critical self-consciousness turn. Thus, the proper criterion should be the narrower one of loss of neocortex function. See Veatch, "Defining Death Anew: Technical and Ethical Problems," in *Ethical Issues in Death and Dying* 19–38. (T. Beachcamp & S. Perlin eds. 1978). The latter criticism argues that loss of brain function should not cavalierly be assumed to be the mark of "death" because this disengages concepts of the "person" too sharply from the living body and may allow the taking of body organs for transplants. Jonas, "Against the Stream: Comments on the Definition and Redefinition of Death," in *Ethical Issues in Death and Dying* 51–60 (T. Beauchamp & S. Perlin eds. 1978). See Schwager, "Life, Death, and the Irreversibly Comatose," in *Ethical Issues in Death and Dying* 38–50 (T. Beachamp & S. Perlin eds. 1978). For a balanced proposal for incorporating brain death into revised legal conceptions of death, see Capron & Kass, "A Statutory Definition of the Standards for Determining Human Death: An Appraisal and a Proposal," in *Ethical Issues in Death and Dying* 60–75 (T. Beauchamp & S. Perlin eds. 1978).

226. Brother Joseph Fox had expressed to close friends both at the time of the Karen Quinlan situation and shortly before being hospitalized his considered view that his life not be sustained if he were in the Quinlan situation. *In re Eichner*, 102 Misc. 2d 184, ____, 423 N.Y.S.2d 580, 586 (1979), modified and aff'd sub nom. *Eichner v. Dillon*, 73 A.D.2d 431, 426 N.Y.S.2d 517 (1980). See note 9, supra. In this Brother Joseph expressly affirmed a Catholic view to which he was, as a religious man, conscientiously committed. In *Quinlan*, Karen Quinlan had not affirmed such a view in so focused and considered a way, but the court found her father's judgment sufficiently based in understanding of his daughter's wishes to warrant his enforcing the privacy right on her behalf. See 70 N.J. at ____, 355 A.2d at 664.

227. See F. Dostoevsky, *The Possessed* 93–98, 524–39 (A. Yarmolinsky trans. 1936).

228. A. Camus, *The Myth of Sisyphus* 3–13, 39–44, 76–83 (J. O'Brien trans. 1955).

229. The perception of absurdity arises from and expresses, as an ultimate meta-

physical fact, a common fact of self-critical evaluation of one's life, namely that a certain range of assumptions of personal significance in which one invests one's energies and aspirations passionately appears, on examination, to lack any justification that one can reasonably affirm. T. Nagel, *Moral Questions* 11–16 (1979). In this case, however, the fact that certain assumptions are shown to be invalid, rather than expressing a perception limited to those assumptions, mistakenly is taken to render invalid, without examination or argument, all alternative assumptions which one might construct or avow.

230. See, e.g., K. Baier, *The Meaning of Life* (1957). See also Edwards, "Life, Meaning and Value of," 4 *Ency. of Phil.* 467–77 (P. Edwards ed. 1967).

231. See K. Baier, supra note 230, at 3–24.

232. See id. at 24–29.

233. See generally S. Schiffer, *Meaning* (1972).

234. See also Tolstoy, "Death and the Meaning of Life," in *Ethical Issues in Death and Dying* 317–24 (T. Beauchamp & S. Perlin eds. 1978).

235. See K. Baier, supra note 230, at 24–29. See also K. Britton, *Philosophy and the Meaning of Life* 51–215 (1969).

236. Sigmund Freud articulated this view:

> It is indeed impossible to imagine our own death; and whenever we attempt to do so we can perceive that we are in fact still present as spectators. Hence the psycho-analytic school could venture on the assertion that at bottom no one believes in his own death, or, to put the same thing in another way, that in the unconscious every one of us is convinced of his own immortality.

Freud, "Thoughts for the Times on War and Death," in 14 *Standard Edition*, supra note 164, at 289.

237. Compare the discussion in Edwards, "My Death," in 5 *Ency. of Phil.* 416–19 (P. Edwards ed. 1967). For a recent example of such a philosopher, see P. Devine, supra note 54, at 24–31.

238. See Edwards, supra note 237. See also M. de Unamuno, *Tragic Sense of Life* 38–57 (1954).

239. See D. Richards, *Reasons for Action*, supra note 13, at 27–48. See also C. Fried, supra note 171, at 155–82.

240. The role of one's death in living an authentic personal life is the central perception of Martin Heidegger's philosophical system. See M. Heidegger, *Being and Time* (J. Mazquarrie & E. Robinson trans. 1962). For forceful criticism, see P. Edwards, *Heidegger on Death: A Critical Evaluation* (Monist Monograph No. 1 1979).

241. H. Fedden, supra note 47, at 285, 287–88, 312.

242. L. Tolstoy, *The Death of Ivan Ilych and Other Stories* 95–156 (A. Maude trans. 1960).

243. See Daube, supra note 99, at 390–94, 399–405.

244. For the range of possible attitudes in the western tradition, see J. Choron, *Death and Western Thought* (1963).

245. See note 134 supra.

246. See notes 47–48, 92, 166 supra.

247. See note 110, supra. For an illustration of Hume's remarkable contentment in his last months, see D. Hume, "My Own Life," in *Hume's Dialogues Concerning Natural Religion* 239 (N. Smith ed. 1935). The letter from Adam Smith to William Strahan describing Hume's last months is reprinted in 2 *The Letters of David Hume* 450–52 (J. Greig ed. 1932). The last-mentioned book contains the remarkable letter from Hume to Edward Gibbon upon reading the first volume of *The Decline and Fall of the Roman Empire*, which appeared while Hume was dying. Id. at 390–11.

248. See J. Hillman, *Suicide and the Soul* (1964).

249. See note 167 supra on the impersonality of contemporary modes of dying. See also G. Gorer, *Death, Grief, and Mourning in Contemporary Britain* (1965); Group for the Advancement of Psychiatry, *The Right to Die: Decision and Decision Makers* (1974).

250. I. Kant, supra note 139, at 153.

251. J. Rousseau, *La Nouvelle Héloïse* 264 (1968).

252. See text accompanying note 139, supra.

253. H. Fedden, supra note 47, at 285, 287–88, 312. This concept of self-willed death, built on rights of the person, has nothing to do with forms of institutional suicide which deny such rights. See id. at 16–26.

254. One perceptive commentator identifies the "suburban spirit" as a form of widespread and unreasoned social prejudice against forms of self-willed death. Id. at 230, 248–49.

255. 137 N.J. Super. 227, 348 A.2d 801 (Ch. Div.), rev'd, 70 N.J. 10, 355 A.2d 647, cert. denied, 429 U.S. 922 (1976).

256. 102 Misc. 2d 184, 423 N.Y.S.2d 580 (1979), modified and aff'd sub nom. *Eichner v. Dillon*, 73 A.D.2d 431, 426 N.Y.S.2d 517 (1980). See note 9, supra.

257. See the address of Pope Pius XII, "The Prolongation of Life, Address of Pope Pius XII to an International Congress of Anesthesiologists," November 24, 1957, *AAS* 49 (1957) (translation from the original French, "The Pope Speaks," Spring 1958, vol. 4, no. 4, pp. 393–98).

258. See notes 71–73 & accompanying text supra. See also notes 83 & accompanying text supra.

259. 73 A.D.2d at___, 426 N.Y.S.2d at 550. The court in *Eichner* adopts the procedure from *Saikewicz*. On the morally problematic facts of *Saikewicz*, see note 224 supra, some such more extraordinary procedure might be required if we assume (which is problematic) that any such procedure at all is justified. The moral status of *Saikewicz* and *Eichner*, however, are completely different, and there is no ground for importing the moral ambiguities of the former into the latter. The New York Court of Appeals, in affirming *Eichner*, supra note 9, made clear that the presence of a court order was optional, not mandatory, in such cases.

260. See, e.g., Fletcher, "Prolonging Life," in *Ethical Issues in Death and Dying* 226–40 (R. Weir ed. 1977).

261. G. Kelly, *Medico-Moral Problems* 20 (1955). See C. McFadden, *Medical Ethics* 27–33 (1962); T. O'Donnell, *Morals in Medicine* 39–44 (1959); N. St. John-Stevas, *The Right to Life* 71 (1963).

262. See, e.g., Foot, "The Problem of Abortion and the Doctrine of Double Effect," in *Killing and Letting Die* 156–65 (B. Steinbock ed. 1980).

263. One criticism of the doctrine expounded in the works cited in note 261 supra, has been that there is no morally relevant distinction *at all* between killing and letting die. See, e.g., Bennett, "Whatever the Consequences," in *Killing and Letting Die* 109–27 (B. Steinbock ed. 1980). However, there appear to be *some* cases in which there is a morally and legally important distinction. See Dinello, "On Killing and Letting Die," in *Killing and Letting Die* 128–31 (B. Steinbock ed. 1980). See also Fitzgerald, "Acting and Refraining," in *Moral Problems in Medicine* 284–89 (S. Gorovitz et al., eds. 1976).

264. Philippa Foot has made this point in terms of more stringent duties of not harming and less stringent duties of rendering aid. See Foot, supra not 262 at 156–65. See also Foot, supra note 51, at 25–32. Foot's way of making the distinction may not be fully accurate. See note 68 supra. See also Davis, "The Priority of Avoiding Harm," in *Killing and Letting Die* 172–214 (B. Steinbock ed. 1980); Russell, "On the Relative Strictness of Negative and Positive Duties," in *Killing and Letting Die* 215–231 (B. Steinbock ed. 1980).

265. See note 264 supra. For example, whereas it might clearly violate nonmaleficence to kill a person, there might be no violation of mutual aid in letting him die if the cost of aid was very high.

266. See, e.g., Rachels, "Euthanasia, Killing and Letting Die," in *Ethical Issues Relating to Life and Death* 146–63 (J. Ladd ed. 1979).

267. See P. Ramsey, *The Patient as Person* 113–64 (1970). Ramsey appears to acknowledge that the force of the prohibition on killing is, for him, a religious ideal about proper dying. Id at 153, 160.

268. Even Ramsey appears to acknowledge some exceptions to the justness of his prohibition on killing. Id. at 161–64.

269. Compare the similar argument in T. Beauchamp & J. Childress, supra note 19, at 112–17.

270. Both Montaigne and St. Thomas More discuss the role of public officials in monitoring decisions to die. See note 166 supra.

271. Such "living wills" currently apply to forms of passive euthanasia. See authorities cited note 201 supra.

272. This might be a way of insuring the voluntariness of the person and absence of overreaching by interested third parties. See Kamisar, supra note 3, at 1011; P. Devine, supra note 54, at 183–84.

273. Such a defense might apply only in the clearest cases of Glanville William's proposed legislative defense. See G. Williams, supra note 1, at 339–46.

274. Compare the role that legislative reform is playing in the area of voluntary passive euthanasia. See note 201 supra.

275. Compare the Switzerland exemption from aiding and abetting suicide for physicians in cases of patient request and terminal illness. See note 86 supra.

276. See note 87 supra. Compare the European practice. See note 86 supra.

6

Concluding Perspectives

We have now completed an argument of some complexity. In Chapter 1, the general form of standard decriminalization argument (including Mill's harm principle) was interpreted in antiutilitarian terms as a consequence of a human rights perspective centering on an autonomy-based interpretation of treating persons as equals; later chapters elaborated this new way of interpreting decriminalization argument in the context of its allegedly powerful consequences for rethinking particular areas of decriminalization controversy: consensual adult sexuality (homosexuality and prostitution), drug use, and claims of a right to die. These later chapters have often been fairly intricate in their argument, in an attempt to unite a theory of proper moral and legal argument with a conception of how these arguments are to be worked out, and often appealed to a kind of sustained empirical inquiry, sometimes including history, literature, anthropology, medicine, psychology, and the like. In this concluding discussion, we will draw back from the disparate details of these separate discussions and discuss the common themes that unify these analyses.

The most obvious common theme in these chapters has been the systematic elaboration and application of a form of moral argument expressing what we have called an autonomy-based interpretation of treating persons as equals. This conception has naturally supplied an alternative interpretation, indeed a far more cogent general justification than doctrinal utilitarianism for the principles of Mill's classic argument against overcriminalization.[1] But in addition and perhaps much more importantly, the conception has been used to work out a determinate set of moral principles against which a particular decriminalization controversy can be reasonably tested and assessed. The idea of harm, rather than being an independent simple test of the moral analysis, appears only as a consequence of the moral analysis: the relevant harms, which may justify criminal sanctions, are defined by the relevant moral principles. We are thus disencumbered in our discussion of these issues of the obscurities and vagaries and perhaps circularity of the harm concept, which may have obscured these discussions unnecessarily. In its place, we have elaborated a forthrightly antiutilitarian form of moral analysis based on Kantian respect for persons.[2] This has enabled us not only to engage seriously and with the respect they deserve the arguments of the traditional exponents of criminalization in the areas of sex, drugs, and death, but to afford a kind of moral analysis that questions the consistency of some of these arguments by great philosophers with the deeper premises of their own moral visions.[3]

Our moral arguments, including our investigations of the moral archeology of the assumptions of overcriminalization, are often complex in a manner uncharacteristic of most arguments against overcriminalization. We have included in our account, for example, relevant moral principles regulating our common institutions (principles of justice, for example) and the moral principles of individual duty (for example, nonmaleficence); and we have argued that certain moral principles (for example, of toleration) have a central place in the practical conception of justice embodied in American constitutional democracy. These complex principles define, it is argued, the most stable and defensible shared values of our society. Advocates of overcriminalization are not mistaken in appealing to shared values as relevant to the reasonable discussion of these issues. Their error, we have argued, often is in their absorption in one cluster of rather specific values that are either sectarian, based on assumptions no longer reasonably defensible, or flatly inconsistent with the deeper moral and constitutional premises of respect for persons.[4] The stability of society, to which they appeal, is a desperate identification of these values, now critically under attack, with the enduring and defensible values of a just society. The more critically vulnerable the values, the most desperate is the appeal. Critical moral reflection enables us to see these arguments for what they are—not the moral reasoning of respect for persons, but the willfulness of an ideology whose moral basis is, in fact, suspect, and seen to be suspect.

In addition to these general themes of the previous chapters, we should remark, first, on a characteristic criticism here made of the assumptions of overcriminalization and, second, on a natural objection to my analysis.

I. HUMAN NATURE AND THE MEANING OF LIFE

The characteristic form of our arguments against the overcriminalization of sex, drugs, and death has been to identify certain assumptions, often Augustinian,[5] about the proper forms of conduct, and to assess critically the moral validity of such assumptions as a basis for criminalization. These standard assumptions reflect determinate notions of our nature as human beings, whether pertaining to sexual activity, drug use, or decisions to die. Often, the idea is stated in terms of the sense in which a certain activity is inconsistent with our human nature, and indeed, reduces us to the level of animals, or even lower still.[6] Thus, the activity in question is condemned because it violates some independently specified form of what it is to be human.

These assumptions constitute a common matrix underlying the overcriminalization of sex, drugs, and death. They share not only a common Augustinian provenance,[7] but have a common form and content: the moral norm of our humanity is defined in some functional way (sex is for procreation, drugs are only for relief of physical pain or cure, our lives are solely for the good of others, human or divine). There is a consequent focus on the will, through the strengthening of which we are enabled to drain our selves of the extraneous (the nonhuman, the animal, the appetitive) and direct our energies to the functions that define our role as humans. The modes of achieving such self-control, whether religious or secular, are various but similar in being technologies of the self, as Foucault observes,[8] ways in which aspects of the natural self are refashioned or denied to conform to the functional norm believed to be ideally human. Such ways of thinking about sex, drugs, and death are distinctive of one aspect of the complex cultural heritage that is western culture. Certainly a foreigner to that culture might perceive the depth of controversy surrounding these areas as symptomatic of uniquely western obsessions, fears, and vulnerabilities.[9]

Still another tradition has arisen within western culture, later in origin than the assumptions just discussed, often uneasily merged with these earlier assumptions, and eventually perceived as in sharp tension with, indeed antagonistic to, them. This is the tradition that stretches at least from Pico Della Mirandola's *Oration*[10] to Sartre,[11] a tradition which denies the above form of the thesis of human nature. Instead it claims that the distinguishing mark of our humanity is precisely that we have no such nature or function or preordained script, that the proper task of a human life, if it has any task at all, is to create oneself, to make a life with the freedom, creative imagination, and rationality that constitute the distinctive dignity of our moral personality. In this book, the motive for our argument has been to connect this tradition with the political perspective of human rights and a deeper moral argument for decriminalization. The focal weight that the Pico-Sartre tradition gives to the freedom and rationality of the individual as the creator of his own life *is* the ideal fundamental to the autonomy-based interpretation of treating persons as equals, the basis of the human rights perspective in politics and law. Our argument has been that some of the greatest philosophers of human rights (for example, Kant) have demonstrably failed to perceive the tension, indeed the inconsistency, between the Augustinian functionalist assumptions and their moral ideal of autonomy.[12] John Stuart Mill's *On Liberty* is a great advance in political theory precisely because it identifies and resolves the inconsistency in a moral argument for decriminalization, which on examination is best explained and justified by a coherent elaboration of the autonomy-based interpretation of treating persons as equals.[13]

This interpretation requires both institutional and individual respect for the capacity of persons, as free and rational beings, to decide, reflect on, and revise the structure of their ends and lives, consistent with a like respect for all. The enforcement of the Augustinian assumptions through overcriminalization is a deep moral wrong because it degrades the capacities of moral personality, enforcing through the criminal law conceptions of a valuable life that do not express, indeed contemptuously frustrate, the higher-order interest of persons in the freedom and rational integrity of their own minds, perspectives, and lives.

In our discussion of the right to die, we stated the criticism of the relevant Augustinian assumptions underlying the overcriminalization of death in terms of the failure to respect the fundamental right of persons to determine the meaning of their own lives. We can now generalize these criticisms to the Augustinian assumptions in general. These assumptions draw their intuitive appeal from a kind of metaphysical picture that the ultimate sense of a human life is functionally defined. Such ideas have a natural and uncontroversial sense when we think of artifacts, like knives or tools, whose functions can be analyzed in terms of the human purposes they serve. But the sense of function, on which the Augustinian assumptions rest, is impersonal: its sense is not defined relative to the interests of persons. Indeed, the technologies of the self, which the assumptions naturally require, often mandate the denial and disfigurement of the most basic critical interests of reflective persons. This conception cannot be squared, indeed is inconsistent with, a human rights perspective that foundationally regards the person as an end in himself; it enforces by law an impersonal ideal that would not naturally be adopted by free and rational persons, and indeed inflicts the indignity of disallowing the right of persons independently to determine the meaning of their own lives.

From the perspective of human rights, life may, in the sense required by the Augustinian assumptions, have no meaning: there may be no impersonal function that a moral life must inevitably serve. But there is another sense in which the life of a person can have meaning: the realization of a free person's critically evaluated conception of a valuable life consistent with a decent respect for the rights of others. The meaning of life, in this sense, is a task to be discovered, experimented with, revised, one that engages and fulfills the deepest interests of one's person. In contrast, the Augustinian assumptions require an impersonal script, which drains life of the personal meaning which alone gives it ethical dignity.

There is an ethically sound ground, then, for Pico's and Sartre's claims that man has no nature; certainly the Augustinian functionalism violates basic rights of the person. If man has a nature, it cannot be functionally specified in the Augustinian way; it must, rather, be sought in the freedom and rationality of moral personality.

II. A NATURAL OBJECTION

Some commentators, clearly not unsympathetic to the general argument for decriminalization here defended, might naturally object that the account here given, although itself critical of various ideals not justly enforced through law, appeals to certain perfectionist ideals of the person.[14] If certain conduct violates these ideals, the argument for decriminalization should not extend to them.[15] And even if certain other forms of conduct should justly be decriminalized for rights-based reasons, perhaps the conduct may violate the underlying ideals of the person to some extent, so that the conduct may be discouraged, even if not prohibited.[16]

The idea of the freedom and rationality of the person, which underlies the autonomy-based interpretation of treating persons as equals, is a regulative moral conception: it is a standard by reference to which we organize our moral judgments. There are real intellectual and practical dangers in confusing so minimal and self-critically abstract a moral concept with any familiar notions of perfectionist ideals, either in the philosophical tradition or in unreflective moral discourse.

Philosophically, this conception of rational autonomy is alien to the kind of moral perfectionism familiar in the works of Aristotle and Nietzsche.[17] Rational autonomy does not identify as morally relevant the kinds of intellectual, artistic, and heroic excellences that these philosophers supposed to deserve preeminent moral weight. Rather, such respect for persons is broadly and radically egalitarian in its mandate. Rational autonomy is certainly not the kind of moral or human ideal that we associate with admirable objects of aspiration in saints and heroes.[18] To the contrary, respect for such autonomy is constitutive of the minimum morality of decency incumbent on all persons.[19]

More importantly, rational autonomy, as a tool of philosophically reflective moral criticism, is far removed from the kinds of intuitive judgments about human perfection that inform some unreflective moral thought. In previous chapters, we have argued at some length and in some detail that various uncritical assumptions about proper human conduct, which pervade American law and conventional ways of thinking, are deeply defective and indeed violate basic conceptions of human rights. Rational autonomy, as a tool of reflective moral analysis, was thus often employed in the criticism of the force these assumptions enjoy in American patterns of unjust overcriminalization.

The natural objection fails, I believe, to give sufficient weight to this critical function of the idea of rational autonomy in the moral criticism of specific forms of overcriminalization. In each case, we have critically examined assumptions fundamental to overcriminalization and assessed them in terms of the conception of a free and rational person that they violate. Often, such analyses have revealed that intuitive judgments of degradation rested on mistakes of fact, erroneous arguments, or idiosyncratic ideals. The reasonable lesson to be drawn from such analyses is, I believe, that we should be skeptical about ad hoc and impressionistic appeals to perfectionist judgments that are often unreflective, ill-considered, and morally unimaginative.[20]

The strongest objection should, on such grounds, be taken to the attempt to delimit the force of valid decriminalization arguments narrowly, suggesting there may still be valid ground for discouraging the conduct in question in other ways.[21] Often, the critical analysis of overcriminalization discloses distorted perceptions of facts, cruel stereotypes, and unreasoning prejudice. In some such cases where the underlying cultural heritage has been one of enforced ignorance and distorting stereotype, the same irrational social hatred, now disallowed as a basis for criminal sanctions, may underlie the judgments of discouraging the conduct, perpetuating precisely the heritage of misunderstanding and prejudice that works such injustice.[22] The appeal to intuitive judgments of degradation, with their tendency to distort facts and hystericalize inferences, should be subjected to the same discipline of reason here as that to which it is increasingly subject in the areas of overcriminalization.[23]

III. IN CONCLUSION

Decriminalization arguments have been, I have argued, much less powerful than they can and should be. Such arguments are most securely grounded in the tradition of human rights, a tradition which, in the United States, enjoys a preeminent status as the background morality of the Constitution. Accordingly, the clarification of the connections of such arguments to the human rights perspective is not merely an exercise of political theory; *pari passu*, it reasonably elaborates the deepest and most reflective values of American constitutional traditions, so that an otherwise mysterious constitutional development, the constitutional right to privacy, is securely grounded.

The arguments for decriminalization, which have gained ground in western culture since the political revolutions initiated in the late eighteenth century, are not accidental features of a liberal constitutionalism that seeks to institutionalize respect for human rights. They are elaborations of its deepest values of respect for persons.

NOTES

1. See Chapter 1, supra.
2. For a recent analysis of Mill's argument, which is consistent with this approach, see C. L. Ten, *Mill on Liberty* (1980).
3. See, especially, the critical discussions of Kant at notes 217–51 and text accompanying, Chapter 3, supra (commercial sex), notes 185–217 and text accompanying, Chapter 4, supra (drug use), and notes 136–53 and text accompanying, Chapter 5, supra (death).
4. For a cogent argument that Mill assumed similar distinctions about the concept of shared values, see C. L. Ten, supra note 2, at 86–108. For further criticism, see notes 106–41 and text accompanying, Chapter 2, supra.
5. See, for example, notes 59–69 and text accompanying, Chapter 2, supra (homosexuality), notes 160–68 and text accompanying, Chapter 4, supra (drug use), and notes 88–135 and text accompanying, Chapter 5, supra (death).
6. See sources at note 80, Chapter 2, supra (homosexuality); notes 185–86 and text accompanying, Chapter 4, supra (drug use); notes 139–40 and text accompanying, Chapter 5, supra (death).
7. The claims did not, of course, all originate with Augustine; the unnaturalness of homosexuality, for example, is discussed philosophically by Plato; see note 80, Chapter 2, supra. But Augustine appears to have transmitted and organized these ideas in a way that was focal for the later development of these ideas in western thought.
8. Foucault introduced these ideas at a faculty seminar given at New York University in the fall term of 1980. For a statement of some of the research findings there discussed, see M. Foucault & R. Sennett, "Sexuality and Solitude," *London Review of Books*,

vol. 3, no. 9, 1981, 3–7. See also M. Foucault, *The History of Sexuality,* vol. 1 (R. Hurley trans. 1978).

9. See sources at note 8, supra.

10. See Giovanni Pico Della Mirandola, *Oration on the Dignity of Man* (A. Robert Caponigri trans. 1956).

11. See Jean-Paul Sartre, "Existentialism is a Humanism," in W. Kaufmann, *Existentialism from Dostoevsky to Sartre* 287–311 (1956).

12. See note 3, supra.

13. See Chapter 1, supra.

14. For a systematic development of this thought, see V. Haksar, *Equality, Liberty, and Perfectionism* (1979). Cf. the similar kinds of argument in J. Finnis, *Natural Law and Natural Rights* (1980).

15. Haksar's leading example is eating excrement, p. 166, Haksar, note 14, supra. But he also mentions heroin use (pp. 146, 186, 190, 294, id.), LSD use (pp. 289, 297, id.), "sexual perversions" (pp. 189, 190, 210, 256–57, 260, 263–64), etc.

16. Haksar mentions, for example, homosexual marriage, p. 260, id., as a case where equal rights might on such grounds not be extended. Cf. p. 297, id.

17. For discussion hereof, see Richards, *A Theory of Reasons for Action* 116–17 (1971). See also note 48, Chapter 2, supra.

18. See Richards, supra note 17, ch. 11.

19. See id., chs. 8–10.

20. Particular objection, on this grounds, might be taken to Haksar's drug examples, note 15, supra. Cf. Finnis, supra note 14, on drug addicts (p. 222) and "anti-procreative" sex acts (p. 124, cf. p. 375). For a sustained criticism of assumptions about the degradation of drug users, see notes 185–217 and text accompanying, Chapter 4, supra.

21. Haksar's disfavor of homosexual marriage, see note 16, supra, seems clearly vulnerable to such objections. For a balanced approach to this question, see T. Honoré, *Sex Law* 10, 41–42, 49, 104 (1978).

22. On the application of this analysis to the supposed propriety of forbidding homosexual teachers of the young, see note 99, Chapter 2, supra.

23. See discussion in notes 21 and 22, supra.

Bibliography

Acton, William. *Prostitution*. Edited by Peter Fryer. New York: Praeger, 1969.

Ad Hoc Committee of the Harvard Medical School to Examine the Definition of Brain Death. "A Definition of Irreversible Coma." Pages 11–18 in *Ethical Issues in Death and Dying*, edited by Tom L. Beauchamp and Seymour Perlin. Englewood Cliffs, N.J.: Prentice-Hall, 1978.

Adler, Freda; Adler, Herbert M. (collaborator); and Levine, Hoag (interviewer). *Sisters in Crime: The Rise of the New Female Criminal*. New York: McGraw-Hill, 1975.

Adler, Polly. *A House Is Not a Home*. New York: Rinehart, 1953.

Adorno, Theodore W., et al. *The Authoritarian Personality*. New York: Harper, 1950.

Akers, Stephen R. "The Living Will: Already a Practical Alternative." *Texas Law Review* 55 (March 1977): 665–717.

Allegro, John Marco. *The Sacred Mushroom and the Cross: A Study of the Nature and Origins of Christianity Within the Fertility Cults of the Ancient Near East*. London: Hodder & Stoughton, 1970.

Alvarez, Alfred. *The Savage God: A Study of Suicide*. New York: Random House, 1972.

"American Psychiatric Association Board of Trustees Removes Homosexuality from List of Mental Diseases." *New York Times*, 16 December 1973, Sec. 1, p. 1.

"American Psychiatric Association Membership Approves Action of APA Board." *New York Times*, 9 April 1974, Sec. 1, p. 12.

Aquinas, St. Thomas. "On the Truth of the Catholic Faith." In *Summa Contra Gentiles*. Translated by V. Bourke. San Diego: Providence, 1946.

———. *Opuscula*. Paris: Lethielleux, 1881.

———. "Summa Theologica." In *Aquinas: Selected Political Writings*. Edited by D'Entreues. Oxford: Basil Blackwell, 1959.

———. "Summa Theologica." Translated by Fathers of the Dominican Province. London: Burne, Oates, and Washburne, 1929.

Arenson, R. J. "Mill versus Paternalism." *Ethics* 90 (1980): 470–89.

Aries, Philippe. *The Hour of Our Death*. Translated by H. Weaver. New York: Alfred A. Knopf, 1981.

———. *Western Attitudes Toward Death: From the Middle Ages to the Present*. Translated by Patricia Rahhm. Baltimore: Johns Hopkins University Press, 1874.

Aristotle. *Nicomachean Ethics*. Translated by H. Rackham. London: Heinemann, 1926.

———. *Politics*. Translated by Benjamin Jowett. Rev. ed. New York: Colonial Press, 1900.

Arrow, Kenneth J. "Gifts and Exchanges." *Philosophy and Public Affairs* 1 (Summer 1972): 343–62.

"Artist's Death: A Last Statement in a Thesis on 'Self-Termination.' " *New York Times*, 17 June 1979, p. 1.

Atkinson, Ronald F. *Sexual Morality*. New York: Harcourt, Brace, and World, 1966.

Augustine, Aurelius Saint. *The City of God Against the Pagans*. Cambridge: Harvard University Press, 1957, 1972.

——. *Concerning the City of God Against the Pagans*. Translated by Henry Bettenson. Harmondsworth: Penguin Books, 1972.

——. *De Ordine*. In *Corpus Scriptorum Ecclesiasticorum Latinorum*, vol. 63. New York: Johnson, 1892.

——. *Enchiridion*. Quoted in Durante White Robertson, *A Preface to Chaucer*, n. 74, p. 429. Princeton, N.J.: Princeton University Press, 1962.

Bach, J.S. "Coffee" Cantata. BWV 211.

Bach, Kurt. *Beyond Words*. New York: Russell Sage, 1972.

Baechler, Jean. *Suicides*. Translated by Barry Cooper. New York: Basic Books, 1979.

Baier, Kurt. *The Meaning of Life*. Canberra: Canberra University College, 1957.

——. *The Moral Point of View: A Rational Basis of Ethics*. Ithaca, N.Y.: Cornell University Press, 1958.

Bailey, D. Sherwin. *Homosexuality and the Western Christian Tradition*. Hamden, Conn.: Shoe String, 1955.

Bailyn, Bernard. *The Ideological Origins of the American Revolution*. Cambridge: Belknap Press, 1967.

Bainton, Roland H. "The Churches and Alcohol." In *Alcohol, Science and Society*, Quarterly Journal of Studies on Alcohol (1945): 287–98.

Balint, Michael. *Primary Love and Psychoanalytic Technique*. Enlarged ed. New York: Liveright Publishing, 1965.

Bandman, Bertram, and Bandman, Elise. "Rights, Justice, and Euthanasia." Pages 81–99 in *Beneficent Euthanasia*, edited by Marvin Kohl. Buffalo, N.Y.: Prometheus, 1975.

Bane, Mary Jo. *Here to Stay: American Families in the Twentieth Century*. New York: Basic Books, 1976.

Barnes, John Arundel. *Three Styles in the Study of Kinship*. Berkeley: University of California Press, 1973.

Barnett, Walter. *Sexual Freedom and the Constitution: An Inquiry into the Constitutionality of Repressive Sex Laws*. Albuquerque: University of New Mexico Press, 1973.

Barr, Pat. *To China with Love: The Lives and Times of Protestant Missionaries in China 1860–1900*. London: Secker & Warburg, 1972.

Barre, Weston la. *The Peyote Cult*. 4th ed. New York: Schocken Books, 1975.

Barrett, Ellen M. "Legal Homophobia and the Christian Church." *Hastings Law Journal* 30 (March 1979): 1019–27.

Barrington, Mary Rose. "Apologia for Suicide." Pages 152–70 in *Euthanasia and the Right to Death*, edited by A. B. Downing. London: Peter Owen, 1969.

Baudelaire, Charles P. "Les Paradis Artificels." Pages 16–40 in *The Drug Experience: First-Person Accounts of Addicts, Writers, Scientists and Others*, edited by David Ebin. New York: Grove Press, 1961.

[Baughman, William H; Bruha, John C.; and Gould, Francis J.] "Survey: Euthanasia: Criminal, Tort, Constitutional and Legislative Considerations." *Notre Dame Lawyer* 48 (June 1973): 1202–60.

Bayer, Ronald. "Heroin Decriminalization and the Ideology of Tolerance: A Critical View." *Law and Society Review* 12 (Winter 1978): 301–18.

Bayer, Ronald. *Homosexuality and American Psychiatry: The Politics of Diagnosis*. New York: Basic Books, 1981.

——. "Methadone Under Attack: An Analysis of Popular Literature." *Contemporary Drug Problems* (Fall 1978): 367–400.

Bean, Philip. *The Social Control of Drugs*. Law in Society Series. New York: John Wiley, 1974.

Beauchamp, T. L. "What Is Suicide?" Pages 97–102 in *Ethical Issues in Death and Dying*, edited by Tom L. Beauchamp and Seymour Perlin. Englewoods Cliffs, N.J.: Prentice-Hall, 1978.

Beauchamp, T. L., and Childress, James F. *Principles of Biomedical Ethics*. New York: Oxford University Press, 1979.

Beauvoir, Simone de. *The Second Sex*. Translated and edited by H. M. Parshley. New York: Bantam Books, 1952.

Bechtel, John Hendricks, ed. *Temperance Selections*. Photographic reprint of 1893 ed. Freeport, N.Y.: Books for Libraries Press, 1970.

Becker, Douglas; Fleming, Robert; and Overstreet, Rebecca. "The Legal Aspects of the Right to Die: Before and After the Quinlan Decision." *Kentucky Law Journal* 65 (1976-77): 823–79.

Becker, Howard Saul. *Outsiders: Studies in the Sociology of Deviance*. London: Free Press of Glencoe, 1963.

Beecher, Lyman. *Six Sermons on the Nature, Occasions, Signs, Evils and Remedy of Intemperance*. New York: American Tract Society, 1827; reprint 6th ed. Boston: T. R. Marvin, 1828.

Beitz, Charles R. *Political and International Relations*. Princeton, N.J.: Princeton University Press, 1979.

Bell, Alan P., and Weinberg, Martin S. *Homosexualities: A Study of Diversity Among Men and Women*. New York: Simon & Schuster, 1975.

Benjamin, Harry. "Prostitution." Pages 869–82 in *The Encyclopedia of Sexual Behavior*, edited by Albert Ellis and Albert Abarbanel. New York: American Elsevier, Hawthorn Books, 1961.

Benjamin, Harry, and Masters, R.E.L. *Prostitution and Morality*. New York: Julian Press, 1964.

Benn, Stanley I. "Freedom, Autonomy and the Concept of A Person." *Proceedings of the Aristotelian Society for the Systematic Study of Philosophy* 76 (1976): 109–30.

———. "Privacy, Freedom and Respect for Persons." Pages 1–25 in *Privacy*, edited by J. Roland Pennock and John W. Chapman. New York: Atherton Press, 1971.

Bennett, Jonathan. *Rationality: An Essay Towards an Analysis*. London: Routledge and K. Paul; New York: Humanities Press, 1964.

———. "Whatever the Consequences." Pages 109–24 in *Killing and Letting Die*, edited by Bonnie Steinbock. Englewood Cliffs, N.J. Prentice-Hall, 1980.

Benthall, Jonathan, and Polhemus, Ted, eds. *The Body as a Medium of Expression: Essays Based on a Course of Lectures Given at the Institute of Contemporary Arts, London*. New York: E. P. Dutton, 1975.

Bentham, Jeremy. "Anarchical Fallacies; Being an Examination of the Declaration of Rights Issued During the French Revolution." Pages 489–534 in *The Works of Jeremy Bentham*, vol. 2. New York: Russell & Russell.

———. "Jeremy Bentham's Essay on 'Paederasty' (Part 1)." Edited by Louis Crompton. *Journal of Homosexuality* 4, no. 1 (Fall 1978): 91–107.

———. "Offenses Against One's Self: Paederasty (Part 2)." Edited by Louis Crompton. *Journal of Homosexuality* 3 (Summer 1978): 389.

Berg, Charles. *Fear, Punishment, Anxiety and the Wolfenden Report*. London: Allen & Unwin, 1959.

Berg, Charles, and Allen, Clifford. *The Problem of Homosexuality*. New York: Citadel Press, 1958.

Berridge, Virginia. "Opium and the Historical Perspective." *The Lancet*, 9 July 1977.

Bertocci, Peter. "The Human Venture in Sex, Love, and Marriage." Pages 218–33 in *Today's Moral Problems*, edited by Richard Wasserstrom. New York: Macmillan, 1975.

Bickel, Alexander M. *The Least Dangerous Branch; The Supreme Court at the Bar of Politics*. Indianapolis: Bobbs-Merrill, 1962.

———. *The Morality of Consent*. New Haven: Yale University Press, 1975.

———. "The Original Understanding and the Segregation Decision." *Howard Law Review* 69 (November 1955): 1–65.

———. *The Supreme Court and the Idea of Progress*. New York: Harper & Row, 1970.

Bieber, Irving, et al. *Homosexuality; A Psychoanalytic Study*. Society of Medical Psychoanalysts. New York: Basic Books, 1962.

Black, Peter Mel. "Definitions of Brain Death." Pages 5–11 in *Ethical Issues in Death and Dying*, edited by Tom L. Beauchamp and Seymour Perlin. Englewoods Cliffs, N.J.: Prentice-Hall, 1978.

Blackstone, Sir William. *Commentaries on the Laws of England*. Edited by William Carey Jones. San Francisco: Bancroft-Whitney, 1915–1916.

Bloustein, Edward J. "Privacy as an Aspect of Human Dignity: An Answer to Dean Prosser." *New York University Law Review* 39 (1964): 962–1007.

Blum, Richard. *Drugs*. Vol. 1; *Society and Drugs*. San Francisco: Jossey-Bass, 1969.

[Bostwick, Gary.] "Comment, A Taxonomy of Privacy: Repose, Sanctuary and Intimate Decision." *California Law Review* 64 (1976): 1447–83.

Boswell, John. *Christianity, Social Tolerance, and Homosexuality: Gay People in Western Europe from the Beginning of the Christian Era to the Fourteenth Century.* Chicago: University of Chicago Press, 1980.

Bouscaren, Timothy L.; Ellis, Adam C.; and Korth, Francis N. *Canon Law; A Text and Commentary.* Milwaukee: Bruce Publishing Co., 1963.

Bowlby, John. *Child Care and the Growth of Love.* 2nd ed. Abridged and edited by Margery Fry, with two new chapters by Mary D. Salter Ainsworth. Baltimore: Penguin Books, 1965.

———. *Attachment and Loss.* Vol. 1: *Attachment*, 1971; Vol. 2: *Separation: Anxiety and Anger*, 1975; Vol. 3: *Loss: Sadness and Depression*, 1980. New York: Basic Books.

Brain, Robert. *Friends and Lovers.* New York: Basic Books, 1976.

Brandt, Richard B. *Ethical Theory.* Englewood Cliffs, N.J.: Prentice-Hall, 1959.

———. "A Moral Principle About Killing." Pages 106–14 in *Beneficent Euthanasia*, edited by Marvin Kohl. Buffalo, N.Y.: Prometheus Books, 1975.

———. "The Morality and Rationality of Suicide." Pages 123–33 in *Ethical Issues in Death and Dying*, edited by Tom L. Beauchamp and Seymour Perlin. Englewood Cliffs, N.J.: Prentice-Hall, 1978.

———. *A Theory of the Good and the Right.* New York: Oxford University Press, 1979.

Brashear, Bruce. "Marijuana Prohibition and the Constitutional Right of Privacy: An Examination of *Ravin v. State.*" *Tulsa Law Journal* 11 (1976): 563–86.

Braverman, Harry. *Labor and Monopoly Capital: The Degradation of Work in the Twentieth Century.* New York: Monthly Review Press, 1974.

Brecher, Edward M. *Licit and Illicit Drugs: The Consumers Union Report on Narcotics, Stimulants, Depressants, Inhalants, Hallucinogens, and Marijuana, Including Caffeine, Nicotine and Alcohol.* Boston: Little, Brown, 1972.

———. *The Sex Researchers.* Boston: Little, Brown, 1969.

Bresnahan, James F. "The Interaction of Religion and Law—A Post-Vatican II Roman Catholic Perspective." *Hastings Law Journal* 29 ([part 2] March-July 1978): 1361–82.

Bristow, Edward J. *Vice and Vigilance: Purity Movements in Britain Since 1700.* Totowa, N.J.: Rowman & Littlefield, 1977.

Britton, Karl. *Philosophy and the Meaning of Life.* London: Cambridge University Press, 1969.

Brown, Barbara A., et al. "The Equal Rights Amendment: A Constitutional Basis for Equal Rights for Women." *Yale Law Journal* 80 (April 1971): 871–985.

Brownmiller, Susan. *Against Our Will: Men, Women, and Rape.* New York: Simon & Schuster, 1975.

———. "Speaking Out on Prostitution." *Notes From the Third Year* (1971): 24–25.

Bullough, Vern L. *Homosexuality, a History.* New York: New American Library, 1979.

Bultena, Louis. *Deviant Behavior in Sweden.* New York: Exposition Press, 1966.

Burket, George E., Jr. "Viewpoints: How Do You Extend Treatment to the Spouse of a Patient with VD?" *Medical Aspects of Human Sexuality* 11 (June 1977): 89–97.

Butler, Joseph. "Upon Resentment." Pages 72–79 in *Fifteen Sermons at the Rolls Chapel*, edited by J. Bernard. London: Macmillan, 1913.

Byrn, Robert M. "Compulsory Lifesaving Treatment for the Competent Adult." *Fordham Law Review* 44 (1975–76): 1–36.

Camus, Albert. *The Myth of Sisyphus.* Translated by Justin O'Brien. New York: Random House, Vintage Books, 1955.

Cantor, Norman L. "A Patient's Decision to Decline Life-Saving Medical Treatment: Bodily Integrity Versus the Preservation of Life." *Rutgers Law Review* 26 (Winter 1973): 228–64.

Capellanus, Andreas, *The Art of Courtly Love.* Translated by John Jay Parry. New York: W. W. Norton, 1941.

Cappelletti, Mauro. *Judicial Review in the Contemporary World.* Indianapolis: Bobbs-Merrill, 1971.

Cappelletti, Mauro, and Adams, John Clarke. "Judicial Review of Legislation: European Antecedents and Adaptions." *Harvard Law Review* 79 (April 1966): 1207–24.

Capron, Alexander Morgan, and Kass, Leon R. "A Statutory Definition of the Standards for Determining Human Death: An Appraisal and a Proposal." Pages 60–75 in *Ethical Issues in Death and Dying*, edited by Tom L. Beauchamp and Seymour Perlin. Englewood Cliffs, N.J.: Prentice-Hall, 1978.

Cardozo, Benjamin N. *The Nature of the Judicial Process.* New Haven: Yale University Press, 1921.

Catullus. Poem 57. In *The Poetry of Catullus.* Translated by C. H. Sisson. New York: Orion, 1967.

Caughey, Madeline S. "Criminal Law—The Principle of Harm and Its Application to Laws Criminalizing Prostitution." *Denver Law Journal* 51 (1974): 235–62.

Chang, Albert. "Quiz: Gonorrhea and Sexual Behavior." *Medical Aspects of Human Sexuality* 11 (April 1977): 48–53.

Chao-Kwang Wu. *The International Aspect of the Missionary Movement in China.* Baltimore: Johns Hopkins University Press, 1960.

Charen, Steven C., and Colangelo, John P. "Criminal Law." *Annual Survey of American Law* (1976): 313–57.

Chein, Isador. "Psychological Functions of Drug Use." In *The Scientific Basis of Drug Dependence*, edited by Hannah Steinberg. New York: Grune & Stratton, 1969.

Chein, Isidor; Gerard, Donald L.; Lee, Robert S.; and Rosenfeld, Eva. *The Road to H.* New York: Basic Books, 1964.

Chesney, Kellow. *The Victorian Underworld.* New York: Schocken, 1970.

Chodorow, Nancy. "Family Structure and Feminine Personality." Pages 43–77 in *Woman, Culture, and Society*, edited by Michelle Zimbalist Rosaldo and Louise Lamphere. Stanford: Stanford University Press, 1974.

Choisy, Maryse. *Psychoanalysis of a Prostitute.* New York: Philosophical Library, 1961.

Choron, Jacques. *Death and Western Thought.* New York: Collier, 1963.

———. *Suicide.* New York: Scribner's, 1972.

Churchill, Wainwright. *Homosexual Behavior Among Males: A Cross-Cultural and Cross-Species Investigation.* New York: American Elsevier, Hawthorn Books, 1971.

Clapp, Raymond. "Social Treatment of Prostitutes and Promiscuous Women." *Federal Probation* 7 (April–June 1943): 23–27.

Clarke-Stewart, Allison. *Child Care in the Family: A Review of Research and Some Propositions for Policy.* New York: Academic Press, 1977.

Cocteau, Jean. *Opium: The Diary of a Cure.* Translated by Margaret Crosland and Sinclair Road. New York: Grove, 1958.

Cohn, Norman. *Europe's Inner Demons.* New York: New American Library, 1977.

———. *The Pursuit of the Millennium.* New York: Harper Torchbooks, 1961.

Coleridge, Samuel Taylor. "Dejection: An Ode." Pages 1107–10 in *The Experience of Literature*, edited by Lionel Trilling. New York: Holt, Rinehart & Winston, 1967.

Colvin, D. Leigh. *Prohibition in the United States.* New York: George H. Doran Co. 1926.

Commager, Henry Steele. *The Empire of Reason: How Europe Imagined and America Realized the Enlightenment.* Garden City, N.Y.: Doubleday, 1977.

"Comment: Discrimination in Private Social Clubs: Freedom of Association and Right to Privacy." *Duke Law Journal* (1970): 1181–1222.

Committee on Homosexual Offenses and Prostitution. *The Wolfenden Report.* New York: Stein & Day, 1963.

"The Constitutionality of Laws Forbidding Private Homosexual Conduct." *Michigan Law Review* 72 (August 1974): 1613–37.

Cooper, William. "Deliverance from the Opium Habit." In *Missionary Review of the World* (December 1908): 922–25.

Cott, Nancy F. *The Bonds of Womanhood.* New Haven: Yale University Press, 1977.

Craven, J. Braxton, Jr. "Personhood: The Right to be Let Alone." *Duke Law Journal* (September 1976): 920–49.

Dante. *Vita Nuova.* Translated by M. Musca. Bloomington: Indiana University Press, 1973.

Daube, David. "The Linguistics of Suicide." *Philosophy and Public Affairs* 1 (Summer 1972): 387-437.

David, Nancy. "The Priority of Avoiding Harm." Pages 173–214 in *Killing and Letting Die,* edited by Bonnie Steinbock. Englewood Cliffs, N.J.: Prentice-Hall, 1980.

Decker, John F. *Prostitution: Regulation and Control.* Littleton, Col.: Fred B. Rothman & Co., 1979.

Deisher, Robert. "Homosexual Prostitution." *Medical Aspects of Human Sexuality* 9 (August 1975): 85–88.

Degler, Carl N. *At Odds: Women and the Family in America from the Revolution to the Present.* New York and London: Oxford University Press, 1980.

———. "What Ought To Be and What Was: Women's Sexuality in the Nineteenth Century." *American Historical Review* 79 (December 1974): 1467–90.

Delgado, Richard. "Euthanasia Reconsidered—The Choice of Death as an Aspect of the Right of Privacy." *Arizona Law Review* 17 (1975): 474–94.

Deutsch, Helene. *The Psychology of Women,* vol. 1. New York: Bantam Books, 1973.

"Developments in the Law—Equal Protection." *Harvard Law Review* 82 (1969): 1065–1192.

Devine, Philip E. *The Ethics of Homicide.* Ithaca, N.Y.: Cornell University Press, 1978.

Devlin, Patrick. *The Enforcement of Morals.* London: Oxford University Press, 1965.

Dinello, Daniel. "On Killing and Letting Die." Pages 128-31 in *Killing and Letting Die,* edited by Bonnie Steinbock. Englewood Cliffs, N.J.: Prentice-Hall, 1980.

Dole, Vincent P. "Addictive Behavior." *Scientific American* 243 (December 1980): 138–54.

Donagan, Alan. *The Theory of Morality.* Chicago: University of Chicago Press, 1978.

Donne, John. *Biathanatos.* New York: The Facsimile Text Society, 1930.

Dostoevsky, Fyodor. *The Possessed.* Translated by Avrahm Yarmolinsky. New York: The Heritage Press, 1959.

Douglas, Ann. *The Feminization of American Culture.* New York: Alfred A. Knopf, 1977.

Douglas, Jack D. *The Social Meanings of Suicide.* Princeton, N.J.: Princeton University Press, 1967.

———. *Youth in Turmoil.* Washington, D.C.: U.S. Government Printing Office, 1970.

Dover, K. J. *Greek Popular Morality in the Time of Plato and Aristotle.* Oxford: Basil Blackwell, 1974.

Drew, Dennis, and Drake, J. *Boys for Sale: A Sociological Study of Boy Prostitution.* New York: Brown Book Co., 1969.

Driver, Samuel. *Deuteronomy.* Edinburgh: Clark, 1896.

Durkheim, Emile. *Suicide: A Study in Sociology.* Translated by John A. Spaulding and George Simpson. New York: Free Press, 1951.

Duster, Troy. *The Legislation of Morality: Law, Drugs, and Moral Judgment.* New York: The Free Press, 1970.

Dworkin, G. "Acting Freely." *Nous* 4 (1970).

———. "Autonomy and Behavior Control." *Hastings Center Report* 6 (February 1976): 23–28.

———. "Paternalism." Pages 107–26 in *Morality and the Law,* edited by Richard A. Wasserstrom. Belmont, Cal.: Wadsworth Publishing Co., 1971.

Dworkin, Ronald. "Liberalism." Pages 113–43 in *Public and Private Morality,* edited by Stuart Hampshire. Cambridge: Cambridge University Press, 1978.

———. "Lord Devlin and the Enforcement of Morals." *Yale Law Journal* 75 (1966): 986.

———. *Taking Rights Seriously.* Cambridge, Mass.: Harvard University Press, 1977.

Educational Broadcasting Corporation. *VD Blues.* New York: Avon Books, 1972.

East, Sir William. *Society and the Criminal.* London: H. M. Stationery Office, 1949.

Edwards, Paul. *Heidegger on Death: A Critical Evaluation* (Monist Monograph No. 1 1979) La Salle, Ill.: The Hegeler Institute, 1979.

———. "Life, Meaning and Value of." Pages 467–77 in vol. 4, *Encyclopedia of Philosophy,* edited by Paul Edwards. New York: Macmillan and the Free Press, 1967.

———. "My Death." Pages 416–19 in vol. 5, *Encyclopedia of Philosophy,* edited by Paul Edwards. New York: Macmillan and the Free Press, 1967.

Eisenberg, Paul D. "From the Forbidden to the Supererogatory: The Basic Ethical Categories in Kant's Tugendlehre." *American Philosophical Quarterly* 3 (October 1966): 255–69.

Elliott, Neil. *Sensuality in Scandinavia.* New York: Weybright and Talley, 1970.

Ellis, Havelock. *Studies in the Psychology of Sex.* Philadelphia: Davis, 1910.

Ely, John Hart. "The Wages of Crying Wolf: A Comment on *Roe v. Wade." Yale Law Journal* 82 (April 1973): 920–49.

Emboden, William. *Narcotic Plants.* New York: Collier Books, 1979.

Engelhardt, H. Tristram, Jr. "Ethical Issues in Aiding the Death of Young Children." Pages 81–91 in *Killing and Letting Die,* edited by Bonnie Steinbock. Englewood Cliffs, N.J.: Prentice-Hall, 1980.

———. "The Ontology of Abortion." Pages 318–34 in *Moral Problems in Medicine,* edited by Samuel Gorovitz et al. Englewood Cliffs, N.J.: Prentice-Hall, 1976.

Engels, Frederick. *The Origin of the Family, Private Property, and the State.* New York: Pathfinder Press, 1972.

Epicurus. "Letter to Menoeceus." Pages 30–33 in *The Stoic and Epicurean Philosophers,* edited by Whitney J. Oates. New York: The Modern Library, 1940.

Epstein, Edward Jay. *Agency of Fear: Opiates and Political Power in America.* New York: G. P. Putnam's Sons, 1977.

"Equal Rights for Women: A Symposium on the Proposed Constitutional Amendment." *Harvard Civil Rights–Civil Liberties Law Review* 6 (March 1971): 215–87.

Ericsson, Lars O. "Charges Against Prostitution: An Attempt at a Philosophical Assessment." *Ethics* 90 (April 1980): 335–66.

Erikson, Erik. *Childhood and Society.* 2nd ed. New York: W. W. Norton, 1963.

Erikson, Kai. *Wayward Puritans.* New York: John Wiley, 1966.

Esselstyn, T. *Prostitution in the United States.* Page 112 in *Sex and Society,* edited by John Edwards. Chicago, Ill.: Markham Publishing Co., 1972.

Euripides. *The Bacchae.* In *The Bacchae and Other Plays,* translated by Philip Vellacott. Harmondsworth: Penguin Books, 1954.

"The Evidence Builds Against Marijuana." *New York Times,* 21 May 1981, p. 1.

Farson, Richard. *Birthrights.* New York: Macmillan, 1974.

Fay, Peter Ward. *The Opium War 1840–1942.* New York: W. W. Norton, 1975.

Fedden, Henry Romilly. *Suicide: A Social and Historical Study.* New York: Benjamin Blom, 1972.

Federal Bureau of Investigation. *Crime in the United States—1972.* Washington, D.C.: Federal Bureau of Investigation, 1974.

Feifel, Herman, et al. "Physicians Consider Death." *Proceedings of the American Psychiatric Society* 2 (1967): 201–2.

Feinberg, Joel. "Abortion." Pages 183–217 in *Matters of Life and Death,* edited by Tom Regan. New York: Random House, 1980.

———. *Doing and Deserving.* Princeton, N.J.: Princeton University Press, 1970.

———. "Harm and Self-Interest." Pages 289–308 in *Law Morality and Society: Essays in Honour of H.L.A. Hart,* edited by P.M.S. Hacker and J. Raz. Oxford: Clarendon Press, 1977.

———. "Legal Paternalism." *Canadian Journal of Philosophy* 1 (1971): 105–24.

Feldman, Harvey W. "Ideological Supports to Becoming and Remaining a Heroin Addict." *Drug Dependence* (March 1970): 3–11.

Feldman, Yehudi. "VD Prophylaxis via Drugs." *Medical Aspects of Human Sexuality* 11 (May 1977): 100.

Fenichel, Otto. *The Psychoanalytic Theory of Neurosis.* New York: W. W. Norton, 1945.

Fingarette, Herbert. "Addiction and Criminal Responsibility." *Yale Law Journal* 84 (January 1975): 413–44.

Finnis, John. *Natural Law and Natural Rights.* Oxford, Clarendon Press, 1980.

Firestone, Shulamith. *The Dialectic of Sex.* New York: Bantam Books, 1972.

Fisher, Seymour. *The Female Orgasm.* New York: Basic Books, 1973.

Fisher, Seymour, and Greenberg, Roger P. *The Scientific Credibility of Freud's Theories and Therapy.* New York: Basic Books, 1977.

Fitzgerald, P. J. "Acting and Refraining." Pages 284–89 in *Moral Problems in Medicine,* edited by Samuel Gorovitz et al. Englewood Cliffs, N.J.: Prentice-Hall, 1976.

Fitzhugh, George. "Sociology for the South." Pages 34–50 in *Slavery Defended,* edited by Eric L. McKitrick. Englewood Cliffs, N.J.: Prentice-Hall, 1963.

Fletcher, George. *Rethinking Criminal Law*. Boston: Little, Brown, 1978.
———. "Prolonging Life." Pages 226–40 in *Ethical Issues in Death and Dying*, edited by Robert F. Weir. New York: Columbia University Press, 1977.
Fletcher, Joseph. *Morals and Medicine*. Princeton, N.J.: Princeton University Press, 1954.
Flew, Anthony. "The Principle of Euthanasia." Pages 30-48 in *Euthanasia and the Right to Death*, edited by A. B. Downing. London: Peter Owen, 1969.
Flexner, Abraham. *Prostitution in Europe*. Montclair, N.J.: Patterson Smith Publishing Corp., 1914.
Foot, P. R. "Euthanasia." Pages 14–40 in *Ethical Issues Relating to Life and Death*, edited by John Ladd. New York-London: Oxford University Press, 1979.
———. "Moral Arguments." *Mind* 67 (October 1958): 502–13.
———. "The Problem of Abortion and the Doctrine of Double Effect." Pages 156–65 in *Killing and Letting Die*, edited by Bonnie Steinbock. Englewood Cliffs, N.J.: Prentice-Hall, Inc., 1980.   .
Foot, P. R., and Harrison, Jonathan. "Symposium: When Is a Principle a Moral Principle." *Aristotelian Society Supplementary* 28 (9–11 July 1954): 95–134.
Ford, Clellan S. "Sex Offences: An Anthropological Perspective." *Law and Contemporary Problems* 25 (Spring 1960): 225–43.
Ford, Clellan S., and Beach, Frank A. *Patterns of Sexual Behavior*. New York: Harper & Row, 1951.
"Former Sponsor of Abolition of French Brothels Seeks Their Reinstitution." *International Herald Tribune*, 25–26 August 1973, p. 5.
Foucault, Michel. *The Archaeology of Knowledge*. Translated by A. M. Sheridan Smith. New York: Harper & Row, 1972.
———. *The History of Sexuality*. Vol. 1: *An Introduction*, trans. by Robert Hurley. New York: Pantheon Books, 1978.
Foucault, Michel, and Sennett, Richard. "Sexuality and Solitude." *London Review of Books* 3, no. 9 (21 May to 3 June 1981): 3–7.
Fourier, Charles. *The Utopian Vision of Charles Fourier*. Translated by Jonathan Beecher and Richard Bienvenu. Boston: Beacon Press, 1971.
Frankel, Viktor E. *Man's Search for Meaning*. New York: Pocket Books, 1959.
Frankfort, Henri, et al. *Before Philosophy*. Baltimore: Penguin Books, 1961.
———. *Kingship and the Gods*. Chicago: University of Chicago Press, 1948.
Frankfurt, Harry G. "Freedom of the Will and the Concept of a Person." *Journal of Philosophy* 68, no. 1 (14 January 1971): 5–20.
"French Brothels." *New York Times*, 16 August 1970, p. 13.
"French Brothels." *Time* Magazine, 9 November 1970, p. 30.
Freud, Anna. *The Ego and the Mechanisms of Defense*. Translated by Cecil Baines. New York: International Universities Press, 1946.
Freud, Sigmund. "The Psychogenesis of a Case of Homosexuality in a Woman." Pages 145–72 in Vol. 18, *The Complete Psychological Works of Sigmund Freud*, trans. by James Strachey. Standard ed. 1920. London: Hogarth Press, 1955.
———. *Civilization and its Discontents*. Pages 64–145 in vol. 21, *The Complete Psychological Works of Sigmund Freud*, trans. by James Strachey. Standard ed. 1939. London: The Hogarth Press, 1961.
———. *'Civilized' Sexual Morality and Modern Nervous Illness*. Pages 181–204 in vol. 9, *The Complete Psychological Works of Sigmund Freud*, trans. by James Strachey. Standard ed. 1908. London: The Hogarth Press, 1959.
———. *The Ego and the Id*. Pages 12–66 in vol. 19, *The Complete Psychological Works of Sigmund Freud*, trans. by James Strachey. Standard ed. 1923. London: The Hogarth Press, 1961.
———. *Inhibitions, Symptoms and Anxiety*. Pages 87–172 in vol. 20, *The Complete Psychological Works of Sigmund Freud*, trans. by James Strachey. Standard ed. 1926. London: The Hogarth Press, 1959.
———. *Introductory Lectures on Psycho-Analysis*. In volumes 15 & 16, *Complete Psychological Works of Sigmund Freud*, trans. by James Strachey. Standard ed. 1915–17. London: The Hogarth Press, 1961, 1963.

———. "Leonardo da Vinci and a Memory of his Childhood." Pages 63–137 in vol. 11, *The Complete Psychological Works of Sigmund Freud*, trans. by James Strachey. Standard ed. 1910. London: The Hogarth Press, 1957.

———. *Letters of Sigmund Freud 1873–1939.* Edited by Ernst Freud. Translated by Tania and James Stern. New York: Basic Books, 1961.

———. "Mourning and Melancolia." Pages 243–58 in vol. 14, *The Standard Edition of the Complete Psychological Works of Sigmund Freud*, trans. by James Stachey. Standard ed. 1917. London: The Hogarth Press, 1957.

———. *New Introductory Lectures on Psycho-Analysis.* Pages 7–182 in vol. 22, *The Complete Psychological Works of Sigmund Freud*, trans. by James Strachey. Standard ed. 1933. London: The Hogarth Press, 1964.

———. *An Outline of Psychoanalysis.* Pages 144–207 in vol. 23, *The Complete Psychological Works of Sigmund Freud*, trans. by James Strachey. Standard ed. 1940. London: The Hogarth Press, 1964.

———. "A Special Type of Choice of Object Made by Men." Pages 165–75 in vol. 11, *The Complete Psychological Works of Sigmund Freud*, trans. by James Strachey. Standard ed. 1910. London: The Hogarth Press, 1957.

———. "On the Universal Tendency to Debasement in the Sphere of Love." Pages 79–90 in vol. 11, *The Complete Psychological Works of Sigmund Freud*, trans. by James Strachey. Standard ed. 1912. London: The Hogarth Press, 1957.

———. "Thoughts for the Times on War and Death." Pages 275–300 in vol. 14, *The Complete Psychological Works of Sigmund Freud*, trans. by James Strachey. Standard ed. 1915. London: The Hogarth Press, 1957.

———. *Three Essays on Sexuality.* Pages 135–243 in vol. 7, *The Complete Psychological Works of Sigmund Freud*, trans. by James Strachey. Standard ed. 1905. London: The Hogarth Press, 1953.

Fried, Charles. *An Anatomy of Values.* Cambridge: Harvard University Press, 1970.

———. *Contract as Promise.* Cambridge: Harvard University Press, 1981.

———. *Right and Wrong.* Cambridge: Harvard University Press, 1978.

Fromm, Erich. *Escape from freedom.* New York: Avon Books, 1941.

Gandy, Patrick, and Deisler, Robert. "Young Male Prostitutes: The Physician's Role in Social Rehabilitation." *Journal of the American Medical Association* 212 (8 June 1970): 1661–66.

Gardiner, Harold C. *Catholic Viewpoint on Censorship.* Garden City, N.Y.: Hanover House, 1958.

———. "Moral Principles Towards a Definition of the Obscene." *Law and Contemporary Problems* 20 (Autumn 1955): 560–71. Durham, N.C.: The Seeman Printery, 1955.

Gauthier, David P. *Practical Reasoning.* Oxford: Clarendon Press, 1963.

Gay Academic Union. *Homosexuality, Intolerance, and Christianity.* Gai Saber Monograph No. 1. New York: Gay Academic Union, 1981.

Gebhard, P.; Pomeroy, W.; and Christenson, C. *Sex Offender.* New York: Harper & Row, 1965.

Gelinas, A. J. Alexis. "*Roe v. Wade* and *Doe v. Bolton:* The Compelling State Interest Test in Substantive Due Process." *Washington and Lee Law Review* 30 (Fall 1973): 628–46.

George, B. J., Jr. "Medical and Psychiatric Considerations in the Control of Prostitution." *Michigan Law Review* 60 (April 1962): 717–60.

Gerety, T. "Redefining Privacy." *Harvard Civil Rights and Civil Liberties Law Review* 12 (1977): 233–96.

Gert, Bernard. *The Moral Rules.* New York: Harper & Row, 1970.

Gewirth, Alan. "The Basis and Content of Human Rights." *Georgia Law Review* 13 (Summer 1979): 1143–70.

———. *Reason and Morality.* Chicago: University of Chicago Press, 1978.

Giannella, Donald. "Religious Liberty, Nonestablishment, and Doctrinal Development: Part I. The Religious Liberty Guarantee." *Harvard Law Review* 80 (May 1967): 1381–1431.

Gillon, R. "Suicide and Voluntary Euthanasia: Historical Perspective." Pages 173–92 in *Euthanasia and the Right to Death*, edited by A. Downing. London: Peter Owen, 1969.

Ginsberg, A. "First Manifesto to End the Bringdown." Pages 230–48 in *The Marihuana Papers,* edited by David Solomon. Indianapolis: Bobbs-Merrill, 1966.

Glover, Edward. *On the Early Development of the Human Mind.* New York: International Universities Press, 1956.

Glover, Jonathan. *Causing Death and Saving Lives.* New York: Penguin Books, 1977.

Goldberg, Herbert. *The Hazards of Being Male.* New York: Nash Publishing, 1976.

Goldstein, Joseph; Freud, Anna; and Solnit, Albert J. *Beyond the Best Interests of the Child .* New York: Free Press, 1973.

Goodman, Louis S., and Gilman, Alfred G. *The Pharmacological Basis of Therapeutics.* 6th Ed. New York: Macmillan, 1980.

Gorer, Geoffrey. *The Danger of Equality .* London: Cresset Press, 1966.

———. *Death, Grief, and Mourning in Contemporary Britain.* London: Cresset Press, 1965.

Graham, Kathleen M. "Security Clearances for Homosexuals." *Stanford Law Review* 25 (February 1973): 403–29.

Greenwald, Harold. *The Elegant Prostitute.* New York: Walker, 1970.

Grey, Thomas C. "Do We Have an Unwritten Constitution?" *Stanford Law Review* 27 (1975): 703–18.

Grice, Geoffrey R. *The Grounds of Moral Judgment.* Cambridge: Cambridge University Press, 1967.

Grinspoon, Lester. *Marihuana Reconsidered.* Cambridge: Harvard University Press, 1971.

Grinspoon, Lester, and Bahalar, James. *Cocaine: A Drug and Its Social Evolution.* New York: Basic Books, 1976.

———. *Psychedelic Drugs Reconsidered.* New York: Basic Books, 1979.

Grotius, Hugo. "Prolegomenon" to *De Jure Belli et Pacis.* Translated by William Whewell. Cambridge: Cambridge University Press, 1853.

Group for the Advancement of Psychiatry. *The Right to Die: Decision and Decision Makers.* New York: Mental Health Materials Center for the Group for the Advancement of Psychiatry, 1973.

Grube, George M. *Plato's Thought.* Boston: Beacon Press, 1964.

Gusfield, Joseph R. "On Legislating Morals: the Symbolic Process of Designating Deviance." *California Law Review* 56 (April 1968): 54–73.

———. *Symbolic Crusade: Status Politics and the American Temperance Movement.* Urbana: University of Illinois Press, 1963.

Gustafson, James M. "Mongolism, Parental Desires, and the Right to Life." Pages 147–72 in *Ethical Issues in Death and Dying,* edited by Robert F. Weir. New York: Columbia University Press, 1977.

Haft, Marilyn G. "Hustling for Rights." *Civil Liberties Review* 1 (Winter/Spring, 1974): 8–26.

Haksar, Vinit. *Equality, Liberty, and Perfectionism.* New York: Oxford University Press, 1979.

Hall, Jerome. *General Principles of Criminal Law.* 2nd ed. Indianapolis: Bobbs-Merrill, 1960.

Haller, John S., and Haller, Robin M. *The Physician and Sexuality in Victorian America.* Urbana: University of Illinois Press, 1974.

Hamburger, Gerd. *The Peking Bomb.* Translated by Sarah Banks Forman. Washington: R. B. Luce, 1975.

Hamilton, Alexander. "Federalist No. 78." In *The Federalist Papers,* by Alexander Hamilton, James Madison, and John Jay. Garden City, N.Y.: Doubleday, 1948.

Hammaker, Wilbur E. et al. *The Christian Case for Abstinence.* New York: Associated Press, 1955.

Hand, Learned. *The Bill of Rights.* Cambridge: Harvard University Press, 1958.

Haney, Robert W. *Comstockery in America.* Boston: Beacon Press, 1960.

"Happy and Healthy Harlots." *Human Behavior* (August 1978), pp. 7–66.

Hare, Richard Mervyn. *Freedom and Reason.* New York: Oxford University Press, 1965.

———. *The Language of Morals.* Oxford: Clarendon Press, 1952.

Harner, Michael J., ed. *Hallucinogens and Shamanism.* New York: Oxford University Press, 1973.

———. *The Way of the Shaman*. San Francisco: Harper & Row, 1980.

Hart, H. L. A. "Are There Any Natural Rights?" Pages 173–86 in *Society, Law and Morality*, edited by Frederick A Olofson. Englewood Cliffs, N.J.: Prentice-Hall, 1961.

———. "Bentham on Legal Rights." Pages 170–201 in *Oxford Essays in Jurisprudence*, edited by Alfred W. Simpson. 2nd series. Oxford: Clarendon Press, 1973.

———. "Between Utility and Rights." In *The Idea of Freedom*, edited by Alan Ryan. New York: Oxford University Press, 1979.

———. *Law, Liberty, and Morality*. Stanford, Cal.: Stanford University Press, 1963.

———. *Punishment and Responsibility*. Oxford: Clarendon Press, 1968.

———. "Social Solidarity and the Enforcement of Morality." *University of Chicago Law Review* 35 (Autumn 1967): 1–12.

Hart,Henry M. "The Aims of the Criminal Law." *Law and Contemporary Problems* 23 (Winter 1958): 401–41.

Hart, Henry M., and Sacks, Albert M. *The Legal Process: Basic Problems in the Making and Application of Law*. Tentative edition. Cambridge, Massachusetts 1958.

Hartmann, Heinz. *Ego Psychology and the Problem of Adaptation*. Translated by David Rapaport. New York: International Universities Press, 1958.

Hatterer, Laurence J. *Changing Homosexuality in the Male*. New York: McGraw-Hill, 1970.

Hayter, Alethea. *Opium and the Romantic Imagination*. Berkeley: University of California Press, 1968.

Heffern, Richard. *Secrets of the Mind-Altering Plants of Mexico*. New York: Pyramid Books, 1974.

(Hegland, Renney.) "Comment, Unauthorized Rendition of Lifesaving Medical Treatment." *California Law Review* 53 (1965): 860–77.

Heidegger, Martin. *Being and Time*. Translated by John Macquarrie and Edward Robinson. New York: Harpers, 1962.

Heilbrun, Carolyn G. *Toward a Recognition of Androgyny*. New York: Alfred A. Knopf, 1973.

Henderson, Jeffrey. *The Maculate Muse: Obscene Language in Attic Comedy*. New Haven: Yale University Press, 1975.

Hendin, Herbert. *The Age of Sensation*. New York: W. W. Norton, 1975.

Henkin, Louis. "Morals and the Constitution." *Columbia Law Review* 63 (March 1963): 391–414.

Henriques, Fernando. *Prostitution and Society*. London: MacGibbon and Kee, 1962.

Henry, George William. *All the Sexes*. New York: Rinehart, 1955.

Herdt, Gilbert H. *Guardians of the Flutes: Idioms of Masculinity*. New York: McGraw-Hill, 1981.

Heroditus. *Histories*. Translated by Henry Cary. New York: Appleton, 1899.

Hill, Christopher. *The World Turned Upside Down: Radical Ideas During the English Revolution*. New York: Viking Press, 1972.

Hillman, James. *Suicide and the Soul*. New York: Harper & Row, 1964.

Hirschfeld, John C. "Criminal Law—Euthanasia—Defendant Allowed to Withdraw Guilty Plea of Manslaughter to Accommodate Finding of Not Guilty on Arraignment." *Notre Dame Lawyer* 34 (May 1959): 460–64.

Hofmann, Albert. *LSD: My Problem Child*. Translated by Jonathan Ott. New York: McGraw-Hill, 1980.

Hoffman, Martin. *The Gay World*. New York: Bantam Books, 1968.

Holmes, Oliver Wendell. *The Common Law*. 2nd Edition. Cambridge, Mass.: Belknap Press, 1963.

———. "The Path of the Law." Pages 167–202 in *Collected Legal Papers*. New York: Harcourt, Brace, and Howe, 1912.

———. "The Path of the Law." *Harvard Law Review* 10 (1897): 457–78.

"Homosexuals Barred from Military." *New York Times* , 23 December 1973, Sec. 4, p. 5.

Honoré, Antony Maurice. *Sex Law*. London: Duckworth, 1978.

Hooker, Evelyn. "The Adjustment of the Male Overt Homosexual." *Journal of Projective Techniques* 21 (March 1957): 18–31.

Hopkins, Gerard Manley. *Poems and Prose*. Edited by W. H. Gardner. Harmondsworth: Penguin Books, 1954.

Hume, David. "The Decline and Fall of the Roman Empire." Pages 309–11 in *The Letters of David Hume*, edited by J. Grieg. Vol. 2. Oxford: Clarendon Press, 1932.

———. "My Own Life." Pages 234–40 in *Hume's Dialogues Concerning Natural Religion*, edited by Norman K. Smith. Oxford: Clarendon Press, 1935.

———. "On Suicide." Pages 593–94 in *Essays Moral, Political, and Literary*. London: Oxford University Press, 1963.

———. *A Treatise of Human Nature*. Book III, Pt. 2, §11. Reprinted in *Society, Law and Morality*, pp. 307–19. Edited by Frederick A. Olafson. Englewood Cliffs, N.J.: Prentice-Hall, 1961.

Humphreys, Laud. *Tearoom Trade*. Chicago: Aldine Publishing Co., 1970.

Huxley, Aldous. *The Doors of Perception*. New York: Harper, 1954.

Ignatius, Saint. *St. Ignatius' Own Story*. Translated by William J. Young, S.J. Chicago: Loyola University Press, 1956.

Irwin, Samuel. "A Rational Approach to Drug Abuse Prevention." *Contemporary Drug Problems* 2 (Spring 1973): 3–46.

Jacobsohn, Gary J. *Pragmatism, Statesmanship, and the Supreme Court*. Ithaca, N.Y.: Cornell University Press, 1977.

James, Jennifer. "Answers to the 20 Questions Most Frequently Asked About Prostitution." In *The Politics of Prostitution*, edited by Jennifer James, Jean Withers, and Sara Theiss. Seattle, Wash.: Social Research Associates, 1975.

———. "Motivations for Entrance into Prostitution." Pages 177–206 in *The Female Offender*, edited by Laura Crites. Lexington, Mass.: Lexington Books, 1976.

James, William. *The Varieties of Religious Experience*. New York: Collier Books, 1961.

Janeway, Elizabeth. *Man's World, Woman's Place*. New York: William Morrow, 1971.

Janus, Sam; Bess, Barbara; and Saltus, Carol. *A Sexual Profile of Men in Power*. Englewood Cliffs, N.J.: Prentice-Hall, 1977.

Jenkins, David. *Sweden and the Price of Progress*. New York: Coward-McCann, 1968.

Jennings, M. Anne. "The Victim as Criminal: A Consideration of California's Prostitution Law." *California Law Review* 64 (September 1976): 1235–84.

Johnson, Bruce D. "Once an Addict, Seldom an Addict." *Contemporary Drug Problems* 7 (Spring 1978): 35–53.

Jonas, Hans. "Against the Stream: Comments on the Definition and Redefinition of Death." Pages 51–60 in *Ethical Issues in Death and Dying*, edited by Tom Beauchamp and Seymour Perlin. Englewood Cliffs, N.J.: Prentice-Hall, 1978.

———. *The Gnostic Religion*. 2d. ed., revised. Boston: Beacon Press, 1963.

Judson, Horace Freeland. *Heroin Addiction in Britain*. New York: Harcourt, Brace, Jovanovich, 1974.

Julien, Robert M. *A Primer of Drug Action*. 2nd ed. San Francisco: W. H. Freeman, 1978.

Junker, John M. "Criminalization and Criminogenesis." *U.C.L.A. Law Review* 19 (April 1972): 697–714.

Kadish, Mortimer R., and Kadish, Sanford H. *Discretion to Disobey*. Stanford, Cal.: Stanford University Press, 1973.

Kadish, Sanford. "The Crisis of Overcriminalization." *Annals* 374 (1967): 157.

———. "More on Overcriminalization: A Reply to Professor Junker." *U.C.L.A. Law Review* 19 (April 1972): 719–22.

Kamisar, Yale. "Some Non-Religious Views Against Proposed 'Mercy-Killing' Legislation." *Minnesota Law Review* 42 (1958): 969–1042.

Kanowitz, Leo. "Buyers of the Bodies of Women." In *Women and Law*, edited by Leo Kanowitz. Albuquerque: University of New Mexico Press, 1969.

———. *Women and the Law*. Albuquerque: University of New Mexico Press, 1969.

Kant, Immanuel. "Concerning the Common Saying: This May Be True in Theory, But Does Not Apply in Practice." Pages 159–72 in *Society, Law and Morality*, edited by Frederick A. Olafson. Englewood Cliffs, N.J.: Prentice-Hall, 1961.

———. *Critique of Practical Reason*. Translated by Lewis White Beck. New York: Liberal Arts Press, 1956.

———. *Foundations of the Metaphysics of Morals*. Translated by Lewis White Beck. New York: Liberal Arts Press, 1959.

———. *Lectures on Ethics*. Translated by Louis Infield. New York: Harper & Row, 1963.

————. *The Metaphysical Principles of Virtue.* Translated by James Ellington. Indianapolis: Bobbs-Merrill, 1964.

————. *The Metaphysics of Morals.* Translated by John Ladd. Indianapolis: Bobbs-Merrill, 1965.

Kaplan, John. *Marijuana: The New Prohibition.* New York: World Publishing Co., 1970.

Kaplan, Ronald P. "Euthanasia Legislation: A Survey and a Model Act." *American Journal of Law and Medicine* 2 (Winter 1976): 41–99.

Kapner, Erik. "Proposed State Euthanasia Statutes: A Philosophical and Legal Analysis." *Hofstra Law Review* 3 (Winter 1975): 115–40.

Karpman, Benjamin. *The Sexual Offender and His Offenses.* New York: Julian Press, 1954.

Karst, K. I. "The Freedom of Intimate Association." *Yale Law Journal* 89 (1980): 624–92.

Katchadourian, Herant, and Lunde, Donald T. *Fundamentals of Human Sexuality.* New York: Holt, Rinehart, & Winston, 1975.

Kauper, Paul G. "The Supreme Court: Hybrid Organ of State." *Southwestern Law Journal* 21 (Summer 1967): 573–90.

Kaye, Harvey E. *Male Survival: Masculinity Without Myth.* New York: Grosset & Dunlap, 1974.

Kearon, Pamela, and Mehrhof, Barbara. "Prostitution." *Notes from the Third Year* (1971): 26–28.

Kelley, G. *Medico-Moral Problems.* Dublin: Clonmore & Reynolds, 1955.

Kelly, Henry Ansgar. *Love and Marriage in the Age of Chaucer.* Ithaca, N.Y.: Cornell University Press, 1975.

Kermode, John Frank. *The Genesis of Secrecy: On the Interpetation of Narrative.* Cambridge: Harvard University Press, 1979.

Kett, Joseph F. *Rites of Passage: Adolescence in America, 1790 to the Present.* New York: Basic Books, 1977.

Kiefer, Otto. *Sexual Life in Ancient Rome.* Translated by Gilbert and Helen Highet. London: Abbey Library, 1934.

Kinsey, Alfred Charles; Pomeroy, Wardell B.; and Martin, Clyde E. *Sexual Behavior in the Human Female.* Philadelphia: W. B. Saunders, Co., 1953.

————. *Sexual Behavior in the Human Male.* Philadelphia: W. B. Saunders, Co., 1948.

"Kinsey Finds Homosexuals Show Deep Predisposition." *New York Times,* 23 August 1981, pp. 1, 30.

"Kinsey May Have Overstated Incidence of Homosexuality." *Playboy,* March 1974 , pp. 54-55.

Kittrie, Nicholas N. *The Right to Be Different.* Baltimore: Johns Hopkins University Press, 1971.

Kluge, Eike-Henner. *The Practice of Death.* New Haven: Yale University Press, 1975.

Kneeland, George Jackson. *Commercialized Prostitution in New York City.* New York: The Century Co., 1913.

Knight, Edward H. "Overt Male Homosexuality." Pages 434–61 in *Sexual Behavior and the Law,* edited by Ralph Slovenko. Springfield, Ill.: Thomos, 1965.

Kobler, John. *Ardent Spirits: The Rise and Fall of Prohibition.* New York: G. P. Putnam's Sons, 1973.

Kohl, Marvin. *The Morality of Killing.* New York: Humanities Press, 1974.

————, ed. *Beneficent Euthanasia.* Buffalo, N.Y.: Prometheus Books, 1975.

Kohlberg, Lawrence. "Education for Justice: A Modern Statement of the Platonic View." Pages 57–83 in *Moral Education: Five Lectures,* edited by T. Sizer. Cambridge: Harvard University Press, 1970.

————. "Moral and Religious Education and the Public Schools: A Developmental View." Pages 164–81 in *Religion and Public Education,* edited by Theodore Sizer. Boston: Houghton Mifflin, 1967.

Korcok, Milan. "The Medical Applications of Marihuana and Heroin: High Time the Laws Were Changed." *Canadian Medical Association Journal* 119 (26 August 1978): 374–380.

Kubler-Ross, Elisabeth. *On Death and Dying.* New York: Macmillan, 1969.

Kurzman, Marc G., and Magell, Hillary. "Decriminalizing Possession of all Controlled

Substances: An Alternative Whose Time Has Come." *Contemporary Drug Problems* 6 (Summer 1977): 245–59.

Kutner, Luis. "Due Process of Euthanasia: The Living Will, A Proposal." *Indiana Law Journal* 44 (Spring 1969): 539–54.

———. "The Living Will: Coping With the Historical Event of Death." *Baylor Law Review* 27 (Winter 1975): 39–53.

La Fave, Wayne L., and Scott, Austin W. *Handbook on Criminal Law.* St. Paul, Minn.: West Publishing Co., 1972.

Lasch, Christopher. *The Culture of Narcissism.* New York: Warner Books, 1979.

Leary, Timothy Francis. *The Politics of Ecstacy.* New York: G. P. Putnam, 1968.

Lecky, William E. *History of European Morals.* New York: D. Appleton and Co., 1900.

Lefebure, Molly. *Samuel Taylor Coleridge: A Bondage of Opium.* New York: Stein & Day, 1974.

"The Legality of Homosexual Marriage." *Yale Law Journal* 82 (January 1973): 573–89.

Lemert, E. M. "Prostitution." In *Problems of Sex Behavior,* edited by Edward Sagarin and Donald E. MacNamara. New York: Crowell, 1968.

Levinson, Daniel J. *The Seasons of a Man's Life.* New York: Alfred A. Knopf, 1978.

Levi-Strauss, Claude. *The Elementary Structures of Kinship.* Translated by James Harle Bell, John Richard von Sturmer, and Rodney Needham. Boston: Beacon Press, 1969.

———. *Structural Anthropology.* Translated by Claire Jacobson and Brooke Schoepf. New York: Basic Books, 1963.

Levy, Donald. "Perversion and the Unnatural as Moral Categories." *Ethics* 90 (1980): 191–202.

Levy, Leonard W. *Legacy of Suppression; Freedom of Speech in Early American History.* Cambridge: Harvard University Press, Belknap Press, 1960.

Lewis, C. S. *The Allegory of Love.* London: Oxford University Press, 1973.

———. *Studies in Words.* Cambridge: Cambridge University Press, 1960.

Lewis, I. M. *Ecstatic Religion.* Harmondsworth: Penguin Books, 1971.

Licht, H. *Sexual Life in Ancient Greece.* Translated by J. H. Freese. London: G. Routledge and Sons, Ltd., 1932.

———. *Sexual Life in Ancient Greece.* Translated by J. H. Freese. New York: Barnes & Noble, 1963.

Lindesmith, Alfred R. *The Addict and the Law.* Bloomington: Indiana University Press, 1965.

———. *Addiction and Opiates.* Chicago: Aldine Publishing Co., 1968.

Linner, Birgitta. *Sex and Society in Sweden.* New York: Pantheon Books, 1967.

Lloyd, Robin. *For Love or Money: Boy Prostitution in America.* New York: Vanguard Press, 1976.

Locke, John. "Second Treatise." Pages 284–446 in *Two Treatises of Government,* edited by Peter Laslett. Cambridge: Cambridge University Press, 1960.

———. *The Second Treatise of Government.* Edited by Thomas P. Peardon. New York: Liberal Arts Press, 1952.

Lowes, Peter D. *The Genesis of International Narcotics Control.* Geneva: Droz, 1966.

Lucretius. *The Nature of the Universe.* Translated by Ronald Latham. Baltimore: Penguin Books, 1961.

Luther, Martin. *Selections From His Writings.* Edited by John Dillenberger. Chicago: Quadrangle Books, 1961.

———. "The Natural Place of Women." Pages 134–43 in *Sexual Love and Western Morality,* edited by Donald P. Verene. New York: Harper & Row, 1972.

Macht, David I. "The History of Opium and Some of Its Preparations and Alkaloids." *Journal of the American Medical Association* 64 (6 February 1915): 477–81.

Mackie, John Leslie. *Ethics: Inventing Right and Wrong.* New York: Penguin Books, 1977.

Mancini, Jean. *Prostitutes and Their Parasites.* London: Elek Books, 1963.

Mandel, Jerry. "Problems With Official Drug Statistics." *Stanford Law Review* 21 (1969): 991–1040.

Mandeville, Bernard. *The Fable of the Bees.* Edited by Philip Harth. Harmondsworth: Penguin, 1970.

Mankoff, Allan. *Mankoff's Lusty Europe.* New York: Simon & Schuster, 1974.

"Many Americans Describe Selves as Addicts." *New York Times,* 27 January 1981, Sec. C., p. 1.

Margolis, Joseph. *Negativities: The Limits of Life.* Columbus, Ohio: Charles E. Merrill Publ. Co., 1975.

———. "The Question of Homosexuality." Pages 288–302 in *Philosophy and Sex,* edited by Robert Baker and Frederick Elliston. Buffalo, N.Y.: Prometheus, 1975.

"The Marijuana Problem in the City of New York: Mayor LaGuardia's Committee on Marijuana." Pages 277–410 in *The Marijuana Papers,* edited by David Solomon. New York: The New American Library, 1968.

Marmor, Judd. "Homosexuality and Sexual Orientation Disturbances." Pages 1510–20 in *Comprehensive Textbook of Psychiatry.* 2nd ed., Vol. 2, edited by Alfred Freeman, Harold Kaplan, and Benjamin Sadock. Baltimore: Williams & Wilkins, 1975.

Marwick, Maxwell, ed. *Witchcraft and Sorcery.* Harmondsworth: Penguin Books, 1970.

Marx, Karl. *Economic and Philosophic Manuscripts of 1844.* Translated by Martin Milligan. New York: International Publishers, 1964.

Masland, John. "Missionary Influence Upon Far Eastern Policy." *Pacific History Review* 5 (1941): 279–96.

Masters, Robert E. L. *Eros and Evil: The Sexual Pathology of Witchcraft.* New York: Julian Press, 1962.

Masters, Robert E. L., and Houston, Jean. *The Varieties of Psychedelic Experience.* New York: Holt, Rinehart & Winston, 1966.

Masters, William H., and Johnson, Virginia E. *Homosexuality in Perspective.* Boston: Little, Brown, 1979.

———. *Human Sexual Inadequacy.* Boston: Little, Brown, 1970.

———. *Human Sexual Response.* Boston: Little, Brown, 1966.

———. *The Pleasure Bond.* Boston: Little, Brown, 1975.

May, Henry Farnham. *The Enlightenment in America.* New York: Oxford University Press, 1976.

McCormick, Richard A. "To Save or Let Die: The Dilemma of Modern Medicine. Pages 173–84 in *Ethical Issues in Death and Dying,* edited by Robert F. Weir. New York: Columbia University Press, 1977.

McFadden, C. *Medical Ethics.* London: Burns & Oates, 1962.

McNeill, John J. *The Church and the Homosexual.* Kansas City: Sheed, Andrews, and McMeel, 1976.

Menninger, Karl Augustus. *Man Against Himself.* New York: Harcourt, Brace, 1938.

Merwin, Samuel. "Drugging a Nation." *Success Magazine,* December, 1907.

Mesarovic, Mikajlo D., and Pestel, Edward. *Mankind at the Turning Point: The Second Report to the Club of Rome.* New York: E. P. Dutton, 1974.

Metzler, Karen M. "Human and Handicapped." Pages 348–52 in *Moral Problems in Medicine,* edited by Samuel Gorovitz et al. Englewood Cliffs, N.J.: Prentice-Hall, 1976.

Mill, John Stuart. *On Liberty.* Edited by A. Castell. Arlington Heights, Ill.: AHM, 1947.

———. "On Liberty." Pages 271–93 in *The Philosophy of John Stuart Mill,* edited by M. Cohen. New York: Modern Library, 1961.

———. *Principles of Political Economy.* 5th ed. New York: D. Appleton and Co., 1864.

———. *The Subjection of Women.* New York: D. Appleton and Co., 1870.

———. *Utilitarianism.* Edited by Oskar Piest. New York: The Liberal Arts Press, 1948.

Millett, Kate. *The Prostitution Papers.* New York: Avon Books, 1973.

———. *Sexual Politics.* Garden City, N.Y.: Doubleday, 1970.

Milton, John. "Areopagitica." In *Areopagitica, and Of Education,* edited by George H. Sabine. New York: Appleton Century-Crofts, 1951.

Mitchell, Basil. *Morality, Religious and Secular: The Dilemma of the Traditional Conscience.* New York: Oxford University Press, 1980.

Mitchell, Juliet. *Woman's Estate.* New York: Pantheon Books, 1971.

Mitchell, Paul Rush. "North Carolina's Natural Death Act: Confronting Death with Dignity." *Wake Forest Law Review* 14 (August 1978): 771–95.

Mitchell, Roger S. *The Homosexual and the Law.* New York: ARCO, 1969.

Mitscherlich, Alexander, and Mitscherlich, Margarete. *The Inability to Mourn.* Translated by Beverley R. Placzek. New York: Grove Press, 1975.

Money, J. *Man and Woman.* Baltimore: Johns Hopkins University Press, 1972.

Money, J; Hampson, J. G.; and Hampson, J. L. "An Examination of Some Basic Sexual Concepts: The Evidence of Human Hermaphroditism." *Bulletin of Johns Hopkins Hospital* 97, (1955): 301–19.

Montaigne, M. "A Custom of the Island of Cea." Pages 251–62 in *The Complete Works of Montaigne.* Stanford, Cal.: Stanford University Press, 1948.

———. "Of Drunkenness." In *The Complete Essays of Montaigne.* Translated by Donald M. Frame. Stanford, Cal.: Stanford University Press, 1967.

Montesquieu, Charles Louis. "The Grandeur and Decline of the Roman Empire." In *The Complete Works.* London: T. Evans and W. Davis, 1777.

———. *The Persian Letters.* Translated by J. Robert Loy. New York: Meridian Books, 1961.

More, Thomas. *Utopia.* Edited by Edward Surtz. New Haven: Yale University Press, 1964.

Morgan, Edmund. *The Challenge of the American Revolution.* New York: W. W. Norton, 1976.

———. "Review of *Inventing America* by Gary Wills." *New York Review of Books* 25 (17 August 1978): 38–40.

Morris, Colin. *The Discovery of the Individual.* London: S.P.C.K. for the Church Historical Society, 1972.

Morris, Norval, and Hawkins, Gordon. *The Honest Politician's Guide to Crime Control.* Chicago: University of Chicago Press, 1970.

Motto, Jerome A. "The Right to Suicide: A Psychiatrist's View." *Life-Threatening Behavior* 2, no. 3 (Fall 1972): 183–88.

Munzer, Stephen R., and Nickel, James W. "Does the Constitution Mean What It Always Meant?" *Columbia Law Review* 77 (November 1977): 1029–62.

Murtagh, John H., and Harris, Sara. *Cast the First Stone.* New York: McGraw-Hill, 1957.

Musto, David F. *The American Disease: Origins of Narcotic Control.* New Haven: Yale University Press, 1973.

Myrdal, Gunnar. *An American Dilemma.* 2nd ed. New York: McGraw-Hill, 1962.

Nagel, Thomas. "The Absurd." Pages 11–23 in *Mortal Questions,* edited by Thomas Nagel. Cambridge: Cambridge University Press, 1979.

———. "Death." Pages 961–70 in *Mortal Questions,* edited by Thomas Nagel. Cambridge: Cambridge University Press, 1979.

Neier, Aryeh. "Public Boozers and Private Smokers." *Civil Liberties Review* 2 (Fall 1975): 41–56.

Neill, Stephen. *The Interpretation of the New Testament 1861–1961.* New York: Oxford University Press, 1966.

A New Catechism. Translated by K. Smith. New York: Herder & Herder, 1967.

"New Life for an Old Profession." *The New Republic* 8, no. 15 (July 1978): 21.

Nichols, Jack. *Men's Liberation: A New Definition of Masculinity.* New York: Penguin Books, 1975.

Nietzsche, Friedrich. *The Antichrist.* Pages 468–656 in *The Portable Nietzsche,* trans. by Walter Kaufmann. New York: Viking Press, 1954.

———. *Beyond Good and Evil: Prelude to a Philosophy of the Future.* Translated by Helen Zimmern. Edinburgh and London: Macmillan, 1907.

———. *Human All-Too-Human.* Translated by Helen Zimmern. New York: Russell & Russell, 1964.

———. *Thus Spoke Zarathustra.* In *The Portable Nietzsche,* trans. by walter Kaufmann. New York: Viking Press, 1954.

———. *Twilight of the Idols.* In *The Portable Nietzsche,* trans. by Walter Kaufmann. New York: Viking Press, 1954.

Noonan, John T. "Tokos and Atokion: An Examination of Natural Law Reasoning Against Usury and Contraception." *Natural Law Forum* 10 (1954): 215–35.

Note, "Native Americans and the Free Exercise Clause." *Hastings Law Journal* 28 (1977): 1509–36.

Oakley, Francis. "Medieval Theories of Natural Law: William of Ockham and the Significance of the Voluntarist Tradition." *Natural Law Forum* 6 (1961): 65–83.

Odegard, Peter H. *Pressure Politics: The Story of the Anti-Saloon League.* New York: Octagon Books, 1966.

O'Donnell, T. *Morals in Medicine.* Westminster, Md.: Newman Press, 1959.

Offit, Avodah K. *The Sexual Self.* Philadelphia: J. B. Lippincott, 1977.

Oliver, Barnard. *Sexual Deviation in American Society.* New Haven: College & University Press, 1967.

Orbon, Margaret J. " 'The Living Will'—An Individual's Exercise of His Rights of Privacy and Self-Determination." *Loyola University Law Journal* 7 (Summer 1976): 714–32.

Ortner, Sherry B. "Is Female to Male as Nature is to Culture?" Pages 67–87 in *Woman, Culture and Society,* edited by Michelle Zimbalist Rosaldo and Louise Lamphere. Stanford, Cal.: Stanford University Press, 1974.

Owen, David. *British Opium Policy in China and India.* New Haven: Yale University Press, 1934.

Packer, Herbert L. *The Limits of the Criminal Sanction.* Stanford, Calif.: Stanford University Press, 1969.

Paine, Thomas. *Rights of Man.* Edited by Henry Collins. Harmondsworth: Penguin Books, 1969.

Panofsky, Erwin. *Meaning in the Visual Arts.* New York: Doubleday Anchor Books, 1955.

Parker, Richard B. "A Definition of Privacy." *Rutgers Law Review* 27 (Winter 1974): 275–96.

Pearson, Michael. *The Age of Consent: Victorian Prostitution and Its Enemies.* Plymouth, England: David & Charles Newton Abbot, 1972.

Peele, Stanton. *Love and Addiction.* New York: Taplinger, 1975.

Perkins, Rollin M. *Criminal Law.* 2nd edition. Mineola, N.Y.: Foundation Press, 1969.

Perry, John, ed. *Personal Identity.* Berkeley and Los Angeles: University of California Press, 1976.

Perry, Michael J. "Abortion, The Public Morals, and the Police Power: The Ethical Function of Substantive Due Process." *University of California Los Angeles Law Review* 23 (April 1970): 689–736.

Pico Della Mirandola, Giovanni. *Oration on the Dignity of Man.* Translated by A. Robert Caponigri. Chicago: Henry Regnery Co., 1956.

Pinzer, Mamie. *The Mamie Papers.* Introduction and edited by Ruth Rosen. Old Westbury, N.Y.: Feminist Press, 1977.

Pius XII. "The Prolongation of Life." *American/Anesthesiological Society* 49 (1956).

Pivar, D. "The New Abolitionism: The Quest for Social Purity, 1876–1900." (Ph.D. dissertation, University of Michigan, 1965.) Available from University Microfilms, Ann Arbor, Mich.

Plato. *Charmides.* In *The Collected Dialogues of Plato.* Edited by Edith Hamilton and Huntington Cairns; translated by Benjamin Jowett. New York: Pantheon, 1961.

———. *Laws.* In *The Collected Dialogues of Plato.* Edited by Edith Hamilton and Huntington Cairns; translated by A. E. Taylor. New York: Pantheon, 1961.

———. *Phaedo.* In *The Collected Dialogues of Plato.* Translated by Hugh Tredennick. New York: Pantheon, 1961.

———. *Phaedrus.* In *The Collected Dialogues of Plato.* Translated by R. Hackworth. New York: Pantheon, 1961.

———. *Symposium.* In *The Collected Dialogues of Plato.* Translated by Michael Joyce. New York: Pantheon, 1961.

Platt, Jerome J., and Labate, Christina. *Heroin Addiction: Theory, Research, and Treatment.* New York: John Wiley & Sons, 1976.

Pleck, Joseph H., and Sawyer, Jack. *Men and Masculinity.* Englewood Cliffs, N.J.: Prentice-Hall, 1974.

Ploscowe, M. *Sex and the Law .* Rev. ed. Englewood Cliffs, N.J.: Prentice-Hall, 1962.

Pomeroy, Sarah B. *Goddesses, Whores, Wives, and Slaves: Women in Classical Antiquity.* New York: Schocken Books, 1975.

———. "Some Aspects of Prostitution." *Journal of Sex Research* 1 (1965): 177–87.

Portwood, Doris. *Common-Sense Suicide: The Final Right.* New York: Dodd, Mead & Co., 1978.

Praz, Mario. *The Romantic Agony*. Translated by Augus Davidson. New York: Oxford University Press 1970.

President's Commission on Law Enforcement and Administration of Justice, Task Force Report. *Organized Crime*. Washington, D.C.: U.S. Government Printing Office, 1967.

Preble, Edward, and Casey, John. "Taking Care of Business; The Heroin Users Life in the Street." Pages 97–118 in *It's So Good Don't Even Try It Once*, edited by David Smith and George Gay. Englewood Cliffs, N.J.: Prentice-Hall 1972.

Price, Richard. *A Review of the Principal Questions in Morals*. Edited by D. D. Raphael. Oxford: Clarendon Press, 1948.

Prosser, William L. "Privacy." *California Law Review* 48 (August 1960): 383–423.

"Prostitutes Demand Decriminalization, Social Security, and Old Age Benefits." *Newsweek*, 23 June 1975, p. 42.

"Prostitution in Seattle." *Washington State Bar News*. August-September 1971, pp. 5, 28.

Quincey, Thomas de. *Confessions of an Opium Eater*. Boston: Ticknor and Fields, 1885.

Quinn, Philip L. *Divine Commands and Moral Requirements*. Oxford: Clarendon Press, 1978.

Quinn, Thomas M., and McLaughlin, Gerald T. "The Evolution and Present Status of New York Drug Control Legislation." *Buffalo Law Review* 22 (1972–73): 705–36.

Quisenberry, W. "Eight Years After the Houses Closed: Was 'Controlled' Prostitution Good for Hawaii?" *Journal of Social Hygiene* 39 (1953): 312–15.

Rachels, James. "Euthanasia, Killing, and Letting Die." Pages 146–63 in *Ethical Issues Relating to Life and Death*, edited by John Ladd. New York: Oxford University Press, 1979.

Raible, A. "The Right to Refuse Treatment and Natural Death Legislation." *Medicolegal News* 5 (1977): 6.

Ramsey, Paul. *The Patient as Person; Explorations in Medical Ethics*. New Haven: Yale University Press, 1970.

Rapoport, R., and Rapoport, R. *Leisure and the Family Life Cycle*. Boston: Routledge & Kegan Paul, 1975.

Rapoport R.; Rapoport, R.; and Strelitz, Z. *Fathers, Mothers and Society: Towards a New Alliance*. New York: Basic Books, 1977.

Rawls, John. "Fairness to Goodness." *Philosophical Review* 84, no. 4 (October 1975): 536–54.

———. "A Kantian Conception of Equality." *Cambridge Review* (February 1975): 94–99.

———. "Kantian Constructivism in Moral Theory." *Journal of Philosophy* 77, no. 9 (September 1980): 515–72.

———. "Reply to Alexander and Musgrave." *Quarterly Journal of Economics* 88 (November 1974): 633–55.

———. *A Theory of Justice*. Cambridge: Harvard University Press, Belknap Press, 1971.

Ray, Oakley S. *Drugs, Society, and Human Behavior*. St. Louis: C. V. Mosby, 1972.

Redlich, Norman. "Are There 'Certain Rights . . . Retained by the People'?" *New York University Law Review* 37 (November 1962): 787–812.

Reich, Wilhelm. *Character Analysis*. Translated by V. Carfagno. New York: Farrar, Straus & Giroux, 1972.

Reichel-Dolmatoff, Gerardo. *The Shaman and the Jaguar: A Study of Narcotic Drugs Among the Indians of Columbia*. Philadelphia: Temple University Press, 1975.

Reuben, David. *Everything You Always Wanted to Know About Sex*. New York: McKay, 1969.

Richards, David A. J. "Equal Opportunity and School Financing: Towards a Moral Theory of Constitutional Adjudication." *University of Chicago Law Review* 41, no. 1 (Fall 1973): 32–71.

———. "Free Speech and Obscenity Law: Toward a Moral Theory of the First Amendment." *University of Pennsylvania Law Review* 123, no. 1 (November 1974): 45–91.

———. "Human Rights and the Moral Foundations of the Substantive Criminal Law." *Georgia Law Review* 13, no. 4 (Summer 1979): 1395–1446.

———. "Human Rights and Moral Ideals: An Essay on the Moral Theory of Liberalism." *Social Theory and Practice* 5, nos. 3–4 (1980): 461–88.

———. "The Individual, the Family, and the Constitution: a Jurisprudential Perspective." *New York University Law Review* 55, no. 1 (April 1980): 1–62.

———. *The Moral Criticism of Law.* Encino, Calif. Dickenson, 1977.

———. "Review of Gary Jacobsohn, '*Pragmatism, Statesmanship, and the Supreme Court.*' " *New York Law School Law Review* 24, no. 1 (1978): 310–21.

———. "Rights and Autonomy." *Ethics* 92, no. 1 (October 1981): 3–20.

———. "Taking 'Taking Rights Seriously' Seriously: Reflections on Dworkin and the American Revival of Natural Law." *New York University Law Review* 52, no. 6 (December 1977): 1265–1340.

———. "The Theory of Adjudication and the Task of the Great Judge." *Cardozo Law Review* 1 (Spring 1979): 171–218.

———. *A Theory of Reasons for Action.* Oxford: Clarendon Press, 1971.

———. "Unnatural Acts and the Constitutional Right to Privacy: a Moral Theory." *Fordham Law Review* 45 (May 1977): 1281–1348.

Riggs, Tom. "*Roe v. Wade*—The Abortion Decision—An Analysis and Its Implication." *San Diego Law Review* 10 (June 1973): 844–56.

Rist, John M. *Stoic Philosophy.* London: Cambridge University Press, 1969.

Rizzo, James J. "The Constitutionality of Sodomy Statutes." *Fordham Law Review* 45 (December 1976): 553–95.

Rivera, Rhonda R. "Our Straight-Laced Judges: The Legal Position of Homosexual Persons in the United States." *Hastings Law Journal* 30 (March 1979): 799–955.

Robertson, Durant Waite. *A Preface to Chaucer; Studies in Medieval Perspectives.* Princeton, N.J.: Princeton University Press, 1962.

Robertson, John A. "Involuntary Euthanasia of Defective Newborns: A Legal Analysis." *Stanford Law Review* 27 (January 1975): 213–69.

Robins, Lee N.; Davis, Darlene H.; and Goodwin, Donald W. "Drug Use by U.S. Army Enlisted Men in Vietnam: A Follow-Up on Their Return Home." *American Journal of Epidemiology* 99 (April 1974): 235–49.

Roby, Pamela, and Kerr, Virginia. "The Politics of Prostitution." *The Nation* 214 (10 April 1972): 463–66.

Rorty, A. O., ed. *The Identities of Persons.* Berkeley: University of California Press, 1976.

Rosaldo, Michelle. "Women, Culture and Society: A Theoretical Overview." In *Woman, Culture, and Society,* edited by Michelle Rosaldo and Louise Lamphere. Stanford: Stanford University Press, 1974.

Rosenbleet, Charles, and Pariente, Barbara J. "The Prostitution of the Criminal Law." *American Criminal Law Review* 11 (Winter 1973): 373–420.

Rosenn, Keith. "Review of *Judicial Review in the Contemporary World* by Mauro Cappelletti." *Yale Law Journal* 81 (1972): 1411–20.

Rothman, David J. *The Discovery of the Asylum: Social Order and Disorder in the New Republic.* Boston: Little, Brown, 1971.

Rougement, Denis de. *Love in the Western World.* Translated by M. Belgion. New York: Pantheon, 1956.

Rousseau, J. J. *La Nouvelle Heloise.* Translated by J. H. McDowell. State College, Pa.: Pennsylvania State University Press, 1968.

———. "The Social Contract." In *The Social Contract and Discourses,* translated by G. D. H. Cole. New York: E. P. Dutton, 1950.

Rubin, Vera D., and Comitas, Lambros. *Ganja in Jamaica: A Medical Anthropological Study of Chronic Marihuana Use.* The Hague: Mouton, 1975.

Runciman, Steven. *The Medieval Manichee, a Study of the Christian Dualist Heresy.* Cambridge: Cambridge University Press, 1947.

Russell, Bertrand. *Marriage and Morals.* New York: Liveright, 1958.

———. "Review of *Sanctity* by Glanville Williams." *Stanford Law Review* 10 (1958): 382–85.

Russell, Bruce. "On the Relative Strictness of Negative and Positive Duties." Pages 215–31 in *Killing and Letting Die,* edited by Bonnie Steinbock. Englewood Cliffs, N.J.: Prentice-Hall, 1980.

Rutter, Michael. *Maternal Deprivation Reassessed.* Harmondsworth: Penguin Books, 1972.

Sagarin, Edward. "Sexual Criminality." Page 138ff in *Current Perspectives on Criminal Behavior,* edited by Abraham Blumberg. New York: Alfred A. Knopf, 1974.

Sager, Lawrence Gene. "Fair Measure: The Legal Status of Underenforced Constitutional Norms." *Harvard Law Review* 91 (April 1978): 1212–64.

Salmon, Robert, and Salmon, Sheila. "The Causes of Heroin Addiction—A Review of the Literature (pts. 1 & 2)." *International Journal of Addictions* 12, nos. 5, 7 (1977): pp. 679–96, 937–51.

Sanders, Joseph. "Euthanasia: None Dare Call It Murder." *Journal of Criminal Law, Criminology, and Police Science* 60 (September 1969): 351–59.

Sanger, William W. *The History of Prostitution: Its Extent, Causes and Effects Throughout the World*. New York: The Medical Publishing Co., 1897.

Sartre, Jean-Paul. "Existentialism is a Humanism." Pages 287–311 in *Existentialism From Dostoevsky to Sartre*, edited by W. Kaufmann. New York: Meridian, 1956.

Saxton, L. *The Individual, Marriage, and the Family*. Belmont, Calif.: Wadsworth, 1972.

Scanlon, T. M. "Due Process." Pages 93–125 in *Due Process: Nomos XVIII*, edited by J. Roland Pennock and John W. Chapman. New York: New York University Press, 1977.

Scheler, Max. *The Nature of Sympathy*. Translated by Peter Heath. London: Routledge & Kegan Paul, Ltd., 1954.

Scher, Edward M. "Legal Aspects of Euthanasia." *Albany Law Review* 36 (1972): 674–97.

Schiffer, Stephen R. *Meaning*. Oxford: Clarendon Press, 1972.

Schneidman, Edward S.; Farberow, Norman L.; and Litman, Robert E. *The Psychology of Suicide*. New York: Jason Aronson, 1970.

Schopenhauer, Arthur. "On Suicide." In *Essays and Aphorisms*. Translated by R. J. Hollingdale. Harmondsworth: Penguin Books, 1970.

———. "On Women." In *Essays and Aphorisms*. Translated by R. J. Hollingdale. Harmondsworth: Penguin Books, 1970.

———. *The World as Will and Representation*. Translated by E. F. J. Payne. New York: Dover Books, 1969.

Schultes, Richard E. "Botanical Sources of the New World Narcotics." Pages 89–110 in *The Psychedelic Reader*, edited by Gunther M. Weil, Ralph Metzner, and Timothy Leary. New Hyde Park, N. Y.: University Books, 1965.

Schur, Edwin. *Law and Society*. New York: Random House, 1968.

———. *Narcotic Addiction in Britain and America*. Bloomington: Indiana University Press, 1962.

Schwager, Robert. "Life, Death, and the Irreversibly Comatose." Pages 38–50 in *Ethical Issues in Death and Dying*, edited by Tom L. Beauchamp and Seymour Perlin. Englewood Cliffs, N.J.: Prentice-Hall, 1978.

Scott, G. *A History of Prostitution: From Antiquity to the Present Day*. New York: AMS, 1936.

———. *Ladies of Vice*. London: Tallis Press, 1968.

Seligman, Edwin. "The Social Evil, With Special Reference to Conditions Existing in the City of New York." Pages 1–143 in *Prostitution in America: Three Investigations, 1902–1917*. New York: Arno, 1976.

Seneca. *Letters from a Stoic*. Translated by Robin Campbell. Harmondsworth: Penguin Books, 1969.

———. *The Stoic Philosophy of Seneca*. Translated by Moses Hadas. Gloucester, Mass.: Peter Smith, 1965.

Sennett, Richard. *The Fall of Public Man*. New York: Vintage Books, 1978.

"Sex Discrimination and Equal Protection: Do We Need a Constitutional Amendment?" *Harvard Law Review* 84 (April 1971): 1499–1524.

Sex Information and Education Council of the United States. *Sexuality and Man*. New York: Charles Scribner's Sons, 1970.

Shakespeare, William. *Hamlet*. In *The Oxford Shakespeare*. London: Oxford University Press, 1966.

———. *Measure for Measure*. Edited by W. Craig. In *The Oxford Shakespeare*. London: Oxford University Press, 1966.

———. *Othello*. Edited by W. Craig. In *The Oxford Shakespeare*. London: Oxford University Press, 1966.

———. *Twelfth Night*. Edited by W. Craig. In *The Oxford Shakespeare*. London: Oxford University Press, 1966.

Shao-Yang, Lin. *A Chinese Appeal to Christendom, Concerning Missions.* New York: Putnam, 1911.

Shaw, George Bernard. *Mrs. Warren's Profession.* Pages 179–286 in *Plays Unpleasant.* Harmondsworth: Penguin Books, 1975.

Sheehy, Gail. *Hustling: Prostitution in Our Wide-Open Society.* New York: Dell Publishing Co., 1973.

Sheinman, Allen. "The Latest Dope on Pot." *High Times* (April 1980): 52–55.

Sherfey, Mary Jane. *The Nature and Evolution of Female Sexuality.* New York: Vintage Books, 1973.

Sherwin, Byron L. "Jewish Views of Euthanasia." Pages 3–11 in *Beneficent Euthanasia,* edited by Marvin Kohl. Buffalo, N.Y.: Prometheus Books, 1975.

Shesgreen, Sean, ed. *Engravings by Hogarth.* New York: Dover Publications, 1973.

Shorter, Edward. *The Making of the Modern Family.* New York: Basic Books, 1975.

Sidel, Ruth. *Women and Child Care in China.* New York: Penguin Books, 1972.

Sidgwick, Henry. *The Methods of Ethics.* 7th ed. London: Macmillan, 1963.

———. *The Principles of Political Economy.* London: Macmillan, 1883.

Siegel, Martin, and Weisner, Paul. "Penicillin-Resistant Gonococcus." *Medical Aspects of Human Sexuality* 11 (May 1977): 105–6.

Siler, J. F., et al. "Marijuana Smoking in Panama." *Military Surgeon* 73 (November 1933): 269–80.

Silverstein, Harry S. "The Evil of Death." *Journal of Philosophy* 77, no. 7 (July 1980): 401–24.

Silving, H. "Euthanasia: A Study in Comparative Criminal Law." *University of Pennsylvania Law Review* 103 (1954): 350–89.

Simmons, Luiz R. S., and Gold, Martin B. "The Myth of International Control: American Foreign Policy and the Heroin Traffic." *International Journal of Addictions* 8, no. 5 (1973): 779–800.

Simon, William, and Gagnon, John. "Femininity in the Lesbian Community." Pages 256–67 in *Sexual Deviance and Sexual Deviants,* edited by Eriche Goude and Richard Troiden. New York: William Morrow, 1974.

Singer, K. "The Choice of Intoxicant Among the Chinese." *British Journal of Addiction* 69 (September 1974): 257–68.

Singer, Peter. *Practical Ethics.* Cambridge: Cambridge University Press, 1979.

Sion, Abraham. *Prostitution and the Law.* London: Faber & Faber, 1977.

Skolnick, Jerome. *Justice Without Trial.* New York: John Wiley & Sons, 1967.

Slater, Philip. *Wealth Addiction.* New York: E. P. Dutton, 1980.

Smith, Adam. "Hume's Last Months." Pages 450–52 in *The Letters of David Hume,* edited by J. Greig. Oxford: Clarendon Press, 1932.

Smith, Alexander, and Pollack, Harriet. *Some Sins Are Not Crimes.* New York: New Viewpoints, 1975.

Smith, James R., and Smith, Lynn G. *Beyond Monogamy.* Baltimore: Johns Hopkins University Press, 1974.

Snaith, N. H., ed. *The Century Bible: Leviticus and Numbers.* London: Thomas Nelson & Sons, 1967.

Socarides, Charles W. *Beyond Sexual Freedom.* New York: Quadrangle/New York Times Book Company, 1975.

Soler, Mark. "Of Cannabis and the Courts: A Critical Examination of Constitutional Challenges to Statutory Marijuana Prohibitions." *Connecticut Law Review* 6 (Summer 1974): 601–723.

Sprott, S. E. *The English Debate on Suicide from Donne to Hume.* La Salle, Ill.: Open Court, 1961.

Standard, David. E. *The Puritan Way of Death.* Oxford: Oxford University Press, 1977.

Stein, Martha. *Lovers, Friends, Slaves . . . The Nine Male Sexual Types.* New York: Berkley Publishing Corp., 1974.

Stengel, Erwin. *Suicide and Attempted Suicide.* Harmondsworth: Penguin Books, 1975.

Stent, Gunther S. *The Coming of the Golden Age: A View of the End of Progress.* Garden City, N.Y.: The Natural History Press, 1969.

Stephen, James Fitzjames. *Liberty, Equality, Fraternity.* Edited by R. J. White. Cambridge: Cambridge University Press, 1967.

―――. "Punishment and Public Morality." In *A History of the Criminal Law of England,* vol. 2. London: Macmillan, 1883.

Stevens, John. *Medieval Romance.* London: Hutchinson, 1973.

St. John-Stevas, N. *Law and Morals.* Windham, Conn.: Hawthorn, 1964.

―――. *The Right to Life.* New York: Holt, Rinehart & Winston, 1963.

Stoller, Robert J. *Perversion: The Erotic Form of Hatred.* New York: Pantheon Books, 1975.

Stone, Lawrence. *The Family, Sex, and Marriage in England, 1500–1800.* New York: Harper & Row, 1977.

Strand, John G. "The 'Living Will': The Right to Death With Dignity?" *Case Western Reserve Law Review* 26 (Winter 1976): 485–526.

Stratton, Robert T. "State Interference With Personhood: The Privacy Right, Necessity Defense, and Proscribed Medical Therapies." *Pacific Law Journal* 10 (1979): 773–800.

Suarez, Francisco. "On Laws and God the Lawgiver." In *Selections from Three Works.* Translated by Williams, Brown, Waldron, and Davis, with introduction by James Brown Scott. Oxford: Clarendon Press, 1944.

Sullivan, Joseph V. "The Immorality of Euthanasia." Pages 12–33 in *Beneficent Euthanasia,* edited by Marvin Kohl. Buffalo, N.Y.: Prometheus Books, 1975.

Swatos, William H. "Opiate Addiction in the Late Nineteenth Century: A Study of the Social Problem, Using Medical Journals of the Period." *International Journal of Addictions* 7(4) (1972): 739–53.

Szasz, Thomas. *Ceremonial Chemistry.* Garden City, N.Y.: Anchor Press/Doubleday, 1974.

Taylor, Arnold H. *American Diplomacy and the Narcotics Traffic, 1900–1939.* Durham, N.C.: Duke University Press, 1969.

Taylor, Gabriele. "Love." Pages 161–82 in *Philosophy As It Is,* edited by Ted Honderich and Myles Burnyeat. New York: Penguin Books, 1979.

Ten, C. L. *Mill on Liberty.* New York: Oxford University Press, 1980.

Terkel, Studs. *Working.* New York: Pantheon, 1974.

Terry, Charles, and Pellens, Mildred. *The Opium Problem.* New York: Committee on Drug Addictions in Collaboration with Bureau of Social Change, 1928.

Thayer, James. B. "The Origin and Scope of the American Doctrine of Constitutional Law." *Harvard Law Review* 7 (25 October 1893): 129–56.

Timberlake, James H. *Prohibition and the Progressive Movement, 1900–1920.* Cambridge: Harvard University Press, 1963.

Tinbergen, Nikolaas. *The Herring Gull's World: A Study of the Social Behavior of Birds.* Revised ed. New York: Basic Books, 1953.

Titmuss, Richard Morris. *The Gift Relationship: From Human Blood to Social Policy.* New York: Pantheon Books, 1971.

Tolstoy, Leo. *The Death of Ivan Ilych.* With a commentary by Arthur C. Carr. Translated by Louise and Aylmer Maude. New York: Health Sciences Publishing Corp., 1973.

―――. "Death and the Meaning of Life." Pages 317–24 in *Ethical Issues in Death and Dying,* edited by T. L. Beauchamp and Seymour Perlin. Englewood Cliffs, N.J.: Prentice-Hall, 1978.

Tooley, Michael. "A Defense of Abortion and Infanticide." Pages 51–91 in *The Problem of Abortion,* edited by Joel Feinberg. Belmont, Calif.: Wadsworth, 1973.

"The Tragic Choice: Termination of Care for Patients in a Permanent Vegetative State." *New York University Law Review* 51 (May 1976): 285–310.

Turner, T. "The Suppression of Prostitution in Relation to Venereal Disease Control in the Army." *Federal Probation* 7 (April–June 1943).

Twining, William L. *Karl Llewellyn and the Realist Movement.* London: Weidenfeld & Nicolson, 1973.

Tribe, Laurence H. *American Constitutional Law.* Mineola, N.Y.: Foundation Press, 1978.

Tripp, C. A. *The Homosexual Matrix.* New York: McGraw-Hill, 1975.

Unamuno, Miguel de. *Tragic Sense of Life.* Translated by J. E. Crawford Flitch. New York: Dover Publications, 1964.

Unger, Roberto Mangabeira. *Knowledge and Politics .* New York: Free Press, 1975.

"The Unhappy Hookers." *Time* Magazine, June 16, 1975, p. 33.

United Nations. Department of Economic and Social Affairs. *Study on Traffic in Persons and Prostitution.* New York: 1959.

Urmson, J. O. "Saints and Heroes." Pages 198–216 in *Essays in Moral Philosophy,* edited by A. Melden. Seattle: Univerity of Washington Press, 1958.

U.S. Congress. Joint Committee on New York Drug Law Evaluation. *The Nation's Toughest Drug Law: Evaluating the New York Experience.* Washington, D.C.: U.S. Government Printing Office, 1978.

———. *Staff Working Papers on the Drug Law Project.* Washington, D.C.: U.S. Government Printing Office, 1978.

U. S. Congress. Senate. Remarks by Rev. W. L. Beard. S. Doc. No. 135, 58th Cong., 3rd Sess. 244–45, 1905.

———. Report of Hearing at State Department on Petitions to the President to Use His Good Offices for the Release of China from Treaty Compulsion to Tolerate the Opium Traffic, with additional Papers, S. Doc. No. 135, 58th Cong., 3rd Sess. 232–56, 1905.

———. Report of the Committee Appointed by the Philippine Commission. S. Doc. No. 265, 59th Cong. 1st Sess. 1905.

Vaillant, George E. *Adaptation to Life.* Boston: Little, Brown, 1977.

———. "The Natural History of Urban Drug Addiction—Some Determinants." In *The Scientific Basis of Drug Dependence,* edited by Hannah Steinberg. New York: Grune and Stratton, 1969.

Valency, Maurice Jacques. *In Praise of Love: An Introduction to the Love-Poetry of the Renaissance.* New York: Macmillan, 1958.

Valente, Michael F. *Sex: The Radical View of a Catholic Theologian.* New York: Bruce Publishing Co., 1970.

Vance, Beverly. "Immunological Factors in Gonorrhea." *Medical Aspects of Human Sexuality* 11 (May 1977): 106–7.

Vanggaard, Thorkil. *Phallos.* New York: International Universities Press, 1972.

Vaughan, Nancy Lee. "The Right to Die." *California Western Law Review* 10 (Spring 1974): 613–27.

Veatch, Robert M. *Death, Dying, and the Biological Revolution: Our Last Quest for Responsibility.* New Haven: Yale University Press, 1976.

———. "Defining Death Anew: Technical and Ethical Problems." Pages 19–38 in *Ethical Issues in Death and Dying* , edited by T. L. Beauchamp and Seymour Perlin. Englewood Cliffs, N.J.: Prentice-Hall, 1978.

Vlastos, Greory. *Platonic Studies.* Princeton: Princeton University Press, 1973.

Voltaire, F. "Of Suicide." In *Works,* vol. 17. Translated by T. Smollett. 4th ed. London: Newbery, 1762.

Vorenberg, Elizabeth, and Vorenberg, James. " 'The Biggest Pimp of All': Prostitution and Some Facts of Life." *Atlantic Monthly* 239 (January 1977): 27–38.

Vorenberg, James. *Criminal Law and Procedure: Cases and Materials.* St. Paul: West Publishing Co., 1975.

Wade, Daniel E. "Prostitution and the Law: Emerging Attacks on the 'Women's Crime.' " *University of Missouri–Kansas City Law Review* 43 (Spring 1975): 413–28.

Walters, Ronald. *Primers for Prudery.* Englewood Cliffs, N.J.: Prentice-Hall, 1974.

Walzer, Michael. *Just and Unjust Wars.* New York: Basic Books, 1977.

Wandling, Therese M. "Decriminalization of Prostitution: The Limits of the Criminal Law." *Oregon Law Review* 55 (1976): 553–66.

Warkany, Josef. *Congenital Malformations.* Chicago: Book Medical Publishers, 1971.

Warner, Marina. "Review of *Vice and Vigilance: Purity Movements in Britian Since 1700* by Edward Bristow." *Times Literary Supplement,* 14 July 1978, p. 793.

Warnock, Geoffrey. *Contemporary Moral Philosophy.* New York: St. Martin's Press, 1967.

———. *The Object of Morality.* London: Methuen, 1971.

Warren, Samuel D., and Brandeis, Louis D. "The Right to Privacy." *Harvard Law Review* 4 (15 December 1890): 193–220.

Wasserstrom, Richard. "Is Adultery Immoral?" Pages 207–21 in *Philosophy and Sex,* edited by R. Baker and F. Elliston. Buffalo, N.Y. Prometheus Books, 1975.

————. "Rights, Human Rights, and Racial Discrimination." *Journal of Philosophy* 61 (1964).

Wasson, Robert. *Soma: Divine Mushroom of Immortality.* New York: Harcourt Brace Jovanovich, 1968.

Wasson, Robert; Hoffman, Albert; and Ruck, Carl. *The Road to Eleusis.* New York: Harcourt Brace Jovanovich, 1978.

Watson, Gary. "Free Agency." *Journal of Philosophy* 72 (24 April 1975): 205–20.

Weil, Andrew. *The Natural Mind.* Boston: Houghton Mifflin, 1972.

Weil, Gunther; Metzner, Ralph; and Leary, Timothy, eds. *The Psychedelic Reader.* New Hyde Park, N.Y.: University Books, 1965.

Weinberg, George H. *Society and the Healthy Homosexual.* New York: St. Martin's Press, 1972.

Weinberg, Martin, and Williams, Colin. *Male Homosexuals.* New York: Oxford University Press, 1974.

Weiss, Jonathan A., and Wizner, Stephen B. "Pot, Prayer, Politics and Privacy: The Right to Cut Your Own Throat in Your Own Way." *Iowa Law Review* 54 (April 1969): 709–35.

Weitz, Shirley. *Nonverbal Communication.* New York: Oxford University Press, 1974.

————. *Sex Roles.* New York: Oxford University Press, 1977.

Wells, Brian. *Psychedelic Drugs.* Forward by Humphry Osmond. Baltimore: Penguin Books, 1974.

West, Donald. *Homosexuality.* Chicago: Aldine Publishing, 1967.

White, Morton. "The Revolt Against Formalism in American Thought in the Twentieth Century." In *Pragmatism and the American Mind.* New York: Oxford University Press, 1973.

White, Robert. *Ego and Reality in Psychological Theory.* New York: International Universities Press, 1963.

————. *Lives in Progress.* New York: Dryden Press, 1952.

Williams, Bernard. "A Critique of Utilitarianism." In *Utilitarianism, For and Against,* edited by James Smart and Bernard Williams. Cambridge: Cambridge University Press, 1973.

————. *Problems of the Self.* Cambridge: Cambridge University Press, 1973.

Williams, Donald H. "The Suppression of Commercialized Prostitution in the City of Vancouver." *Journal of Social Hygiene* 27 (October 1941): 364–72.

Williams, George Huntston. *The Radical Reformation.* Philadelphia: Westminster Press, 1962.

Williams, Glanville. *Criminal Law: The General Part.* 2d ed. London: Stevens, 1961.

————. "Euthanasia Legislation; A Rejoinder to the Non-Religious Objections." Pages 134–47 in *Euthanasia and the Right to Death,* edited by A. Downing. London: Owen, 1969.

————. *The Sanctity of Life and the Criminal Law.* Foreword by William C. Warren. New York: Alfred A. Knopf, 1957.

Williams, Ralph C. "Diagnosing Disseminated Gonorrhea." *Medical Aspects of Human Sexuality* 11 (May 1977): 57–58.

Wills, Garry. *Inventing America: Jefferson's Declaration of Independence.* Garden City, N.Y.: Doubleday, 1978.

Wilson, James Q. *Thinking About Crime.* New York: Vintage Books, 1975.

Wilson, John. *Logic and Sexual Morality.* Harmondsworth: Penguin Books, 1965.

Wilson, Paul R. *The Sexual Dilemma: Abortion, Homosexuality, Prostitution, and the Criminal Threshold.* St. Lucia: University of Queensland Press, 1971.

Winick, Charles. "Maturing Out of Narcotic Addiction." *Bulletin on Narcotics* 14 (January–March 1962): 1–7.

————. "The Use of Drugs by Jazz Musicians." *Social Problems* 7 (Winter 1959–60): 240–53.

Winick, Charles, and Kinsie, Paul M. *The Lively Commerce: Prostitution in the United States.* Chicago: Quadrangle Books, 1971.

Wolfe, Tom. *The Electric Kool-Aid Acid Test.* New York: Farrar, Straus, & Giroux, 1968.

Wolfgang, Marvin E.; Figlio, Robert M.; and Sellin, Thorsten. *Delinquency in a Birth Cohort.* Chicago: University of Chicago Press, 1972.

Wollstonecraft, Mary. *A Vindication of the Rights of Women.* Edited by Carol Poston. New York: W. W. Norton, 1975.

Women Endorsing Decriminalization. "Prostitution: A Non-Victim Crime?" *Issues in Criminality* 8 (1973) 137–62.

Wood, Gordon. *The Creation of the American Republic, 1776–1787.* New York: W. W. Norton, 1969.

Woolf, Virginia. *A Room of One's Own.* New York: Harcourt, Brace & Co., 1929.

Wordsworth, William. *The Prelude.* Edited by E. Reynolds. London: Macmillan, 1932.

Zabriskie, Alexander Clinton. *Bishop Brent: Crusader for Christian Unity.* Philadelphia: Westminster Press, 1948.

Zachary, R. B. "Ethical and Social Aspects of Treatment of Spina Bifida." Pages 342–48 in *Moral Problems in Medicine,* edited by S. Gorovitz et. al. Englewood Cliffs, N.J.: Prentice-Hall, 1976.

Zaehner, Robert. *Mysticism, Sacred and Profane: An Inquiry into Some Varieties of Praeter-Natural Experience.* Oxford: Clarendon Press, 1969.

———. *Zen, Drugs and Mysticism.* New York: Pantheon Books, 1972.

Zinberg, Norman Earl, and Robertson, John A. *Drugs and Public Use.* New York: Simon & Schuster, 1972.

Table of Cases

Table of Statutes

International

Convention for the Suppression of the Traffic in Persons and of the Exploitation of the Prostitution of Others, British Foreign Office and State Papers 157, 482, United Nations Treaty Series, 96, 271

International Convention for the Suppression of the Traffic in Women and Children, British Foreign Service and State Papers 116, 547 League of Nations Treaty Series 9, 415 (September 30, 1921).

Protocol to Amend the Convention for the Suppression of the Traffic in Women and Children of September 30, 1921, British Foreign Office and State Papers 14, 871, United Nations Treaty Series 53, 13 (November 12, 1947)

Austria

Strafrechtsanderungsgesetz (Penal Law Reform), Article 3 Zehntes, Federal Laws Registry I, 313 (April 7, 1970)

France

France, Declaration of the Rights of Man and of Citizens

Penal Code, secs. 330–40

Germany

German Penal Code of 1871, Ch. 3, secs. 180–81

Great Britain

Great Britain, Laws, Statutes, etc. 5 Eliz. 1, c 17 (1562)

————9 Geo. 4, C. 31 (1828)

————25 Hen. 8, C.6 (1533)

Netherlands

Amsterdam, Regulations of Amsterdam, Art. 223 (1973)

Wetbock Van Strafrecht (Code of Criminal Law of Holland) art. 250 (1973)

Rome

Justinian, Novelle 77, 141

Ulpian, Digest, XLVIII, 13, 5

United States—Federal

Comprehensive Drug Abuse Prevention and Control Act, U.S. Code, Vol. secs. 801–966 (1976)

International Agreement for the Suppression of the "White Slave Traffic," Statutes at Large 35, 1979, Treaties Series, No. 391, League of Nations Treaties Series 1, 83 (March 18, 1904)

Marihuana Exise Tax Act Public Law No. 75-238, Statutes at Large 50, 551 (1937) (superseded 1939)

Opium and Coca Importer and Seller Registration and Tax Act, Public Law No. 63-223, Statutes at Large 38, 785 (1914) (superseded 1914)

Protocol Amending the International Agreements and Conventions on the White Slave Traffic, United States Treaties and Other International Agreements, Vol. 2, T.I.A.S. No. 2332, United Nations Treaties Series, Vol. 30, 4 May 1949

U.S. Constitution, Art. I, sec. 2 cl. 3; Art. I, sec. 9, cl. 1; Art. VI, sec. 2 cl. 3; Amends. IV, V, VI, VII

United States—State

Georgia, Code Annotated, secs. 26-2002 (1970)

Massachusetts, Annotated Laws, Ch. 272, Sec. 34 (1968)

New York, New York Penal Code, secs. 220.00–220.60 (McKinney 1980)

————, Uniform Controlled Substances Act, New York Public Health Law, Secs. 3300-3396 (McKinney 1980)

Wisconsin, Annotated Statutes, Sec. 944.17 (1958)

United States—Model Codes

Model Penal Code, sec. 207.1-6, Comments (Tentative Draft No. 4, 1955)

Index